THE CAMBRIDGE COMPANION TO
GREEK AND ROMAN PHILOSOPHY

The Cambridge Companion to Greek and Roman Philosophy is a wide-ranging introduction to the study of philosophy in the ancient world. A team of leading specialists surveys the developments of the period and evaluates a comprehensive series of major thinkers, ranging from Pythagoras to Epicurus. There are also separate chapters on how philosophy in the ancient world interacted with religion, literature and science, and a final chapter traces the seminal influence of Greek and Roman philosophy down to the seventeenth century. Practical elements such as tables, illustrations, a glossary, and extensive advice on further reading make it an ideal book to accompany survey courses on the history of ancient philosophy. It will be an invaluable guide for all who are interested in the philosophical thought of this rich and formative period.

OTHER VOLUMES IN THE SERIES OF CAMBRIDGE COMPANIONS

AQUINAS *Edited by* NORMAN KRETZMANN *and* ELEONORE STUMP

HANNAH ARENDT *Edited by* DANA VILLA

ARISTOTLE *Edited by* JONATHAN BARNES

AUGUSTINE *Edited by* ELEONORE STUMP *and* NORMAN KRETZMANN

BACON *Edited by* MARKKU PELTONEN

SIMONE DE BEAUVOIR *Edited by* CLAUDIA CARD

DARWIN *Edited by* JONATHAN HODGE *and* GREGORY RADICK

DESCARTES *Edited by* JOHN COTTINGHAM

DUNS SCOTUS *Edited by* THOMAS WILLIAMS

EARLY GREEK PHILOSOPHY *Edited by* A. A. LONG

FEMINISM IN PHILOSOPHY *Edited by* MIRANDA FRICKER *and* JENNIFER HORNSBY

FOUCAULT *Edited by* GARY GUTTING

FREUD *Edited by* JEROME NEU

GADAMER *Edited by* ROBERT J. DOSTAL

GALILEO *Edited by* PETER MACHAMER

GERMAN IDEALISM *Edited by* KARL AMERIKS

HABERMAS *Edited by* STEPHEN K. WHITE

HEGEL *Edited by* FREDERICK BEISER

HEIDEGGER *Edited by* CHARLES GUIGNON

HOBBES *Edited by* TOM SORELL

HUME *Edited by* DAVID FATE NORTON

HUSSERL *Edited by* BARRY SMITH *and* DAVID WOODRUFF SMITH

WILLIAM JAMES *Edited by* RUTH ANNA PUTNAM

KANT *Edited by* PAUL GUYER

KIERKEGAARD *Edited by* ALASTAIR HANNAY *and* GORDON MARINO

LEIBNIZ *Edited by* NICHOLAS JOLLEY

LEVINAS *Edited by* SIMON CRITCHLEY *and* ROBERT BERNASCONI

LOCKE *Edited by* VERE CHAPPELL

MALEBRANCHE *Edited by* STEVEN NADLER

The Cambridge Companion to
GREEK AND ROMAN PHILOSOPHY

Edited by
David Sedley
University of Cambridge

CAMBRIDGE
UNIVERSITY PRESS

PUBLISHED BY THE PRESS SYNDICATE OF THE UNIVERSITY OF CAMBRIDGE
The Pitt Building, Trumpington Street, Cambridge, United Kingdom

CAMBRIDGE UNIVERSITY PRESS
The Edinburgh Building, Cambridge, CB2 2RU, UK
40 West 20th Street, New York, NY 10011–4211, USA
477 Williamstown Road, Port Melbourne, VIC 3207, Australia
Ruiz de Alarcón 13, 28014 Madrid, Spain
Dock House, The Waterfront, Cape Town 8001, South Africa

http://www.cambridge.org

First published 2003
Reprinted 2004

Printed in the United Kingdom at the University Press, Cambridge

Typeface Trump Medieval 10/13 pt.   *System* LaTeX 2_ε [TB]

A catalogue record for this book is available from the British Library

ISBN 0 521 77285 0 hardback
ISBN 0 521 77503 5 paperback

CONTENTS

vii

ILLUSTRATIONS AND CHARTS

CONTRIBUTORS

JONATHAN BARNES is Professor of Ancient Philosophy at the University of Paris-IV Sorbonne, having previously taught at the University of Oxford for twenty-five years, and subsequently at the University of Geneva. His most recent books are *Sextus Empiricus, Outlines of Scepticism* (with Julia Annas, 1994), *The Cambridge Companion to Aristotle* (ed., 1995), *Logic and the Imperial Stoa* (1997), *The Cambridge History of Hellenistic Philosophy* (co-edited with Keimpe Algra, Jaap Mansfeld and Malcolm Schofield, 1999), and *Porphyry, Introduction* (2003).

SARAH BROADIE is Professor of Philosophy at the University of St Andrews. Her earlier work (as Sarah Waterlow) included *Nature, Agency and Change in Aristotle's Physics* (1982) and *Passage and Possibility: A Study of Aristotle's Modal Concepts* (1982). More recently she has published *Ethics with Aristotle* (1991), and a commentary on Aristotle's *Nicomachean Ethics* accompanying a new translation by Christopher Rowe (2002). She is currently working on Plato.

JACQUES BRUNSCHWIG is Professor Emeritus of Ancient Philosophy at the University of Paris-I. He is the author of *Aristote, Topiques* (vol. I, 1967; vol. II currently in progress), and his most recent books are *Papers in Hellenistic Philosophy* (1994) and (co-edited with G. E. R. Lloyd) *Greek Thought: A Guide to Classical Knowledge* (2000). His main current interests are Aristotle and Stoicism.

JOHN M. COOPER is Stuart Professor of Philosophy at Princeton University. His most recent books are *Plato: Complete Works* (ed., 1997), and *Reason and Emotion: Essays on Ancient Moral*

Psychology and Ethical Theory (1999). A second collection of his papers, *Stoic Autonomy and Other Essays on Ancient Philosophy*, is forthcoming.

FRANS A. J. DE HAAS is Professor of Ancient and Medieval Philosophy at the University of Leiden. He is the author of *John Philoponus' New Definition of Prime Matter. Aspects of its Background in Neoplatonism and the Ancient Commentary Tradition* (1997). He is currently working on Aristotle's *Posterior Analytics* and its impact on late ancient philosophy, and in particular the notions of induction, division and definition.

R. J. HANKINSON is Professor of Philosophy at the University of Texas, Austin. His most recent books are *The Sceptics* (1995), *Cause and Explanation in the Ancient Greek World* (1998), and *Galen on Antecedent Causes* (1998). He is currently editing *The Cambridge Companion to Galen*.

JILL KRAYE is Reader in the History of Renaissance Philosophy and Librarian of the Warburg Institute, the School of Advanced Study, University of London. She is the editor of *The Cambridge Companion to Renaissance Humanism* (1997), and of *Cambridge Translations of Renaissance Philosophical Texts: Moral and Political Philosophy*, 2 vols. (1997) and, together with M. W. F. Stone, of *Humanism and Early Modern Philosophy* (2000). A collection of her articles has been published under the title *Classical Traditions in Renaissance Philosophy* (2002). She is currently preparing translations of Cristoforo Landino's *Camaldulensian Disputations* and Justus Lipsius' *Guide to Stoic Philosophy*, as well as researching the cultural history of Stoicism from the Renaissance to the seventeenth century.

A. A. LONG is Professor of Classics and Irving Stone Professor of Literature at the University of California, Berkeley. He is the author of *Hellenistic Philosophy* (1974, 1986), *The Hellenistic Philosophers* (with David Sedley, 1987), *Stoic Studies* (1996), and *Epictetus. A Stoic and Socratic Guide to Life* (2002). He is also the editor of the *Cambridge Companion to Early Greek Philosophy* (1999). He is currently working on a book about cosmology, theology and human identity in Greek thought.

GLENN W. MOST is Professor of Greek Philology at the Scuola Normale Superiore, Pisa and Professor in the Committee on Social Thought of the University of Chicago. In addition to the many volumes that he has edited, his own publications include *The Measures of Praise: Structure and Function in Pindar's Second Pythian and Seventh Nemean Odes* (1985), *Théophraste, Métaphysique* (with A. Laks, 1993), and *Raffael, Die Schule von Athen* (1999) = *Leggere Raffaello: 'La Scuola di Atene' e il suo pretesto*, 2001). He is currently completing the new Loeb edition of Hesiod, and a study of the traditions concerning Doubting Thomas, and collaborating on a new textual edition of Aristotle's *Metaphysics*.

MARTHA C. NUSSBAUM is Ernst Freund Distinguished Service Professor of Law and Ethics at the University of Chicago. Her most recent books are *Women and Human Development: The Capabilities Approach* (2000), *Upheavals of Thought: The Intelligence of Emotions* (2001), and *The Sleep of Reason: Erotic Experience and Sexual Ethics in Ancient Greece and Rome* (co-edited with Juha Sihvola, 2002). She is currently writing a book about the influence of Stoic cosmopolitanism on the modern tradition of political philosophy and on international law.

CHRISTOPHER ROWE is Professor of Greek at the University of Durham, and currently holds a Leverhulme Personal Research Professorship. He has edited Plato's *Phaedrus* (1986), *Phaedo* (1993), *Statesman* (1995) and *Symposium* (1998). His most recent books are *The Cambridge History of Greek and Roman Political Thought* (co-edited with Malcolm Schofield, 2000), a new translation of Aristotle's *Nicomachean Ethics* (with commentary by Sarah Broadie, 2002), and *New Perspectives on Plato, Modern and Ancient* (co-edited with Julia Annas, 2002). He is currently completing a book on Plato's *Lysis* (with Terry Penner), and a study of Plato's theory and practice in the writing of philosophy.

MALCOLM SCHOFIELD is Professor of Ancient Philosophy at the University of Cambridge. In addition to the many volumes that he has edited, his most recent books are *The Stoic Idea of the City* (1991; expanded edition, 1999), *Saving the City* (1999), *The Cambridge History of Hellenistic Philosophy* (co-edited with Keimpe Algra, Jonathan Barnes and Jaap Mansfeld, 1999), and *The Cambridge*

History of Greek and Roman Political Thought (co-edited with
Christopher Rowe, 2000).

DAVID SEDLEY is Laurence Professor of Ancient Philosophy at
the University of Cambridge. He is the author of *The Hellenistic
Philosophers* (with A. A. Long, 1987), and of *Lucretius and the Transformation of Greek Wisdom* (1998). He works on Greek philosophical papyri, is editor of *Oxford Studies in Ancient Philosophy*, and
has recently completed two books on Plato (on the *Cratylus* and
Theaetetus respectively).

ACKNOWLEDGEMENTS

I would like to express my gratitude to all contributors to this volume, not only for their own chapters but also for their invaluable suggestions pertaining to other aspects of the volume; to Liba Taub for her comments on an early draft of the introduction; and above all to Hilary Gaskin of Cambridge University Press, who has been an unfailing source of wise advice from the day she first proposed the project.

I would also like to thank the British Library for permission to reproduce *P. Petrie I*; the Bodleian Library, University of Oxford for permission to reproduce M.S. E. D. Clarke 39; and Candace H. Smith for permission to reproduce the sketch of the Athenian philosophical schools which she originally drew for A. A. Long and D. N. Sedley, *The Hellenistic Philosophers* (Cambridge 1987).

David Sedley

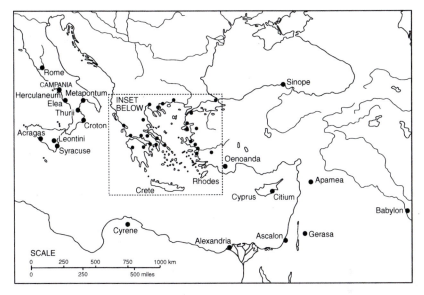

Map of the Greek world

Introduction

Compare the following two questions, both of which greatly exercised ancient Greek and Roman thinkers:

1 What is a good human life?
2 Why isn't the earth falling?

They appear about as different as any two questions could be. The first is one that most of us continue to consider important today. The second is not a question we are likely even to think worth asking: however little physics we know, we know enough to realize that the question itself rests on false suppositions.

Despite this and other contrasts, those who manage to get inside the subject – Greek and Roman philosophy – to which this book aims to provide an entry route should find that the two questions come to exercise an equal fascination. They may even find that the two of them have more in common than at first appears, as I shall suggest below.

Take the first of them, what a good human life is. How would you react to the answer that it should in principle be no harder to work out what makes a human life a good one than it is to work out what makes a doctor, a scalpel, an operation or an eye a good one? The latter kind of question is answered by first determining what the essential *function* of a doctor, a scalpel, an operation or an eye is, a good one simply being any that is such as to be successful in performing that function. Analogously, then, find out what is the function of a human being, or of a human life, and you will know what it is to be a good human being and to have a good human life. If, for example, man's natural function is fundamentally social, a human life's goodness will be defined accordingly; if intellectual, in a different way;

if pleasure-seeking, in yet another way. Despite their very various answers, nearly all the major philosophers of antiquity were united in this same fundamental conviction: by studying human nature we can aspire to determine the true character of a good human life.

One common and understandable modern reaction is to protest that this kind of functional analogy confuses two radically different kinds of good, one moral, the other non-moral: the functional 'goodness' of a scalpel has nothing in common with the moral 'goodness' of a person, an action or a life. Some may go so far as to congratulate themselves that we today are no longer deaf to an equivocation that tricked even the greatest thinkers of antiquity.

But why be so confident that there *are* these two incommensurable kinds of good? The confidence arises – as the history of ancient philosophy reveals – because we are ourselves heirs to a tradition in ethics which emerged relatively late on in antiquity. It was the Stoics of the third century BC who, building on a set of insights provided by their figurehead Socrates, set the standard for what is to count as 'good' so high that only moral virtue could satisfy it; all other, conventional uses of 'good', they inferred, as applied for example to what is merely practically advantageous, represent a different and strictly incorrect sense of the term. The Stoics did not themselves go on to infer that the (genuine) goodness of a life is not something given in nature, but their distinction is nevertheless the very earliest forerunner of that radical division between kinds of goodness.

Once we have reconstructed where and how our own presupposition began its long career, it becomes not only easier, but also potentially liberating, to put the clock back and consider the advantages of the earlier outlook, where 'good' was not roped off into moral and functional senses. It was from such a unified starting point, for example, that Aristotle was able to compose an ethical treatise, the *Nicomachean Ethics*, which has still not in two and a half millennia been superseded by any rival.

Another common reaction to the same treatment of moral goodness as some kind of functional goodness is to protest that, unlike a scalpel, a human being cannot be assumed to have any function at all – not, at any rate, without supplying some contentious theological presuppositions. Here too there is much to learn from Aristotle, who made a powerful case for understanding living beings, humans included, and their parts in terms of their natural functions, without for a moment admitting divine design or government.

My point is not to insinuate that our intuition is wrong and that the ancients were right about the nature of good (or for that matter that the reverse is true). It is to underline how retracing the early history of our own philosophical concepts and assumptions is almost bound to be enlightening, not only about our forerunners but also about ourselves.

My second example, the earth's stability, could hardly be more different. Understanding why the ancients thought it a problem in the first place is already half the challenge. Immobile heavy objects, such as buildings and boulders, are immobile precisely because they rest on solid earth. All the more reason, then, to be confident that the earth, which provides that immobility, is itself immobile. But some further reflection – exactly the kind of reflection that kick-started philosophical thought in the sixth century BC – undermines this initial confidence. The heavier an object is, the harder it will fall downwards when dropped; and since earth is itself a heavy substance, won't that comprehensive amalgam of it, *the* earth, be the likeliest object of all to hurtle downwards, this time without any obstacle to stop it? Showing why, in the face of this danger, the earth stays still was one of the earliest and most persisting challenges for those thinkers committed to explaining the regularity and orderly arrangement of the world. The Greek for this 'order' is *kosmos*, and the word came to signify the world-order taken as a whole, embracing the earth, the surrounding heaven, and everything in between. Thus it is that explaining the earth's stability was a focal question in the emergence of *cosmology* as an area of inquiry.

The problem, once posed, attracted all manner of answers. That none of them will strike us as entirely correct is somewhat less important than the variety of explanatory devices and models that were devised in the process of getting it wrong. One kind of answer was the mechanical model: even very heavy objects can float on a fluid, as wood does on water, as leaves do on the wind, and as a saucepan lid does over steam. Perhaps then the earth floats on water (Thales), or air (Anaximenes), in which case there may also be grounds for regarding this same fluid as the ultimate pool of stuff on which our world depends. A second mode of solution invoked equilibrium (Anaximander): the world is a mathematically symmetrical structure surrounded by a spherical heaven and with the earth at its exact centre, where it consequently has no more reason to move off in one direction than in any other. A third suggestion (Xenophanes) is that the earth is stable because it rests on more earth, and that earth on yet more earth, and so on *ad infinitum*. However far down you were to dig, you would never come to a portion of earth that, because unsupported by more earth, was liable to fall. It is earth all the way down.

All these suggestions predate the fifth century BC. In the fifth century itself, yet other models emerged. Some philosophers, for example, pointed to the way that in a vortex the heavy material will naturally gravitate to the centre, and suggested that the cosmic vortex, evidenced by the perpetual rotation of the heavens, in some comparable way forces the earth to the centre. Around the same time a more mathematical alternative became current. Not only the world but also the earth, located at its centre, is spherical. The direction which we call 'down' represents in reality the natural motion of all heavy objects, not in parallel vertical lines, but towards that centre. If not yet the Newtonian theory of gravity, this was an impressive forerunner to it, and it proved to explain the astronomical and other data more successfully than any of its rivals.

Yet another twist was added by Plato, who, in a classic passage of his *Phaedo*, presents Socrates arguing that no such explanation of the earth's stability achieves much until it shows why it is *better* that the cosmic order, the earth's fixed location in it included, should be as it is. Socrates is assuming here that the world-order is the product of intelligence, and he compares a merely mechanistic explanation of this order to someone answering, when asked why Socrates is sitting here in prison (where he is awaiting his own execution), that it is because of his bones, muscles etc. being arranged in a certain way, with no mention of his rational decision that it is *better* not to escape but to stay and face the death penalty. Likewise if the earth is, say, a sphere in equipoise at the centre, the only adequate explanation will be one that among other things tells why that arrangement is 'better' than any alternative. But how might a cosmic arrangement be 'better'? Plato's idea seems to be that such an explanation would reveal how the world's arrangement maximizes the chances of its inhabitants' own self-improvement – for example through studying mathematical astronomy, or through appropriate relocation in each successive incarnation that a soul undergoes. In such ways, even the cosmological puzzle of the world's stability may bring us back to the issue of goodness, and to the all-important issue of what makes a life a good life (see further, pp. 112–13 below).

More significant from the point of view of philosophical history is the fact that Plato, in setting this challenge, was announcing a new agenda for *teleological* explanation. That agenda was thereafter to dominate scientific thinking until at least the seventeenth century. The evidence of design in the world, once Plato had drawn attention to it, became extraordinarily hard to discount or ignore. In antiquity there remained those, such as the atomists, who were prepared to argue that chance on a large enough scale could account for apparent purposiveness. But, as R. J. Hankinson's chapter on 'Philosophy and Science' brings out, the teleologists were by and large to have the better of the ancient debate.

The business of cataloguing these solutions to the problem of the earth's stability belongs primarily to the domain of intellectual history. What we are likely to appreciate is less the specific solutions than the development of increasingly sophisticated explanatory strategies. However, it also illustrates a second cardinal point about the value of studying ancient philosophy. In reconstructing the thought of the ancients, we need not be seeking to vindicate their beliefs, whether by assimilating our ideas to theirs or theirs to ours. But what we can always fruitfully do is find out *what it would be like* to face the questions that they faced and to think as they thought. Learning to strip off our own assumptions and to try on the thought processes of others who lacked them is almost invariably an enlightening and mind-stretching exercise.

For a variety of reasons, the Greek and Roman philosophers are supremely suitable subjects for the kind of enterprise I have been sketching. For one thing, as inaugurators of the tradition to which most of us are heirs they inevitably have a very special place in our understanding of our own intellectual make-up. For another, their brilliance, originality and diversity would be hard to parallel in any other single culture. Even if this volume had chosen to focus just on the extraordinary trio of Socrates, his pupil Plato, and *his* pupil Aristotle, it would be dealing with three utterly diverse but equally seminal thinkers, each of whom over the next two millennia was to inspire more than one entire philosophical movement. Yet to concentrate on these three would be to leave out of account a large part of the ancient world's legacy, as well as to impoverish our understanding even of them, by isolating them from their historical milieu.

It is unlikely that any other philosophical texts have been subjected to the minute analysis that the writings of these philosophers, and especially those of Plato and Aristotle, have enjoyed from the first century BC to the present day. Yet this tradition of philosophical exegesis is very far from having led to a convergence of views about how best to interpret them. It is hard for us not to recreate our philosophical predecessors to some degree in our own image, since to read them wherever possible as believing what we ourselves take to be true or at least sensible is an application of the commendable Principle of Charity, whereby of two or more competing and equally well-founded interpretations the one to be preferred is whichever makes the philosopher under scrutiny come out looking better. However, philosophical truth (even on the unlikely hypothesis that we are privileged arbiters of this) is only one criterion of a charitable reading: others include internal consistency, argumentative soundness, and, by no means least, historical plausibility. Again and again it turns out that, when all these factors are weighed against each other, the view we must attribute to the philosopher is strangely unlike anything we ourselves would be inclined to believe, but for that very reason all the more valuable both to acknowledge and to seek to understand from the inside.

The Cambridge Companion to Greek and Roman Philosophy has been designed, not to take readers all the way to this goal, but to provide a suitable entry route.

It offers overviews of the main philosophical movements and trends, written by leading specialists as the fruit of many years' close study: the Presocratics (Malcolm Schofield), the Sophists and Socrates (Sarah Broadie), Plato (Christopher Rowe), Aristotle (John Cooper), Hellenistic philosophy (Jacques Brunschwig, in partnership with myself), Roman philosophy (A. A. Long), and late ancient philosophy (Frans de Haas). In addition, Jonathan Barnes surveys the place of argument in ancient philosophical thinking, and Jill Kraye surveys the part played by ancient philosophy in the classical tradition down to the seventeenth century. Three further chapters examine the relation of philosophy to other dominant aspects of ancient culture: literature (Martha Nussbaum), science (R. J. Hankinson), and religion (Glenn Most). If the twelve chapters differ considerably from each other in focus and approach, that reflects to some degree the varying nature of the material, and to a greater extent the personal methods and priorities of those writing, which it would have been counterproductive to obliterate by excessive homogenization.

In addition to this introductory function, the book also has a secondary function as a handbook. You will not find in it constant instructions directing you to the primary texts, since it is conceived as a survey to read *before* moving on to the closer study of the subject. But you will find, in addition to the historical surveys, the following aids. (a) Advice on how best to gain access to the original philosophical writings and sources in English translation. (b) An introductory bibliography, concentrating on the sort of books, in English, that you will want to acquaint yourself with in order to move deeper into the subject. (Please do not take this restriction to English as xenophobic or anglocentric. A vast part of the modern scholarship on which this volume draws and depends is in other languages. The restriction is motivated purely by didactic and practical considerations.) (c) A glossary, to which you can refer when pursuing this further reading. (d) Various charts, throughout the book, setting out the chief philosophical authors and their work in accessible tabular form.

There are many ways to divide up the history of ancient philosophy. The one followed in this book is fairly conventional, except in its separate treatment of Roman philosophy. Starting from the celebrated episode, in 155 BC, when three leading Greek philosophers landed in Rome and kindled a passion for their discipline among the local intelligentsia, Roman philosophy took its lead from the Greeks – so much so that it is easy to view it as nothing more than Greek philosophy in translation. However, Roman philosophy – whether written in Latin or in Greek – does in certain ways constitute an autonomous tradition, harnessed to an indigenous moral code, to the dynamics of Roman political life, and to home-grown literary genres. It has very rarely been displayed as an integral whole, and A. A. Long's chapter, 'Roman philosophy', offers a taste of what we have been missing. However, this perspective will not be allowed to obscure the fact that there is also, and perhaps in a stronger sense, a *single* tradition of ancient philosophy, of which the Roman philosophers have to be recognized as integral voices. If their absorption into the single tradition can look less than complete, and their relation to it one-sided, that is because virtually no Greek philosopher ever shows signs of turning to Latin texts, whereas nearly all Roman philosophers were immersed in Greek texts. In this sense, ancient philosophy remained a Greek-dominated enterprise, and if we call it 'Greek philosophy' we are not doing any major injustice.

There is one somewhat artificial constraint to which this book is unavoidably subject. The period covered by it, which runs from the sixth century BC to the sixth century AD, incorporates the entire history of the western Roman empire, a history that saw momentous developments in Judaeo-Christian culture, among others. The birth, rise and eventual triumph of Christianity is an integral part of the philosophical history of the empire, and not least of Rome itself. Patristic writers of the calibre of Origen, Eusebius, Augustine and Boethius were immersed in contemporary pagan philosophy, and interacted with it on many levels. To understand the nature of early Christianity, it is imperative to relate it to the philosophical culture of late antiquity, of which it is indeed an inseparable part, just as, conversely, understanding the meaning of ancient philosophy itself requires contextualizing it within the religious culture of the ancient world, as Glenn Most explains in the final section of his chapter on 'Philosophy and religion'. However, it would be an unrealistically ambitious undertaking to include Christianity within these same covers. The broad unity of the pagan–Christian philosophical culture of the Roman empire will emerge occasionally, particularly in Jonathan Barnes' chapter on 'Argument in ancient philosophy', and to a lesser extent in the chapters on 'Roman philosophy', 'Late ancient philosophy' and 'Philosophy and religion'. But it will not be among the official themes of the book.

The main phases separated by the book's chapter divisions are:

(a) Presocratic philosophy: the phase philosophically prior to (although chronologically overlapping with) Socrates, whose own activity falls into the second half of the fifth century BC.
(b) The sophists: a heterogeneous collection of professional intellectuals roughly contemporary with Socrates.
(c) Socrates himself.
(d) Plato: early to mid fourth century BC.
(e) Aristotle: mid to late fourth century BC.

(f) Hellenistic philosophy: third to first century BC: Epicureans, Stoics and sceptics.

(g) Roman philosophy: second or first century BC to sixth century AD.

(h) Late ancient philosophy: first century BC to sixth century AD: the re-emergence and eventual dominance of Platonism.

The historian of ancient philosophy is the victim of a curious irony. The division between (a), (b) and (c) was in effect invented by (d), Plato, and represents very much his own perspective; yet so dominant has been Plato's influence on the history of Western philosophy (which A. N. Whitehead famously called a series of 'footnotes to Plato') that however hard we may try to manage without Plato's divisions we usually end up coming back to them. Because history is written by the winners, Plato can be said to have *made* these divisions true. That is, the way that philosophy progressed under Plato's influence determined that, in retrospect, the threefold division of his predecessors into Presocratics, sophists and Socrates *was* the relevant one to make when seeking to understand where he and the subsequent tradition were coming from.

It was Plato who singled out his own master, Socrates, as representing a radical break from the existing tradition, both Presocratic and sophistic, thanks to two factors. The first of these was Socrates' departure from the physical focus that can, with considerable oversimplification, be said to characterize the astonishingly diverse range of early thinkers from Thales in the early sixth century BC to Democritus in the late fifth and early fourth. Socrates, as presented by Plato (in stark contrast to the image of him created in the Athenian mind by Aristophanes' delightfully wicked portrayal in the *Clouds*), abandoned all interest in the cosmos at large, and turned his attention to the human soul, in the process developing the philosophical method that Plato named dialectic. The second factor, in Plato's eyes, was the polar opposition between Socrates, humble open-minded inquirer and critic, and the sophists, opinionated high-charging self-styled experts on everything under the sun. So simplistic a distinction will not survive a reading of Sarah Broadie's chapter 'The sophists and Socrates'. But like it or not, Plato's distinction is still with us, both in the convention embodied in her chapter's title (imposed by the editor, not the author), and in our persisting pejorative

The Athenian philosophical schools (Academy, Garden, Lyceum, Stoa), © Candace H. Smith

uses of 'sophist', 'sophistry' and 'sophistical' – even if the more positive connotations of 'sophisticated' may offer some consolation. Readers of this volume can gain amusement by working out how a whole set of other English words similarly embodies, at best, half-truths about ancient philosophy: 'platonic', 'stoical', 'epicure', 'cynical', and 'sceptical'.

The point of the above paragraph is not to reject Plato's map of the existing philosophical landscape, but to remind readers that it is only one map among many possible. A much later boundary on the map that should be treated with equal caution is that between 'Hellenistic' and 'late ancient' philosophy, the subjects of two distinct chapters in this book. The Hellenistic period is politically defined: it ends with the birth of the Roman empire in 27 BC. Now it is quite true that the new dominance of Rome was a key factor in the transformation that brought Hellenistic philosophy to an end, but the major development had occurred around sixty years before the start of the Roman empire, when the Roman general Sulla subjected Athens to a long and devastating siege. The result was the virtual break-up of the remaining Athenian philosophical schools, ending an era in which they had been in effect the international headquarters of philosophy, and accelerating an already growing diaspora of philosophers to other centres around the Mediterranean world, including Rome itself. The effect of the change was dramatic. Instead of participating in the activities of the Stoa, the Academy, or some other Athenian school – schools which had seen themselves as the living continuation of the philosophical work of their respective founders – philosophy students henceforth were interpreters of the august texts that these schools, far off in both space and time, had once generated. The new era, in which the writing of commentaries on Plato and Aristotle typified the activity of the philosopher, is portrayed in Frans de Haas's chapter 'Late ancient philosophy'. Although such is the way that philosophical study formally viewed itself for the next half-millennium (during which the patristic writers who developed Christian dogma throughout most of the same period were engaged in a closely analogous enterprise), in no way does the change of attitude represent any decline in the quality or importance of the work done by philosophers. Some of the greatest and most original minds of antiquity were working within this new framework, including Plotinus, whose version of Platonism – Neoplatonism, as we now call it – became the dominant one in late antiquity, and remained so until the seventeenth century, as charted in Jill Kraye's chapter, 'The legacy of ancient philosophy'.

One other disadvantage of the unavoidable but regrettable compartmentalizaton of ancient philosophy is that 'minor' schools and individuals get squeezed out. Such fourth-century BC schools as the Cynics, the Megarians and the Cyrenaics, all of them working in the tradition inaugurated by Socrates, will be mentioned in the ensuing chapters only in passing, without treatment under their own headings: they can be found by use of the book's index. They and others like them were important parts of the philosophical landscape, and their contribution deserves to be explored in much greater detail than has been possible here.

To some extent it is the poor state of the evidence we have about these and other minor schools that has pushed them to the margins. The philosophical texts that survived intact from antiquity, thanks to being lovingly copied and preserved in mediaeval codices, partly represent a canon consisting of those thinkers who could be sufficiently reconciled with Christianity to justify their preservation. But this is only one part of the truth. We should for example not – as is sometimes done – blame the Christian tradition for the loss of the writings of the materialist Democritus: the very considerable modern finds of papyri in Egypt, dating from the third century BC to the end of antiquity, show that the works of Democritus and other Presocratic writers had already more or less ceased to circulate, at least in this part of the Hellenized world, which we have no reason to think was untypical. The recent discovery in an Egyptian papyrus of a first-century AD copy of Empedocles, reported by Malcolm Schofield in his chapter on 'The Presocratics', gives us what may well be the only exemplar ever found of an original Presocratic work dating from the classical or post-classical period (although copies of *Truth* by the sophist Antiphon have been found too). The pattern of post-classical survival largely represents the intellectual fashions that already prevailed in later antiquity, fashions which led to widespread circulation and study of both Plato and Aristotle, along with their more recent interpreters, while for example the writings of the early Stoics, just as easily reconcilable with Christianity, had largely vanished from view. The pattern of papyrus finds largely confirms this picture, although it does also show that Plato (partly because of his literary pre-eminence, on which see pp. 228–34 of Martha Nussbaum's chapter 'Philosophy and literature') was being very much more widely read than *any* other philosopher, Aristotle included. Not much has changed: a recent international survey among philosophy students shows that still today Plato remains the philosopher they most want to read.

In learning about ancient philosophy, we do not usually have the luxury of fully preserved texts, and are therefore obliged to weigh up a range of indirect sources. Almost every philosopher must be studied at least partly through 'fragments' and 'testimonia'. A fragment is strictly speaking a verbatim quotation of a now-lost original text, while a testimonium is an indirect report or indication of what some philosopher wrote, said or did. But the distinction is often an unavoidably loose one in practice. Neither Greek nor Latin authors tend to mark clearly the difference between direct and indirect quotation (punctuation, including the ancient equivalent of quotation marks, was used irregularly if at all), and even when they are quoting directly it is frequently from memory. Besides, an author reporting some predecessor in either direct or indirect form usually has an agenda of his own, whether hostile or benign, and often is assuming his own construal of the now-lost context from which the quotation, if that is what it really is, has been torn. All this means that reconstruction of a philosopher's work via the evaluation of fragments and testimonia is both an extremely skilled and a somewhat unscientific undertaking. The nature and complexity of the task, which sometimes involves looking back through several strata of transmission and potential contamination, is briefly illustrated by Malcolm Schofield in the opening section of his chapter 'The Presocratics'. But in a book with the scope of this one it is not possible to exhibit such source-evaluation problems on a regular basis, and they will by and large be left in the background.

Even where a philosophical text has come down to us intact, its meaning can rarely be straightforwardly read off from it. The most prominent such case is that of Plato. His philosophical writings are thought to survive in their entirety, but this fact has not prevented scholars from being deeply divided over their interpretation for two and a half millennia, and, as Christopher Rowe's 'Plato' chapter brings out, there is even less sign of convergence now than there was in antiquity. This is not in any way a fault of Plato's, as if he had tried but somehow failed to make clear what he was trying to say. Such a suspicion would rest, among other mistakes, on a serious underestimation of his subtlety as a writer of philosophical dialogues. But to a considerable extent what applies to Plato applies to all philosophical authors: *any* classic work of philosophy has to be reinterpreted by every generation of every culture that has absorbed it into its heritage, and even within a single generation there will be numerous perspectives from which a given text is going to be approached.

However, the reasons why the meaning of these texts cannot simply be read off are more complex and various than that. In particular, it is not really true that any of them has come down to us 'intact'. The very fact of their survival between their original composition and the Renaissance attests repeated copying, by hand, from exemplar to exemplar. From an early date variant readings crept in. Such divergences, although inevitable anyway, were encouraged by ancient writing practices: a typical book in the classical period was a scroll containing columns of writing, maybe 30 lines in height and 20 letters in width, the letters written continuously with no signalled breaks between words, even at line ends, and little if any punctuation. Although it becomes surprisingly easy to learn to read fluently from a text written this way, the fact remains that mechanical errors, such as haplography (reading a repeated sequence of letters as if it occurred only once), happened very easily. Some ancient scholars, like their modern counterparts, had hopes of repairing corrupted texts, but that too was capable of leading to unwarranted interference, sometimes ideologically motivated. Comparable factors continued to influence the continued hand-copying of these same texts in codices (manuscripts bound as books) after the end of antiquity, with the result that the multiple medieval manuscripts of a single work usually divide up into distinct 'families', whose history of progressive divergence from a single archetype can be speculatively reconstructed. The picture is further complicated by the survival of translations, based on now-lost original exemplars, into Latin, Arabic, Syriac, Armenian, and a number of other languages, all of which provide supplementary data for the reconstruction.

At the foot of a page of Greek or Latin text in a modern edition there sits the 'apparatus criticus', affectionately known to classical scholars as the 'app. crit.': a tersely coded summary of the complex manuscript data and editorial speculations from which the printed text has been synthesized. Getting back to *the* original reading is an ideal that can probably never be fully attained – even if one ignores the not negligible possibility that some of the competing variants may have been introduced to the tradition by the original author himself.

TRANSMISSION OF A TEXT

Plato, Phaedo *83b4–7: four lines of text, over 23 centuries:*

1   *A third-century* BC *papyrus copy (P.Petrie 1 5–8).*

2   *A direct transcript of 1 (letters entirely missing through damage are in square brackets).*

> TAYTEIOY[NTHI]
> ΛΥΣΕΙΟ[ΥΚΟΙ]ΟΜΕΝΗΔΕΙΝΕΝΑΝΤΙ
> ΟΥΣΘΑΙΗΤΟΥΩΣΑΛΗΘΩΣΦΙΛΟΣΟΦΟΥ
> ΨΥΧΗΟΥΤΩΑΠΕΧΕΤΑΙΤΩΝΗΔΟ
> Ν[ΩΝ]ΤΕΚΑΙΕΠΙΘΥΜΙΩΝΚΑΙΛΥΠΩΝ
> ΚΑΘΟΣΟΝΔΥΝΑΤΑ[Ι

3 *The same passage in a medieval manuscript (Bodleian Library, MS E. D. Clarke 39), dated to AD 895.*

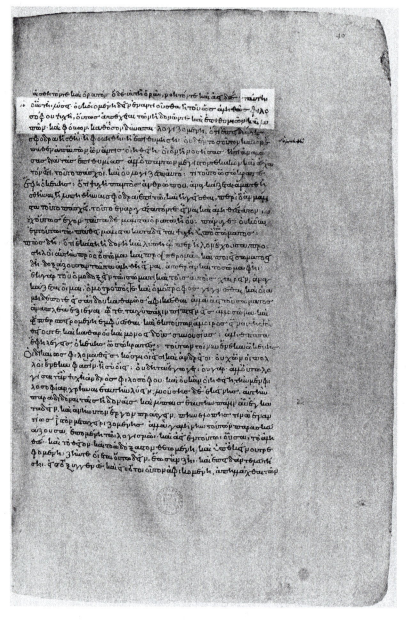

4 The same passage in the Stephanus edition (Henri Estienne's 1574 edition of Plato, from which all modern numbering is taken), Greek text with Latin translation.

5   *The same passage as edited by C. Strachan, in the 1995 revised edition of the Oxford Classical Text of Plato, with accompanying 'apparatus criticus'.*

> ταύτῃ οὖν τῇ λύσει οὐκ οἰομένη
> δεῖν ἐναντιοῦσθαι ἡ τοῦ ὡς ἀληθῶς φιλοσόφου ψυχὴ   5
> οὕτως ἀπέχεται τῶν ἡδονῶν τε καὶ ἐπιθυμιῶν καὶ λυπῶν
> καὶ φόβων καθ᾽ ὅσον δύναται
>
> b4 οὖν βTV Iambl.: δ᾽οὖν WΛ: δὲ PQB¹   b6 ἐπιθυμιῶν καὶ λυπῶν βT Π2 Iambl.: λυπῶν
> καὶ ἐπιθυμιῶν δ   b7 καὶ φόβων βδ, add. in mg. T² vel T m. 1: om. T Π2 Iambl.

6   *The same passage in English translation by D. Gallop (Oxford, 1975).*

> It is, then, because it believes it should not oppose this release that the soul of the true philosopher abstains from pleasures and desires and pains,* so far as it can.
>
> *Bracketing καὶ φόβων (83b7), with Burnet

Naturally the app. crit. can be used only by readers with some classical training, but even they are likely to find it only too easy to ignore most of the time, as if it were no more than a set of rough workings, now superseded by the integral text which the editor has recovered out of them. Nothing could be further from the truth. Not only are editors compelled to choose, often questionably, between attested variants, they also introduce further editorial changes to these, usually recording such interventions only in the app. crit. where they easily pass unnoticed. Much superb work has been done over many generations on the improvement of classical texts, but it is important to keep reminding ourselves that no editor's decisions are authoritative, and that what looks like the original meaning, recovered by editorial skill, may in reality represent the editor's prior assumptions about that meaning, now endowed with a spurious authority by being enshrined in the letter of the text.

This caution about the indeterminate state of our texts should be set alongside the earlier ones about source evaluation and the perpetually self-renewing character of philosophical interpretation. The point is not to arouse general scepticism about the historical claims made in this book, but to help explain why the recovery of ancient philosophy is not a finite task that might in principle one day be completed and consigned to the bookshelf. So long as the humanities continue to be taught and researched, this process of constantly rethinking and enriching the understanding of our philosophical origins will remain an integral part of them.

1 Argument in ancient philosophy

At the beginning of Book Gamma of his *Metaphysics*, Aristotle announces the existence of a peculiar branch of knowledge:

There is a certain science which considers the things which exist insofar as they exist, and what holds of them in their own right. It is not the same as any of the particular sciences; for none of them investigates universally about the things which exist insofar as they exist – rather, they cut off a certain part of these things and consider what holds of this part (so, for example, the mathematical sciences). (*Metaphysics* 1003a21–6)[1]

The science which considers everything which exists, insofar as it exists, Aristotle calls first philosophy. It is usually named metaphysics.

Most things about Aristotelian metaphysics are contested. But at any rate it is a science. Alexander of Aphrodisias (pp. 243–4 below), who held the imperial Chair in Aristotelian philosophy at Athens in the early third century AD, took the word 'science' in a strict and Aristotelian sense. An Aristotelian science is an organized body of truths. Its scope and subject-matter are defined by the genus or class of items with which it deals and by the aspects of those items which interest it. Its foundations or first principles are laid down in the form of axioms and definitions. Its remaining truths – its theorems – are deduced from these principles by formal syllogisms. The geometry presented in Euclid's *Elements* (pp. 288–9 below) is a paradigm of an Aristotelian science. Metaphysics, according to Alexander, is also an Aristotelian science; and a metaphysician is, or ought to be, engaged in the construction of an *Elements of Metaphysics*.

Alexander introduces his view without trumpets, apparently taking it to be uncontroversial (see *On Aristotle's Metaphysics* 239.6–9).

And if he thought metaphysics a science, then he assigned the same status to the other branches of philosophy – not only to physics, but also to ethics and to politics. To be sure, these latter sciences will not share the rigour of geometry:

> When speaking about such things and on the basis of such things it is enough to indicate the truth roughly and in outline – that is to say, when speaking about what holds for the most part and on the basis of such things it is enough to conclude to such things.
>
> (Aristotle, *Nicomachean Ethics* 1094b19–22)

The genus with which the science of ethics is concerned collects truths which hold 'for the most part' rather than by an iron necessity; and in that sense ethics is less rigorous than geometry.

It does not follow, and Aristotle does not affirm, that ethics is not, in principle, an organized and axiomatized science. And Alexander knows that

> many arts are conjectural and syllogize their propositions on the basis of what is possible in this sense [i.e. as holding for the most part] – e.g. medicine, navigation, gymnastics. In general, matters which involve deliberation are shown by way of this sort of possibility: e.g. if someone were wondering whether he should now put to sea and were to urge that, when the wind is favourable, then for the most part those who sail are safe; but now the winds are favourable; therefore those who put to sea now will for the most part be safe. Aristotle calls probative a syllogism which someone might use when he wants to show something.   (*On Aristotle's Prior Analytics* 165.8–15)

The arts and sciences proceed by probative syllogizing even if the component propositions of their syllogisms are not necessary truths.

An Aristotelian science is purple with proofs. To be sure, its first principles must somehow be magicked into position; but after that, all scientific truths are proved. Now a proof is a sort of syllogism, and a syllogism is a formally valid deduction. The discipline which the ancients called logic comprehended more than the modern discipline of the same name, but the study of formally valid deductions was always at its centre. All Aristotelian sciences, metaphysics among them, therefore depend on logic.

Alexander urged that logic is an instrument or tool of philosophy and the other sciences; and he argued against a rival thesis which made logic a part of philosophy (*On Aristotle's Prior Analytics*

1.7–4.29). The dispute was not a piece of arid scholasticism: it had momentous consequences for the study of syllogisms.

As for those items about which Aristotle said nothing but which the more recent thinkers discuss, they are useless for proof, and it is clear that he omitted them because of their uselessness and not because of his own ignorance . . . For the measure of any instrument is its utility with regard to what is shown or produced by it. What is not useful is not an instrument: an adze which is no use to a carpenter is not an adze at all – except in a different sense.   (On Aristotle's Prior Analytics 164.27–165.2)

If the task of a logician is to provide the tools with which scientists can make their deductions, then he is to them as a harness-maker is to horsemen; and a harness-maker has no business to fabricate exotic equipment which can serve no rider's needs.

Alexander's austere – or philistine – view of logic was not idiosyncratic. But neither was it widely shared, and it became a platitude of post-Aristotelian philosophy that logic is one of the three main parts of philosophy, alongside physics and ethics (see p. 166 below). But despite Alexander's insinuations, no one who maintained that logic was a part of philosophy, and therefore a legitimate object of study in its own right, disputed the idea that logic also supplied the sciences with its instruments.

Mastery of the instruments was taught to their potential users. In antiquity, logic was not an esoteric discipline, reserved – like medicine or the higher mathematics – for a few specialists. Rather, it was a standard part of the school curriculum, the first subject to be tackled by a young man once he had escaped from the hands of the grammarian and the rhetorician.

You read out of the book. You listen in silence while the master explains it. You nod to show that you understand. Then the others read. You doze off. You hear 'What's the first? what's the second?', again and again. The windows are open. Someone hammers out: 'If it is day, it is light . . .'
                                                       (Fronto, On Eloquence v 4)

So Marcus Cornelius Fronto, the statesman and stylist who taught the Emperor Marcus Aurelius his rhetoric; and no doubt logic exercises bored many students to distraction. But the subject sometimes proved beguiling, and even exciting – and there are tales of glib young men who vexed their elders at the dinner-table by ostentatious and inappropriate logic-chopping. In any event, every educated man was soaked in logic; and just as grammar was an undisputed foundation for the appreciation of literature, so logic was an uncontested basis for the study of science and philosophy.

Logic, as it was standardly taught, had two parts. There was 'categorical' syllogistic, which had been invented by Aristotle (pp. 132–6 below) and which was concerned with those formal deductions the validity of which turns on the sense of the quantifying expressions 'all' and 'some'. For example:

> All philosophers are intelligent.
> Some emperors are philosophers.
> Therefore: some emperors are intelligent.

Secondly, there was 'hypothetical' syllogistic, associated primarily with the Stoics (p. 168 below), which investigated those inferences where validity turns on the sense of the connecting particles 'if', 'or' and 'and'. Thus:

> If it is day, it is light.
> It is day.
> Therefore: it is light.

Such stuff is worth knowing. Galen (see pp. 295–8 below), whom Marcus Aurelius saluted as the most eminent doctor and the leading philosopher of the age, held, like Alexander, that logic was an instrument of the sciences. Science, he opined, cannot be done by someone who has no grounding in logic – and this holds of his own eminently practical science of medicine as well as of other, more theoretical, sciences. A doctor must learn logic. Logic will, first of all, protect him from error: he will not be misled by the fallacies of his less capable colleagues, and he will not fall into fallacy himself. And secondly, logic will give him the power to elaborate his own science, to prove its constituent theorems. The sciences are probative sciences; and their practitioners must drill themselves in the probative methods.

'Philosophy is a probative science': the notion may seem alchimerical, a vapour distilled in the alembic of some Peripatetic brain and having little connection with the solid reality of actual philosophizing.

To be sure, late antiquity offers a finished instance of the thing. Proclus, head of the Platonic school at Athens in the second half of the fifth century AD (p. 245 below), was at home in Aristotelian philosophy. His commentary on Euclid's *Elements* shows that he had reflected on the nature of an axiomatized deductive system; his *Elements of Physics* put the theoretical reflections into practice; and the *Elements of Theology* is nothing less than an attempt to write a science of metaphysics, 'theology' being another name for that polyonymous discipline.

Perhaps Proclus had Aristotle in mind. Surely he had a passage from Plato's *Republic* in mind:

Reason treats these hypotheses not as principles but as genuine hypotheses – as it were, stepping-stones or starting-points – in order that it may go to what is not hypothetical and reach the principle of everything. Having touched this principle, it then again takes hold of what depends upon it and thus descends to a conclusion ...   (511b)

What is the second part of this up-and-down procedure if not a deductive and probative science? Does not Plato adumbrate the conception of scientific philosophy which Aristotle was later to elaborate? Come to that, Proclus might have reflected that there had been a Presocratic pioneer in the science of first philosophy; for in the mid fifth century BC Parmenides' *Way of Truth*, having laid down that anything which can be the subject of inquiry exists, had then proceeded to establish, in rigorously deductive fashion, a sequence of properties which must hold of every existent item insofar as it exists (pp. 43–4, 61–4 below).

And yet few of the philosophers of antiquity produced, or seem to have aspired to produce, sciences of this sort. Was Epicurean physics a science? Or Stoic ethics? Or Plotinian metaphysics?

Certainly, no philosopher started work by casting round for first principles. But then no scientist worked like that. Greek geometers began *in mediis rebus*, with some particular problem or in some special part of their subject. They fastened upon some truths, or apparent truths, in the domain; they worked down from those putative theorems by deducing their consequences; and they worked upwards, seeking truths from which the theorems might be derived. The upward path might eventually hit upon some axioms. The *Elements* of Euclid amalgamated and systematized the results of such piecemeal research. So too in philosophy: research is piecemeal; consolidation into an *Elements* comes later.

In the *Republic* Plato does not profess to use the up and down procedure which he there describes – it is a 'longer path' which cannot yet be followed (504b). The path had been mentioned in connection with the question of whether souls have three parts to them:

> You must know, Glaucon, that in my opinion we shall never obtain a precise answer from the sort of methods which we now use in our arguments; for it is another longer and greater path which leads to such things.   (435d)

Socrates and his friends, the speakers in this dialogue, will not arrive at a precise psychology inasmuch as they cannot, or will not, use the appropriate methods. Nonetheless, the methods which they do use will yield proofs – or at any rate proofs of a sort (504b). And earlier in the dialogue (436a–441b) Socrates urges – or proves – that souls have three parts.

The argument is intricate; but its general structure is not hard to make out. It begins with what looks for all the world like an axiom or first principle:

> The same thing will not at one and the same time do or undergo opposites in the same respect and in relation to the same thing.   (436b)

Then there is some material to which the principle can be applied:

> What about assenting and dissenting, wanting to get and rejecting, taking and pushing away – would you not say that all these are mutual opposites, whether they are doings or undergoings?   (437b)

And finally, the soul:

> – Now the soul of a thirsty man, insofar as he is thirsty, wants nothing else than to drink, and yearns for this and starts towards it?
> – Evidently.
> – So if something drags it away when it is thirsty, that will be something in it different from what thirsts and drives it like a beast to drink? For we say that the same thing does not at one and the same time do opposite things with the same part of itself in relation to the same thing.   (439b)

You may be thirsty and at the same time desire not to drink. Hence the soul has at least two parts – a part which thirsts (and in general, desires) and a part which cautions (and in general, reasons).

The argument is cited here for its promise, not for its performance. It is a sketch for a page in a book which Plato was never to write, an outline of a proof which was to form part of a scientific philosophy. Such preparatory work, in philosophy as in geometry, contains, or consists of, syllogisms.

The Stoa was notorious for its philosophical syllogisms. Zeno of Citium, the school's first head, started the fashion. Here is one of his little deductions:

The rational is superior to the irrational. But nothing is superior to the world. Therefore the world is rational.   (Sextus, *Against the Professors* IX 104)

Zeno's successors imitated him. Galen reports that the following argument was advanced by the second-century BC Stoic Diogenes of Babylon:

The voice passes through the throat. If it passed from the brain it would not pass through the throat. But the voice passes from the same place as the reason. The reason passes from the intellect. Hence the intellect is not in the brain.   (*On the Doctrines of Hippocrates and Plato* V 241)

These syllogisms are simple, and the Stoics were proud of the fact. Other texts offer more elaborate deductions. Sextus Empiricus, a Sceptical philosopher of the late second century AD, transcribes an argument which his Sceptical predecessor Aenesidemus had proposed some two and a half centuries earlier:

If what is apparent appears in the same way to everyone who is disposed in the same way, and if signs are apparent, then signs appear in the same way to everyone who is disposed in the same way. But signs do not appear in the same way to everyone who is disposed in the same way. But what is apparent appears in the same way to everyone who is disposed in the same way. Therefore signs are not apparent.

This argument is compounded from a second and a third unproved syllogism, as we can learn from an analysis – which will be clearer if we expound it in terms of an argument schema, thus:

> If the first and the second, then the third.
> But not the third.
> But the first.
> Therefore, not the second.   (*Against the Professors* VIII 234–5)

The analysis, which is couched in the technical terminology of Stoic syllogistic, continues for a page or so.

Such texts are remarkable for their pedantry: literary elegance is of no account – what matters is logical structure. Formality of this sort does not appeal to every taste. Alexander remarks that some people will add unnecessary flourishes to their syllogisms in order to 'avoid the dry and naked impression which technicality makes' (*On Aristotle's Prior Analytics* 279.24–5). And some authors offer both a formal and an informal, a naked and a clothed, version of their reasoning. The best examples are found in Christian texts. Thus in his *Eranistes*, the fifth-century Bishop of Cyrrhus, Theodoretus, first presents a sequence of theological considerations in prose, and then sets out what purports to be a fully syllogized version of them.

It is true that formal syllogizing is hardly the rule in ancient philosophical writings. Plato's dialogues, for example, contain innumerable arguments; but with rare exceptions – the most notable of which fill the second half of his *Parmenides* – Plato does not set them out with dry formality. Here is a little argument in its Platonic clothing:

– Well, I said, don't you think that everything to which a function is assigned also has an excellence (*aretē*)? Let's look at the same examples again. We say that eyes have a function?
– Yes.
– So do eyes also have an excellence?
– They also have an excellence.
– Well, do ears have a function?
– Yes.
– And also an excellence?
– And also an excellence.
– And what about all the rest? Isn't it the same?
– The same.   (*Republic* 353b)

The logic of this argument will be glanced at later. Here it is quoted for its form.

Plato sets it out in a dialogue; and, thus expressed, it best corresponds – in Plato's view – to the thought which it represents. For Plato conceived of thought as an interior dialogue, not as an interior monologue (*Sophist* 264a). Members of his school, the Academy, trained their private faculties in public dialogues, for which various rules were laid down. The rules made up the art of 'dialectic' (Aristotle sets them out in his *Topics*); and this art had a permanent influence on the terminology of later Greek logic. (For example, a standard term for 'to propound (an argument)' means literally 'to ask'.)

Nonetheless, the dialogue form is extrinsic, in this sense: Plato's arguments can all be turned into monologues without any logical or philosophical loss. The ancient commentators were aware of this; and they frequently bared Plato's arguments of their conversational clothing in order to reveal their logical force. An anonymous commentary on the *Theaetetus*, partially preserved on papyrus and dating perhaps from the first century AD, contains this morsel:

When you look at the matter, he propounds the argument according to the third figure.
>   As things appear to each man, so are they for him,
and
>   As they appear, so does he perceive them.
From which it is concluded:
>   As each man perceives things, so are they for him.
>   (anon., *On Plato's Theaetetus* LXVI 11–22)

The commentator purports to find an Aristotelian syllogism (the 'third figure', see p. 136 below) underlying Plato's text. In the same vein Alcinous, who wrote an introductory handbook to Platonism in the second century AD, assures his readers that Plato knew all the syllogisms of the Peripatetics and the Stoics, and he duly cites illustrative passages from the dialogues in which this or that syllogism is exemplified (*Handbook of Platonism* 158.17–159.30). And according to Proclus, some interpreters had analysed the whole of Plato's *Alcibiades* into ten syllogisms (*On Plato's Alcibiades* 12–13).

Syllogistic analysis might have a critical as well as an exegetical function. Thus Alexander has this to say about a celebrated Epicurean argument:

In some cases a different conclusion is inferred, not the one which is concluded from the premises. Thus it is in the argument propounded ['asked'] by Epicurus:
>   Death is nothing to us. For what is dissolved does
>   not perceive, and what does not perceive is nothing to us.
This is not the conclusion – rather, that what is dissolved is nothing to us (in the first figure).   (*On Aristotle's Prior Analytics* 346.14–17)

More generally, logic will serve philosophers in their refutations as well as in their proofs. So it is, *passim*, in the works of the Sceptical Sextus – an example has already been quoted.

So it was – or seems to have been – in the work of the Presocratic Zeno, whom Aristotle is reported to have called the originator of dialectic. For example:

If several things exist, it is necessary for them to be as many as they are, and neither more nor fewer. But if they are as many as they are, they will be limited in number. Again, if several things exist, the things which exist are unlimited in number. For there are always others between the things which exist, and again others between them. And thus the things which exist are unlimited in number.   (fragment B3)

Hence if several things exist, they are both limited and unlimited in number. But that is impossible. Hence it is not the case that several things exist.

The Aristotelian conception of a scientific philosophy was not elaborated before Aristotle. But the general notion which underlies it – the notion that a philosopher must offer rigorous proofs of his theses – had been understood from at least the time of Parmenides; and it is found again and again in ancient texts.

True, Galen thought that the notion was not sufficiently prized: he liked to berate his contemporaries for being 'slaves to their sects', for spurning proof and accepting on trust the doctrines of a Master and a School. True, in the dying years of pagan philosophy, Greek thinkers – and in particular Greek Platonists – are often supposed to have surrendered reason to trust and proof to authority. Yet if there were some intellectual slaves – and perhaps a few happy slaves – slavery was not a common condition among philosophers.

Olympiodorus, who taught in Alexandria in the sixth century AD, tells an anecdote about his teacher Ammonius:

Plato himself commands us not to trust him simply and at haphazard but to seek out the truth. Thus the philosopher Ammonius says: 'Perhaps I am wrong, but when someone was giving a talk and said "Plato said so", I said to him: "He did not say so; and in any case – may Plato forgive me – even if he did say so, I do not trust him unless there is a proof."'
                                               (On Plato's Gorgias xli 9)

It is one thing to accept what Plato says, another to accept it on his say-so. Ammonius saw the difference. There is no reason to think that he was unusual.

Proof contrasts with trust (or with faith as the Greek word is often translated). A modern – and an ancient – platitude contrasts the trust (or faith) of Christians with the reason of pagans. So, for example, Galen – in one of the earliest pagan texts to take notice of the Christian religion – reprobates his colleague Archigenes for offering unproved assertions:

It would have been far better to have added something – if not a solid proof then at least an adequate argument...so that you would not at the very beginning – as though you had entered a school of Christ or of Moses – read out unproved laws...   (*On Types of Pulse* VIII 579)

Christians preferred trust to proof: every pagan opponent of the new philosophy repeated the accusation.

The Christians vigorously rebutted the charge. Their philosophers set things out in syllogisms; they used all the devices of pagan logic in proof of orthodox doctrine – and in refutation of heresy and of paganism. Eusebius, Bishop of Caesarea in the early fourth century AD, was a devotee of proof. Near the beginning of his vast *Proof of the Gospel* he writes thus:

They say that we provide nothing by way of proof but require that those who come to us rely on trust alone. Against this slander the present treatise may be a not irrational reply.   (*Proof of the Gospel* I 1.12–13)

The suggestion that Christianity is a philosophy of trust is a slander.

Eusebius was not the last Christian to vaunt his probative prowess, nor the first. Justin, who was martyred under the Emperor Hadrian, is his most remarkable predecessor. In the long *Dialogue with Trypho*, in which Justin defends the Christian reading of the Old Testament against Jewish objectors, the words 'proof' and 'prove' pepper the discussion – no ancient text makes more frequent or more insistent use of them.

Reason, not custom or trust, is the instrument of philosophy: such was the view of Presocratics and Postsocratics, of Platonists and Peripatetics, of pagans and Christians. And after all, there is nothing very remarkable about the view. Philosophy is not a matter of obedience to authority; nor is it an historical enterprise or a collecting of empirical data. In that case, it can only be a rational venture; and if it is a rational venture, then it is a matter of amassing proofs – and, at bottom, of logic. And so it may come to seem that the Aristotelian thesis which makes a science of philosophy is no more than the elaboration of a simple truth. That is the tapestry: it is time to unpick it.

First, the discipline of logic had its ancient detractors. For every Christian writer who pretended to good logical method there is a Christian writer – often the same writer – who purported to despise the quibbles of Chrysippus and the snares of Aristotle. In his diatribe against the dead Emperor Julian, Gregory of Nazianzus mocks the pagan:

Give me your royal and sophistical syllogisms and your enthymemes, and let us see how our fishermen and farmers speak.   (*Orations* v 30.1)

His friend Gregory of Nyssa concurred:

As for confirming our doctrines by way of the dialectical art, through syllogisms and analytical science, we abjure that form of discourse as rotten and suspect with regard to the proof of the truth.   (*PG* xl vi 52B)

Logic was an invention of the fallen angels – and a device of the heretics. According to Jerome,

Eutychius and Eunomius...attempt with syllogisms – and with sophisms and Liars and Sorites – to confirm the errors which others have invented.
                                                        (*On Amos* i 1.4)

(For the 'Liar' and 'Sorites' paradoxes, see p. 169 below.) Such sentiments are a constant feature of Christian polemic from its earliest days.

Nor are they limited to Christian texts. Some late Platonists left the logical plains of Aristotle below them as their hot-air balloons lifted them into the blue Platonic empyrean. Damascius, the last head of the Platonic school of Athens in the early sixth century AD, records in his diverting *Life of Isidore* that his hero, when he found a particularly gifted pupil, would entice him away from the syllogisms of Aristotle (fragment 338 Zintzen). For Isidore – again according to Damascius –

did not want simply to compel himself and his companions by syllogisms to follow an unseen truth, being driven by reason to travel down a single road and following the right path like a blind man; rather, he always endeavoured to persuade and to put insight in the soul – or better, to purify the insight which it already contains.   (Photius, *Library* cod. 242, 339a29–34)

Long before Isidore's time, hard-nosed doctors of Galen's acquaintance found that logic was a trivial pursuit. Galen lambasted them –

They know nothing whatever of philosophy itself but consider it the most useless of all studies, like drilling holes in millet seeds.

(*On Prognosis* xiv 606)

More generally, standard histories of philosophy reported that certain schools – not only the Pyrrhonist sceptics but the Cynics, the Cyrenaics, the Epicureans, even some Stoics – 'rejected logic'.

Much of the opposition to logic was bluster. Gregory of Nazianzus fulminated against logic – and lauded Basil for his logical prowess (*Orations* XLIII 23). Jerome detested spiny syllogisms – and was affronted when a pushy young man dared to criticize his own deductions:

You say that ... this dialectician, a pillar of your city and of the family of the Plautii, has not even read the *Categories* of Aristotle, nor his *De interpretatione*, nor the *Analytics*, nor indeed Cicero's *Topics*; but in the circles of the ignorant and at tea-parties of little women he weaves his unsyllogistic syllogisms and by cunning argumentation unravels what he calls my sophisms. ... In vain did I turn the pages of Alexander's commentaries, in vain did my learned teacher introduce me to logic by way of Porphyry's *Introduction* ...   (*Letters* 50.1)

Even when the objection to logic was more than puff and wind, it did not necessarily touch the thesis that syllogizing is essential to philosophical inquiry. Thus some denounced logic in the same breath as rhetoric; and they were concerned with style rather than with method. According to Eusebius' contemporary Lactantius,

divine learning has no need for logic, since wisdom is not in the tongue but in the heart, and it is of no account what style you use – it is things not words which we seek.   (*Divine Institutes* III 13)

There are innumerable parallels. Many ancient authors who 'reject logic' were against the vulgar parade of logical jargon: they were not against the unostentatious application of logical expertise.

Again, some authors objected that formal arguments rarely have much persuasive force, that they fail to grip the minds of their audience. Seneca, the severe Stoic moralist who advised the Emperor Nero, jeered at the little reasonings of the founder of his own school:

'No evil is glorious. Death is glorious. Therefore death is not an evil.' – Congratulations: I am free of the fear of death. Now I shall not hesitate to stretch out my neck on the block. To tell the truth, it is not easy to say who is the more futile: someone who thinks that such an argument can extinguish the fear of death, or someone who tries to refute the argument as though it had some bearing on reality.   (*Letters* 82.9)

Seneca claims that Zeno's syllogisms do not move the mind to assent. No doubt he is right, and perhaps his observation has some importance for teachers of philosophy. But it has no interest for philosophers – or for geometers. Euclid was not in the business of persuading the multitude that Pythagoras' theorem is true: he wanted to prove its truth. A Stoic philosopher had to prove the truths of Stoicism – how those truths are best commended to the world is another question.

There is more to the matter. Galen's anti-logical contemporaries might have asked him why he thought that without logical expertise a scientist could get nowhere. Hippocrates, whom Galen himself admired beyond measure, had made some progress in medical science before logic had been invented. As for Euclid and his successors, was their paradigmatic success really dependent on the work done by Aristotle and Chrysippus? In short, concede that philosophy and the other sciences are essentially deductive systems: why infer that formal logic is of utility to them?

Two very different considerations are pertinent here. The first concerns the state of the logical art in antiquity. Galen reports that

I put myself into the hands of all the reputable Stoics and Peripatetics of the age. I learned a great many logical theorems which, when I later scrutinized them, I found to be useless for proofs; and I learned very few which they had usefully discovered and which might serve the goal I had set myself – and even those were disputed among them, and some went contrary to our natural notions. Indeed, as far as my teachers went, I would have fallen into a Pyrrhonian puzzlement had I not taken a hold of geometry and arithmetic and calculation...   (*On My Own Books* XIX 39–40)

The standard curriculum in logic, Galen claims, contained much useless material – material which could not serve the needs of the sciences; and what is more, it was collectively inadequate to those needs.

Galen himself, reflecting on 'geometry and arithmetic and calculation', came to add 'a third genus of syllogisms' to the traditional two:

There is another, third, genus of syllogisms useful for proofs which I say come about in respect of relational items – although the Aristotelians insist on enumerating them among the categorical syllogisms.

(Introduction to Logic 16.1)

In the proof of his first theorem, Euclid uses an argument of this form:

A is equal to B.
C is equal to B.
Therefore A is equal to C.

This is a formally valid deduction, according to Galen; but it is neither a categorical nor a hypothetical syllogism – it belongs to a third genus of syllogisms, a genus of syllogisms the validity of which is determined by the properties of certain relations.

Galen has been applauded for his insight. But he did little with his relational syllogisms. He offers a ragbag of examples rather than a theory. Still less did he try to unite all three sorts of syllogism into a single system. In other words, formal logic, despite the achievements of Aristotle, Chrysippus and Galen, was an imperfect science and offered an imperfect instrument to the scientist. Alexander might pretend that Euclidean proofs could be conducted within the confines of Aristotelian syllogistic; but geometers knew better. And if some scientists and philosophers were unimpressed by the claims of formal logic to ground their work, then part of the reason might be found in the imperfection of the discipline.

The second consideration is this. You might concede that science and philosophy are essentially deductive systems, and that any philosopher must therefore be capable of producing good arguments and detecting bad. But, given that men argued rationally before Aristotle discovered the syllogism, it is evident that an expertise in logic is not a necessary condition for competent ratiocination. It is equally evident that expert logicians do not always excel in argument: logical expertise is not a sufficient condition for competent ratiocination. A philosopher who wants to make syllogisms has no need for formal logic: he may rely on his natural faculties.

This view of logic was common in early modern philosophy. There is an ancient affirmation of it in a text by Theodoretus:

The Persians are extremely syllogistic – not because they have read the mazes of Chrysippus and of Aristotle, nor because Socrates and Plato have educated them in this area; for they have not been fed on rhetorical and philosophical arguments – their only teacher is nature.

(The Cure of Greek Diseases v 72)

If someone is trained in logic, it does not follow that he will argue well – nor even that he will argue better than someone not so trained. If someone argues well, it does not follow that he has been trained in logic. And – as the meetings of any Department of Philosophy demonstrate – it is not true that, as a matter of fact, someone argues better if and only if he has had some logical training.

All this is linked to a central fact about logic: the art is extraordinarily easy to master. The Methodical school of medicine boasted that it could teach the art of medicine in three months. Galen exploded with rage. But you could learn the art of logic in three days – or in three hours, if you were quick witted. Aristotelian syllogistic, once its modal parts are set aside (and all later logicians did set them aside), reduces to some twenty valid forms. The whole system can be set down in a few pages – and it is so set down later in this volume (pp. 133–6). As Proclus put it,

The analytics of the Peripatos, and its culmination – the theory of proof – are evident and easily grasped by anyone who is not utterly obfuscated or drowning in the waters of Lethe.   *(On Plato's Cratylus* 2)

And the same holds of Stoic syllogistic.

Galen, it is true, more than once declares that long and arduous training in the logical methods is essential. But he does not thereby contradict the thesis that logic is quickly learned. The training is needed, not in order to master the logical schemata, but in order to apply them – to spot deductive structure in a piece of informal reasoning, to see how a sequence of syllogisms may be concatenated into a complex proof, and so on.

The simplicity of ancient syllogistic is not a sign of the primitive state of the art. Modern logic, of the elementary kind which is all that a scientist will ever need, is equally straight-forward. Gottlob Frege, who invented the business in 1879, set it all out in twenty pages; it consists of a couple of forms of deduction and half a dozen axioms; a few hours and it is understood. For logic – this elementary part of logic – contains nothing esoteric. It is a matter of articulated common sense. John Locke's washerwoman, relying on her native wit, had natural access to all the schemes of the logicians.

Thus a philosopher might 'reject logic' in the expectation that nature and practice would meet all his deductive requirements. Epicurus 'rejected logic' in this sense. He pooh-poohed syllogistic theorizing, not syllogisms. The existence of empty space, for example, is one of the pillars of Epicurean physics. It is not an evident fact of experience – it had to be inferred:

Epicurus says that there is empty space (which is something unclear) and justifies it by an evident fact, namely motion; for if there were no empty space, there would be no movement.

(Sextus, *Against the Professors* VII 213)

In other words:

If there is no empty space, there is no movement.
There is movement.
Therefore: there is empty space.

This is a hypothetical syllogism of the sort which the Stoics called a 'second unproved' (p. 168). Epicurus did not need a course in logic in order to employ it.

Or did Epicurus use the second unproved? The question may be approached obliquely.

It is a familiar observation that the theory of proof which Aristotle develops in his *Posterior Analytics* finds little echo in his philosophical and scientific treatises. Those works are not stuffed with syllogisms; and in general they make little use of the logic of the *Analytics*. Some scholars have urged that the treatises should be considered 'dialectical' rather than 'analytical', that their logical background is to be found in the *Topics* rather than in the *Analytics*. But the suggestion does little to resolve the issue. To be sure, if you use the term 'dialectical' in a sufficiently vague sense, Aristotle's works are dialectical – and so is everything else. Aristotelian dialectic, in the sense of the *Topics*, is 'a method by which we shall be able to syllogize, on any subject which may be proposed, on the basis of reputable propositions' (*Topics* 100a18–20). The term 'syllogism' has its standard Aristotelian sense. So the treatises are dialectical to the extent that they contain syllogisms; and they are not stuffed with syllogisms.

Different and complementary explanations have been offered for this fact. One of them runs like this. Not all arguments are formal deductions; and although philosophy may be a science, and an argumentative science, it does not follow that the syllogism is its main instrument. There are arguments in Aristotle – and in every ancient philosophical text. But in the general run of things, the arguments which philosophers use are informal – not merely are a philosopher's premises not invariably marked by geometrical necessity; in addition, and more importantly, the link between the premises of a philosophical argument and its conclusion is not invariably a formal deductive link.

The existence of non-formal arguments was no secret. The Stoics recognized a class of deductions which 'conclude non-methodically'. Among them is the following:

It is day.
You say that it is day.
Therefore: you speak the truth.

This is a valid deduction – if its premises are true, then and for that reason its conclusion must be true. But its validity does not depend on its logical structure or on the sense of any formal particles which it exploits; rather, its validity depends on the nature of its 'matter' – on the sense of its constituent terms (and here, on the sense of the term 'true'). Formal logic has nothing to say about such non-formal or material deductions; but material deduction is a common sort of argument in philosophical texts.

Take the following passage from Plotinus – the leading Platonist of the third century AD – which purports to show that the soul, the item which perceives, is not corporeal:

If what perceives is a body, perception can only come about in the way in which a seal is impressed on wax from a seal-ring – whether the objects of perception are impressed on blood or on air. And if they are impressed on liquid bodies (which is plausible) they will run together as though in water and there will be no such thing as memory. If the impressions stay, then either – since they occupy the place – it is not possible for others to be impressed, so that there will be no further perceptions, or else when others come along the former impressions will perish, so that it will not be possible to remember anything.   (*Enneads* IV 8.6.37–46)

Plotinus here produces no syllogisms. But he produces an argument, and his argument is deductive in intent – it involves 'non-methodical' deductions which turn in particular on the concept of an impression.

Non-methodical deductions are one sort of informal argument. There are others – the ancient philosophers talked of inductions, of sign-inferences, of paradigm-arguments. Such things are not deductions at all; rather, they amass reasons, or evidence, or considerations, in favour of a thesis. Parts of the passage from Plotinus just cited seem to present non-deductive argumentation; and the phenomenon is ubiquitous. Take Plato's argument at *Republic* 353b (above, p. 27). It might be set out – in the style of the ancient commentators – like this:

Eyes have a function, and also an excellence.
Ears have a function, and also an excellence.
And so on.
Hence everything which has a function has an excellence.

Construed as a deduction, the argument is lamentable – for it is evident that the premisses do not necessitate the conclusion. But the argument is not to be construed as a deduction: it is an induction – that is to say, it infers a general truth from a number of individual cases. Whether it is a good or bad induction is a question. But the question is not answered by observing that the argument is not a deduction.

A dogged logician will not yet throw in the sponge. Although he must acknowledge that real philosophy and real science are full of non-syllogistic arguments, he will be quick to observe that non-methodical deductions and non-deductive inferences can always be transformed into syllogisms. Different transformations suggest themselves for different arguments; but the universal thesis is readily proved. Take any non-syllogistic argument whatsoever. It will have a conclusion, and a certain number of premisses; so it can be put in the following shape:

$P_1, P_2, \ldots, P_n$: therefore Q.

Form the conjunction of the n premisses,

P_1 and P_2 and ... and P_n,

and then make a conditional proposition with this conjunction as antecedent and the conclusion of the original argument as consequent:

If P_1 and P_2 and ... and P_n, then Q.

The original argument can now be transformed into the inference:

If P_1 and P_2 and ... and P_n, then Q.
P_1 and P_2 and ... and P_n.
Therefore, Q.

This is a syllogism – a Stoic 'first unproved'. Moreover, the syllogism will be a proof that Q if and only if the original argument is a proof that Q.

Transformations of this sort have a purpose; but they do not show that every informal argument may be reduced without remainder to a syllogism. In the original argument, half the effort will go into showing that each of the premisses is true and the other half into showing that the premisses provide sufficient reason for accepting the conclusion. In the syllogism, no work is needed to forge the link between premisses and conclusion; rather, half the effort will go into showing that the conjunctive premiss is true and the other half into showing that the conditional premiss is true – and that second half is neither more nor less than the effort of showing that the premisses of the original argument provide a sufficient reason for accepting its conclusion.

Epicurus argued roughly thus:

Things move.
So there is empty space.

You may transmogrify this into a second unproved – or into a first unproved:

If things move, there is empty space.
Things move.
Therefore: there is empty space.

The problematical aspect of the informal argument, and the part of the argument which Epicurus must strain every nerve to defend, is the link between its premiss and its conclusion. Does the fact that things move provide a sufficient reason for postulating the existence of empty space? If there is movement, is there therefore empty space? The problematical aspect of the syllogized argument is its conditional premiss. Is it true that if things move then there is empty space? The transformation of Epicurus' argument into a Stoic syllogism resolves no problems – it displaces them.

There is a final step to be taken. Often enough, philosophy is not only not a matter of deductive argument – it is not a matter of argument at all. A philosopher may want not to prove a theorem but to describe a state of affairs, not to demonstrate how things must be but to point out how they are. How this sort of activity is best characterized I do not know. Some speak of analysis, some of phenomenology, some of descriptive metaphysics, and I have heard the phrase 'conceptual hoovering'. Anyone who has read a few pages of philosophy knows what I have in mind. Take, for example, the account of the 'moral virtues' in Aristotle's *Nicomachean Ethics*. His analysis of the virtue of magnificence begins like this:

It would seem to be appropriate next to discuss magnificence; for this too seems to be a virtue concerned with money. But unlike generosity it does not extend to all monetary dealings but only to expenditure – and here it exceeds generosity in grandeur. For as its name hints, it is a fitting expenditure on a grand scale. But grandeur is a relational matter . . .   (1122a18–24)

And so on. Aristotle's account of his virtues is all description – even if the descriptions are sometimes tricked out with reasons and generally aim at a certain coherence. It is hard to characterize what Aristotle is up to. But he is plainly up to something which philosophers are often up to; and he is plainly not tracking down long arguments, or deducing theorems from axioms, or elaborating a deductive system.

'Philosophy is a science. A science is a series of proofs. Proofs are deductive inferences. Deductive inferences are the province of logic.' Such was the tapestry suggested by a passage in Aristotle's *Metaphysics*. It has its charms, but each aspect of it is less attractive than at first it seems.

In order to understand deductive inferences you do not need to be a logician: native wit is, in most actual cases, quite enough to decide the validity of a philosopher's deductions. Proofs are not, or need not be, deductive inferences: in the general run of things, a philosopher's proofs – that is to say, the reasons which he gives for his theses – will not be syllogisms nor even deductions; and although they can always be recast as deductively valid inferences, that fact is of little significance. Sciences – let it be added – need not be conceived of as essentially probative and axiomatizable: geography and palaeontology, for example, are not like that. And finally, why think that philosophy is a science?

Logic is an instrument of philosophy and of the sciences. But it is an instrument which a scientist will rarely have occasion to use.

Logic – *pace* Alexander and Galen – is also a part of philosophy. Indeed, it is the most respectable part of that rather louche discipline. (And it is the part which ancient philosophers did most to develop.) To that extent any half-decent philosopher will be a logician.

And what of the science of the things which exist insofar as they exist? Aristotle says that 'there is a science...', but he means not that the science was actually established, like geometry, but that someone with sufficient flair and energy might develop it. He did not develop it himself. (The *Metaphysics*, whatever else it may be, is not a sample of the science which it announces.) Proclus' *Elements* is a splendid failure. Perhaps the project is absurd? As well teach ravens to fly underwater. Well, the peculiar Aristotelian science is not an absurdity. It is part of what is now called logic; and it was established in 1879.

NOTE

1   For the forms of citations used in this chapter see: for Aristotle pp. 127–9, for Plato pp. 99–103, for Galen p. 299 n.3, and for the commentators on Aristotle p. 249. '*PG*' refers to J. P. Migne, *Patrologia Graeca* (1857–66), the ency- clopaedic compilation of Greek patristic writings.

2   The Presocratics

INTRODUCTION. FROM FOSSILS TO PHILOSOPHY

Hippolytus, antipope in the early third century AD, has this to tell us in the course of the survey of pagan Greek philosophy he presents in the first book of his *Refutation of all Heresies* (exhibit A):

Xenophanes thinks that a mixture of the land with the sea occurs, and that in time the land is dissolved by wetness. He claims he has demonstrations of the following kind: shells are found inland and in the mountains. Moreover he says that in Syracuse an impression of a fish and of seaweed has been found in the quarries; in Paros an impression of a bay-leaf in the depth of the rock; and in Malta laminae of all marine life. These came into being, he says, when everything was long ago covered with mud, and the impression was dried in the mud. All mankind is destroyed when the land is carried down into the sea and becomes mud. Subsequently the land starts again on its genesis. And for all worlds genesis takes place through a process of change.   (KRS 184)[1]

You might think that Xenophanes' heresy was to have been someone who left God out of the creation story. But that does not seem to have been a point Hippolytus was wanting to make. What leaps out of his report is the picture it paints of Xenophanes as pioneer practitioner of the scientific method. And although Hippolytus could not have put it in these terms, I fancy that it was Xenophanes' scientific imagination that fascinated him too. Here is a bold conjecture – for which he is the only source – about the history of the earth supported by a body of empirical evidence, including fossil evidence from specified locations; a conjecture deployed in its turn to support a further hypothesis about the conditions of creation in *all* worlds: what we might call proto-science rather than philosophy.

Xenophanes (c.570–c.475 BC) was a native of Colophon in what is now western Asiatic Turkey, located not far from Miletus, the maritime trading city which was home to the sixth-century thinkers later Greeks from before Aristotle claimed as their first philosophers: Thales, Anaximander, Anaximenes. Colophon is a long way from Elea, on the coast of Italy some distance south of the bay of Naples, and the native city of Parmenides, who was active early in the fifth century, and author of exhibit B – which is preserved only in commentaries on Plato's *Timaeus* and Aristotle's *Physics* respectively by two Athenian Neoplatonist philosophers even later than Hippolytus: Proclus, head of the Academy in the fifth century AD, and Simplicius, who was working there in AD 529, the year the emperor Justinian issued an edict ordering the closure of pagan philosophical schools. Exhibit B is a vastly different specimen from exhibit A: A talks of empirical proof, B works within a highly *a priori* framework and is expressed as the deliverance of divine revelation. And although the difference will not be apparent from the translation of B which follows, whereas A is in prose, B consists of seven and a bit lines of hexameter verse:

Come now, and I will tell you (and you must convey my account away once you have heard it) the only ways of inquiry that are to be thought of. The one, that a thing is and that it is impossible for it not to be, is the path of Persuasion (for she attends upon Truth); the other, that a thing is not and that there is a requirement that it should not be, this I declare to you is an altogether indiscernible track – for you could not know what is not (that cannot be done) nor point it out.   (KRS 291)

Exhibit A was proto-science. Exhibit B is unquestionably philosophy: a dense and on first acquaintance mysterious exercise in epistemology, employing something like logic (or more specifically the Law of Excluded Middle) to enunciate the metaphysical conditions of all successful inquiry – presumably including proto-scientific inquiry of the kind Xenophanes was engaged in. Parmenides seems to be proposing that with respect to any subject of inquiry whatever, there are in principle two and only two logically exclusive assumptions we can coherently make: either that it exists (is something or other), or that it does not exist (is nothing at all). And he then presents an argument for ruling out the second assumption: to make it is to be committed to attempting to find out something where nothing can be found out. He will go on in subsequent fragments to argue further that there are severe constraints on the interpretation of what is compatible with saying of something that it exists. Anything which exists must be uncreated and imperishable, changeless and perfect. What emerges is a radical form of monism: it certainly transpires that everything there is must have one and the same character; and it is doubtful whether in fact anything could have that character except reality as a whole. Readers have often been put in mind of Descartes' 'I think, therefore I am', and his attempt in the *Meditations* to find in that proposition a secure foundation for knowledge immune to the assaults of sceptical doubt.

Modern treatments of the Presocratics (or – as they might in a way more appropriately be called – Preplatonics) unsurprisingly find little reason to talk of Xenophanes and Parmenides in the same breath. Xenophanes is often seen as fitting into the early Ionian tradition of inquiry – heir to Thales and Anaximander, forerunner of the historians Hecataeus and Herodotus – whereas Parmenides figures as a pre-eminent critic of that tradition, and above all of its assumption that the natural world of birth, change and death is the real world. Xenophanes has some things to say in a monistic vein about the true conception of god which seem to find at least verbal echoes in some of Parmenides' verses about true reality; and the two thinkers share a theoretical preoccupation with the limitations of ordinary human understanding – 'the opinions of mortals' as Parmenides puts it. But it is nowadays commonly supposed that Parmenides was a creative genius not much in debt to anybody.

Yet Xenophanes spent much of his long life in Sicily and (very likely) southern Italy, after expulsion from Colophon in early manhood. Diogenes Laertius (early third century AD) reproduces the claim that he composed a poem on the original settlement of the colony at Elea; and although this is not apparent from Hippolytus' report in exhibit A, like Parmenides Xenophanes wrote his philosophy in verse (to judge from what survives of his writing he was in fact a much more versatile and prolific poet than Parmenides, and he may actually have earned his living as a rhapsode, i.e. performer of poetry). All this makes it likely enough that Parmenides knew him and fell under his influence. In any event, both Plato and Aristotle represent Xenophanes as a metaphysical monist precursor of Parmenides, with Aristotle recording the suggestion that Parmenides was his pupil, and Plato making the Eleatic philosophical 'family' originate with Xenophanes. Hippolytus' survey in Book I of the *Refutation* includes Parmenides as well as Xenophanes, and evidently relies on a source which put the two of them in one and the same philosophical tradition.

There is something troubling here. In the assessment of the relationship between two such major figures as Xenophanes and Parmenides, modern scholarship – which knows these thinkers only through fragments and later reports and paraphrases – is at odds with the towering minds of Plato and Aristotle, who could read their writings intact. Where antiquity saw intellectual traditions at work, moderns invoke the idea of originality. Of course, even great thinkers operate within those of the intellectual paradigms of their time and culture which they do not seek to overturn. But so too – like the critical anthropological observer – does the modern scholar.

The project of reconstructing Presocratic thought, whether in its main lines of development or in detail, is therefore a precarious business, as this introductory sketch has sought to emphasize. A catalogue of doubts would however be a pusillanimous response to the undisputed boldness of Presocratic speculation. In the rest of this chapter I shall forge ahead and offer an account which constitutes not a brief history of Presocratic thought, but an attempt to etch the different modes and focuses of inquiry which successive generations of thinkers made their distinctive concerns. And I shall not for the most part comment further on the manifold complexities and shortcomings of the evidence supporting the account, apart from indicating what we can assert with relative confidence and what less so. The figures with whom we shall be concerned are these:

Presocratic	Birthplace	Date	Key ideas	Comment
Thales	Miletus	Early 6C	Measurement as technique in astronomy	Made water the origin of things
Pherecydes	Syros	Early/mid 6C	Rationalized theological cosmogony	Author of first treatise ever written in prose

(cont.)

(cont.)

Presocratic	Birthplace	Date	Key ideas	Comment
Anaximander	Miletus	Early/mid 6C	Symmetry; analogical and indifference reasoning	Pupil of Thales; author of a prose treatise
Anaximenes	Miletus	Mid 6C	Material monism (air the sole basic substance)	Pupil of Anaximander; also writes in prose
Xenophanes	Colophon	Mid/late 6C	Monotheism; epistemological pessimism; fossil evidence	Practises philosophy in South Italy; verse writer
Pythagoras	Samos	Later 6C	Transmigration of the soul; number as key to cosmology	Founds religious sect in South Italy; writes nothing
Heraclitus	Ephesus	Turn of 6/5C	Unity of opposites	Writes prose aphorisms
Parmenides	Elea	Turn of 6/5C	Radical metaphysical monist	Author of a single poem in hexameters
Zeno	Elea	Earlier 5C	Paradoxes: Achilles, the Arrow, etc.	Pupil of Parmenides; writes in prose
Anaxagoras	Clazomenae	Earlier/mid 5C	Mind as first cause in cosmology	Teaches in Athens, where he is accused of impiety; one prose book
Empedocles	Acragas	Earlier/mid 5C	Combines Pythagorean religion and physical theory	Two hexameter poems: On Nature and Purifications; new papyrus

Presocratic	Birthplace	Date	Key ideas	Comment
Melissus	Samos	Mid 5C	Revises Parmenidean monism	Admiral; one prose book
Archelaus	Athens	Mid 5C	Revises Anaxagorean cosmology	Teacher of Socrates
Leucippus	(disputed)	Mid 5C	Invents atomism	
Philolaus	Croton	Mid/late 5C	Develops Pythagorean cosmology	First known Pythagorean book (in prose)
Diogenes	Apollonia	Late 5C	Eclectic material monist	At least one prose book
Metrodorus	Lampsacus	Late 5C	Allegorist	Associate of Anaxagoras
Anon., the Derveni Papyrus	(unknown; scroll found near Thessaloniki)	Late 5C	Cosmogony	In the form of allegorical commentary on an Orphic hymn
Democritus	Abdera	Late 5C–early 4C	Develops atomism	Associate of Leucippus; prolific prose author

THE MILESIANS

It is as intellectual pioneers that the Presocratics in general – not just Xenophanes and Parmenides – exert their fascination. All practitioners of a pursuit, intellectual or otherwise, need their heroes. The Presocratics are the heroes who set western science and philosophy on their way: heroes not just to us but to the later Greeks, who were no more immune than we are to curiosity about origins or admiration for originators. Here for example is Diogenes Laertius on Thales:

Some think he was the first to do astronomy and to foretell eclipses of the sun and solstices, as Eudemus says in his history of astronomy – hence

the admiration he won from both Xenophanes and Herodotus. And both
Heraclitus and Democritus report favourably on him.   (KRS 75)

And here is Proclus:

Thales, who had travelled to Egypt, was the first to introduce geometry
into Greece. He made many discoveries himself and taught his successors
the principles for many other discoveries, treating some things in a more
universal way, others more in terms of perception.   (KRS 68)

As for Thales' follower Anaximander, later geographical writers tell
us that:

Anaximander the Milesian, a disciple of Thales, was the first to venture
to draw the inhabited world on a tablet. After him Hecataeus, who travelled a lot, made it more detailed, with the result that it became a focus of
wonder.   (KRS 98)

How much of all this we should believe is disputable. Anaximander's production of a map is generally accepted, as is Thales' employ-
ment – if not discovery – of some device or other for working out
the variable period of the solstices (Anaximander is specifically if
questionably credited with discovery of the *gnōmōn*, a vertical rod
used to work out e.g. the direction and height of the sun from the
shadow it casts). The prediction of a solar eclipse (datable to 585 BC)
which is imputed to him remains an issue of fierce disagreement,
between scholars who for various reasons judge such an accomplishment impossible for a Greek of his time and place, and others who
regard it as feasible provided Thales had some contact with contemporary Babylonian astronomers. Whether Thales' alleged discoveries
in geometry are any more than later retrojections, based on feats of
mensuration reinterpreted to create a suitably distinguished pedigree
for geometry, is likewise a matter of dispute.

What is hard to doubt is an explosion of energy and ingenuity
harnessed to the project of measuring the earth and the heavens –
although why it should have occurred when and where and as it did
in early sixth-century Miletus will doubtless always remain something of a mystery. When Anaximander could not measure, he speculated about symmetries, as notably in his radically deconstructionist
account of the heavenly bodies:

The heavenly bodies come into being as circles of fire separated off from
the fire in the world, and enclosed by air. There are breathing-holes, certain

pipe-like passages, at which the heavenly bodies show themselves. So when the breathing-holes are blocked off eclipses occur. The moon is seen now waxing, now waning, due to the blocking or opening of the passages. The circle of the sun is 27 times the earth, that of the moon 18 times. The sun is highest, the circles of the fixed stars lowest. (KRS 125)

The apparently chaotic variety of the heavens is here reduced to the simplest scheme of geometrical and arithmetical relationships: circles and multiples of the number 9. The scheme is as economical as it is simple. *Circles* account for the diurnal revolutions of sun and moon and the alternation of day and night. Circles of *fire enveloped in air* permit explanation of why they do not fall – they are not in fact solid bodies. And by the subsidiary hypothesis of variable *orifices* in the air Anaximander proposes a physics not just for the light of the moon and the other heavenly bodies but for its phases too and for eclipses of sun and moon. Even bolder was Anaximander's thoroughly geocentric attempt to understand the stability of a cylindrical earth (its depth three times its diameter), most authoritatively described in Aristotle's treatise *On the Heavens*:

There are some like Anaximander among the ancients who say that the earth stays put because of likeness. For it is appropriate for something set firm at the centre to have no more tendency to move up or down or sideways; but it is impossible for it to make a motion in opposite directions; so of necessity it stays put. (KRS 123)

In appealing to an indifference principle Anaximander appeals once again to geometrical reasoning: by virtue solely of its equidistance from everything else a thing so positioned can have no sufficient reason to travel to one point that is not a sufficient reason for it to travel to a point opposite. (For Anaximander's theoretical speculations on the basic stuff of the universe, 'the indefinite', see chapter 10, p. 272 below.)

There is not much in all this that anticipates the empiricist spirit of Xenophanes' exploitation of his collection of fossil evidence, although Anaximander like him thought that the sea was currently drying out, and engaged – perhaps connectedly – in some intriguing speculations about the amphibious origins of human life (he thought humans must have developed initially in embryonic form inside fish or 'creatures very like fish'). What Thales and Anaximander offer is another kind of appeal to experience. Thales' best attested contribution to cosmology is his proposal that the earth lies on water and 'stays in place because it is buoyant, like wood or something similar' (see further, chapter 10, p. 271 below). Anaximander's guesses about sun, moon and earth are likewise full of vivid analogies. He is reported to have said that the shape of the earth resembled a stone column (or perhaps column base); and he is on record as comparing the largest of his celestial circles to a chariot wheel, its rim hollow and full of fire, and the orifice at which the light of the sun appears to the nozzle of a bellows. His follower Anaximenes – last and least of the Milesian triad – evidently disagreed with Anaximander's conjectures on these topics. But he too had analogies to hand: the stars have been fixed like nails into the sky, while the sun and moon move not under the earth but round it, like a felt cap turned about one's head (see, for more examples, p. 272 below). On the other hand Anaximenes seems to have accepted Anaximander's basic approach to the explanation of 'meteorological' phenomena such as thunder and lightning, with or without modification. His own most distinctive contribution was the addition of a comparison: the effect is rather like the flashing of the sea as it is cut up by oars.

In our information about Anaximenes there is no trace of the zest for measurement or geometrical reasoning attested for Thales and Anaximander. Moreover his basic strategy for explaining physical change looks to have been quite different from Anaximander's. Anaximander sees the universe as a battleground on which in every region war is being waged between great cosmic forces: 'they pay penalty and retribution to each other for their injustice', he said, 'according to the ordinance of time'. For example, at the very origins of our world the hot (in the form of flame) encases the cold (air) 'like bark round a tree', but air in due course breaks the casing and encloses fire in what become the circles of sun, moon and stars. By contrast Anaximenes is a monist: air is the one basic stuff, and its transformations by the fundamental processes of compression and expansion are the mechanisms he invokes to account for everything else:

Through becoming denser or finer it has different appearances. When it is dissolved into something finer it becomes fire, but winds by contrast are air that is becoming condensed, and cloud is produced from air by felting. When it is condensed still more, water is produced; and with yet further condensing earth; and when condensed as far as possible stones. (KRS 141)

This pattern of explanation seems to have been much admired by later Ionian philosophers with monistic leanings such as Anaxagoras (in the first half of the fifth century BC) and Diogenes of Apollonia (later fifth century) – but not perhaps by Xenophanes. At any rate, when Xenophanes too couches virtually all his explanations of astronomical and meteorological phenomena in terms not of air but of cloud, it is tempting to diagnose parody, especially when we hear specifically of 'felting' at work in his account of the moon and the earth.

PYTHAGORAS

Anaximenes was in any event not the only butt of Xenophanes' satire. Pythagoras is said to have been the target of a still surviving elegiac quatrain:

Once they say that he was passing by when a puppy was being whipped, and he took pity and said: 'Stop, do not beat it; for it is the soul of a friend that I recognised when I heard it giving tongue.'   (KRS 260)

Xenophanes picks on the doctrine with which Pythagoras' name is most often associated in the earliest evidence about him: the transmigration of the soul (*psychē*), or more generally its survival after death.

   In Pythagoras' preoccupation about the soul (or as we might say, the self) we encounter a third mode of Presocratic theorizing: neither proto-science nor philosophy, but religious speculation and indeed indoctrination. For to understand Pythagoras' teaching on the soul, conceived above all as source of life, we need to set it in its religious context – the context of what Plato's Socrates in the *Republic* says was still called the Pythagorean way of life in his own day (an indicative description: we never hear of an Anaximandrian or a Xenophanean way of life). The geographical setting, as with Xenophanes, is no longer the Ionian seaboard, for although the island of Samos in the eastern Aegean was Pythagoras' place of origin, he emigrated around 525 BC to Croton in southern Italy. There and subsequently in neighbouring cities his followers formed groups or coteries dedicated to the practice of a morally and religiously austere and exclusive life-style, and came to exercise considerable political influence during the period 500–450 BC. We know something about

their rituals and the form and content of their characteristic teachings. And we can guess at something of the character of their veneration for Pythagoras from the miracle stories which soon accumulated
about him:

Aristotle says that Pythagoras was called 'the Hyperborean Apollo' by the
people of Croton. The son of Nicomachus [i.e. Aristotle] adds that he was
once seen by many people on the same day and at the same hour in both
Metapontum and Croton; and that at Olympia, during the games, he got
up in the theatre and revealed that one of his thighs was golden. The same
writer says that while crossing the Cosas he was hailed by the river, and he
says many people heard this greeting.   (KRS 273)

One clue to the distinctive focus of the Pythagorean way of life
is the fact that Herodotus associated it with the rites and writings
of Orphic religion. By the fifth century BC the name of Orpheus
had become attached to the doctrine that the body is a prison in
which the soul serves out its punishment for sin, and to practices
designed to purify initiates and ensure their happiness before and
after death (these included renunciation of animal sacrifice). A similar belief as to why and how the soul must be purified if it is to achieve
ultimate escape from the cycle of reincarnation is what seems to
have animated Pythagoreanism. Much of its teaching was evidently
couched in the form of maxims (known as *akusmata*, 'things heard',
or *symbola*, 'passwords'), which recruits would probably have been
required to memorize as a catechism and as testimony to their status as initiates. Iamblichus, author of a late third century AD *Life
of Pythagoras*, preserves a classification of *akusmata*: 'some of them
signify what a thing is, some what is the most such and such, some
what one must do or not do'. He gives as examples of the first category: 'What are the isles of the blessed? Sun and moon. What is the oracle at Delphi? The *tetraktys*: which is the attunement (*harmonia*) in
which the Sirens sing.' Both these sayings sound as though they may
be very ancient, and both represent rationalizing explanations of conceptions of traditional religious thought and discourse; in taking up
an eschatological theme the first discloses a preoccupation evidenced
elsewhere, e.g. in Aristotle's observation (probably reflecting another
akusma) that 'if it thunders, then if what the Pythagoreans say is
true, that is to threaten those in Tartarus, so that they may be afraid'.
Iamblichus begins the list in his second category as follows: 'What

is the most just thing? To sacrifice. What is the wisest? Number.'
Most notorious of the Pythagorean *akusmata*, however, are some
of those in his third category, above all the injunction to abstain
from beans, whose rationale was much debated, conceivably even
among Pythagoreans themselves. Many sound like bits of prover-
bial wisdom, even if sometimes given a new moral or religious or
other interpretation by the Pythagoreans: e.g. 'Don't turn back on
a journey' – don't cling on to life when you're dying; 'Don't break
a loaf into bits' – here rival moral, eschatological and cosmological
explanations were mentioned by Aristotle.

The Pythagoras who inspired ideas and practices such as these
sounds as though he must have been more charismatic guru than
proto-scientist or the mathematical pioneer who was later in antiquity to be credited anecdotally with the discovery of the famous
theorem about the square of the hypotenuse of a right-angled trian-
gle. Or is that a false dichotomy? An important if elusive piece of
evidence on this issue is supplied by the contemporary Presocratic
Heraclitus when he writes:

Pythagoras son of Mnesarchus pursued inquiry (*historiē*)[2] further than any
other men – and selecting these 'compositions' (*syngraphai*) made up his
own wisdom: prolific learning (*polymathiē*), craft of deceit.   (KRS 256)[3]

In his opening clause Heraclitus talks as though adopting the wholly
unaccustomed mode of high praise. So we smell a rat; and the second half of the saying confirms the rightness of our suspicions.
Pythagoras' version of inquiry turns out to consist in nothing but
appropriating the contents of other thinkers' writings, and turning
them into a plagiarized 'wisdom' of his own – a wisdom that is then
twice redescribed: first as *polymathiē*, jackdaw accumulation of information; then as a craft – but only of deceit (I imagine Heraclitus
has his eye on the Pythagorean promise of a means of securing immortal happiness). So Heraclitus represents Pythagoras as a charlatan. The question is: what sort of charlatan?

Two things in particular suggest that Heraclitus perceived or pretended to perceive Pythagoras as someone who worked or pretended
to work in the Ionian tradition of inquiry illustrated in our previous two sections. First is the very use of the expression 'inquiry',
as the pursuit characteristic of 'other men'. Second is the reference
to 'compositions', plundered by Pythagoras. A *syngraphē* seems to

have been a very specific form of composition: a systematic composition in prose of a theoretical character – something still so new
and so rare that Heraclitus, writing at the end of the sixth century
BC, could expect his sneering but anonymous reference to 'these
"compositions" ' to be instantly intelligible. What he would have had
principally in his sights were the earlier sixth-century cosmological
treatises of Pherecydes (author of a revisionist theological account
of the universe and its origins), Anaximander and Anaximenes. We
can, I think, draw an inference. For Heraclitus' critique to have had
any plausibility, it must be true that (a) Pythagoras was generally
believed to have had opinions on all manner of topics (not just the
soul), and more specifically (b) he was known to have engaged in
cosmological speculation in some way reminiscent of writers like
Pherecydes, Anaximander and Anaximenes. We need not suppose
Pythagoras himself wrote a book or books: the scholarly consensus
is that he did not – certainly if he did write anything it must have been
lost very soon. Nor need we suppose that his 'prolific learning' much
resembled e.g. Xenophanes'. In another saying dismissive of poly-
mathic learning Heraclitus couples Pythagoras with Hesiod, active
around 700 BC, and author of two didactic poems on the moral basis of
society (*Works and Days*) and the theological history of the universe
(*Theogony*): which is intelligible enough if one thing Pythagoras attempted was a comprehensive rationalization of the cosmological
dimension of traditional religion, something at least suggested by
what we are told – admittedly at second hand – of Aristotle's reports
about him in this connection.

As it happens a cosmological system is precisely what Aristotle
ascribes to the early Pythagoreans. He is careful not to claim Pythagoras himself as its author – indeed he speaks of the 'so-called'
Pythagoreans, as if to flag the need for caution about its relationship
to anything Pythagoras himself may have taught. The key which according to these thinkers unlocked the secrets of the universe and
indeed of much else besides was number, particularly as it figures in
the expression of musical intervals as ratios:

Since of these principles [i.e. the principles of all things] numbers are by
nature the first, and in numbers they thought they saw many resemblances
to the things that exist and come into being – more than in fire and earth
and water (such and such a modification of numbers being justice, another
being soul and intellect, another being opportunity – and similarly almost

all things being numerically expressible); since again they saw that the attributes and the ratios of the attunements were expressible in numbers;
since, then, all other things in the whole of nature seemed to be modelled
after numbers, and numbers seemed to be the first things in the whole of
nature, they supposed the elements of numbers to be the elements of all
things, and the whole heaven to be an attunement and a number. And all
the properties of numbers and attunements they could show to agree with
the attributes and parts and the whole arrangement of the heavens, they
collected and fitted into their scheme; and if there was a gap anywhere, they
readily made additions so as to make their whole theory coherent. E.g. as
the number 10 is thought to be perfect and to comprise the whole nature of
numbers, they say that the bodies which move through the heavens are ten,
but as the visible bodies are only nine, to meet this they invent a tenth – the
counter-earth.   (KRS 430)

The number 10 was accorded special significance by the Pythagoreans, as the last sentence in Aristotle's account suggests, and as is
indicated also by the *akusma* about the *tetraktys*: i.e. the 'foursome'
consisting of the first four natural numbers, which sum to ten and
are also those needed to express the fundamental musical ratios of
fourth (4 to 3), fifth (3 to 2) and octave (2 to 1). These ratios were
given astronomical significance in Pythagorean theory: 'the attunement in which the Sirens sing' was identified as 'the music of the
spheres' – it was proposed that the relative speeds of the movements of the heavenly bodies stood in the same ratios as musical
concords.

No doubt the detailed and systematic working out of explanations of things in terms of number and the musical ratios is something more plausibly ascribed to his followers than to Pythagoras
himself. The astronomical scheme is in fact explicitly ascribed elsewhere to Philolaus of Croton, a Pythagorean active in the second
half of the fifth century BC, and author of some important surviving fragments (see further, p. 278 below). Yet it is likely enough
that Pythagoras conceived the basic idea of interpreting the universe
on this model. If so, Heraclitus might understandably have thought
he saw here only something derivative: an unacknowledged reflection of Anaximander's symbolic use of numbers in *his* astronomical
scheme. Pythagorean speculation on origins of the universe is similarly reminiscent of what he would have found in the *syngraphai*. A
report ultimately dependent on Aristotle tells us that according to
the Pythagoreans 'from the unlimited there are drawn in time, breath

and the void'. This again sounds like adaptation of Anaximander, though the elemental roles in cosmology it assigns to time and breath make one think also of Pherecydes and Anaximenes respectively. (On Pythagorean mathematical science, see further, chapter 10, pp. 278–9 below.)

Ancient authors represent Pythagoras as someone who introduced the Greeks to mysterious oriental ideas. Herodotus in the fifth century BC speaks of 'Egyptian and Pythagorean' practices in a single phrase; according to Aristotle in the fourth the people of Croton called Pythagoras 'the Hyperborean Apollo' – i.e. from beyond the northern limits of the civilized world; Hippolytus in the third century AD suggests that he derived elements of his teaching on the soul and his prohibition on eating beans from 'Zaratas the Chaldaean', i.e. Zoroaster/Zarathustra. It is certainly tempting to see in Pythagoreanism an attempt to harness the purely theoretical speculation characteristic of the Milesians to a broader agenda in which the practical concerns of religion and particularly eschatology become uppermost – a religion moreover dominated by an intense preoccupation with sin and its consequences in reincarnation which has oriental parallels but no Greek antecedents. There are clearly larger issues here of the whole relationship between ancient Greek culture and the civilizations of the Near East, and of 'western' and 'eastern' conceptions of what should count as philosophy or science. Pythagoreanism shows no detectable interest in measurement or the use of evidence or experience in painting its picture of the universe. But by application of the idea of numerical ratio it would doubtless have claimed to have discovered much more rationality than did the Ionians, not just in nature but in the whole framework of human life and death.

METAPHYSICS, ARGUMENT AND THE REFLEXIVE TURN

Xenophanes. Xenophanes did not restrict his penchant for criticism to philosophical targets. His most remarkable surviving verses attack anthropomorphic conceptions of the gods, particularly as evidenced in Homer and Hesiod, whom he accused of attributing all manner of human faults to them (KRS 166, quoted below, pp. 309–10). Self-projection – as he comments elsewhere – is what shapes human constructions of deity. Xenophanes supports the charge with ethnographic observation – 'The Ethiopians say that their gods are snub-nosed and black, the Thracians that theirs have light-blue eyes and red hair' (KRS 168) – and with counterfactual ingenuity: if non-human animals could depict gods of their own, these would come out resembling *them* in form (KRS 169, quoted p. 306 below).

But in Xenophanes as in Heraclitus and Parmenides after him critique of a common human propensity to self-deception is coupled with metaphysical assertion of how things really are:

One god, greatest among men and gods, not like mortals either in body or
thought.   (KRS 170)

All of him sees, all thinks, and all hears.   (KRS 172)

Always he remains in the same place, moving not at all; nor is it fitting for
him to go to different places at different times, but without toil he shakes
all things by the thought of his mind.   (KRS 171)

What status Xenophanes ascribed to these claims we do not know. It seems unlikely that he thought their superior rationality conferred on them any kind of certainty. For we possess some further verses of his which reflect soberly on the limitations intrinsic to human understanding:

No man knows, or ever will know, the clear truth about the gods and what
I say about all things. For even if someone surpassed himself by happening
to say it complete, still he himself does not know that: opinion is what gets
constructed over all things.   (KRS 186)

Later writers interpreted these lines as a programmatic declaration of philosophical scepticism. But elsewhere we catch Xenophanes saying optimistically that 'the gods have not revealed all things to mortals from the beginning, but by inquiring they find out better over time' (KRS 188). And closely examined KRS 186 does not deny the possibility of knowledge or true belief, but only that we could ever know that we know, or achieve a direct or unfailingly reliable grasp of the truth about gods and the causes of natural phenomena.

Heraclitus. Xenophanes was dismissed by Heraclitus as just one more polymath. But in some ways Heraclitus looks like nothing so much as Xenophanes' most attentive student (it is worth noting that he was from Ephesus, only a few miles southeast of Colophon). Heraclitus shares Xenophanes' taste for polemic, not least against Homer and Hesiod. Like him he implicitly rejects a good deal of Milesian cosmology in both substance and method, with a similar penchant for naive or faux-naive physical explanations, such as the idea – advanced by both thinkers – that the sun is new every day; and like Xenophanes he issues ethical and political imperatives, something not attested for the Milesians. Heraclitus too takes a gloomy view of ordinary human understanding of things, as imprisoned within its own perspective, and he too offers an alternative vision. As in Xenophanes, the understanding he promises has a monistic and theological cast: 'listening not to me but to the account it is wise to agree that all things are one'.

The multiple reflexivity of Heraclitus' riddling and paradoxical style is aggressively communicated in the opening sentences of his book of prose aphorisms:

Although this account holds for ever, humans forever prove to be uncomprehending – both before they hear it and when first they have heard it. For although all things happen in accordance with this account, it is as if they have never experienced them before when they have a go at words and practices such as those I am explaining, as I distinguish each according to its nature and indicate how it is. Other people are as unaware of what they are doing when they are awake as they are forgetful of what they do in their sleep.   (KRS 194)

Heraclitus does not begin by announcing the principal truths which constitute his account (*logos*) of things. He refers instead to the status of the account. That might lead one to expect that epistemological or metaphysical or methodological reflections on this second-order topic will be a major preoccupation – and such indeed proves to be the case. But the reference to the account is confined here to a subordinate clause (as also in the second sentence), which helps to thrust the emphasis on to something else again: the third-order contrast between the incomprehension of ordinary humanity and the universal applicability of the account as it is articulated by Heraclitus. This third-order theme is what Heraclitus develops in the fragment. On the one hand, the account explains 'words and practices' – presumably Heraclitus means by that the nature of language and of human behaviour. But on the other, a failure in reflectiveness prevents people from understanding these phenomena. People in general have no awareness of their own linguistic and non-linguistic behaviour, of what *they themselves* are *doing*. 'Although the account is common property', as Heraclitus says in another fragment, 'most

people live as though understanding were something private to them'
(KRS 195).

Perhaps Heraclitus' most famous illustration of the account and
(by implication) of human deafness to it is his aphorism about rivers:

You would not step twice into the same river.   (KRS 215)

Or in what is probably the more authentic formulation:

Over those who step into the same rivers the waters that flow are different
and again different.   (KRS 214)

This remark was very early taken as a metaphor for the truth about
reality in general, with Heracliteanism being construed in Plato as
the doctrine that all things are in flux. But the point is rather one
about the unity and diversity of things as we encounter them in our
behaviour. Our experience is of diversity: the water flowing over us
at one moment is different from that flowing over us at the next. But
that diversity is really a function of a more fundamental identity: the
dynamic form of unity constituted by a river. No doubt people usually assume that difference and contrariety preclude unity. To stir us
from our dogmatic slumbers, Heraclitus presents example after example designed to get us to see that once we engage in metaphysical
reflection, we recognize that – contrary to the popular incomprehension – they don't and we don't actually think they do. Here are just
two sample aphorisms:

They do not understand how in differing with itself it agrees with itself: a
backward-turning structure of attunement, like that of bow and lyre.
                                                                (KRS 209)

Most people accept Hesiod as their teacher. Their understanding is that he
knows more than anyone – someone who did not recognise day and night:
for they are one.   (fr. 57 Diels–Kranz)[4]

Elsewhere Heraclitus stresses that the likes of Hesiod go wrong not
in trusting their senses ('whatever comes from sight, hearing, experience, this I privilege' (KRS 197)), but in misinterpreting them: 'Bad
witnesses are eyes and ears for humans whose souls do not understand their language' (KRS 198).

Even where Heraclitus is not explicitly attacking assumptions
made by other writers and thinkers or by people at large, there may

be an implicit critique, as in his principal surviving aphorism on the nature of the universe:

The world-order (*kosmos*) – the same for all – no god or human made it. Always it was and is and will be, an everliving fire, catching alight in measures and being extinguished in measures.   (KRS 217)

'The same for all' hints once again at the contrast between the universal objectivity of the truth expressed by 'the account' and the private unreal worlds inhabited by the unenlightened; denial that there was a creation contradicts not just the theology of Hesiod's *Theogony* but the proto-scientific speculation of an Anaximander. The meaning of the assertion about fire is harder to decode, but I take it that the fragment as a whole draws attention once again to the unity of a dynamic process as what governs the pattern of diversity and change on the cosmic scale, and more specifically to the regulation of night and day and the seasons by the heavenly bodies, and above all by the sun as it rises ('catches light') and sets ('is extinguished'). Aristotle represents him as treating fire – like Anaximenes' air – as the material stuff underlying all else. Other sayings about the 'turnings' of fire into sea and earth and back again make this an unlikely interpretation, as does his remark:

For fire all things are an exchange and fire for all things – as for gold are goods and goods for gold.   (KRS 219)

This sounds like an attempt to characterize physical processes in terms of transformation of energy rather than of the expansion or compression of gases.

An analogous story is intimated in Heraclitus' quite numerous aphorisms on life and death. The thought that life and death are in some sense the same is explicated in the following saying:

The same: living and dead, what is awake and what sleeps, young and old – for these changed around are those, and those changed around are these.
                                    (KRS 202)

These opposites count as the same because they share the same *form of change*: each member of each pair changes into the other. The sleeper wakes up, and subsequently goes to sleep again; the younger generation not only becomes old in due course, but itself took the place of the older generation before it; as his grandfather dies a grandson is born to take his place in the family, destined to die himself in due course. In all three cases the significant thing is the dynamic process: the polarities make no sense except as interchangeable phases within it. The deepest of all Heraclitus' sayings about life and death has been called 'the most perfectly symmetrical of all the fragments':

Immortals mortals, mortals immortals, living their death and dying their life.   (KRS 239)

Whatever else should be said about this fragment, its main point – conveyed by the multiple ambiguities of its syntax – must be its suggestion that the very categories of mortality and immortality, life and death, collapse into each other. It threatens both traditional religion, with its confident separation of mortals and immortals, and Pythagoreanism, with its consoling promise that there is really no such thing as mortality, merely different forms or phases of immortality.

In this last aphorism Heraclitus gestures towards a transcendent perspective which he sometimes identifies as the vantage point of wisdom or the divine ('the wise is one thing alone, unwilling and willing to be spoken of by the name of Zeus' (KRS 228)). God is where all polarities can exist and be understood simultaneously:

The god: day and night, winter and summer, war and peace, plenty and famine.   (KRS 204)

Parmenides. In Parmenides a comparable conception of the transcendent perspective is presented in dramatized form. The philosopher poet makes a mystical journey through and beyond the realm of day and night, to be greeted by a goddess who then explains that he must 'learn all things: both the unshaken heart of well-rounded truth, and the opinions of mortals in which there is no true reliance' (KRS 288.28–30). The goddess represents a logical space in which it is possible to articulate and reflect upon other radically differing perspectives: that of rationality, and that of ordinary human belief. On Parmenides' finding the key strength of the one and the cardinal weakness of the other turn on a single consideration.

Parmenidean reason takes the starting point that inquiry must presuppose either the existence or the non-existence of whatever it proposes to investigate, and that a decision between the two needs to be made. On the grounds (quoted on p. 43 above) that what is not cannot be known or successfully referred to, the second option is ruled out as an 'altogether indiscernible track'. 'Is' is the only remaining option, and reason is left with the task of working out what is involved in commitment to choice of that path. Where does 'mortal opinion' stand on this same decision? According to Parmenides, most humans never articulate the decision as a decision at all. In a daze they drift 'two-headed' between thinking and saying things that imply existence or being and things that imply non-existence or not-being. It is sometimes suggested that on Parmenides' diagnosis where people go wrong is in trusting not reason but the senses. But what Parmenides criticizes is use of an *aimless eye* and 'hearing and tongue *full of noise*' – which is represented as the inevitable *consequence* of letting habit not rational decision govern talk and thought.

The role of the decision between 'is' and 'is not' in Parmenides' philosophy is what gives his metaphysical monism a distinctive character very different from Heraclitus' version of monism, despite striking similarities in the overall epistemological structure of their two intellectual projects. While both thinkers reject 'mortal opinion' as uncritical and unreflective, Parmenidean monism is the outcome of *exclusion* (hence the stress on decision), whereas Heraclitus makes ultimate unity a function of difference and contrariety and conflict (so what is required is not a decision between alternatives but a more inclusive understanding of why alternatives are not in the end alternatives). The basis for the possibility of saying and thinking 'is not' is argument; and Parmenides' pervasive use of deductive argument as the instrument of rational decision and of consequential metaphysical exploration is quite different from anything in Heraclitus, whose resort to paradox, riddle and the like is what is more appropriate to his very different conception of philosophical understanding.

At the beginning of a long passage from his poem excerpted by the sixth-century AD Aristotle commentator Simplicius, Parmenides announces a number of 'signs' that mark the path 'is': what is is ungenerated and imperishable, wholly and uniformly itself, unchangeable, and perfect (KRS 295). The greater part of the rest of this fragment (KRS 296–9) is then taken up with a series of proofs of each of these properties in turn. Some at least of the subsequent proofs assume the results of their predecessors, but the mainspring of each is the original decision for a conception of being which excludes non-existence at any point in time or space. It will suffice to quote from the first and last of these deductions. The key lines of the first run as follows:

For what birth will you seek for it? How and whence did it grow? I shall not allow you to say nor to think from not being: for it is not to be said or thought that it is not; and what would have driven it to grow later rather than earlier, beginning from nothing? Thus it must either be completely or not at all. (KRS 296)

Parmenides assumes that the only reasonable answer to 'whence?' could be: 'from not existing', which he rejects as already excluded by his argument against 'is not'. In his treatment of 'how?' he appeals to the principle of sufficient reason. Suppose we waive the objection to speaking of what is not. Why should something which does not exist start its journey into existence sooner rather than later?

In the lines that follow Parmenides enunciates the reflection that 'justice has never loosed her fetters to allow it [i.e. what exists] to come to be or to perish, but holds it fast'. The talk of fetters – or (elsewhere in the fragment) binding limits – is his way of expressing the further inference that what exists does so necessarily and determinately. This conclusion then some sections later becomes the premiss of his proof of perfection:

But since there is a furthest limit, it is perfected, like the bulk of a ball well-rounded on every side, equally balanced in every direction from the centre. For it cannot be bigger or smaller here or there. For neither is it non-existent, which would stop it from reaching its like, nor is it existent in such a way that there would be more being here, less there, since it is all inviolate: for being equal to itself on every side, it lies uniformly within its limits. (KRS 299)

There is a good deal that is puzzling in this train of thought, notably the assumption that the metaphysical constraint ensuring that what exists *must* exist is also to be conceived as a spatial boundary making all reality a finite sphere. What is clear is its overall logical structure, pointed up by the iteration of the inferential conjunctions 'since' and 'for': first the conclusion: 'it is perfected'; then the premiss from which the conclusion is derived; then the considerations which underpin the truth of the premiss – here Parmenides lays particular stress on the way what exists lies 'inviolate' within its limits, as anticipated in the very first words of the section ('since there is a furthest limit').

Parmenides' idea that reason discloses true reality as something eternal, homogeneous and changeless was the key factor shaping both the atomism of Leucippus and Democritus and Plato's metaphysics of the Forms (and thereby indirectly much of Greek philosophy thereafter); and it surely helped to give these thinkers some of the confidence they will have needed to propose first principles far removed from the phenomena of experience. Nor did Parmenides lack adherents more or less faithful to his distinctive monistic vision. We possess fragments and other information relating to two mid-fifth century 'Eleatic' philosophers in particular: Melissus of Samos, who commanded the island's fleet in a victory over the Athenians in 441 BC, and Parmenides' younger companion Zeno, like Parmenides from Elea in South Italy, where he was said to have shown courage under torture after an abortive coup against the tyrannical regime of the city's ruler. Neither emulated Parmenides' choice of verse as vehicle of communication.

Melissus. Melissus was evidently troubled by Parmenides' conception of reality as finite. He began his own sustained deduction of the properties of reality with a proof that if it is without beginning and end in time (as he argued on grounds not specifically Parmenidean), then it can have no spatial beginning or end either – it must be infinite. Aristotle thought this argument crassly fallacious, but it can be understood more charitably and persuasively as designed merely to remove a possible objection (that temporal stops and starts imply spatial analogues) to the idea of infinite extension: an idea Ionian readers might well have been prepared to grant as the default position in cosmology. Melissus' subsequent proofs cover much the same ground as Parmenides', but generally a lot more lucidly and sometimes expansively. The highlight is probably his argument – influential by virtue of its premiss about motion and void – that what exists cannot move, because void is a precondition of motion, and if what exists is 'full' there can be no void.

Zeno. Zeno's contribution to Eleaticism was altogether more quizzical. In fact so far as we can see, it consisted of nothing but puzzles – including one of the most famous philosophical puzzles ever constructed: the paradox of Achilles and the tortoise (as later writers report it). Achilles decides to race against a tortoise, but gives it a head start. The consequence, so Zeno argues, is that he can never catch it. For although he runs a lot faster than it does, when he reaches the point at which the tortoise began moving, the tortoise has moved on to a further point. When he reaches that in turn, the tortoise has moved ahead yet again. And so *ad infinitum.* Zeno has articulated a powerful problem about the application of the notion of infinity to the physical world: to complete a journey someone both must and cannot complete an infinite series of sub-journeys. Another notable puzzle was the Arrow. Right now – and indeed at every moment in its flight – a flying arrow must be at rest. For right now it will be occupying a space exactly equal to its own length, which gives it no room to move. This paradox poses an incisive challenge to the idea that motion must occur in the present. It trades on two incompatible conceptions of the present: the notion of a present duration (when motion is occurring), and the notion of an indivisible instant (indivisibility excludes the possibility of anything divisible – such as movement – actually going on in such an instant).

Plato construed Zeno's paradoxes as an indirect defence of Parmenidean monism. No better conjecture about their purpose has ever been proposed. But it leaves a good deal of scope for further debate. Was Zeno a *doctrinal* Parmenidean, intent on proving that the alternative to monism – belief in a world of plurality and change – was riddled with contradictions more lethal than might be suggested by Parmenides' rather swift and compressed strictures on 'mortal opinion'? Or are the paradoxes conceived less as demonstrations than as proto-sceptical questions? Whatever the objections to the Eleatic one, is the hypothesis of plurality and change any less objectionable? Indeed, for all its apparent validation by experience, is it any less of a hypothesis, any less in need of rational defence, than Parmenides' conception of reality?

SOME FIFTH-CENTURY COSMOLOGISTS

The atomists. It is Aristotle who is our main authority for the claim that Eleatic metaphysics was a major shaping influence on Presocratic atomism – and indeed, given the non-survival of any substantial fragments of Leucippus' or Democritus' writings on physics, he is the principal source of our knowledge of the chief tenets of their system. Neither he nor any other ancient reporter uses the designation 'atomist' conventional in modern presentations of these thinkers, nor do they characterize the system primarily in terms of the atomistic hypothesis. For Aristotle, Leucippus and Democritus were *dualists*, whose dualism was an in-house rebellion against Eleatic monism. They accept the Eleatic idea that what is real is not subject to birth or death and is complete and unchangeable in its reality. Their radical move is to posit the existence of something else: unreality, characterized as empty or (as we say) void, and as 'rare' or permeable. Unreality or void separates one real being from another, and is what makes locomotion possible. This way, says Aristotle, Leucippus found a means of 'agreeing with the appearances', i.e. of explaining how contrary to Eleatic metaphysics there could be birth and death, and a plurality of real beings in motion.

Having proposed the existence of void, Leucippus and Democritus then go on to posit an infinite number of separated indestructible Eleatic beings moving in it. When these beings come together in such a way as to get intertwined into a compound (on account of salient differences in their shapes), they create larger bodies – which, however, can be dissolved and destroyed if penetrated by further solid or non-permeable beings. Diogenes Laertius preserves an elaborate account of how the innumerable worlds postulated by Leucippus and Democritus come to be created as perishable compounds of just such a kind, through the operation of a vortex which produces a spherical structure or 'membrane' made up of entangled primary beings. These primary indestructible beings were indeed described by Democritus at any rate as 'atoms', i.e. indivisibles, invisible – in our world, at least – to the naked eye. Aristotle saw the idea of the atom as a further sign of Eleatic influence: Zeno's arguments in particular had been designed to exhibit the logical incoherences implicit in the view that magnitudes are divisible, whether *ad finitum* or otherwise; so Leucippus and Democritus simply ruled that their primary beings were *in*divisible (although why and how they could be so is something given different explanations in presentations of their system in later accounts, and remains a subject of scholarly disagreement).

It is generally accepted that while it was Leucippus who worked out the basics of this theory, his younger associate Democritus (born c.460 BC at Abdera in northern Greece), a prolific author, developed particular dimensions of it, such as the exploration of epistemological issues and a detailed account of sense perception (a topic extensively discussed by all the major thinkers considered in this section – their speculations on human physiology bear comparison also with ideas in contemporary medical writings preserved in the Hippocratic corpus).

By convention (*nomos*) sweet, by convention bitter, by convention hot, by convention cold, by convention colour; but in reality atoms and void.

(KRS 549)

On Democritus' finding, the senses tell us very few truths about the world (see further chapter 10, p. 274 below). But they 'confirm' the theory of atoms and void. For example, if one and the same wind feels hot to you but cold to me, so far from presenting us with a troubling contradiction that effect is just what the theory would lead one to expect. It is readily explained by the supposition that there are subtle variations in the atomic structure both in the wind and in different individuals' sensory equipment (after all, Democritus remarked, tragedies and comedies are composed from the same alphabet). He was particularly intrigued by the prospects for application of what is sometimes called indifference reasoning. Why, for example, should bodies or worlds exist in one area of the void rather than some other? On this basis he argued for the existence of an infinite number of worlds. Hippolytus for one was evidently captivated by Democritus' elaborations of this theme

He said that there are innumerable worlds differing in size. In some there is no sun or moon, in others they are larger than those in our world, in others more numerous. The intervals between the worlds are unequal – in some parts there are more worlds, in others fewer. Some are growing, some are at their peak, others are declining. In some parts they are coming into existence, in others they are failing. They are destroyed through colliding into each other. There are some worlds devoid of living creatures or plants or any moisture.   (KRS 565)

Plato never mentions the names of Leucippus and Democritus, nor is there much sign in his dialogues of reference to their doctrines. Yet their influence lived on through a succession of fourth-century thinkers, culminating in Epicurus and his major restatement of atomist physics (see chapter 6).

Anaxagoras. Plato gives the impression that the figure who dominated fifth-century cosmology was the Ionian Anaxagoras (500–428 BC), from Clazomenae near Colophon, but the first major thinker to take up residence in Athens until he left in the 430s to avoid an impiety trial. Anaxagoras' detailed account of the structure and contents of the universe (mostly known from Hippolytus and other late reports) and of the processes which brought them into being shows him to have been a theorist working squarely within the Milesian tradition. The interest of his work lies more in the novel categories of explanation and analysis he applied to the conduct of what was by now a traditional project.

Plato's Socrates simultaneously applauds and deplores what he represents as Anaxagoras' major achievement: the decision to postulate mind as the first cause of cosmic order is saluted as a potentially decisive advance, but it was evidently not supported by the detailed demonstrations of why things are for the best which Socrates says he had hoped for. The sustained passage of elevated prose in which Anaxagoras set out his thesis about mind is preserved by Simplicius, as are the famous opening words of his book:

All things were together, infinite in respect of both number and smallness; for the small too was infinite. And all being together, nothing was manifest on account of smallness. For air and aether enveloped and dominated all things, both of them being infinite – for these are the greatest in the sum of things, both in number and in magnitude.   (KRS 467)

Anaxagoras' conception of the original condition of matter contrasts with the atomists' at every point. It constitutes a single inert infinitely divisible mixture, made up of all the stuffs and powers which will eventually become apparent in the single differentiated world that mind's separating activity is to create. For Anaxagoras sweet, bitter, hot, cold, colour are not mere conventions, but part of the basic furniture of the universe: anything which subsequently emerges must have been latent all along ('in everything a portion of everything', as his slogan puts it).

The legacy of Anaxagoras. We can document Anaxagoras' influence on subsequent fifth-century thinkers. Socrates is said to have sat at the feet of Anaxagoras' follower Archelaus (like Socrates an Athenian) in his youth; and Hippolytus presents an extended account of his highly derivative theories. A more impressive figure is Diogenes of Apollonia, active some time in the latter half of the fifth century; his idea that air is the divine first principle is mocked by Aristophanes in the *Clouds* (423 BC). A number of fragments are preserved (mostly by Simplicius). Diogenes argued the monist thesis that things could not interact with each other unless all were differentiated out of the same basic substance. That does not sound particularly Anaxagorean, but in having air permeate all other things Diogenes made it organize and control them, and he argued that its optimal disposition of day and night and the seasons reveals its intelligence, as also does its role in sustaining animal life, which he worked out in a detailed psychology and physiology that thanks to Aristotle and Theophrastus is still largely accessible to us. In other words, Diogenes accepted from Anaxagoras that cosmic order and the phenomena of life require explanation in terms of mind, but he construed mind as a predicate, not an independent substance.

A third and very different writer who appropriates Anaxagoras' hypothesis of a dominant cosmic role for mind is the author of the Derveni papyrus. This extraordinary document, discovered as recently as 1962 in the remains of a funeral pyre at an ancient tomb complex near Thessaloniki in northern Greece, contains in fragmentary form an allegorical commentary on an Orphic hymn about the origins of the universe, probably composed around the end of the fifth century. There is much debate about its religious and intellectual purpose, but what is undeniable is the author's absorption in Presocratic physics, as well as his use of a range of etymological and other similarly questionable philological techniques to decode the Orphic verses as cryptic expressions of cosmological theory. In this respect the exegetical ambitions of the commentator resemble those attested for Metrodorus of Lampsacus (in the Dardanelles), said to have been close to Anaxagoras, who reportedly ended his days at Lampsacus in high public esteem.

Empedocles. The most celebrated modern discovery of Presocratic material is even more recent. In 1994 the Belgian scholar Alain Martin announced the identification of over seventy lines or part lines of Empedocles – many previously unknown – in fragments of a papyrus roll (from Egypt, but since 1905 in the university library at Strasbourg) which once formed a stiff strip with copper pasted on, and apparently intended to function as a coronet for a deceased person. Empedocles, born c.495 in the Sicilian city of Acragas (modern Agrigento), wrote at least two poems in epic hexameter verse known to later antiquity as *On Nature* and *Purifications*. Numerous fragments survive (greater in bulk than for any other Presocratic), but many key issues of interpretation are still vigorously disputed. Scholars have been hoping that the new evidence, now presented in a magnificent edition by Martin and his German colleague Oliver Primavesi, might help settle some of them, e.g. the relation of religion to philosophy in Empedocles' thought. For while a good deal of Empedoclean theory – e.g. his ideas about the formation of the heavenly bodies, or his account of sense perception – is comparable with atomist and Anaxagorean treatment of such topics, Pythagorean preoccupations with the soul and its reincarnation also much engage him. The scholarship of the last few decades has made it increasingly unlikely that the physics of *On Nature* is insulated from Empedocles' religious convictions; and there is much less confidence than once there was that all the fragments pertaining to reincarnation are to be assigned to *Purifications*.

On the reasonable (but not universally accepted) assumption that the newly reconstructed verses all belong to the same poem, there is indeed further confirmation that *On Nature* had an overarching religious purpose: to situate the soul and its fate within a cosmic history, a cycle of alternate harmonization of elemental powers into unity followed by their dissolution into plurality, endlessly repeated. One of the new passages is concerned with the fall of the soul, or the *daimōn*, as Empedocles prefers to say – and incidentally includes remains of two lines which enable us to establish an improved text of the already existing two-line fragment KRS 416 (quoted by the Neoplatonist Porphyry). But the other three passages which can be reconstituted all overlap with existing fragments of Empedocles' philosophical poem *On Nature*. There is therefore a probability that the passage on the soul too belongs to the same part of *On Nature*, not to the religious poem *Purifications* to which Diels assigned KRS 416. In which case we can infer that *On Nature* combined the concerns of a nature theorist with those of Pythagorean religion, as many have already suspected.

Something of the unique intensity of Empedocles' vision of the world is conveyed in the best preserved lines[5] in the Strasbourg papyrus, a passage previously unknown to us:

But when Strife reaches transgressively the depths of the vortex, and Love comes to be at the middle of the whirlpool, then under her [i.e. Love] do all these things [i.e. elements] come together to be only one. Exert yourself – so that the account reach not only your ears – and as you listen look upon the unerring evidences that are around you. I will show your eyes, too, where things [i.e. elements] find a larger body: first the coming together and un-folding [i.e. proliferation] that breeding consists in, and all the variety that is now still left in this phase of generation, whether among the wild species of mountain roaming beasts, or with the twin offspring of humans [i.e. the two sexes], or with the progeny of root-bearing fields and the cluster of grapes mounting upon the vine. From these accounts convey to your mind un-deceitful proofs: for you will *see* the coming together and unfolding that breeding consists in.   (a(ii) 18–30, Martin and Primavesi edition)

Empedocles posits as his framing idea a Heraclitean clash between the great cosmic forces of Strife and Love, operating between poles of unity and plurality in their effects on the four elements he made canonical: fire, air, water, earth. What he seeks to capture in these verses is Love's creative energy at work in the world as it is now, following a decisive moment in the conflict. In diction sometimes reminiscent of Parmenides he promises a proof which will be based on the evidence of our very eyes: we shall *see* union bringing prolif-eration about, and the earth in consequence fruitful and multiply-ing. On one reading, Empedocles here devotes himself to confirming theory with sensory evidence. On another, his tactic is at once more cunning and more intuitive: so to picture the world as to render us incapable of seeing it except as exemplifying the rhythms of Love and Strife his theory postulates. Perhaps we should not be surprised that his most notable student was Gorgias of Leontini, the celebrated fifth-century rhetorician whose dazzling artificial display orations *Palamedes* and the *Praise of Helen* still survive, and who will be among the principal figures featured in the next chapter.

Empedocles' most memorable contribution to speculation about nature was his theory of the origin of species. He posited a sequence of stages (much debated by scholars) in the emergence of animal forms, starting at a point when Strife was even more dominant than it is now. First came a phase when 'many faces sprang up with-out necks, arms wandered without shoulders, unattached, and eyes strayed alone, in need of foreheads' (KRS 376). This was followed by a generation of monsters, such as bulls with human faces and 'ox-headed offspring of man'. After that the picture is less clear. What is well attested is Empedocles' frequent appeal to chance in spelling the theory out; and Aristotle suggests that he proposed an idea of the survival of the fittest: from amongst the monsters of the second generation, only those that happened to be biologically viable survived and reproduced their kind. Aristotle had greater admiration for Empedocles' perception of homologous functions in the living beings of our present zoological phase ('the same things are hair and leaves and the close-packed feathers of birds and the scales which come to be on sturdy limbs' (KRS 383)). He quotes quite sustained Empedoclean passages on vision and respiration. And on the last page of his principal discussion of the Presocratics he implies that in Empedocles' account of the constitution of bone there is a closer approximation than in any other of his predecessors to an understanding of the role of form and essence in physical explanation. On this upbeat note we too may appropriately take our leave of the Presocratics.

NOTES

1   All citations are by KRS number where available (i.e. as in Kirk, Raven and Schofield, *The Presocratic Philosophers*; see Bibliography [10]), whose version of the Greek text is followed except where specifically noted otherwise; translations, however, sometimes diverge from those in KRS, as in the present case. The text of this passage (Hipp. *Ref.* 1.14.5–6) is corrupt or doubtful at various points. I translate the KRS version, except for the final word where for the MSS *kataballein* I propose *kata to metaballein*.

2   *Historiē* in due course becomes our 'history', but originally history was only one among several forms of *historiē*.

3   I translate the text given in the manuscripts, restoring the words *tas syngraphas* excised in KRS.

4   This fragment, not included in KRS, is cited from Diels–Kranz, *Die Fragmente der Vorsokratiker* (ed. 6, 1952), the fundamental modern collection (original texts with German translation of fragments but not testimonia).

5   Line endings are mostly missing: restorations largely speculative.

3 The Sophists and Socrates

THE SOPHISTS

The fifth-century sophists were the first exponents of higher education in the West. 'Sophist' means 'professional practitioner of wisdom (*sophia*)'. To call someone 'wise' (*sophos*) without qualification was to ascribe the highest, most desirable, expertise. And in the relentlessly political atmosphere of the fifth-century Greek city-states, the expertise most at a premium was skill in civic speech: debate, exhortation, pleading, formal eulogy. Whether the context was council-chamber or law-court, democratic assembly or a prince's cabinet, mediation at home or diplomacy abroad, success hinged on excellent communication. In this climate the sophists emerged and flourished.

Since most of what they wrote is lost, and since in any case much of their work consisted in teaching, not writing, our picture of the sophists is necessarily fragmentary and speculative. Fortunately, however, enough actual sophistic rhetoric survives to give a rich impression of the skills these men – and those who paid them – held dear. From Gorgias of Leontini we have some highly artificial speeches composed for demonstration; from Antiphon of Rhamnous near Athens we have speeches written for real-life protagonists in the law-courts, as well as some demonstration-speeches. There are also the speeches which the contemporary historian Thucydides assigns to historical agents in his account of the Peloponnesian War. Thucydides was not a sophist (a paid professional) himself, but we know he created his speeches not merely to explain motives and decisions that affected that particular war, but as models of political and strategic thinking that would be useful in future situations.

73

If one came to sophists like Gorgias and Antiphon as an intelligent aspirant to the skills they taught, what would one learn? Study of their speeches shows that one would learn to marshal thoughts so as to reach conclusions logically from fairly obvious premises; to make clear transitions from each point to the next; to frame analogies; to split a subject into categories and deal with them effectively one by one: e.g. a defendant argues that even if he had wanted to commit the crime, (a) he could not, and (b) even if he could he would not have wanted to. Under (a) he might make a division between lack of means and lack of opportunity, and under (b) between possible motives, each of which he shows was absent. The student would learn to bring a subject under control with a set of questions applicable to just about anything: 'Where?', 'When?', 'For how long?', 'Who?', 'How many?', 'By what means?', and so on. In short, one would learn to master a range of *formal* devices. These were not, mainly, the *aesthetic* formalities of word-music – rhythm, alliteration, assonance – although, studying Gorgias in particular, a newcomer to rhetoric might have been surprised, and at first delighted, at how those ornamentations of poetry can make prose magnificent too.

One would learn that a case can usually be forged on both sides of a question, since if the matter were obvious there would be no need to persuade through skilful speech. One would therefore learn to anticipate opposing arguments. One would learn that precision and logical tightness not only can be elegant, but make the discourse both impermeable and transparent. One would learn to distinguish observation and conjecture, certainty and probability; and to compare probabilities of alternatives. One would begin to engage conceptual issues, such as the difference in legal cases between determining facts and determining guilt, and problems of deciding who, or what, *initiated* the important event. One would absorb generalizations about how different kinds of person act in various situations, and one would learn that there are exceptions. These assumptions about human psychology would help one adjust a speech to a given audience's probable reactions, and present plausible accounts of how a plaintiff or defendant, a political ally or enemy, or oneself in any of these roles, might have acted or be expected to act.

The sophists' staple, then, was the study and teaching of communication-skills for exercise in various fairly well defined civic situations. But they also stand for something larger and more nebulous, and their originality far outran innovations immediately relevant to producing good speakers for existing contexts. The sophists were pioneers of systematic reflection on the nature of human *logos* (which variously means 'speech', 'language', 'argument', 'reason'). They worked for control of the power of *logos* in the interest of familiar objectives, but they also rode with it into an entire new space of intellectual possibility. The key element of this brave new world was awareness of human mentality as a force with its own nature and laws of development, which moulds itself by means of its products, namely culture and institutions. Paradoxically, these realities exist only because we believe in them, yet they shape and fashion us every bit as much as do the forces of non-human nature. But we need not be at their mercy. These forces too can be harnessed, and inventions and improvements brought to birth. This dual realization, of our power over *logos* and its power over us, was the fundamental insight of the sophists.

Many contemporaries viewed the sophists as exploiters, whose defining interest lay in tapping or teaching how to tap the power of *logos* for material advantage. The impression was fed by the fact that they charged for their courses in rhetoric – in some cases very high fees. This was a constant theme of their early detractors, who included not only ordinary people suspicious of intellectuals and new thinking, and fearful – not unreasonably – that sophistic education drove a wedge between the youth and parental authority, but also Plato, a revolutionary thinker himself. Again and again in his dialogues Plato endorsed the vulgar image of the 'sophist', and it was his authority that stamped that word with its connotation of shallow and mercenary trickster.[1] For instance, he ends his dialogue *Sophist* with this characterization of sophistic activity:

> Imitation of the contrary-speech-producing, insincere and unknowing sort, of the appearance-making kind of copy-making, the word-juggling part of production that's marked off as human and not divine. Anyone who says the sophist is of this 'blood and family' will be saying, it seems, the absolute truth.   (Trans. N. P. White)

Even so, Plato's portraits of individual sophists are not all negative caricatures. His portrayal of Protagoras of Abdera makes clear even while poking fun that this great sophist was not only accomplished, but high-minded and serious. In reality, the sophists, far from simply being mercenaries, represented love of intellectual accomplishment for its own sake. The perfectionism and sense of vocation shown in Plato's picture of Protagoras, and in some of Gorgias' surviving work, suggest that these men and their associates were connoisseurs of the intellect to whom the civic needs which their craft subserved were less opportunities for gain than occasions for engaging in a splendid human activity. And in any case, the sophists were much more than professional teachers of rhetoric. They were free-ranging inquirers, deeply and productively fascinated by the human condition. Curious, creative, thought-provoking, they wondered, speculated, and wrote (in numerous works, of which only fragments now survive) about the natures and origins of society, law, religion and values; about language, truth, belief or opinion (*doxa*), illusion, the imagination, and human agency; and in some cases about physics. In short, by any modern standard they were, among other things, philosophers.

GORGIAS

Let us illustrate first from two displays of logical craft by Gorgias, *Praise of Helen* and *On What Is Not*. Both prove the power of *logos* by demonstrating paradoxes. In *On What Is Not* Gorgias argues:

(1) 'Nothing is';
(2) 'Even if 1 is false, what is is not an object for our grasping';
(3) 'Even if 1 and 2 are false, what is cannot be conveyed by *logos* to others'.

(Here (2) is logical rather than epistemological. It opposes not the assumption that cognition is possible, for Gorgias allows for perceptual cognition, but Parmenides' insistence that only 'what is' can be an object of thought, on which see above pp. 61–2.) Evidently Gorgias means to show that his own reasoning is as powerful as that of Parmenides and Melissus in favour of 'what is' (above, pp. 61–4). We do not know whether Gorgias means to refute those philosophers, or just to make the contrary case so as to show how *logos* can compel the mind in opposite directions.

The *Praise of Helen* is less praise than exoneration. Tradition blamed Helen for the Trojan War, which was started by her adulterous elopement with Paris to Troy. Gorgias argues that Helen's behaviour was due to one of four causes: divine decree or fate, physical overpowerment, persuasion by *logos*, or erotic passion; but in each case Helen was a victim and did nothing shameful. Gorgias assumes that all the causes are kinds of necessitation, and that necessitation nullifies responsibility. It is noteworthy that he exonerates agents driven by divine decree. Not uncommonly in Homer and ancient tragedy, an action for which a human is responsible is also the work of gods furthering their own agenda. It was not clear cut that being a pawn of the gods negates responsibility any more than it is clear to us today that being psychologically damaged negates it. But Gorgias draws a sharp line: if the gods were responsible, Helen was not. Surely he meant the contrapositive too: if Helen was responsible, the gods were not. That is: if man is a cause, this cause is as autonomous and ultimate for explanation as the gods. And man *is* a cause, never more distinctively so than when persuading by *logos*. This, then, in Gorgias' division stands co-ordinate with divine decree.

Accordingly, Gorgias signalled his distance from the philosopher-poets Parmenides and Empedocles (the latter of whom had been his teacher) by advertising his own human autonomy. Parmenides was guided by goddesses to the Way of Truth, and Empedocles began *On Nature* by praying to the Muse for assistance. But Gorgias starts *On What Is Not* with *himself*, declaring in short order that he 'will establish' the first of his conclusions, 'will make clear' the second, and 'will teach' the third. At the beginning of *Helen*, too, it is he himself who by introducing reasoning (*logismos*) into his *logos* will simultaneously rescue Helen from universal infamy (a level of challenge apt, with Socrates or Plato, to elicit a prayer for divine assistance), and her detractors from their ignorance. He ends *Helen*, too, on himself, asserting that this *logos* designed to rehabilitate a heroine and re-educate the Greeks has been 'Helen's praise and my diversion'. Scholars have understood 'diversion' as a warning to take the *logos* playfully. More plausibly, perhaps, Gorgias is explaining what *he* gets out of creating it: not rehabilitation nor re-education, but pleasure. He has made and presented it for its own sake, not in hope of blessings from the spirit of Helen, or favour from her descendants, or release from a curse. (The seventh- to sixth-century poet Stesichorus was said to have gone blind after telling the traditional Helen story, and to have regained his sight on recanting it.)

One Gorgianic innovation, then, is to celebrate the autonomy of human *logos*, which is its own kind of cause and in its more exquisite

manifestations an end in itself for its human author. The contrast
has been with divine causation, and with human creation of beautiful
things as offerings to the gods. But Gorgias also brings out the *sui
generis* nature of *logos* by a contrast with the corporeal. Let us approach this via another innovation, his scrapping of the traditional
contrast between persuasion by *logos* and compulsion (*anankē*). This
opposition hinges on the thought that compelled I go willy nilly,
persuaded I go voluntarily, the difference being between acting from
oneself and being forced from outside. It is assumed that 'voluntary'
implies that even if I was persuaded, the persuader secured *my own
agreement* to the action, an agreement flowing from some attitude
already in me all along, which the persuader activated or turned towards a new situation. To the extent that my antecedent attitude is
cause of the action, I cannot be excused responsibility on grounds
that someone else persuaded me. But when Gorgias maintains that
being persuaded exonerates, he implies that foreign persuasion takes
the soul over, planting in it new springs of action that do the persuader's will. He compares the effect of *logos* on the soul to that
of medications on the body, and says that although persuasion does
not have the form or appearance of compulsion (compulsion being
paradigmatically equated here with physical force (*bia*)), it is equally
powerful.[2] As for the difference in form, he explains this by a new
opposition between corporeal and incorporeal. The power of *logos*
stands in no proportion to physical magnitude, say volume of breath
exhaled in speech or size of written characters. In a related thought
in *On What Is Not*, Gorgias asserts that grasp of *logos* has its own
'organ'; *logos* cannot be taken in by the organs that take in objects
of sense any more than vision can take in sounds.

Gorgias is pondering how linguistic meaning and our understanding of it relate to the physical and our cognition of the physical, and he
is reaching towards the contrast of 'sensible' with 'intelligible' which
will be central for Plato. But whereas Plato postulated extra-mental
incorporeal realities to be what *logos* essentially reveals, Gorgias assumes that the only realities (apart from *logos* itself) are corporeal
and perceptible. So even though sense perception stirs up in us *logoi*
for sensible things, these *logoi*, being utterly different in nature from
their referents, cannot transmit to anyone the characters of the latter.
If we put together these findings of *Praise of Helen* and *On What Is*

Not, we seem to have the result that when *logos* constrains and determines the soul, it does so not as a medium through which metaphysically prior determining realities make themselves present to us, but in its own right by uninherited authority. As Gorgias says, '*Logos* is a powerful lord' (*Helen*, 8). Even so, he allows that it can be true or false, for he means to teach the truth and remove falsehood about Helen. However, he does not explain what truth of a *logos* consists in. But plainly the truth-making realities do not reach out and grab us by means of their *logos* so that in accepting *it* we receive *them*; for if so, a false *logos* could have no power over us. At times Gorgias seems to write as if persuasion is essentially false. But he surely means not that its message is necessarily false, but that it works by deceiving us into accepting the message not as unstable, obscure, opinion (*doxa*) which is the most it can be, but as solid, clear, self-presentation of the opined realities themselves, so that they affect us as if they were actually there. And this is not necessarily a bad thing or a symptom of our weakness. In one context, at least, as Gorgias observed, the following paradox is true: 'Deluder excels non-deluder in justice, and deluded non-deluded in wisdom.' The context is that of tragic drama, where the good producer does his just duty of deluding, and the good audience are not so stupid as to be impervious to tragic illusion.

Philosophers of mind and language today are still not free of the puzzling that began with these Gorgianic insights: that *logos* is not something we grasp as we grasp objects of sense; that *logos* cannot literally transmit such objects to us; that what instead it can do, in persuasion, is make us not notice its own role in persuading us, so that we open ourselves up (so we think) directly to the objects it is 'about'; and that this is exactly what ought to happen if *logos*, a human contrivance, were really what in persuasion it works by pretending to be: a natural transparent medium through which realities naturally appear.

PROTAGORAS

Let us turn now to Protagoras, chronologically first of the sophists and generally considered the greatest. According to ancient sources, his was a mind of astonishing originality. Among the innovations attributed to him were: teaching that there is a pair of opposed arguments on every question; asserting that contradiction is impossible (presumably because the two sides are really talking about different things); arguing by questions (the method later made famous by Socrates); distinguishing the tenses of the verb; dividing *logos* into basic types of speech-act such as entreaty, question, answer, command. Of his writings almost nothing survives apart from two memorable opening sentences, one from his work called *Truth* or *Refutations*, the other from *On Gods*. The latter starts: 'Concerning the gods, I cannot know either that they exist or that they do not exist or what form they might have, for there is much to prevent one's knowing: the obscurity of the subject [or possibly: their [sc. the gods'] imperceptibility] and the shortness of man's life.' From this decisively agnostic beginning, it would seem that the bulk of *On Gods* must have been about human religion, rather than about divinities themselves. It was a work of anthropology, not theology. Protagoras may have surveyed beliefs and cultic practices; he may have examined the psychological and social effects of belief and disbelief in gods; he may have speculated on the origin of religion. One thing is clear: since it would have been obvious to him that belief in gods is all but universal, his own agnosticism would have told him that a belief that is humanly irrepressible, even partly definitive of human nature, may simply *not be true* – if by 'true' we mean made so by an independently existing reality to which it conforms. Protagoras would have seen that religious belief makes exactly the same difference to the world, in and through lives of believers, whether it is true or not in the above sense. And since, if external gods do not exist, we must somehow have generated entirely by ourselves the belief in them, it is reasonable to suppose that if, instead, external gods do exist, it is not on account of that (human nature itself being the same) that men believe, but, as before, because it is human nature to fashion this belief for itself. Just as for Gorgias sheer *logos* is the 'powerful lord' – becoming no more powerful over men when truth is added to it – so for Protagoras with belief and imagination.

However, Protagoras seems to have thought that 'truth' (*alētheia*) should mean not undetectable correspondence with something whose non-existence could make no difference, but a desirable state, one in which the soul is, so to speak, properly switched on to what concerns it. If so, and if he adhered to the logical point that truth represents things as they are whether positive or negative, then since what concerns us does so because of *our* nature, not purely through its own, for him it follows that what counts as being and what counts as not being are not, as we may once have assumed, controlled by a set of wholly independently present or absent realities, but are a function of the way *we* are. As Protagoras declares in the first sentence of his *Truth*: 'Of all things the measure is man, of things that are that [or 'how'] they are, and of things that are not that [or 'how'] they are not.'

According to Plato's presentation of this Protagorean dictum (*Theaetetus* 151e ff.), it summarizes the theory that for each individual things are/are not as he or she at that moment takes them to be/not be. Plato, however, is not writing scientific history of philosophy, but using 'Protagoras' to represent a doctrine he will refute; and it is difficult to believe that the highly respected and practical Protagoras based his teaching on the view that any answer thrown out to any question was automatically on target, factually speaking. More likely he was concerned with human affairs, and with areas in which there is practical disagreement or divergence because people (1) are struck by different features of a complex situation owing to their different material needs and interests, or (2) see something in different lights owing to their different cultural values. Protagoras may not have distinguished these scenarios. The first can be convincingly dealt with by saying that each party grasps as much of the real state of affairs as is possible from their particular perspective, whereas for the second it may seem more reasonable to say that there is no objective fact of the matter, for instance as to whether the dead should be buried or cremated.

But then doesn't 'Man the measure' imply that no one is ever wiser than another – can give no better advice? This would make nonsense of Protagoras' life. He was a long-time friend of the great Athenian leader Pericles, who showed his trust in Protagoras' wisdom and judgement by assigning him the task of framing laws for Thurii, an important new colony. And of course as teacher Protagoras promised improvement. He would assure the prospective pupil that he would learn from Protagoras good judgement (*euboulia*) in his own affairs, so that he may manage his own household in the best way, and good judgement in the affairs of the city, so that he may be most capable in action and in speech in matters concerning the city.   (Plato, *Protagoras* 318a–d, trans. S. Lombardo and K. Bell)

Elsewhere Plato makes Protagoras explain that although what appears to each person is *true* enough, as it answers to the condition the subject is in, some appearances are more *beneficial* than others; and Protagoras' skill, which he professes to teach, is in seeing better than most people which appearances would be beneficial in a given case, and in persuading men to let go of unhelpful appearances and take on helpful ones.

Probably Protagoras had a common-sense understanding of 'more/less beneficial'. There are fundamental human needs and desires, say for health, security, livelihood, the company of loved ones, pleasure; and focusing on a given aspect of a situation, or following a given set of *mores*, may for individual or group be more or less conducive to these desiderata. One who is skilful at improving (by this standard) the way people look at things must be highly experienced and intelligent so as to identify and understand different perspectives, and highly articulate so as to formulate explanations that make it easier for people to move to initially unacceptable positions.

In offering to teach this kind of good judgement, Protagoras surely did not pretend to make an exact science of it. True, the enthusiasm he aroused in students and would-be students like young Hippocrates in Plato's *Protagoras* might lead us to think that what the sophist claimed to deliver was a cut and dried package of ingenious principles offering miraculously sure and easy, though of course illusory, quick fixes on every social and civic question. For, we might wonder, what could all the excitement have been about if not about promises to teach some kind of superhuman method whose nature one can only fantasize? No doubt some of Protagoras' young followers were so inexperienced as to expect that it would all be as easy as magic; but the main cause of excitement, and source of the sophists' glamour, was something we today might fail to appreciate, positioned as we are to take for granted the reality of higher education in politics, economics, law, sociology, government, business management, and so on: it was the shattering newness, when Protagoras began his career, of the very idea that education by professionals can develop the potential for leadership. Before, it had simply been assumed that the qualities of a leader were a sort of hereditary endowment naturally developed through imitative osmosis from elders and betters in and round the family: rich sources of practice and precept, but not of explanation and analysis.

Although in the first scene of Plato's *Protagoras* Hippocrates is almost beside himself with rapture at the thought of learning mighty new things from the sophist, the body of the dialogue shows Protagoras at pains to present his teaching as continuous with familiar, traditional, elements of the culture. He describes himself as carrying forward the role of the poets, who were standardly used as sources of instruction on how to live. And he argues that his and his students' teaching and learning of civic excellence is not a new-fangled, revolutionary, activity, but an extension of what in families and communities has always gone on under the heading of bringing up children ever since civil society began. To the challenge that if excellence can be taught, paragons like Pericles would have taught or had it taught to their sons, who in fact were not outstanding, the Protagorean response was to compare man socialized with man as he would be without socialization. From this point of view it is clear that every member of society, even though some are better than others, has absorbed a large measure of 'justice' and 'respect', the twin elements of civic decency; and that this has come about through teaching and learning, since individuals do not acquire these qualities left to themselves.

This argument, while obviously meant to allay traditionalist suspicions about sophistic education, also reflects solid thinking about human nature and the origins of society. We know that the historical Protagoras wrote a work *On Government* (*Peri politeas*; the same noun recurs as the title of Plato's *Republic*), and one *On the Original State of Things* (that is, of human affairs); and an ancient source accuses Plato of having plagiarized the ideas of his *Republic* from Protagoras. Certainly Plato in the *Republic* completely concurred with and may have been inspired by Protagoras' vision of the human soul as not merely persuadable by *logos* to do, think, or feel, this or that particular thing, but as educable in respect of those underlying moral and intellectual dispositions that come to be 'second nature', in that they determine our particular actions, thoughts, feelings, and responses to persuasion. The *Republic* works out in monumental breadth and penetrating detail the Protagorean insight that human individuals are shaped through and through by the institutions of their society.

LANGUAGE

Much sophistic debate over the meaning and authority of human institutions was framed in terms of the contrast of *physis* (nature) with *nomos* (law, custom, convention, established practice). For example, language is clearly natural to human beings; human beings are part of the natural world, biological organisms in a physical environment; and words of language relate referentially to objects in nature. Hence some thinkers theorized that there is or is recoverable a natural 'correctness of names' whereby characteristics of words reflect in nonarbitrary fashion the characteristics of things. Words may have been thought of by analogy with sense impressions, on a naive realist view: objects somehow cause us to frame words that non-arbitrarily represent them. At any rate, Protagoras apparently held that objects in general have genders (because all nouns do in Greek), which we can identify independently of actual words for them and which words should be made to reflect. (Thus he held that the standardly feminine word *mēnis*, meaning 'wrath' and notable as the first word of the *Iliad*, should be masculine, presumably because the emotion is a masculine thing.) The sophist Prodicus of Ceos was a butt of humour for distinguishing between synonyms and near-synonyms such as 'debate' and 'dispute', 'doing' and 'working'. He may have theorized that language is naturally tailored to its function, and that it therefore would not provide different words unless there were significant differences in meaning. Like Protagoras he proposed revisions of standard usage, refusing to call phlegm (a cold 'humour') by that name as the etymology implies having been heated. The sophistic thinker Cratylus of Athens apparently held that the fundamental words phonetically mimic fundamental natural movements and forces. On the other side, of course, were those who held that correctness of names depends on human convention and agreement. With logic in its infancy, this view, obvious to us, was not necessarily easy to defend. By convention a certain Greek word, considered as a set of phonemes, means 'dog', while a statement in Greek that dogs are carnivorous is true because of canine nature. But not only was the distinction as yet undiscovered between meaning and reference; none had even been clearly drawn between statements and words. In fact, a statement could seem to be a complex name. In this state of things, the commonsensical premiss that correctness of names is a matter of arbitrary human convention could seem to carry the shocking consequence that the truth of statements is arbitrary too.

The debate over natural correctness of names may have focused first on etymology and onomatopoeia. The anti-naturalist could point out that onomatopoeia cannot be the principle of natural correctness since so few words are onomatopoeic, and that etymology cannot be the principle either since so many mean something different from what etymology suggests. There was, however, potential for taking the debate to a new level, that of categories or forms. The author of the Hippocratic treatise *On Expertise*, probably written near the end of the fifth century, held that although names are imposed by human *nomos*, the different branches of knowledge capture the forms (*eidē*) of things, and these are 'offspring of nature'. So if knowledge is couched in language, its linguistic expression might be expected to reflect natural structures in the subject-matter. For example, the entailment by 'fire' of 'hot' (a connection not restricted to any given language, and not dependent on phonetics or etymology) might seem a manifestation in *logos* of a connection in the world of nature. Hence perhaps by studying indubitable linguistic truths, we can find out about extra-linguistic reality.[3] But in light of Gorgias' sweeping denial of the ability of *logos* to convey reality, someone was bound to come forward with the opposing view that linguistic forms are wholly internal to language: they do not reflect the natures of things. Such a view could limit itself to warning that the study of linguistic and logical form cannot of itself increase our knowledge about things in nature, while allowing that the senses afford us cognition. This may have been the view of the sophist Antiphon,[4] who said, for instance, that time is only a thought or a measurement. (In light of Protagoras' work on tense, it would have been natural to wonder whether time, as tense, is a trick of language.) Antiphon too wrote a work called *Truth*, where he declared it barbaric to contrast Greeks with barbarians, patricians with plebeians: these human concepts do not reflect natural kinds.

One could, however, progress to the extreme position that *nothing* extra-linguistic has anything remotely resembling the stability and definiteness of linguistic and logical structures – which seems to put the extra-linguistic world completely beyond human comprehension. Its seeming comprehensibility will then be an illusion generated by *logos*, just as to Gorgias the seeming presence to us of things through *logos* was another illusion from the same source.

JUSTICE

The fact that custom and law, like language, differ for different societies, together with the assumption that what is lawful is what is right, suggested to some that right and wrong, just and unjust, are relative to the society, while to others it suggested that there is a natural justice and injustice over and above the man-made systems. According to an old and popular view, which was endorsed by the sophist Hippias of Elis, there is natural justice in the sense of a set of moral principles valid for all nations. Plato would develop this into the doctrine that natural justice is an eternal essence which human justice 'imitates' (cf. pp. 104–5). According to a very different interpretation, natural justice is exploitation of weaker by stronger. This is what we see throughout the animal kingdom; and on some views it ought to be the law of human life as well. Such is the position of the character (probably fictional) of Callicles in Plato's *Gorgias*. Elements of this view surface in the *Republic* too, voiced by Thrasymachus (an historical sophist, from Chalcedon), and by Plato's brother Glaucon. According to this sort of view, an individual who is strong and clever enough to take advantage of his neighbours' weakness but refrains out of justice and respect, betrays his own nature and natural inheritance. In fact he has been made artificially weak by the naturally weak many (*hoi polloi*), who for self-protection have conditioned men into accepting the myth that true justice requires individuals to sacrifice their own well-being for others.

This myth of morality, as these thinkers saw it, has been bolstered by further artifices: punitive state sanctions and fictitious threats of divine punishment. Several maintained that the gods themselves are a fiction. There were, however, important variations in this view. Prodicus, for instance, held that men naturally and spontaneously worship, as beneficent deities, the natural forces that sustain life, such as earth and sun. It was also suggested, however, that righteous gods are humanly crafted propaganda devised by some individuals in order to subjugate others. An extreme but logical version of this is voiced by a character in the lost play *Sisyphus* (variously attributed to Euripides and to the Athenian politician Critias), who declares the fiction of righteous gods to be the *single-handed* invention of a brilliant human despot. (The less logical alternative would be that the feeble-minded many successfully deceive the super-intelligent few as well as – somehow – each other.)

The sort of doctrine favoured by Callicles and Thrasymachus, while sharing roots with theories of Protagoras, moves in a very different direction. For Protagoras, human nature is perfected through social institutions, even if no one set of institutions is objectively the best. But according to Callicles and Thrasymachus, society represses the best natures, fostering the weak without improving them individually, and encouraging the cult of mediocrity. Different again, it seems, was the view of Antiphon. Like Callicles and Thrasymachus, Antiphon sharply contrasts the humanly lawful with the naturally advantageous, but unlike them he seems in some sense to accept the rule of man-made law. In his *Truth*, he declares that a man profits by conforming to *nomos* only when witnesses are present; the causal connection between, for example, crime and punishment depends on whether, and how, the deed *appears to others.* By contrast, the effects on one of going against nature are the same whether anybody else notices it or not; this causal nexus is a matter of 'truth', i.e. opinion-independent reality. What *nomos* forbids and what it permits are equally natural actions. It was Antiphon, not Rousseau, who first spoke of custom and law as 'fetters' on natural human freedom. On the other hand, Antiphon does not go along with Callicles and Thrasymachus in their rhapsodizing on unfettered despotism as the ideal of human happiness. Presumably Antiphon sees unfettered despotism as fantasy. He asserts that only a fool imagines he can wrong another without retaliation. Antiphon is also more pessimistic and realistic than Callicles and Glaucon about the degree to which law protects the weak, pointing out that an injured party has no guarantee that he will convince the jury. And Antiphon sees injustice, and therefore self-contradiction, in the legal enforcement of justice. *A* can be punished for/ deterred from wronging *B* only if an uninvolved party, *C*, can/ would testify against *A*; but this requires *C* to commit against *A* the injustice of deliberately harming someone who has not harmed him. By the same token, and even

more paradoxically, disinterested judges and arbitrators are necessarily unjust, since their rulings must harm one who never harmed
them, i.e. the losing party in the case.

SOCRATES

Let us turn now to Socrates, surely the best-known figure in ancient
Greek philosophy.

Both Plato and Xenophon wrote Socratic dialogues, and so did several of their contemporaries. The 'Socratic dialogue' became a recognized genre. But except for a few fragments only those of Plato and
Xenophon survive. From the pages of Plato, and to a lesser extent
from the pages of Xenophon, Socrates leaps out at us. We are even
shown his appearance: his broad face, snub nose, and protruding eyes;
and his going about barefoot wearing a skimpy old cloak winter and
summer. We are shown his extraordinary personality: his utter faith
in the power of reason to save men's souls, his conviction that he
must get his fellow citizens to join him in this faith, his addiction
to step-by-step puzzling over the deepest questions in the plainest
words using no device or ornament but close logic and homespun
analogies. Alongside this profound rationalism of his, we also learn
of something quite peculiar and mysterious but of the utmost importance to him and about him: namely, his visitation (quite often,
it seems) by a 'divine sign' which only ever told him to refrain from
something he was about to do, and which he obeyed without question. Our composite portrait also affords many glimpses of Socrates'
legendary self-control and courage, and of his affection and steady
concern for the young men round him. It shows the mesmerizing
effect he had on those who were drawn in by him, and how he was
adored by some of the most brilliant, beautiful and aristocratic figures of his time. It shows him displaying a dazzling range of intellectual and verbal skills in jousts with such sophists as Protagoras,
Gorgias and Hippias. We also see Socrates framed by certain definitive events: the Delphic oracle's pronouncement that no one was
wiser than he; his trial on trumped up charges of impiety and corrupting the young; his refusal, when the verdict went against him,
to beg to be spared the death sentence (since in his view he deserved
honour, not leniency); his refusal to escape from prison when it was
possible; his philosophizing among his friends up to the last; his

final calm downing of the hemlock drink by which he was executed. All in all, Socrates is the best known of the ancient Greek philosophers because, beginning with Plato and Xenophon, generation after generation has seen in him the model of the philosophical life. And philosophers of many different stripes have made Socrates their tutelary figure: Platonists, sceptics, Stoics and still others.

So it is not for nothing that we feel a familiarity with the uniquely seminal Socrates. But we must be wary. Socrates wrote nothing himself, and almost everything we know about him comes to us through the lenses of his younger associates, Plato and Xenophon. (Another, highly distorting, lens is that of the comedian Aristophanes, Socrates' contemporary, who caricatured him in his *Clouds*.) Neither Plato nor Xenophon was trying to write historical biography, and each had an other than strictly historical agenda. They were trying, rather, to present what they thought Socrates stood for, and to make him an exemplar and inspiration for 'cultivation of the soul'.

Apparently as a young man Socrates was interested in natural science; but his great contribution was to ethical thought. He fastened on the fact that the fundamental assumptions of practical life lie almost completely unexamined by all of us, even though nothing should matter to us more than that these assumptions be true and the guidance they give us be right. These are the assumptions which begin to be revealed if we start to ask questions like 'How should we live?', 'What things are really worth caring about?', 'What is wisdom, what is virtue?', and 'How are those qualities to be attained?' Socrates saw that these questions can be discussed logically and systematically, and that such discussion can yield progress. For even if positive answers cannot be established beyond doubt, discussion can help one shed false views. It seems that Socrates assumed that if we are right-minded and really care about living well ourselves, then once we realize that this sort of inquiry is possible, we shall be eager to have it scrutinize the principles underlying our own practice. Thus by his own light Socrates was doing himself and others a great favour when he engaged them in these discussions. In conversation after conversation he would put his questions step by step. Again and again not merely his interlocutors, but often also a ring of fascinated silent listeners, were confronted with their own inability to give clear, consistent, answers to Socrates' questioning. In many cases the interlocutors became embarrassed and even angry at being shown up by Socrates. But their predicament of ignorance was one which Socrates loved to confess he shared. People often could not believe he was sincere in his protestation of not being in the know about the answers to his own questions. They thought it was a trick he played in order to fool them and thereby steal the advantage in debate. This was probably because the pattern of the sophists had led many to assume that the point of engaging in systematic discourse was to demonstrate one's superior expertise on the topics in question. It was an extraordinary novelty, Socrates' insistence that if he was wiser than others this was only because, on the most important matters in life, he unlike others knew that he did not know.

Socrates and sophists in conversation

This table shows a selection of Socrates' conversations – the majority of them with sophists, and all of them bearing on issues considered in this chapter – as portrayed, reconstructed, or imagined by Plato and Xenophon. In the final column, names in quotation marks indicate people represented in the conversation but not present at it.[5]

Author	Work	Topic	Participants include
Plato	*Charmides*	What is temperance?	Socrates, Critias
Plato	*Cratylus*	Correctness of names	Socrates, Hermogenes, Cratylus
Plato	*Crito*	Should obedience to the law be absolute?	Socrates, Crito, 'the laws'
Plato	*Euthydemus*	Displays of sophistic argument	Socrates, Euthydemus, Dionysodorus
Plato	*Euthyphro*	What is piety?	Socrates, Euthyphro
Plato	*Gorgias*	What is rhetoric for? Natural vs artificial justice	Socrates, Gorgias, Callicles, Polus
Plato	*Greater Hippias*	What is the fine (or beautiful)?	Socrates, Hippias
Plato	*Laches*	What is courage?	Socrates, the two generals Laches and Nicias

Author	Work	Topic	Participants include
Plato	*Lesser Hippias*	Is wisdom a two-way power?	Socrates, Hippias
Plato	*Protagoras*	Virtue and wisdom; is virtue teachable?	Socrates, Protagoras, Hippias, Prodicus, 'the many'
Plato	*Republic* I	Might is right	Socrates, Thrasymachus
Plato	*Theaetetus*	What is knowledge?	Socrates, 'Protagoras'
Xenophon	*Memoirs* I 5–6	Socrates on his own life and work	Socrates, Antiphon
Xenophon	*Memoirs* II 1	Self-control	Socrates, Aristippus, 'Prodicus'
Xenophon	*Memoirs* III 8	The good and the fine	Socrates, Aristippus
Xenophon	*Memoirs* IV 3–4	Justice and lawfulness	Socrates, Hippias

According to Plato's *Apology* (i.e. *Defence*) *of Socrates*, Socrates approached first the political figures in Athens, then the poets, finally the various craftsmen, and subjected them to his questioning. It is a pity if these facts have become too familiar to us to seem surprising. For surely it is remarkable that Socrates managed to engage enough interlocutors up and down the city on enough occasions over many years to make it a notorious life-style for himself. His doing so tells us not just something about Socrates – about the power of his personality – but something about the extent to which contemporary Athens had become intellectualized by the sophists. For why did so many of those approached by Socrates 'abide the question' in the first place, and accept the burden of answering? Out of self-respect. But why was that? Why didn't most of these good burghers simply brush him off, confident of being as wise as they needed to be, whether or not they could talk back well Socratically – talk of this kind being a waste of time anyway? That significantly many of them did not react like that is a measure of the spread of sophistication (in the original sense) in Athens in the mid to late fifth century.

And it was natural for Socrates' contemporaries to think of him too as a sophist. Like the sophists, he assumed that the highest form of self-improvement is a training in and by means of subtly constructed *logoi*. For him too the purpose was to inculcate virtue (*aretē*) and wisdom, terms which for him and the (other) sophists were all but synonymous. Like the sophists, he saw this virtue and wisdom as a kind of intellectual mastery that could not automatically develop just through common sense, ordinary experience and traditional intuitions. Socrates too was a sort of professional educator, even though he flatly denied being a 'teacher' in the sense of someone possessed of authoritative answers. He made it his vocation to introduce into Athens his own kind of intellectual discipline. He was contemptuous of demanding fees (as if the paid sophists were concerned with their students only as a source of income), but his main business was disseminating his kind of cultivation, and he went about it in a focused and purposeful way for a considerable part of his fairly long life, apparently neglecting his private affairs. Because of the strangeness of what he was doing and the enthusiasm he aroused in his followers, Socrates no less than the sophists was a target of anxiety on the part of traditional-minded parents and mentors.

This fact no doubt helped to create the atmosphere in which he was charged with impiety and corrupting the young. But the main motive for bringing the charges was surely political. Though neither rich nor aristocratic himself, Socrates had friends, admirers and disciples from amongst leading Athenian families. There was perennial discord in Athens between democrats and supporters of oligarchic government, and this trouble came to a particularly ugly head near the end of the fifth century. In 404, when Athens had suffered final defeat in the Peloponnesian War, the democracy was suspended and power passed to a group known as the 'Thirty Tyrants'. In less than a year they were violently overthrown and democracy restored, but not before they had killed or exiled thousands of citizens. Socrates had prominent adherents, and therefore prominent enemies too, on both sides of the political divide. His trial, conviction and death came in 399.

But for all his intellectual innovation and the apparent subversiveness of his questioning, Socrates also stood forth as a champion, in a way, of traditional values. Not only was he himself a person of exceptional moral integrity, proved through a variety of testing moments in his life, but in his pedagogy he never departed from the assumption that the all-important excellence which he was dedicated to cultivating comprised justice and respect for law, along with piety, courage, good sense and moderation. He saw the excellence to which he was dedicated as somehow, in the limit, consisting in a kind of intellectual clarity on ethical questions: an intellectual clarity that somehow subsumed and united in itself the traditional practical virtues.

Along with this intellectualism Socrates introduced a new interpretation of the value of upright conduct. The tradition, of course, preached uncompromising rejection of wrongdoing as shameful; and Socrates left this unquestioned. But he took a momentous further step in insisting that wrongdoing is not only shameful, but extremely *harmful*, to the doer. One is *worse off* doing wrong than suffering it. Thus Socrates rejected common sense's multi-focused awareness of two kinds of practical claim, the claim of morality and the claim of personal well-being, whose radical disparity allows for soul-destroying dilemmas in which the agent will do what is right only at terrible cost to himself. The point here is not that Socrates saw the claim of morality as supreme – for this does not set him apart from common sense – but that he refused to see possible conflict between morality and well-being, on the ground that nothing is as truly advantageous and beneficial to the agent as upright conduct whatever the circumstances. In effect, then, Socrates rejected Antiphon's view that the link between wrongdoing and harm to the doer depends on the contingencies of human witnesses and the non-miscarriage of man-made law. Or, rather, Socrates implied that whereas Antiphon's view may be true of empirically recognizable harms such as execution, prison, fines, exile, hostility of neighbours etc., it fails in face of an incomparably worse kind of harm – a kind undreamt of in Antiphon's philosophy. To commit wrong is to do to *oneself* the greatest conceivable damage.

Socrates' conviction that this is so seems not to have led him to speculate at any length on how it can be so. It was already clear from Antiphon's arguments that *if* there is such a necessary connection between wrongdoing and harm to the agent, it is not a physical or natural tie, nor yet a man-made one. Socrates was a devout man, but he seems to have been agnostic about a life after death in which the harm would be dealt out by god as punishment. It was left to Plato to bring out the implications of Socrates' faith that the wrongdoer does himself a terrible harm: for instance, the implication that the soul is (as we would put it) a metaphysical entity, locus of a non-empirical and supremely important kind of well-being and harm; and the implication that since the connection does not emanate from nature nor from human contrivance, it must be grounded in a divine super-reality: a reality such that the natural world now looks as insubstantial and adventitious by comparison with it as human institutions looked to certain sophists by comparison with the natural world.

Let us return to the uniquely Socratic synthesis of intellectual discipline with excellence as it was traditionally understood. It is instructive to see how, in the ambiguous light of this proposed combination, one and the same view can shift between seeming an obvious truth and seeming an outrageous paradox. Take, for example, Socrates' famous assertion that 'No one goes wrong willingly.' If 'going wrong' is understood to mean an intellectual failure like a slip in geometrical reasoning, or, for that matter, in Socratic inquiry, then the view seems clearly true and unsurprising. We make wrong intellectual moves just because we fail to realize that they are mistakes. We avoid such error if we realize in time. Thus on this level we go wrong only through ignorance of our going wrong, which implies we do not go wrong 'willingly'. But if Socrates' dictum applies to moral wrong-doing, i.e. failure to live up to the standards defining traditional excellence, it seems so obviously false as to be absurd. For (from a commonsense perspective) one sometimes knows perfectly well that a given action is wrong – unjust, cowardly or greedy – yet one does it freely all the same. Thus in such a case an agent's clearheaded knowledge (as we might normally call it) of a particular error does not save him from committing it. And it may seem more obvious still that the kind of knowledge Socrates was after, namely the ability to give well-grounded answers to *universal* ethical questions, is compatible with wrongdoing; for its abstractness, universality, and logical strength would seem to make it a *theoretical* sort of knowledge, and how can *that* of itself preserve one from moral wrongdoing? Of course, no one has yet attained such knowledge, in Socrates' view, but this does not make it easier to understand how we would be morally better if we had it. Even Socrates himself was sometimes inclined to admit that mere 'true opinion (*doxa*)' is sufficient for moral goodness, 'true opinion' being the set of unsystematized

decent attitudes that ordinary good upbringing is meant to inculcate. In fact this is simply a return to common sense – except that
common sense would not have described the goal of good upbringing
as 'true opinion', a phrase which gets its point by contrast with the
ideal of a scientific knowledge of values.

But now Socrates' intellectual, discursive, approach hardly seems
even a necessary condition for attaining the excellence that typifies
the upright person. What, then, was the value of Socrates' method?
Was it just a quixotic dream, his extraordinary faith that uprightness is somehow intimately dependent on systematic reflection on
values? Not at all. True, if we simply consider individual cases, and
abstract from historical context, it is obvious that uprightness may
flourish in the absence of Socratic questioning. It is also fairly obvious, as several of Plato's dialogues seem meant among other things to
demonstrate, that Socratic probing which confronts the interlocutor
with his own ignorance is powerless on its own to change dyed-in-
the-wool moral foolishness into moral wisdom. It might seem from
this that what Socrates was doing was rather pointless, however interesting it may be to read about it. To see why this is not so, we
must look at him in historical context. We must consider the effect
of sophistic influence on the general moral climate.

THE SOPHISTIC CONTEXT

There was reason to be nervous about this influence: not because
it was new, not because it dealt in *logoi*, not because the sophists
were bad men individually (there is no particular ground for believing that); but because sophistic training in rhetoric brought power
without responsibility or direction, and was delivered and received
in an atmosphere of uncritical admiration for rhetorical skill as such.
This enthusiasm was entirely natural given that rhetorical art was
necessary equipment for the all-important world of contemporary
politics. It was also entirely natural given the absence then of any
other intellectual discipline of comparable appeal. In effect, there existed an intellectual vacuum wherein could flourish the illusion that
what the sophists taught was not merely useful, even indispensable,
preparation for the civic scene, but the peak of mental accomplishment and the sovereign art of political life.[6] This self-inflation is
understandable as a phenomenon, but it had perilous implications.

For if rhetoric is the supreme expertise, it must be its own highest authority, not subservient to any prior expertise. But rhetorical skill is skill in *persuasion* – in getting people to accept one set of appearances rather than another. It is not expertise in discovering realities behind the appearances. Suppose there were such an expertise, one for discovering realities in those areas where it matters most to be able to persuade, i.e. in the big questions of life: such an expertise would or ought to be sovereign over rhetoric, directing rhetoric's creation of appearances so that they reflect the higher expert's knowledge of ethical and political realities. Hence if rhetoric is sovereign, there can be no such expertise about the realities.

Now if no such expertise about realities is available, this could be for one of two reasons. According to one, knowledge of the realities is so easy to come by and to hold on to that possessing it cannot be considered an *expertise*. In that case, although that knowledge ought surely to guide our use of rhetoric, it will not supplant rhetoric as the highest expertise. According to the other, in these areas there simply *are* no realities to be objects of knowledge or expertise.

The sophists could hardly embrace the first alternative. If knowledge of the most important things is so easily available to everyone, why is there so much dissension? And what need after all can there be for the sophists' art of persuasion? One who already knows does not require to be persuaded of the truth, and cannot be persuaded into believing anything different. So for those who idolized rhetoric, the second alternative was the only way to go, whether they fully realized it or not. Their hyperbolic devotion makes sense only if there are no realities beyond the appearances of good and bad, right and wrong, and any appearance is as true as any other. This was the view to which the intellectual authorities of the day were committed – if sophists were rightly considered the intellectual authorities.

These implications of the sophistic movement are displayed with brilliant sharpness in Plato's dialogues. It may even have been Plato rather than Socrates who first saw clearly the full comprehensive import of the craze for rhetoric, constructing his 'Socrates' character as vehicle for a critique he elaborated himself after his master's death. But even if the worked out critique came from Plato, we can be certain that it came because of the impact on him of the life and death of the actual Socrates. The actual Socrates, with his firmness about the real difference between good and bad, his insistence that one think things out for oneself, and his stubborn systematic ethical questioning, stood for the contrary of the sophists according to the sketch just given; and the contrast brought both sides out into the open. Socrates' life made sense only if the human intellect can reach ethical answers in a scientific way, answers which are objectively more adequate than others (even if infallible answers remain elusive). But once this is allowed, we see that rhetoric's place is only ancillary, and that the human intellect, especially on the profoundest questions of life, must not be satisfied with appearances.

NOTES

1   See Plato, *Sophist* 218b–233c for a series of divisions resulting in unflattering definitions of the sophist. See also 267e–268d. However, 226d–231b defines the 'noble sophistry' represented by Socrates.

2   This follows Diels' reconstruction of the text.

3   See Plato, *Phaedo* 99d–100a; cf. 103c–e.

4   According to one tradition he was a different person from Antiphon of Rhamnous, the rhetorician (see above, p. 000), but today many scholars identify them as one and the same.

5   See also Plato, *Symposium* 214e ff., which gives us, not a Socratic conversation, but Alcibiades' 'encomium' of Socrates.

6   See Plato's declaration at *Sophist* 216b–217c that, confusing appearances notwithstanding, the sophist, the statesman and the philosopher are three distinct kinds. (The word 'philosophy' at this time meant nothing much more precise than 'the highest intellectual activity'. It was Socrates' and Plato's view about 'philosophy' in this broad sense that led to its being understood more narrowly, in terms of the rational search for objective truth.)

4   Plato

THE PLATONIC CORPUS

From any perspective, Plato's dialogues are extraordinary. Others have tried to write philosophical dialogues, frequently in imitation of his. Indeed other associates of Socrates had already used the genre before Plato adopted it; bits and pieces, along with titles, remain. But the *Platonic* dialogues remain essentially *sui generis*, whether taken singly or as a whole. There are somewhere between twenty-five and thirty-five genuine works which, while always returning to ethics and politics, between them cover a vast range of topics, and cover them in often startlingly different ways; always, however, using a cast of characters that excludes the author, even in disguise. A main feature is that they define – and would later be taken as having defined – what philosophy itself is, not just in terms of its subject-matter but in terms of method and attitude or approach. This they do chiefly by exhibiting philosophy in action; or rather, typically, by exhibiting a philosopher – usually Socrates – going about his business, often in confrontation with others (teachers of rhetoric, sophists, politicians, poets) who dealt with the same subject-matter but in different, non-philosophical ways.

Quite what this thing 'philosophy' is, on Plato's account, will emerge in due course. First, it will be helpful to review the extent of the corpus, the parts of which are laid out below in an ancient ordering. (The ordering – at least of the first thirty-six items, arranged in nine 'tetralogies' – is probably due to the Platonist Thrasyllus of Alexandria in the first century AD.)

Diagram A: The contents of the Platonic corpus

Approximate lengths are given in 'Stephanus' pages. These are the page numbers of the several volumes of Henri Estienne's 1574 edition of Plato, used by all modern editions and translations to provide a standard referencing system. (Each Stephanus page – see p. 17 – is divided into five sections, a–e; however, line numbers within sections are frequently specific to particular editions, so may vary.) One Stephanus page typically contains around 530 words, slightly more than the equivalent of one page of this book. Alternative titles, and some obscurer but regularly used abbreviations are given in square brackets.

Diagram A

Title	Topic	Main speaker(s)	Pages
1 *Euthyphro*	On piety	Socrates	14
2 *Apology*	Defence speeches at trial, re-created (not a dialogue)	Socrates	25
3 *Crito*	On the citizen and the law	Socrates	12
4 *Phaedo* (*Phd.*, *Phdo*)	On the soul: does it survive death?	Socrates	61
5 *Cratylus*	On the relationship of language to reality	Socrates	58
6 *Theaetetus* (*Tht.*)	Three formally unsuccessful attempts to define knowledge	Socrates	69
7 *Sophist*	(Sequel to *Theaetetus*.) What is a sophist? Falsity, not-being	Visitor from Elea	53
8 *Statesman* (*Politicus*, *Pol.*, *Plt.*)	(Sequel to *Sophist*.) What is it to be a statesman?	Visitor from Elea	55

(*cont.*)

(cont.)

Title	Topic	Main speaker(s)	Pages
9 *Parmenides*	On 'Forms'; with philosophical training exercises	Parmenides (from Elea), Socrates	41
10 *Philebus (Phlb.)*	On pleasure and the good; method	Socrates	57
11 *Symposium*	On *erōs* (passionate love); speeches at a drinking party held at Agathon's house	Aristophanes, Agathon, Socrates, Alcibiades et al.	52
12 *Phaedrus (Phdr.)*	On *erōs* (passionate love) and the art of *logoi* (speaking and writing)	Socrates	53
13 *Alcibiades (First Alcibiades, Alc. I)*	A kind of introduction to Platonic philosophy?	Socrates	32
14 *Second Alcibiades (Alc. II)*	A miniature version of *Alcibiades?*	Socrates	14
15 *Hipparchus*	On greed	Socrates	8
16 *(Rival) Lovers*	On knowledge and authority	Socrates	7
17 *Theages*	On Socrates and his 'divine sign'	Socrates	10
18 *Charmides*	On *sōphrosynē* ('self-control'?)	Socrates	24
19 *Laches*	On courage	Socrates	23
20 *Lysis*	On 'love' (or 'friendship': *philia*) and human motivation	Socrates	20

Title	Topic	Main speaker(s)	Pages
21 *Euthydemus* (*Euthyd., Eud.*)	Philosophy meets 'eristic' sophistry	Socrates	37
22 *Protagoras*	On knowledge and excellence/virtue: philosopher meets sophist	Socrates, Protagoras	53
23 *Gorgias*	On rhetoric: philosopher meets sophist (Gorgias) and pupils	Socrates	81
24 *Meno*	On excellence/virtue, and whether it can be taught	Socrates	30
25 *Greater Hippias* (*Hippias Major, Hi. Ma.*)	On beauty/fineness: philosopher meets sophist	Socrates	24
26 *Lesser Hippias* (*Hippias Minor, Hi. Mi.*)	Better to go wrong deliberately or without meaning to?	Socrates	14
27 *Ion*	On poets, poetry, knowledge: philosopher meets rhapsode (performer of epic)	Socrates	12
28 *Menexenus* (*Mx.*)	A funeral oration (said to come from Aspasia, Pericles' mistress)	Socrates	16
29 *Clitopho*	On Socrates' shortcomings as teacher	Clitopho	5
30 *Republic* (*Rep., Resp.*)	On whether justice pays; construction of an idealized city; tripartite soul; theory of education	Socrates	295 (in 10 books)

(*cont.*)

(cont.)

Title	Topic	Main speaker(s)	Pages
31 *Timaeus*	An early Athenian 'history'; the cosmos and the origins of mankind	Timaeus (mostly a monologue)	76
32 *Critias*	(Fragment, continuing *Timaeus*.) Ancient Athens' defeat of Atlantis	Critias	16
33 *Minos*	On the nature of law	Socrates	9
34 *Laws* (*Leges, Leg., Lg.*)	An imaginary city constructed, with legal system and theory; extended theological excursus in book x	An Athenian visitor to Crete	345 (in 12 books)
35 *Epinomis*	(Appendix to *Laws*.) On wisdom, and how it is to be achieved by the governing council of the city	The Athenian visitor (as in *Laws*)	20
36 *Letters* (*Epist., Ep.*)	[Ranging from one fifth of a page to 28 pages]	Plato (alleged author)	55 (13 letters)
37 *Definitions*	Some Academic definitions of philosophically important items		6
38 *On Justice*	Various questions about justice	Socrates	3
39 *On Virtue*	Can virtue be taught?	Socrates	4
40 *Demodocus*	A small collection of Academic discussions?	Socrates	7
41 *Sisyphus*	On knowledge and deliberation	Socrates	5

Title	Topic	Main speaker(s)	Pages
42 *Halcyon*	Interpretation of a myth	Socrates	[2]
43 *Eryxias*	Is money a good thing?	Socrates	14
44 *Axiochus*	On the prospect of death	Socrates	8

With probably or certainly spurious items removed, the list looks like this, in a fairly standard modern ordering:

> *Diagram B: A standard modern ordering of the undoubtedly genuine Platonic works*

Diagram B

Early (alphabetical order)
Apology, Charmides, Crito, Euthyphro, Gorgias, Lesser Hippias, Ion, Laches, Protagoras, Republic (Book I); plus ('transitional'?) *Euthydemus, Greater Hippias, Lysis, Menexenus, Meno*

Middle (suggested chronological order)
Cratylus, Phaedo, Symposium, Republic (Books II–X), *Phaedrus, Parmenides, Theaetetus*

Late (suggested chronological order)
Timaeus–Critias, Sophist, Statesman, Philebus, Laws

Or, in the ordering given by mainly nineteenth-century studies of Plato's style ('stylometry'), which begin from the reasonably firmly established fact that *Laws* was written last:

> *Diagram C: The undoubtedly genuine Platonic works as grouped according to purely stylistic criteria*

Each group, until the last-placed *Laws*, is in alphabetical order.

Diagram C

Group I (presumed earlier)
Apology, Charmides, Cratylus, Crito, Euthydemus, Euthyphro, Gorgias, Greater Hippias, Lesser Hippias, Ion, Laches, Lysis, Menexenus, Meno, Phaedo, Protagoras, Symposium

---

Group II (presumed transitional to later dialogues)
Phaedrus, Parmenides, Republic, Theaetetus

Group III (later):
Philebus, Sophist, Statesman, Timaeus–Critias, Laws

PLATO'S LIFE

Diagram B makes more ambitious claims than Diagram C about the shape of the corpus, by connecting it with a particular view about the way Plato's thought developed; that is, by ordering the dialogues at least partly according to 'doctrinal' content. Two theses in particular have been seen by modern scholars as relevant to establishing relative dates of composition. One is the thesis that the soul has three parts or aspects, the relevance and importance of which for issues of dating will be discussed on pp. 120–2 below. The other thesis is about the existence of a special set of entities collectively called 'Forms' (*eidē*) or 'Ideas' (*ideai*) that lie beyond ordinary phenomenal existence. This thesis is so fundamental to any reading of Plato that it requires immediate introduction; but in any case a basic understanding of the concept of a Platonic 'Form' is needed for the argument of the present section.

What, then, are Platonic Forms? This is not an easy question to answer. One reason is that Plato never presents us with a single, comprehensive account of the 'theory' (as scholars frequently call it) – that is not his style (see especially p. 108 below). Another is that he may perhaps not have anything stable enough to be called a 'theory' at all (pp. 113–19 below). But this much one can say. Forms are, first of all, those things that the philosopher aims to grasp when he or she attempts to understand anything important, whether goodness, or beauty, or justice (i.e. what it is to be good, beautiful, or just), or the cosmos as a whole (see p. 109 below). Secondly, each Form is what explains, is even cause of, those particular things at the phenomenal level that share its name, and 'participate in' or 'resemble' it. But, thirdly, Forms exist independently, not only of particular, phenomenal things but also of minds, whether human or divine. They can be pictured as located in some region beyond the reach of the senses, although in fact they are non-spatial and non-temporal, as well as non-corporeal. Insofar as they are eternal, they are themselves divine; and unlike phenomenal objects, which change and come into and pass out of existence, they are and remain exactly what they are, thus representing an appropriately stable set of objects for knowledge. Aristotle, looking back from the perspective of his own views, tends to treat Platonic Forms simply as objects of definition, universals, that have been mistakenly 'separated' from particulars, but the true picture will certainly have been more complicated. In different contexts in Plato, Forms have different faces: sometimes they do indeed look like universals, but perhaps more often they look like ideal paradigms or limiting cases (as e.g. when particulars are said to 'resemble' them); sometimes they may plausibly be interpreted as an underlying ordered structure resembling a set of physical laws (see p. 110 below).

For present purposes, however, what matters is that it is the perceived moment, or process, of the introduction of Forms as clearly independent of, and prior to, particulars that primarily determines the shape and membership of the group of dialogues called 'middle' in Diagram B. On the view that this diagram represents (a view which by contrast generally downplays the importance, in this or any other context, of the introduction of the tripartite soul), the early or 'Socratic' dialogues make no significant metaphysical commitments. But then, in the 'middle' dialogues, Plato moves decisively away from his teacher, to develop – among other things – the hallmark, 'classical', theory of Forms. The shift from 'middle' to 'late', too, has frequently been seen as an extension of the same story: now Plato allegedly starts to have doubts about, or even rejects, the 'classical' idea of Forms (see pp. 115, 116 below, on the *Parmenides*), along with other constructions of the 'middle' period.

This reading is undoubtedly psychologically plausible, but is rather weakly supported. For example, while Diagram C is compatible with Diagram B, it falls short of corroborating it: three of the main 'middle' dialogues, *Cratylus*, *Phaedo* and *Symposium*, actually belong to the first stylistic group. A second and perhaps more serious consideration is that we have hardly any reliable and independent evidence about the way Plato's life and thinking developed; and to infer – in the way the proposed reading does, almost entirely – from the dialogues' content to the history of the creative mind behind it comes dangerously close to the methods of the ancient biographers, who with hard facts unavailable tended to fill out anecdotal evidence with whatever it seemed plausible to derive from the corpus.

Nonetheless, as we shall see (pp. 119–22 below), a modified evolutionary or 'developmental' model of interpretation remains a useful – perhaps even necessary – alternative to the opposite, or 'unitarian', pole of interpretation, even granted that the latter would in itself be perfectly compatible with the stylometrists' discoveries (Diagram C). The unitarian tendency, treating the corpus as a more or less static unity, was in fact the norm until the modern period, which in terms of the interpretation of Plato begins in the nineteenth century. Despite this, 'developmentalism' too has historical roots of a sort (in Aristotle), and in any case it would surely be surprising if someone who lived and thought – philosophically – until the age of about eighty did not sometimes find it necessary to change his views.

The important things we know for sure about the author of the works collected under the name 'Plato' are roughly these: that he was born in the early 420s BC to a wealthy father by the name of Ariston (his mother's name is in some doubt); that he had a close relationship, at least on an intellectual level, with Socrates; that he spent the larger part of his life in Athens, without interference from the authorities despite the profoundly anti-democratic nature of his extensive political writing; that he founded a philosophical 'school', the Academy, which was to survive as an institution for research and reflection, and for teaching, for at least three centuries; that from 367 until his death, he had Aristotle with him in the Academy; and that he died in 347.[1] Later chapters in this volume will deal with the fortunes of Platonism in its various forms, and, most immediately, with Aristotle, who was in many ways the most faithful Platonist of them all, despite some central points of disagreement. However elusive Plato may be, and have been, from a biographer's point of view, there is no doubting the difference he made, as a single individual, to the history of philosophy. Even Stoicism, that great rival of Platonism in the early days of both, can be detected rifling Platonic dialogues to provide material for its own systematic constructions.

FORMS, THE PHENOMENAL WORLD, AND PHILOSOPHY'S SEARCH FOR THE GOOD: SOME CENTRAL PLATONIC IDEAS

Astonishingly, we appear to have all the works that Plato ever wrote and wanted read. The dialogues are also the first complete philosophical works that we possess from the ancient world; practically everything from before then, and much of what comes after, we have only in the form of fragments. In terms of preservation Plato fared much better even than the three canonical Athenian tragedians, only a selection of whose work survived (Aristotle did better in terms of volume, but only because he wrote more). This by itself is testimony to Plato's importance for later generations. Even those works that our evidence tells us were less read than others survived along with the rest, and new works – more or less Platonic, but not by Plato – went on being added until the first century BC.

That Plato's texts survived so well is a reflection not only of his status, but of the nature of the corpus itself. Firstly, its parts seem to have been designed to be circulated, some widely, some perhaps less widely. Secondly, whatever it is that Plato stands for, it is not easily to be got from any single dialogue or set of dialogues (indeed, because of the kind of writing these represent, it is not easily to be got at all: see below). No two dialogues cover exactly the same ground, and as Diagram A will confirm (pp. 99–102 above), not many either significantly overlap or even refer to each other. In this sense knowing Plato means reading him all. Every dialogue tends to be surprisingly different from every other, except in the sense that each puts the same heavy demands on readers. To put it another way, it is hard to know what to *discard*; and presumably all the harder if you are inclined, as many readers of Plato have been, to suppose that the corpus as a whole contains a systematic world view.

Such a reading is encouraged by both the range and the nature of Plato's coverage. His topics, or those of his characters, stretch from the macrocosm, the cosmos itself, down to the microcosm of the individual human soul; and any index to the Platonic corpus will include substantial reference to any serious subject that would have been familiar to an educated ancient audience, as well as many that would not. At the same time the treatment of each of those subjects will tend to be connected, somehow, to that of others. When the eponymous main speaker of the *Timaeus* claims that the world is as 'good' as it can be, what he means is essentially that its parts compose an ordered system, and this pair of associations, of things in the world with 'goodness' and of 'goodness' with order, is fundamental to the Platonic project as a whole. What that project seems to promise above all is a *synoptic* account of everything – something far more ambitious even than any search, in modern science, for a unified field theory, insofar as the aim was to explain individual and society in the same breath as the cosmos itself, and using the same or similar principles.

At the same time the parts of the Platonic corpus themselves are strikingly *un*systematic. The extended, continuous account of the physical world in the *Timaeus* is practically unparalleled; for the rest, readers must put things together for themselves from conversations or snatches of conversation here and there. Thus if the corpus *does* contain a worked-out system, it has an odd way of showing it. Indeed main speakers, and especially Socrates, typically qualify whatever positive ideas they may advance as provisional and lacking authority. It is an enduring characteristic of Plato's Socrates that he claims to know nothing, and to have got anything substantial from somewhere else; even Timaeus' account is only a 'likely story', or 'likely account' (see below, p. 110), even if we are told to 'look for nothing further' (*Timaeus* 29d). It is perhaps the main challenge for the interpreter of Plato to explain this paradox of a promise of system combined with a form of exposition that seems almost designed to exclude it.

That, however, is a topic for other sections (pp. 116–22 below). For now, it is sufficient to note that there are explanations available, the oldest of which exploits the nature of Socratic teaching as portrayed in the dialogues: a kind of teaching that helps the recipient to find his own way, first or simultaneously purifying him of his mistaken conceptions. So too, the claim is, Plato intends his readers to do the hard work for themselves. This, we may note, will also provide a 'unitarian'-style explanation of the mixture in the corpus of so-called 'Socratic' dialogues, often apparently negative in outcome, with more positive works like the *Timaeus*. Interpreters who take this sort of line, as most did for two millennia, can then safely get on with looking for Platonic 'doctrines'. (What follows is merely one perspective on such 'doctrines'; there is no implication that this is how the Platonic interpreters in question saw them.)

The world, then, makes sense in terms of system, order, harmony. From here the trail leads in several directions. Firstly there is a strong mathematizing strand in Plato, which expresses itself especially in talk about principles, appropriated from Pythagoreanism: Limit, or the One, and the Unlimited (also, or later, called the 'Indefinite Dyad'), with countable plurality emerging from the 'imposition' of the former upon the latter. This is the kind of talk found in the *Philebus* (16c ff.), and according to Aristotle's and other evidence was much in vogue in the Academy after Plato's death. The *Timaeus* also provides mathematical accounts of the structure of the rational World Soul and of the elements and their relationships (see below, chapter 10, p. 279).

But parallel with this mathematical approach, and perhaps in principle or aspiration ultimately reducible to it, are two others. The Form of the Good, described in the *Republic* as 'beyond being, in authority and in power' (VI, 509b: perhaps because *explaining* the existence of other things?),[2] is compared in the same context to the sun, giving rise to everything intelligible as the sun gives rise to everything that comes-to-be in the physical realm; at the same time it is Forms – once these, or rather 'copies' of them, have been 'received' by the Receptacle, the obscure 'place' that allows them to acquire physical location (*Timaeus* 48e–53c) – that somehow explain the particular phenomenal objects which share their names with them. The emergence of the physical universe can then also be described, again in the *Timaeus*, as a process of the co-operation of reason and necessity, with reason as a divine and provident Craftsman or 'Demiurge' imposing a pattern (the Forms) on recalcitrant materials (27e ff., 47e ff.; cf. chapter 10, p. 279). 'Necessity' is represented both by the fact that the realization of the Creator's intentions frequently requires purely instrumental and in themselves undesirable means, and, secondly, by the inherent instability of the 'Receptacle', which the Creator took over already containing 'traces' of the elements in disordered motion (52d–53b: he imposes the mathematical structures).

If this is still only a 'likely story', what it describes will never-theless be something *like* the truth, at the level of ultimate reality. Forms in the *Timaeus* are represented centrally by the Form of Living Creature, the model for the cosmos, itself a living creature animated by a rational soul, whose motions are made visible by the heavenly bodies. The Form of Living Creature encapsulates the structured rela-tionships that are assumed to exist between Forms, and are mirrored in the relationships between things in the phenomenal world. Being an image, or a likeness, of this Form, the world is capable of revealing something of the nature of the Form; all the same, a likeness is not the same as its original, and an account based exclusively on a like-ness will similarly fall short of one based on the corresponding orig-inal (it will be merely 'likely').[3] When Socrates bans observational astronomy from the higher mathematical education of the future philosopher-rulers in the *Republic*, in favour of a study of 'real move-ments', 'true number' and 'true figures' (VII, 529c–d), he is perhaps relying on the same distinction between embodied structures and relationships and the same structures and relationships considered in isolation from such embodiment, and so in purely mathematical terms. This is the context of Plato's challenge – or of the story of his challenge – to the mathematicians to find a model that would account for the actual movements of the heavens (see chapter 10, p. 291).

The individual, as a compound of body and soul, is an organic part of the physical universe. At the same time the soul, in its best state, will mirror the order of that universe, with the movements of its rational part mimicking the movements of the World Soul. Souls inhabit bodies, but are themselves incorporeal; divine souls move the heavenly bodies. All of this gives a literal sense to the ideal of 'becoming like god' (*homoiōsis theōi*), most eloquently expressed in the *Theaetetus* (176a–177a). Interpreted more generally, 'becoming like god' means becoming as rational as possible, gods being purely rational entities.

The analogy can also go the other way, as it does in the myth – fantasy – of the reversal of the world in the *Statesman* (268d–274e). In the middle of the long series of divisions (on the method see pp. 115–16 below) that will ultimately lead to a definition of the true statesman, the Visitor from Elea embarks on a story which, he ad-mits, is out of proportion to the job it is introduced to do (illustrating a wrong turning in the divisions). 'You remember those old stories', he says to Socrates' younger namesake, 'about the portent that appeared during the dispute about the kingship between Atreus and Thyestes – the reversal of the movements of the heavenly bodies? Well, the truth about this has never been told...' There are, it seems, two recurring eras in world history, one golden, belonging to Cronus, and one belonging to Zeus, in which we ourselves live; and these two eras are separated by a shorter period of reversal,[4] when the deity has 'let go of the steering oars of the universe', at the appointed time. In this period, which begins and ends with great destruction, dead bodies come back to life from the earth, and get smaller as time goes by, until they disappear altogether. What causes the reversal? We are given two explanations: firstly, we are told that the cause is the bodily nature of the whole – nothing bodily can remain in the same condition for ever. This explanation fits well enough with the *Timaeus*. But the second seems rather different. The reversal is now attributed to the 'innate desire' of the physical universe (272e), pent up during the time the guiding deity has been in control; ultimately, however, the universe remembers the teaching of its 'craftsman and father', 'the one who put it together' (273b), and returns to its proper course. This second explanation recalls a common image in Plato, of a divided soul in which the natural rule of the rational part is permanently under threat from the desires of the irrational part or parts.[5] In the *Statesman* myth, the world is not just a living creature, as in the *Timaeus*, but like a human creature, its instability caused not by 'necessity' and the imperfection of a craftsman's materials, but by its own desire, which takes it in the direction opposite to the one favoured by reason. However the metaphor of the *Statesman*, which treats the cosmos as if it were a human agent, is natural enough if we take into account that according to the *Timaeus* the lower parts of the soul are themselves a product of necessity (that is, specifically, a by-product of the insertion of reason into a body), and that irrational desires can be treated – as they are in the *Phaedo* – as the desires of the body.

Society too can be analysed along the same lines. The great thought-experiment of the *Republic*, in which Socrates designs a city or *polis* from the ground up, establishes a direct analogy between city and individual souls (Books II–IV). City and soul each consist of three parts, rational, 'spirited' and appetitive: the city naturally consists of

wise rulers, brave soldiers, effective producers, while internal conflicts in the soul show *it* to contain three separate kinds of desires
with separate sorts of objects,[6] the rational kind of desires being naturally dominant over the other two.[7] Allow either of the two lower
parts – but especially the appetitive – to get out of hand and usurp
the ruling function of reason, and the result will be a diseased city[8]
and a diseased individual. Since many individuals' own reason is too
weak to exercise its natural rule, reason's rule must be established
over them from outside; and that will mean *philosophical* rule, exercised by those who have successfully emerged from the cave in which
the rest of humanity finds itself, into the light of truth, and of the
Good.[9]

   The universe, then, of which we are parts, is structured; it is as
the Socrates of the *Phaedo* hoped to find it, 'bound together by the
good' (99c–d). And the good that binds the whole is the same good
that we all seek in our lives, insofar as we are rational. Nor is this a
mere question of coincidence of structures. A series of arguments in
different dialogues attempt to show that our souls will survive our
deaths, and indeed will last for ever, passing on from one incarnation to another (for the Pythagorean origins of this doctrine, cf. p. 51
above). Insofar as 'we' are identical with our souls, we are no mere
ephemeral creatures, but permanent parts of the universe. What
is more, when freed from the body the soul can either take flight
through the heavens or plumb the depths of the earth, depending on
the quality of its conduct in its previous incarnations. The eschatological myths in *Gorgias, Phaedo, Republic* and *Phaedrus* depict a
cosmos which might have been designed to provide for the appropriate reward and punishment of human beings. They are, of course,
myths, and we should expect myths not to tell us literal truths (the
Statesman myth is a case in point). Moreover, they differ in tone,
in register, and in the degree to which they borrow motifs from traditional myths. All the same, as Socrates suggests in the context of
the *Phaedo* myth, the truth will be that or something *like* that,[10]
and indeed in the Platonic universe there is nowhere much else for
discarnate souls to go except up or down.[11] What such stories suggest, without their having to establish it, is the idea of a universe
whose structure somehow exhibits the goodness, justice and beauty
that – as Plato's Socrates urges – should be exhibited in human lives;
and exhibits them even (perhaps) to the extent of providing, through
its geography or in other ways, those rewards and punishments

that human institutions may fail to provide for lives well or badly lived.

Thus even if man is not the highest thing in the world, nevertheless on Plato's account he has a central role in it. Thanks to his dual nature, he can become like god, remain merely human, or even become an animal. What makes the difference between a first-grade life and a less successful one is *philosophy*, which is both what enables one to see what a good life actually is, and the main constituent of such a life. (The irrational parts will function meanwhile, but tamed in the way that the state education system of the 'beautiful city' of the *Republic* is envisaged as taming its citizens; similarly in the Magnesia of the *Laws*.) *Philosophy* makes the difference, for even granted everything that is claimed by Socrates and others about the way things are in the universe, that will provide no more than a rough framework for deciding how exactly we are to live our lives from day to day. Being told that one should live a good/structured/harmonious/rational life, in imitation of god/nature, is all well and fine; but what exactly is to count as that kind of life, and how do I ensure that the particular decisions I take from day to day will contribute to it? No wonder Socrates goes on refusing to claim any knowledge, and insisting on the need for further thought. No wonder, either, that the importance of philosophy is *the* central theme of the Platonic corpus as a whole. We may identify as many other 'doctrines' in Plato as we like, but to miss this one is to miss the main point.

PHILOSOPHY AND TRUTH

Discovering the good will require systematic rational inquiry, and this is what the dialogues above all illustrate and promote. Such inquiry is nearly always in Plato treated as involving face-to-face discussion – conversation – with others; indeed expertise in rational inquiry is just the 'art of conversation', or 'dialectic' (*dialektikē technē*), and even internal thought takes the form of posing and answering questions (see chapter 1, p. 27). What the philosopher wants is to know the truth; since he doesn't have it, he must go looking for it; and where better than in other people? But he can't assume they have it either. He will test and challenge them as closely as he tests and challenges himself, and will allow them to do the same to him.[12]

Given this emphasis on the importance of talking to others, there might be a temptation to attribute some kind of intersubjective notion of truth to Plato; and all the more so in that he seems to reserve real wisdom for gods alone. If a 'god's-eye view' is forever beyond us, then perhaps we shall have to settle for what we, as sharing at least in a part of the gods' rationality, may agree (rationally) with each other to be the case. Yet in the end this looks an unlikely diagnosis of Plato's position, given his evident commitment to Forms as the ultimate objects of knowledge: the Good Itself, Beauty Itself, the Just Itself, and so on. Plato is a 'platonist', who believes in objective truths.

How then do we acquire access to these, if at all? It cannot be just by talking to people, because others, like the sophist brothers Euthydemus and Dionysodorus whom Socrates encounters in the *Euthydemus*, also spend their time in conversation. What matters is the *kind* of conversation one has. The brothers are mere experts in the 'eristic' branch of sophistry, the art of verbal dispute, and the *Euthydemus* shows at some length what the difference is between this and real dialectic: most importantly, the real dialectician, the philosopher, will be interested in making distinctions where the 'eristic' deliberately avoids making them – even if he understands them – because all he wants is to *win* the debate.

In short, the philosopher argues *philosophically*, that is, with the aim of finding the truth (the *philosophos* is, literally, the 'lover of truth'), whereas the eristic argues to win. What Plato's Socrates is after is arguments that would convince any rational person, just by virtue of that person's being rational. Given that there are only people to try arguments out on, and that human capacities are limited, no agreement between particular individuals that a point has been won can be counted as final. Nor does the fact that a conclusion has not so far been refuted mean that it will not be refuted in the future. Socrates' habit of 'examining myself and others' (*Apology* 38a) is often treated by moderns as if it were a kind of therapy; but purification from false belief is only a condition, and side-product, of the search for truth. The question Socrates puts to himself and others is 'Do we have *reason* for believing that?' And there can be no better standard than what reason has *so far* demonstrated (*Crito*, e.g. 46b), the strongest conclusions *so far* reached (*Phaedo* 100a). It is consistent with this that about the only figures recognized unqualifiedly as

philosophers in Plato apart from Socrates are Parmenides and a visitor from Parmenides' home city of Elea (modern Velia). Parmenides
stands out for the austere rigour of his argument, even though Plato
thought his conclusions wrong, and spent a significant chunk of
the *Sophist* letting the visitor from Elea show why (namely that a
proper handling of being and *difference* will offer a way in which
'what is not' can be – something that Parmenides had denied).[13]
In the dialogue named after him, Parmenides becomes the critic of
Socrates' handling of Forms, while admitting that they are a necessary condition of thinking and speaking. The second and larger part
of the dialogue consists in what is announced as a training exercise
(135d–136a) in deduction, starting from certain hypotheses ('if (the)
one is...'; 'if (the) one is not...'); only Parmenides could give Socrates
such lessons in argument. Protagoras is treated with some respect,
especially in the *Theaetetus*, but practically every other available
figure with any intellectual pretensions tends to be dispatched –
along with, and because of, their methods and/or aims – with the
full force of Socratic irony. The second part of the *Phaedrus* introduces a theory of philosophically based rhetoric that will allow the
truly expert speaker to cater for different kinds of audiences (as Plato
does, implicitly, himself?); story-telling, not teaching, is said in the
Statesman to be appropriate for the masses (304c–d); and the *Laws*
advocates that the laws themselves be accompanied by persuasive
preludes, the given examples of which surely fall short of the kind of
hard argument associated with the philosophical enterprise in other
dialogues. But otherwise that hard argument is treated as *the* requirement, however elusive really definitive arguments may seem
to be.[14]

If the philosopher/dialectician will evidently always employ
question-and-answer, question-and-answer can employ different
types of systematic method: one or more kinds of hypothetical
method (*Meno, Phaedo, Republic*), and the method of 'collection and
division' that *Phaedrus* and – more allusively – *Philebus* describe
and *Sophist* and *Statesman* employ. The latter method is one of definition: 'collection' is a matter of trying to identify the most general
item under which the definiendum falls, while division breaks down
that item in successive stages until the definiendum is reached, the
definition consisting of whatever it is in each division that is kept
for further division. But of course 'below' the definiendum, which

will itself be a general item, will be the indeterminate plurality of particular instances of it. The method clearly presupposes a stable and structured reality, to provide the material for division; there is layer upon connected layer stretching down from the highest unity to (what we might call) the *infima species*, which – as Socrates puts it in the *Philebus* – it is our task as philosophers to uncover before 'abandoning unity to infinity' (16e), i.e. the phenomenal world that results from the imposition of limit or unity, in its various forms, on the unlimited.

But dialectic is still a matter of *talk*, of using language, and neither language nor the mind that uses it obviously possess any natural or necessary connection with the things to which they purport to refer. This problem Plato had inherited.[15] One solution, appearing in *Meno*, *Phaedo* and *Phaedrus*, is that our souls have 'seen' the objects of knowledge before being born into bodies but forgotten them at birth, so that 'learning' about them is really a matter of recollection (*anamnēsis*): a kind of theory of innate ideas. The proposal immediately defuses any problem of separation between language and Forms, or between human souls/minds and Forms. If such a theory is hardly visible outside *Meno*, *Phaedo* and *Phaedrus*, that may be because Plato elsewhere does not have in mind the kind of radical separation between Forms and particulars which the theory was designed to overcome – and which Parmenides criticizes in the *Parmenides*. Here is one case, at least, where there may be an advantage in not attributing 'doctrines' to Plato. Philosophers more than anyone should surely be allowed not only to change their minds, but to entertain doubts, as Plato's own philosopher – Socrates – always does.

READING PLATO

None of the above, however, gives much of an idea of what it is actually like to *read* Plato. An external description of a Platonic dialogue must be as far from the real thing as, say, a prose paraphrase of a poem. Among the things inevitably missed is the *indirectness* of Plato's technique. If the author never appears (he is twice referred to, fleetingly), by and large it is not difficult to locate the authorial voice, usually behind the main speaker. But this does not mean that one can read through the text to the authorial *mind*. The strategies of the character Socrates are often less than straightforward; at least in the shorter dialogues they are typically responses to particular interlocutors in particular contexts, and reading off more general outcomes can be a ticklish matter. The longer dialogues can appear more transparent, and perhaps they are, but then their sheer variety, combined with the fact that most are formally independent of each other, makes life hardly any easier for the interpreter. And then, on top of this, there is the way in which they tend to mimic – or pretend to mimic – the unpredictability of ordinary conversations. All of this illustrates the point made earlier about the unsystematic nature of the corpus, its essential *messiness*. That does not necessarily mean that the thought behind it is messy (though it might be), but it is as well to be aware of the appearance of the original material.

Consider now, by way of example, three shorter dialogues and two longer:

(a) *Euthyphro*. Euthyphro and Socrates are both involved with the Athenian legal authorities: Euthyphro is prosecuting his own father for homicide, while Socrates will soon be in court on trial for his life. Euthyphro is something of a religious expert, just the sort of person to discuss the nature of *hosiotēs* (piety/propriety?) with Socrates. Asked what *hosiotēs* is, a typical form of question in the shorter dialogues (though also asked in longer ones, such as *Theaetetus*), he begins with the proposal that it's what he's doing now, prosecuting his father. When this fails, he comes up with other proposals, mostly prompted by Socrates, but none stands up to scrutiny, and at the end the conversation comes full circle; Socrates suggests they need to start all over again, but Euthyphro has urgent business elsewhere. In fact, several philosophical points have been made along the way, and near the end Socrates suggests, without explaining, that Euthyphro was *almost* there. Questions: (1) Does he mean it? (2) If he does, which bit was almost right? And (3) why does Plato allow the conversation to stop there?

(b) *Crito*. Socrates is in prison awaiting execution, and his close associate Crito comes to urge him to escape. Socrates instead takes the opportunity to do some philosophy: are Crito's reasons for his escaping any good, and do they trump the rational conclusions they'd reached in previous discussions? It's never good to harm anyone, even in return for harm, and breaking agreements with people does harm to them; his escaping when condemned by due process would break an agreement with, and harm, the laws (he imagines them addressing him); so it won't be a good thing for him to escape, even if he was condemned unjustly. And the reader knows that he is in fact executed. Modern liberal-minded readers, wanting to take Socrates as a model, often find themselves embarrassed by what appears to be an implied blanket argument against resistance to the state even when the state is wrong. The laws' arguments do not obviously look strong, yet Socrates' says that they are 'buzzing in his ears', and preventing him from hearing anything else. So did he die unnecessarily? Or is Plato's own real point a different one?

(c) *Lysis*. Socrates finds himself in a new gymnasium, where he meets Hippothales, lover of the boy Lysis, then Lysis and Lysis' friend Menexenus. Socrates starts by teaching Hippothales a lesson about how to talk to a beloved, i.e. by humbling him. Socrates, Lysis and Menexenus then discuss what it is that loves and what is loved. What we love is evidently that for which we say we love other things, the 'first friend', something good not loved for the sake of something else; what loves is the neither good (knowledgeable) nor bad (wholly ignorant). The final conclusion of the main argument is that the true lover, sc. the one who truly loves what he says he loves, must necessarily be loved by the beloved (222a) – and after all, who would not love someone who loves them and knows what is truly lovable? (Hippothales, understanding nothing, is delighted.) But now the participants reach an impasse, apparently because the two boys ultimately cannot accept the paradoxical results of the argument. Readers, too, are faced with the choice: accept the argument, or go with the boys and say what's *wrong* with the argument.

(d) *Phaedrus*. Socrates meets Phaedrus, in an idyllic setting outside the city-walls; Phaedrus, a devotee of the orator Lysias, has a speech of Lysias' tucked under his clothes. After reading the speech, on 'Why a beloved should give in to someone who doesn't love him rather than someone who does', Socrates responds with two speeches of his own, one for the thesis and one – an inspired speech – against it. The second speech first argues for the soul's immortality, and then in mythical mode compares the tripartite soul to a charioteer and his pair of horses, white and black, promising at least temporary escape from incarnation for the true lover, the soul that has lived three successive philosophical lives with no concessions to the black horse of appetite. Such a soul will soar through the heavens with the gods, and will hope to get another sight of the Forms, beyond the heavens, at the ten-thousand-yearly feast the gods enjoy.

After this speech, Socrates discusses with Phaedrus what makes for good and bad writing and speaking, developing a theory of philosophical rhetoric, and finally devaluing writing by comparison with living dialectic and its capacity to collect and divide: the expert dialectician is the true sower of immortal seed in others' souls.

(e) *Philebus*. The eponymous Philebus supports pleasure as the candidate for what constitutes the Good in the good life; Socrates supports knowledge. The dialogue begins with these protagonists at loggerheads, and with one Protarchus taking over Philebus' case. The conversation ends, however, with the conclusion that, although knowledge ranks ahead of pleasure, the Good itself is neither of these but the combination of beauty, measure and truth that regulates their mixture. The dialogue mostly consists in a detailed analysis of pleasure and pleasures, preceded by a – dialogical – excursus on method and its metaphysical presuppositions: the passage on Limit and the Unlimited (see above, pp. 109, 115–16), which also have a product and a cause. The excursus seems to go considerably beyond what is required for the discussion that follows, and in many respects is more suggestive than explicit. Is this because Plato has more up his sleeve than he is telling us, or because he hasn't?

ALTERNATIVE READINGS

The lack of determinacy in the Platonic texts, and their variety and complexity, have unsurprisingly spawned numerous interpretative strategies. Of these, the oldest and most general may be labelled respectively the 'dogmatic' (or 'doctrinal') and the 'sceptical' tendencies. Plato's immediate successors in the Academy continued with the kind of ambitious metaphysical schemes hinted at in the *Philebus*; but not so long afterwards the 'New' Academy (see chapter 6) was treating Plato as a sceptic – an approach which, like its opposite, can easily be justified by privileging some parts of the corpus and downplaying others. 'Dogmatic' types of interpretation then regained the ascendancy, giving rise to what we label as the 'Middle Platonists' and the Neoplatonists, whose idea of Platonism remained the one most widely accepted until the modern period.

Both 'dogmatic' and 'sceptical' modes of interpretation have their modern analogues: the former, for example, in the 'esoteric' reading of Plato, or in the Straussian, the latter in what may broadly be termed the 'analytical' reading, which probably still dominates in the English-speaking world. 'Esoteric' interpreters find the core of Plato in his oral teaching, what Aristotle calls, and documents as, the 'unwritten doctrines'; the dialogues are more or less explicit invitations to the dance. For the 'Straussians' (followers of the Platonic scholar and political philosopher Leo Strauss), Plato's indirectness is concealment: the real, subversive meaning of the philosopher – who must always stand in fear of suffering the fate of a Socrates – needs to be looked for, by the trained reader, under the surface.

A caricature of an 'analytical' interpreter would identify him as one who formalizes whatever can be formalized and discards the rest; or who sees no difference between a dialogical argument and its monological counterpart. The extreme form of self-consciously 'literary' interpretations will, by contrast, tend to treat the arguments of the dialogues as secondary.

It is the analytical interpreters who have probably most enthusiastically embraced the 'developmental' model referred to at pp. 104–6 above, partly because of a fundamental commitment to the idea of progress in philosophy: development in this case implies improvement, and correction of mistakes, perhaps even the abandonment of metaphysics; and in any case for the analytical Plato it is finally *argument* that matters, not grand conclusions.

Esoterists, Straussians and others are essentially 'unitarian' in tendency – as, again, all the ancients were. That in itself may seem an impressive fact, though of course the ancients in question were committed Platonists, with their own axes to grind, in a way that most modern readers have not been. (Nor had ancient interpreters invented stylometry, for what that is worth.)

There is, however, what looks like a major obstacle to any unitarian interpretation: the presence, and active deployment, in a number of dialogues of a philosophical theory that is inconsistent with a significant proportion of the ideas described as 'Platonic' at pp. 109–13 above. In this group of works – which happens more or less to coincide with Group 1 in Diagram C (p. 104) – the starting-point, or the end-point, is a view of human motivation which either explicitly or implicitly denies that we can be 'overcome by (irrational) desire'; we cannot 'willingly go wrong'.[16] So most directly in the *Protagoras* (351b ff.), but also in the *Lysis*, which argues that even the most basic, physiological desires are directed to what is truly good for us; also in the *Symposium*, where Diotima the priestess and Socrates' teacher sponsors a similar argument, and in the 'dialogues of definition', which tend consistently to assimilate the 'virtues' (excellences) to knowledge (the *Charmides* treats even *sōphrosynē* like this, an excellence typically understood, and treated in *Republic* IV, as 'self-control' – a notion for which there will in fact be no room, if there is none for 'weakness of will'). On this theory, what motivates every action we perform, except under external compulsion, is our desire for what is, overall, good for us; and the only relevant difference between us as individuals is what we happen to believe will contribute to that good. (We shall also probably be attracted by other things, but will not go for them unless we think that best. The quality of our actions, then, is determined by the quality of our beliefs; hence the name given to the theory, 'intellectualism'.)

To be human, in this case, will be simply to be rational: there is no beast in us, to be whipped, cajoled or conditioned into quietness, and the only way of changing people's behaviour will be to talk to them, to give them *reasons* for changing. This is the position against which Plato's Socrates appears to be arguing in Book IV of the *Republic*, when he introduces the tripartite soul, one third rational and two thirds irrational;[17] for he specifically argues both that the desires of the irrational 'parts' have their own, non-rational, objects, and that they are capable of overcoming our rational, good-directed desires. (So now there *will* be a need for irrational modes of control. The political dimension in Plato, and indeed many other aspects of his thinking, seem vitally dependent on the argument of *Republic* IV. The intellectualist Socrates is no political theorist; nor, as it happens, does he have much interest in science, or in the idea of an immortal soul.)

Aristotle is familiar with this kind of theory, which he consistently attributes to the real Socrates. But, like many moderns, he does not think much of it, discovering the real difference between Socrates and Plato in the latter's 'separation' of Forms (see pp. 104–5, 109–10 above). Here too Aristotle's judgement has been influential, for the distinction between 'early' and 'middle' in Diagram B (p. 103 above) is essentially based on this point of his (i.e. about 'separation'). Socratic intellectualism, for its part, is nowadays frequently held to be easily falsifiable and therefore uninteresting. Yet *Plato* evidently did not easily dismiss the Socratic theory – partly, perhaps, because he understood it better. Aristotle complains, among other things (and moderns have again taken up the refrain), that it leaves out the factor of motivation and/or emotion, which – as Plato works it out – it plainly does not: what drives us, on the theory in question, is precisely desire for the good. It may even be that Plato thought he was improving on Socrates in *Republic* IV, not abandoning him, insofar as his substantive views on the nature of the good life remained unaltered. Again, even if he thought – or came to think – that not all desires were for the good, he nevertheless still thought that every *soul*, every person, desires the good, *qua* rational (the idea of desire for the merely apparent good is an Aristotelian invention). But the consequences of the shift in other respects are considerable – and much greater than those of metaphysical 'separation' (from *Aristotle*'s point of view, 'separated' Forms represent a massive philosophical mistake, but there seem to be few implications for ethics).

If Plato thought there was continuity even here between himself and Socrates, then perhaps honours will yet be even between developmentalists and unitarians. However the more important point, in the present context, is that Plato himself seems finally to have decided against the 'intellectualist' view. It is of course conceivable that he *started* with the anti-intellectualist, irrationalist, model of the human mind, and later moved into what Aristotle firmly identifies as the Socratic camp; but if stylometry shows anything, it seems consistently to show that Plato's interest in the intellectualist position came earlier rather than later. And it is the general theme of a conflict between reason and unreason that dominates works like *Republic, Phaedrus, Statesman, Timaeus–Critias* and *Laws* – and through them, the corpus as a whole. This, together with the belief in philosophy and the difference it makes to life (because contributing to the victory of reason over unreason, of order over disorder) has every claim to be called properly 'Platonic'.

NOTES

1   The *Seventh Letter*, even if not genuine, will probably add to this scant list of biographical items three visits to Syracuse in Sicily and some sort of political involvement there. The author of the letter echoes Socrates' famous declaration in the *Republic* that 'until philosophers rule as kings or those presently called kings...philosophize...cities will have no

respite from evils' (473c–d), and has Plato unsuccessfully attempting to turn the young Syracusan tyrant Dionysius II into a philosopher (cf. pp. 107–13 below, and *Republic* VI, especially 502a–b). Maybe it was on his Italian travels that Plato encountered Pythagoreanism (though there were also Pythagoreans visiting and resident in mainland Greece) For other more certainly fictional travels attributed to Plato, see chapter 9, pp. 251–2.

2 Cf. Hankinson, p. 282 this volume, for a contrast of such teleological explanation with mere 'mechanistic causes'. These latter, on the Platonic account, will belong to the sphere of 'necessity', on which see p. 109.

3 To the extent that the existence of the Demiurge is inferred from the 'goodness' of the phenomenal world, it too will be subject to the same caveat, i.e. 'likely' but not certain; and in fact the gods are one of only two examples Timaeus uses in spelling out his point about the mere 'likeliness' of the following account ('so in many cases about many things, about gods and the coming-into-being of the all': 29c). So the evidence is that there was a creation, and a Creator, but the evidence is not *that* good.

4 A more usual interpretation of the myth has just two stages in each cycle, with the world – puzzlingly – in reverse for the whole of the (ideal?) age of Cronus.

5 'Irrationality' here is defined by opposition to the dictates of reason. Reason is naturally directed towards the good; 'appetitive' desires are for food, drink, sex, and so on, without reference to whether these objects are good or not. See further below, and p. 121.

6 The second, 'spirited', part, though the natural ally of reason, is also irrational and also has projects of its own: the maintenance of self-esteem, winning, and so on.

7 The extended argument to this effect in Book IV of the *Republic* has a good claim to being one of the most important in Plato. See pp. 120–2 below, and p. 25 above, where part of the argument is cited.

8 A 'healthy' city will be a wise one, ruled by wisdom and reason in its rulers; it will in fact be one where all three constituent groups, rulers, soldiers and producers, do 'what belongs to them' – and so will also be 'just', 'justice' being defined as 'doing one's own'. Courage it will have from its properly trained – and obedient – soldiers, and 'self-control' from the agreement of all three groups about who should rule. All the 'political' virtues thus relate essentially to the single factor of the rule of wisdom.

9 The 'Cave' reference is to the great simile (514a–518d) that rounds off the group of three in *Republic* VI–VII. If the gap between rulers and ruled is much narrower in Plato's other imaginary city, in the *Laws*,

this evidently has as much to do with the exclusion of ordinary people from the citizen-body as with any relaxation in the requirements for rulership (as laid out in their most extreme form in the *Statesman*).

10   *Phaedo* 114d. This is rather different from the 'likelihood' of the *Timaeus'* cosmology: there the account was (only) 'likely' because of problems with the evidence, whereas here the problem is that there is no evidence at all – which is one reason for moving into 'mythical' mode.

11   The universe for Plato is a sphere of limited size (its boundary being marked by the fixed stars), and there is no other dimension for things to enter; souls must evidently always be located somewhere within the universe itself. From this point of view, once given that souls are immortal, the Pythagorean theory of their 'transmigration' from body to body looks economical enough.

12   'Testing', 'examining', and 'refuting' all fall within the scope of the central Greek root in this area: *elench-*, as in the verb *elenchein*, and the noun *elenchos*.

13   Being and difference, along with sameness, motion and rest, constitute the five 'greatest kinds' (*megista genē*) on whose complex interrelation the *Sophist* relies for its solution to the problem of how false statement is possible.

14   The *Phaedo* neatly illustrates the essential points: four arguments (roughly) for immortality, each successive argument designed to improve on its predecessor(s), and a final one that – Socrates promises (107b) – will deliver the goods, with some further work.

15   See especially *Cratylus*. Contrast also the frequent talk of 'seeing' the objects of knowledge in Books VI–VII of the *Republic* with the subsequent description in Book VII of what dialectic can actually achieve: a grasp that consists of statements not so far refuted (534b–c).

16   See chapter 3, p. 94 above. How much of the working-out of the theory we find in Plato had already been done by Socrates is impossible to tell; if it was mostly done by Plato, still it is evidently what the original Socratic position required, and so may to that extent count as genuinely Socratic.

17   Tripartition in Plato sometimes gives way to bipartition, as e.g. in the *Laws*, where he shows less interest in treating the aggressive/ competitive as a distinct aspect of humanity's irrational side.

5   Aristotle

LIFE

Aristotle (384–322 BC) was a wealthy native of Stagira, a Greek coastal city on the Chalcidice peninsula of Macedonia, not far from modern Thessaloniki. His father, who died in Aristotle's childhood, was physician to the Macedonian king. In 367 Aristotle was sent to Athens, at the age of seventeen, to complete his education at Plato's school, the Academy. Instead, he remained there until Plato's death in 347, studying, writing and lecturing over a wide range of philosophical subjects having roots in Plato's own work – the theory of rhetorical argument and persuasion, logical theory, ethics, and questions of metaphysics, among others. At Plato's death he, together with Xenocrates, another of the leading members of the school, left Athens for the north-western coast of Asia Minor, where the local ruler Hermias (whose daughter Aristotle married – later the mother of his two children) established them at the town of Assos. Aristotle continued his work there, and afterwards for a time at Mytilene on the nearby island of Lesbos, where he apparently first collaborated with the younger philosopher Theophrastus: it appears that his most important researches on sea animals date from this period. In 343 King Philip II of Macedon called him (accompanied by Theophrastus and others) to the royal court to become tutor to his son Alexander ('the Great'). Aristotle seems to have stayed in Macedon until 335, by which time Alexander, who had succeeded to the throne in 336, had secured Macedonian hegemony over Athens and the rest of Greece. Aristotle returned to Athens as a resident alien, opening his own school in the exercise-grounds of the Lyceum just outside the city-walls – rather than rejoining his former colleagues at the Academy

on the opposite side of the city. For the next thirteen years he wrote
and lectured in the Lyceum, until in the summer of 323 word reached
Athens of Alexander's death in Babylon. With anti-Macedonian sentiment high at Athens and the threat of a rebellion, he withdrew to
family estates at Chalcis on Euboea off the northeast coast of Attica,
where he himself died the next year, at the age of 63.

WORKS

Ancient sources tell us of dialogues by Aristotle, in the tradition
of Plato, and of other more widely accessible ('exoteric') works,
from which however only isolated quotations have survived. All
Aristotle's surviving works are 'esoteric' texts of professional philosophy and science, written in an unadorned prose replete with philosophical technicalities and for the most part presupposing familiarity with philosophy and its prior history. They are for specialists, or
advanced students. They may derive ultimately, as scholars have traditionally thought, from the collection of Aristotle's works prepared
at Athens (or perhaps it was at Rome) by Andronicus of Rhodes at
some undetermined time in the mid-first century BC; but Andronicus' role in establishing Aristotle's 'esoteric' texts has recently been
the subject of controversy. At any rate, the titles of the works together with the number and grouping of their constituent books that
we find in our manuscripts differ greatly from what is reported in
the surviving ancient lists of Aristotle's works – the latter seem to
antedate Andronicus' work or at any rate to be based on library collections organized independently of it, if the traditional view of his
role in establishing our text of Aristotle is correct. However that
may be, the arrangement of the Corpus Aristotelicum (the 'body' of
Aristotle's works) as we know it today derives only from the edition
of Aristotle's works by I. Bekker (Berlin 1831).

Aristotle's longer works, in common with other longer ancient
writings, were divided by early editors into 'books' (the length of
a book being roughly determined by the standard length of one
of the rolled-up papyrus scrolls on which literary and other works
were written) – something like fifteen to twenty pages of a densely
printed modern book. These books were later themselves divided
into 'chapters'.

The Corpus begins with an 'Organon' or 'instrument' for philosophical inquiry consisting of six works devoted to logical studies (15 books in toto), followed by twenty-nine works on nature and natural philosophy, including the study of animals and plants (more than 80 books or the equivalent), then by the *Metaphysics* (the title literally means 'After the physical writings') in 14 books, three ethical treatises (17 books) together with a short spurious work *On Virtues and Vices*, and the works on politics, household or estate management ('economics'), rhetoric, and poetics (16 books); in modern editions the *Constitution of the Athenians*, recovered in papyrus only at the end of the nineteenth century, is included in this last section. Thus, even after spurious works are excluded, by far the largest portion of the Aristotelian Corpus is devoted to studies in natural science and the philosophy of nature.

Below, in tabular form, are the titles of Aristotle's surviving works, together with their most commonly encountered Latinizations and the abbreviations of these. A single asterisk indicates a work of doubtful authenticity, a double one a work universally agreed not to be by Aristotle.

Organon

Categories (*Cat.*)
De interpretatione (*Int.*)
Prior Analytics (i, ii) (*An. Pr., Pr. An.*)
Posterior Analytics (i, ii) (*An. Post., Post. An.*)
Topics (i–viii) (*Top.*)
Sophistical Refutations[1] (*SE, Soph. El.*)

Physics

Physics (i–viii) (*Phys.*)
On the Heavens (*De caelo*) (i–iv) (*Cael.*)
On Coming-to-be and Passing Away (*De generatione et corruptione*) (i, ii) (*GC*)
Meteorology (i–iv) (*Meteor.*)
**On the Universe* (*Mund.*)
On the Soul (*De anima*) (i–iii) (*DA, de An.*)

On Sensation and the Objects of the Senses (Sens.)
On Memory (Mem.)
On Sleep (Somn.)
On Dreams (Insomn.)
On Divination in Sleep (Div. Somn.)
On Length and Shortness of Life (Long. vit.)
On Youth, Old Age, Life and Death, and Respiration (Juv. and Resp.)
***On Breath (Spir.)*

Zoology

History of Animals (Historia animalium) (I–X)² (HA)
Parts of Animals (De partibus animalium) (I–IV) (PA)
On the Movement of Animals (De motu animalium) (MA, de Motu)
On Progression of Animals (De incessu animalium) (IA)
Generation of Animals (I–V) (GA)

Miscellaneous physical treatises (mainly inauthentic)

***On Colours (Col.)*
***On the Objects of Hearing (Aud.)*
***Physiognomonics (Physiog.)*
***On Plants (I, II) (Plant.)*
***On Marvellous Things Heard (Mir.)*
***Mechanics (Mech.)*
**Physical Problems (I–XXXVIII)³ (Prob.)*
***On Indivisible Lines (Lin. insec.)*
***The Situations and Names of Winds (Vent.)*
***On Melissus, Xenophanes, and Gorgias (MXG)*

Metaphysics

Metaphysics (I–XIV) (Metaph.)

Ethics, politics, aesthetics

Nicomachean Ethics (I–X)⁴ (EN, NE)
**Magna moralia (I, II)⁵ (MM)*

Eudemian Ethics (ɪ–vɪɪɪ) (*EE*)
**On Virtues and Vices* (*VV*)
Politics (ɪ–vɪɪɪ) (*Pol.*)
**Economics* (ɪ–ɪɪɪ) (*Ec.*)
Rhetoric (ɪ–ɪɪɪ) (*Rhet.*)
***Rhetoric to Alexander* (*Rhet. Al.*)
Poetics (*Poet.*)
Constitution of the Athenians[6] (*Ath. pol.*)

In scholarly writings these works, with the exception of the last, are standardly cited by the pages, columns (a and b), and lines of Bekker's edition, where they are printed in the order given above; the Bekker numeration is printed in the margins of all subsequent editions of the Greek texts of Aristotle's works, and in translations as well. The traditional division into books (usually Roman numerals) and chapters (usually arabic numerals) is regularly used alongside this system of more exact citation. Thus a full citation might read 'Aristotle, *NE* x 7, 1177b33': that is, *Nicomachean Ethics* book x chapter 7, Bekker page 1177, column b line 33.

Among the lost works the most important that have significant fragmentary remains (generally held to be early works) are the dialogue *Eudemus* or *On the Soul*, the works in uncertain format *On Philosophy* (three books) and *Protrepticus* (an invitation and encouragement to philosophy and the philosophical life), and the treatises *On the Good* (three books, a report and discussion of Plato's late metaphysical doctrines) and *On Ideas* (containing arguments against Plato's theory of Forms).[7]

INFLUENCE IN ANTIQUITY

Except for the lost 'exoteric' works, Aristotle's writings were not, as all of Plato's were, copied and circulated by booksellers during and immediately after his lifetime. His own school in the Lyceum, headed after his death by Theophrastus and from that time onwards called the 'Peripatos' (named after the covered walkway on the grounds of the school), preserved copies. In addition, in the period immediately following his death and thereafter, copies of at least some of his works were found in other centres of philosophical teaching and research, such as at Rhodes and in Alexandria. It is unclear, however, to what extent leading philosophers of the next generations who were not Peripatetics, such as Epicurus and the early Stoics (most notably Zeno and Chrysippus), were familiar with them. Since these philosophers all lived and taught in Athens, and there was ample interchange among the schools of philosophy, they certainly could have had access to Aristotle's works. It has been argued that in developing his theory of atomism Epicurus was taking account of and responding to arguments Aristotle had advanced in his *Physics* against Democritus' atomism; and that Epicurus' views on moral responsibility owe a great deal to Aristotle's own theories in the *Ethics* about moral character and its role in responsibility. But in his extant writings Epicurus does not cite Aristotle. And it has been plausibly maintained that the many features of early Stoic logic, metaphysics, physics and ethical theory that might invite comparison (or contrast) with Aristotle's derive not from reading his works but (at best) from reading Plato's and from associating with those in the Academy who carried forward in their own way the same Platonic theories to which Aristotle was heir in the development of his own. (We do not hear of specific mentions of Aristotle's writings or philosophical opinions by any of the early Stoics, though we do hear of discussions of and disagreements with Plato's views.) The Peripatetics Theophrastus (died 287) and (to a lesser extent) his successor as head of the school Strato (died 269) did continue to do original work within an Aristotelian framework in logic, the investigation of the natural world, metaphysics, ethics, and the theory of rhetoric, but the then-dominant philosophical systems of Epicurus and the Stoics were largely constructed on new foundations owing little to Aristotle's work. After Theophrastus, Peripateticism was a minor player in the world of Hellenistic philosophy.

It was only towards the end of the second century BC that philosophers began again to read Aristotle's 'esoteric' works and to take account of his views and arguments in developing their own ideas. The Stoic philosophers Panaetius and his pupil Posidonius (see below, p. 165), whose school was in Rhodes, began to treat Aristotle, as well as Plato, as authoritative thinkers – divine, inspired. They softened and adjusted traditional Stoic teaching in various ways to accommodate the 'truth' to be found in these classical, more ancient predecessors of the earliest Stoics. We hear of full-fledged commentaries on works of Aristotle beginning already during Posidonius' lifetime, in the middle of the first century BC – further indication of the authoritative status being accorded during that time to his works. Gradually over the next centuries increasing numbers of philosophers made the study and explication of texts of Aristotle (and Plato) integral, central elements in the practice of philosophy and in the formation and development of their own philosophical ideas. Towards the end of the second century AD and into the third the great Aristotelian philosopher Alexander of Aphrodisias (see pp. 243–4 below) wrote vast, detailed, paragraph-by-paragraph and sentence-by-sentence, enormously acute commentaries (many of which still survive) on Aristotle's *De interpretatione* (lost), *Topics*, *Sophistical Refutations*, *Prior Analytics* I, *Posterior Analytics*, *Physics* (lost), *On the Heavens* (lost), *Meteorology*, *On Sensation*, and *Metaphysics* (the first five books survive), together with independent works *On Fate*, *On the Soul*, *On Mixture*, and various *Problems* and *Questions*, all aimed at establishing the views of Aristotle, updated as needed to take account of Stoic and other alternatives, as the best and most defensible current (second to third centuries AD) ideas on their subjects. For Alexander, the inspired genius of Aristotle's writings was a sufficient basis, if they were properly interpreted, explicated, and fleshed out, to resolve with complete satisfaction all the questions debated among philosophers of varying schools in his own time.

However, in Alexander's time and in the previous several generations, a powerful movement was under way to connect current philosophy rather all the way back to Plato, Aristotle's forebear. Plato, not Aristotle, was to be the divine genius whose authority would provide the contact that thinkers needed with the ancient, original 'truth' that Hellenistic philosophers (Epicurean, Stoic, neo-Aristotelian) had abandoned or obfuscated, if they were to deal adequately with the philosophical (and spiritual) problems of their own age. By the end of the third century, with the work of Plotinus (see p. 244 below), all the Greek philosophers were, or professed to be, Platonists (virtually none called themselves Peripatetics or Aristotelians), engaged in recovering from or at least tracing back to Plato's writings the solutions to all the problems of philosophy. The tradition of reading and commenting on Aristotle's works nonetheless continued and indeed entrenched itself in this new uniformly Platonist intellectual world. Plotinus' pupil and biographer Porphyry (p. 244 below) with the reinforcement of his own pupil Iamblichus, established a long-lasting tradition of harmonizing Aristotle with Plato (despite the awkward and rather obvious fact of Aristotle's rejection of Plato's theory of separate, purely intellectual Forms). Through his writings in logic, natural philosophy, ethics, metaphysics, even politics and rhetoric, Aristotle would provide the systematically developed and deployed, detailed accounts of the physical, sensible world and our life within it, which had been neglected by Plato himself. These were taken to flesh out and apply the Platonic insights into the super-sensible world of Forms, the Divine Mind, and the ultimate source of everything, the One, that, for these Neoplatonists, were the indispensable core of Plato's philosophy and of the ancient 'truth' itself. It is from this Platonizing point of view that the great series of commentaries on Aristotle of the fourth through sixth centuries were written: see the catalogue of these on pp. 246–9 below.

LOGIC

Logic is the systematic study of arguments or argumentation: the study of what *follows* from given premises, and *why* it follows (and of what does not follow, though it might appear to). As he himself observes (*SE* 34), Aristotle is the earliest thinker to conceive of logic as a subject for study. Thus he is the first logician, the inventor of logic – i.e. of the study (not of course the *use!*) of arguments. However, he concentrates his study upon argumentation in two specific contexts, so that his remarkable, pioneering achievements in logic also have severe limitations. It is certainly far from being the 'complete' system of logic that his followers later tried to claim. First, we have the context of 'dialectical' argument, argument or debate in which one person attempts to force another to draw some conclusion simply on the basis of conceding certain other propositions. Socrates in the 'Socratic' dialogues of Plato – dialogues such as *Crito* or *Laches*, or the first part of *Meno* – illustrates this, when he asks his interlocutor a series of questions, gaining concessions, and then gets the interlocutor to see that his answers logically commit him to some unwelcome conclusion, something that he had previously denied. To the study of such dialectical arguments Aristotle devotes his *Topics* and *Sophistical Refutations*. Second, there is what Aristotle calls 'demonstration' in the sciences. Aristotle accepted the mathematical disciplines of arithmetic and geometry as models for all scientific knowledge and understanding, including what we would regard as empirical and experimental sciences such as medicine or biology or physics. Geometry presents itself in the form of rigorous proofs, starting from basic first principles (axioms), for a systematic series of theorems setting out the properties of all the various objects studied by the science (the geometrical figures – triangles, squares and the like). So likewise, Aristotle thought, each of the other sciences should ideally be presented as starting from a small set of basic truths which establish the fundamental nature of the specific kinds of things that that science studies, and deriving from those 'principles' by demonstration or proof the rest of the truths in the science (its 'theorems'). In his *Prior* and *Posterior Analytics* Aristotle studies demonstrative argument in the sciences, ideally so conceived. When and why do the conclusions of scientific arguments (the ones stating the 'theorems') actually follow from their premises? What further conditions, beyond simply having conclusions that follow logically from their premises, must arguments in the sciences fulfil? (See further, chapter 10, pp. 286–8 below.)

It is in his study of scientific argumentation that Aristotle made his most celebrated discovery – his theory of 'syllogistic'. He takes it for granted that every assertion in any of the sciences has the form of a subject–predicate statement, in which something (a predicate) is either affirmed or denied of some subject. Furthermore, in the sciences the subjects are always kinds of thing, rather than individuals: isosceles triangles, rather than the one whose equal sides are two inches in length, human beings rather than Socrates or Plato. (Even if the sciences do have things to say about individuals, it is about them as members of given kinds – kinds which are, from the scientific point of view, the basic subjects of the predicates in question. So any such assertions can be disregarded, as derivative from the main business of science, which is concerned with kinds or 'universals'.) With these severely limiting assumptions in place, Aristotle notes that scientific assertions will always be of one of four forms, depending upon whether the predicate is affirmed or denied of all of the subject, or only of part of it. Thus, using a convention introduced in the Middle Ages to designate these types of assertion, every scientific assertion will be of one of the following four forms (*a, e, i* or *o* respectively). (I illustrate each of these with what is intended to be a truth, but of course there are plenty of false examples of each as well.)

A belongs to all (every) B.	AaB	'Every human is two-footed.'
A belongs to no B.	AeB	'No fish has feathers.'
A belongs to some (of) B.	AiB	'Some lilies are white.'
A does not belong to some (of) B.	AoB	'Some lilies are not white.'

Thus each of the premisses and the conclusion of each and every scientific argument will be of one or another of these four forms.

Now in the first chapter of the *Prior Analytics* Aristotle defines the arguments which he calls in Greek *syllogismoi* (singular: *syllogismos*), of which scientific arguments are, according to him, a special case, as follows:

A *syllogismos* is an argument in which, certain things being posited, something else different from the things posited results of necessity because of their being so.　　　　　　　　　　　　　　　(*Pr. An.* I 1, 24b18–20)

Thus a *syllogismos* is, in modern terminology, a deductively valid argument (i.e. one such that if or whenever its premisses are true the conclusion necessarily *must* be true as well), and moreover one of a particular kind, namely one where the conclusion is *different* from its premiss or premisses.[8] Our word 'syllogism' was in fact adopted into English simply as a transliteration of Aristotle's *syllogismos*, yet it is always used in such a way that there are *both* valid *and* invalid syllogisms (i.e. valid and invalid arguments of a certain determinate form). So, paradoxically, it is desirable in discussing Aristotle's syllogistic not to use 'syllogism' to translate his Greek: instead, it is better to speak of the intended subject of the definition I have just quoted as (valid) *deductions* (of a certain type – i.e. ones where the conclusion is distinct from any of the premisses). Now, it is evident that, with some obvious exceptions, no single proposition of any of the forms *a, e, i,* or *o* can logically imply any other *different* proposition of any of those forms.[9] Thus any deduction (*syllogismos*) involving only propositions of these four forms will have to have, at a minimum, two premises. Moreover, it is also evident that no pair of propositions of those forms can imply a third one unless each has at least one term in common with the other (whether as its subject or its predicate): otherwise, each will say something logically quite unrelated to what the other says. So, taking all possible combinations of two distinct *a*, *e*, *i*, or *o* propositions having exactly one common term, Aristotle asks which of them are, and which of them are not, premisses which lead, via (valid) deductions of the required type, to some *a*, *e*, *i*, or *o* conclusion, or rather (in particular) to some *a*, *e*, *i*, or *o* conclusion having just the terms that the premisses do *not* have in common. His answers to this question constitute his theory of syllogistic.

He groups all possible pairs of *a*, *e*, *i*, or *o* propositions having precisely one common term into three sets, three so-called 'figures'. Either (1) the subject of one proposition is the predicate of the other – this is the 'first figure' – or (2) the two propositions have the same predicate – the 'second figure' – or (3) the two propositions have the same subject – the 'third figure'.

First Figure		Second Figure		Third Figure	
Predicate	Subject	Predicate	Subject	Predicate	Subject
A	B	A	B	A	B
B	C	A	C	C	B

Taking each figure in turn, Aristotle then asks which pairs of propositions, each of which is of one of the forms *a*, *e*, *i*, or *o*, imply some conclusion different from either of the premises, i.e. an *a*, *e*, *i*, or *o* conclusion having as its terms the two terms that the premisses do not have in common.[10] Working systematically through the sixteen possible premiss pairs in each figure, he proves, for each of the four forms *a*, *e*, *i*, and *o*, that a conclusion in that form either follows or does not follow from the given premisses. Leaving aside, for lack of space, consideration of these proofs (and their methods), we can summarize the resulting theory of the valid deductions (the ones that Aristotle calls the 'moods'), in the table below. I add the medieval names for each mood; they are a useful mnemonic, since the three vowels in each name indicate to which of the forms *a*, *e*, *i*, or *o* each of the three propositions, in order, belongs. Some but not all the consonants function to indicate the method of proof, but this beginner's exposition omits such refinements.[11]

First Figure[12]

AaB, BaC; therefore AaC   *Barbara*
AeB, BaC; therefore AeC   *Celarent*
AaB, BiC; therefore AiC   *Darii*
AeB, BiC; therefore AoC   *Ferio*

Second Figure

MaN, MeX; therefore NeX   *Camestres*
MeN, MaX; therefore NeX   *Cesare*
MeN, MiX; therefore NoX   *Festino*
MaN, MoX; therefore NoX   *Baroco*

Third Figure

PaS, RaS; therefore PiR   *Darapti*
PeS, RaS; therefore PoR   *Felapton*
PiS, RaS; therefore PiR   *Disamis*
PaS, RiS; therefore PiR   *Datisi*
PoS, RaS; therefore PoR   *Bocardo*
PeS, RiS; therefore PoR   *Ferison*

The *Analytics* contains a great deal else of great interest besides this basic theory of the categorical syllogistic (syllogistic dealing with simple categorical propositions): there is a modal syllogistic too (dealing with arguments having one or more premises where the predicate's belonging to the subject is qualified as necessary or possible), and a number of discussions of what we would nowadays call a 'metalogical' kind, to do with the structural properties of Aristotle's deductive system – and much else. But this is all we have room for here; it is enough to suggest why, from the revival of Platonism and Aristotelianism in later antiquity and all through the Middle Ages (when the important contributions of the Stoics to logical theory were neglected) – in fact, until the beginnings of modern mathematical logic through Frege's work in the late nineteenth century – Aristotle's logic simply *was* logic. It was as if Aristotle had virtually completed the whole of logic once and for all, even while establishing it for the first time as a subject of study. Only with the development of modern mathematical logic were the severe limitations of Aristotle's logic generally recognized.

For the issues addressed in this section, see also chapter 1 above.

NATURAL PHILOSOPHY AND NATURAL SCIENCE

I said above that the largest portion by far of the Corpus Aristotelicum is devoted to the study of nature in general and of various specific natural phenomena, including pre-eminently the world's animal population. Perhaps the most useful introduction to this part of Aristotle's work would be to discuss briefly the objectives and main contents of the major works falling under this heading, with some remarks also on the relationship of these works to one another, and to Aristotle's overall ambitions with regard to knowledge of the natural world.

It is often remarked, correctly, that despite Aristotle's ambitious account in the *Posterior Analytics* of all sciences as consisting of demonstrations of 'theorems' starting from primitive conceptions ('axioms' definitive of their particular subject matters), none of his works in natural philosophy and science presents its results in that format. So far as the *Physics* is concerned, that is because its function is rather to explain and defend certain specific analyses of the actual conceptions that Aristotle thinks are fundamental to the study of nature overall, and in all its branches. The argumentation that he employs, instead of being scientific demonstration as that is explained in the *Analytics*, is much closer to the dialectical argumentation set forth in the *Topics*. In Book I, for example, he develops a general account of what *change* is (change of quality, of quantity, of place, of nature or substance), and defends against the objections of certain Presocratic philosophers the basic assumption (on which all study of nature depends) that things do change in all these ways. His aim is to show that these fundamental notions can be expressed clearly and coherently – in such a way as to free them from all philosophical doubts about their coherence and applicability to the objects and phenomena of nature. In Book II he does the same thing with the crucial notions, first, of a thing's *nature*: in what does the nature of a thing that exists by nature in fact consist? Then, that of a 'cause' – whatever it is, in a given case, that explains either a change that something undergoes, or any of the ways that it *is* and remains. Here (II 3) he introduces his famous and vastly influential distinction between four basic sorts of 'cause': *material* (the matter a thing is made of insofar as that is responsible for certain of its properties), *formal* (the thing's nature or 'form' as a factor responsible for others of its properties – an apple tree's having flowers or fruit of a certain kind), 'efficient' (this terminology, though traditional, does not correspond to any term Aristotle himself uses – he usually speaks here of 'the source of the change', whatever it is that sets off a change whenever anything changes in any way), and 'final' (the thing's intended or natural function or purpose – its 'for the sake of which' or 'end', as when we say that taking a walk after eating is for the sake of health – our walking is to be explained by reference to that – or that the specific construction of the eye is for the sake of seeing). For the fundamental importance of this teleological principle in Aristotle's natural philosophy, see chapter 10, pp. 283, 286 below.

Books III and IV offer detailed analyses of five further concepts that are central to the study of nature and natural objects, as we ordinarily understand them: (a) *change* itself (what a process of change actually *is* – a question not addressed in Book I), (b) the sort of '*infinity*' that characterizes the magnitudes studied in physics (physical magnitudes, change itself, time), (c) how we should understand the *place* of a thing (every natural object, it would seem, has to be *some*where at each moment), (d) whether we need to think that there are any *void* spaces in the natural world (e.g. to make movement possible), (e) what *time* (something required if there is to be change at all) actually *is*. Aristotle raises difficulties for each of these concepts, ones that if unresolved threaten their coherence and applicability; discusses these difficulties in thorough and brilliant fashion; and proposes his own final account intended to respond to and accommodate the bases of objection while offering (with two exceptions) refined, clear and coherent conceptions suitable for unworried use by anyone who wishes to study nature and natural objects. (He rejects the notion of a void space as thoroughly incoherent, but also unnecessary; and while accepting that the magnitudes presupposed in physics are 'infinite' in some ways, he rejects the idea, again as incoherent, that there is any infinitely extended physical magnitude, and argues that no one concerned with physics has any need for such an idea anyhow.) *Physics* V–VIII discuss further puzzles about change (the dynamics of motion in particular), and develop (VIII) the idea that the world, which is, as a whole, subject to constant change, cannot have come into being but must be eternal, though it depends for its continued functioning upon some otherwise undetermined 'unmoved mover' or ultimate source of this constant change, which is itself free from all change, and lies outside the physical system altogether.

Having thus established clear and coherent versions of the basic concepts applicable to all natural objects, he goes on to use these concepts, so understood, in a series of specialized studies of particular parts and aspects of the physical world. *On the Heavens* and *On Coming-to-be and Passing Away* discuss the four basic sorts of matter (earth, air, fire and water) which ultimately compose all bodies other than the sun, moon and other heavenly bodies – these, on Aristotle's view, are made of a separate 'fifth body', called 'aether', endowed with a natural circular motion. Aristotle also considers the modes of transformation into one another of earth, air, fire and water, their 'natural places' and 'natural motions'. *Meteorology* as its name implies discusses and offers explanations of all sorts of meteorological and other natural phenomena: rainbows, shooting stars, clouds, snow, winds, earthquakes, thunderbolts, rivers, springs, etc. On all this, see further, chapter 10, pp. 280–1 below.

Aristotle applies the same principles in further studies, too – of living things. But in their case additional principles are needed, since many of the facts and phenomena to be understood and explained in this area cannot, he thinks, be adequately dealt with entirely in terms of the various materials of which these natural objects are composed. We must also understand living things specifically as *alive* – and that means, for him, in terms of their souls. A soul (*psychē*) is precisely what anything that is alive (even plants) possesses simply in virtue of being alive, and that to which, ultimately, all the behaviours which constitute its specific type of life are to be traced: its absorption of food, growth and physical self-maintenance, its eating and sleeping and breathing (if it is an animal), its moving about from place to place.

On the Soul offers a general investigation and account of all the varied life-functions of living things (plants as well as animals) and the types of organs needed for performing them – nutrition and reproduction (these apply to virtually all living things), sensation and movement from place to place (virtually all animals), and mentality and thought (humans). For Aristotle the soul of a type of animal or plant can be equated with its 'form', that is, the principle of specific bodily organization, self-maintenance and continued functioning that constitutes it as precisely *that* sort of natural object – a blade of grass, an oyster, a starling, a horse, a human being.[13] Aristotle devotes special attention to animals in general, and indeed to the human being: he gives fascinating, detailed accounts of the five senses, in terms of their different essential objects (colours for sight, odours for smell, etc.), and of how the senses and sense organs function to obtain information about physical objects and their properties (II 5–III 2). He also discusses the higher 'cognitive' powers of *phantasia* ('imagination', as it usually translated – animals' capacity to receive appearances or impressions of things, and to form images, for example in dreams; III 3) and *nous* (mind, i.e. the human capacity for scientific and philosophical knowledge; III 4–7); here he formulates his famous, but obscure, distinction between active and passive mind, and expounds his thesis that in active knowing the mind is identical with the object known. Finally, he discusses animal locomotion, and its source within the capacities that make up the animal soul (III 9–11).

In this way, *On the Soul* serves as the source of the additional basic concepts needed, beyond those provided in the *Physics*, for the study of living things, and Aristotle applies these in a long series of works devoted to varied aspects of (especially) animals and animal life – his 'psychological' writings on sensation and the senses, memory, sleep, dreams, etc., and the astonishingly rich, pioneering works of his biology (primary among them the *History of Animals*, *Parts of Animals*, and *Generation of Animals*). In antiquity Aristotle was famous as the most 'aetiological' of philosophers – the most given (over-ambitiously, many thought) to inquiring into and offering explanations of all kinds of natural phenomena – and it is in the cleverness and inventiveness of his explanations in biology that this feature of his mind and his work is best displayed.

METAPHYSICS

The fourteen books of Aristotle's *Metaphysics* were first assembled into a single work only some three centuries after his death.[14] Our word 'metaphysics' derives from this title. Aristotle himself speaks of 'first philosophy' at several places in the *Metaph.* and elsewhere as a study that lies in intellectual value above natural science and mathematics. He begins *Metaph.* Alpha (chapters 1–2) with a discussion of

'wisdom' (*sophia*), as a branch or type of knowledge the precise specification and explication of which is his objective in the investigation
being launched there. It emerges that this 'science' is the knowledge
of the *first* 'causes and principles', i.e. the causes and principles that
lie ultimately behind *everything*, and so have nothing lying behind
them. Aristotle further identifies this knowledge as the one that
deals with 'things that are divine' and the one that, among types of
knowledge, is itself entitled to be called 'most divine'. In *Metaph.*
Gamma 2 he describes this knowledge as knowledge of 'being *qua*
being', or being simply as such – knowledge of what belongs to anything that has being in any way, i.e. that exists and is anything at all
(whatever that might be), simply insofar as it *is*. And in Epsilon 1 he
further names this science as theology, and ranks it above the various
mathematical and physical sciences, as concerned universally with
everything, whereas the mathematical and physical sciences, starting somehow from the results of this highest science, inquire into
and get to know special particular parts of what is, via principles
that relate, in particular, to those particular parts (and, in the first
instance, only to them). Thus we learn that Aristotle recognized a
philosophy or science, 'first philosophy', dealing with god or divinity
as the first 'cause or principle', which has universal and equal application to everything that is, just insofar as it is, i.e. to anything that
has being in any way or is anything at all. Our collection called the
Metaphysics is the result of Aristotle's earliest editors' search among
his surviving writings for items written within this perspective.

Aristotle's conception of god as the absolutely first cause and principle greatly influenced the development of Jewish, Christian and
Muslim theology during late antiquity and the Middle Ages. Modern
readers coming from those traditions have to understand, however,
that Aristotle's god or divinity is not to be conceived as a person –
a father or mother who loves and, as such, is concerned in some
personal way with what happens to human beings and the rest of
nature, and has hopes and expectations, or who has any power of
punishment in case something happens that he or she disapproves
of or has forbidden. God for Aristotle is an eternally existing, extra-
physical and non-material entity, whose activity is the original and
fundamental model of what it is to *be* in any way or respect, and
which as such serves as the foundation for the being of everything
in the physical world – and as the source of the constantly renewing

series of changes that keep the world unified and functioning as a single whole over the vast expanse of time. Unfortunately, if Aristotle ever did write up a full account of this divinity and its activities, it was lost before his earliest editors did their work. What remained to them (and us) is a very sketchy account (in book Lambda, 6–10) of this 'god' as an entity that consists of nothing but thinking – its activity is that of pure knowing, knowing about *itself* as the source of being to everything else.

The various books of the *Metaphysics*, as we now have it, are essays in the study of being, where that study is conceived as focusing on divinity and its role in relation to the rest of what there is.[15] However, the reference to divinity recedes sometimes to the point of virtual invisibility, and this is particularly so with the intricate, probing analyses of the 'being' of physical objects and their properties which we find in the so-called 'middle books' of the work, books Zeta, Eta and Theta. Aristotle is concerned here to work out in detail, and give philosophical grounding to, two fundamental metaphysical contentions. (a) Among the entities making up the physical world it is the living beings – the plants and animals – that are ontologically basic. That is, the being of other things (the various kinds of inorganic matter that there are, and the various properties of colour, weight, size etc. that characterize both the materials of the world and these living beings) comes to them derivatively from the being of the living things; the latter, therefore, constitute the 'substances' or basic beings of the physical world. Thus, on Aristotle's theory, it is through their relationships to the natural substances (the living things) that the being of these other entities is to be conceived. (b) As to the substances, it is their 'forms', not their material make-up, and not so to speak *themselves* (as unities of their matter taken together with their forms), that have the priority. *What* they are, and *that* they have being at all, is given to them by their forms. These forms are what Aristotle calls full *actualities*, as opposed to the material embodiment of forms in flesh, blood, bone etc. of special sorts (depending on the needs of the given species): the materials only have being *potentially*, as making up living things under the specifications given by the forms. As Aristotle puts it, the material constitution of a natural substance is in potentiality what that substance's form is in actuality. So, in the natural world, the basic beings are the forms that shape and direct the lives of the living things that the world contains.

Aristotle's metaphysics of form and matter, set out at its deepest in these 'middle books' (and in *On the Soul*) has recently come in for a great deal of intense and appreciative study. For the most part, however, this has proceeded with little consideration of the place and function of these books within the framework provided by Aristotle's conception of first philosophy as the study of the absolutely first causes and principles. Even within these books we find a clear indication (Zeta 11, 1037a 10–20) that Aristotle's examination of the being of physical objects, taken on their own, is undertaken with a view to the knowledge of the being of non-physical substances. Presumably, then, one mostly implicit lesson we are to learn from the studies of the 'middle books' is that, however much more basic the being of the forms of the world's plants and animals may be than the being of everything else in the physical world (all of which depend immediately upon those forms for their being), these forms are not responsible for their own being; for the absolutely *first* causes and principles of being we must look behind or above them, to the transcendent being of god.

ETHICS, POLITICS, RHETORIC AND POETICS

The Corpus Aristotelicum contains three comprehensive treatments of ethical topics – the substance and nature of *eudaimonia* (the overall and final good for a human being and a human life), the moral virtues of courage, justice, temperance and the rest, and their place in such a life, the value of subsidiary goods such as pleasure, and so on: the *Nicomachean* and *Eudemian Ethics* and the *Magna moralia*. (Aristotle's son was named Nicomachus, as was his father, and Eudemus of Rhodes was a famous pupil and associate of Aristotle's in his later years: scholars presume that Nicomachus and Eudemus were responsible respectively for the preparation of the two treatises bearing their names, apparently from lecture notes of Aristotle's for two distinct lecture-series.) By contrast, the Corpus includes just one comprehensive political treatise, and one (genuine) one on rhetoric; the *Poetics* is only half-preserved, since the single-book work under that title deals exclusively with ancient tragedy of the classical period (fifth to fourth centuries BC; the plays of Aeschylus, Sophocles, Euripides and other tragedians whose plays did not survive the end of antiquity), whereas in fact Aristotle continued his discussion in a lost second book dealing with classical comedy.

In the *Politics* Aristotle frequently refers to or draws upon analyses and discussions in the ethical writings (calling them simply 'the *Ethics*'); it seems clear that, without exception, the texts in question belong to the *Eudemian*, not the *Nicomachean*, *Ethics*. On the other hand, among other differences of emphasis or even of doctrine, the *Nicomachean* (but not the *Eudemian*) treatise presents ethical theory as itself *part* of political philosophy (see I 1–2, x 9). On the *Nicomachean* view, its ten books establish the nature of the human good and the place of moral virtue within a life led in successful pursuit of that good, and do so on the fundamental presupposition that all human beings by nature need to live their lives (if they are to be acceptable lives at all) in a well-bound-up context of social and political relations with other people, with whom they live and co-operate as fellow-citizens. The *Politics* is conceived as following directly and immediately upon the *NE*, with the task of working out just how the social and political arrangements presupposed in the *NE* should legitimately be arranged, given the authoritative account provided in *NE* of the human good. The best political structures will be those that advance the citizens' individual well-being by providing appropriate contexts for them to develop the personal qualities and abilities that will permit them individually and collectively to lead the best human life. Thus, the way that ethics is part of political philosophy, on Aristotle's view, does not subsume ethics under politics, as actually practised in any city or state; rather, ethics establishes *for* politics the concrete goals that, if properly conducted, it must be oriented toward. For Aristotle, ethics is the foundation of politics; the order of dependence does not go in the other direction.

It appears, then, that the 'Eudemian' lectures on ethics were worked out and written down before Aristotle had established and elaborated the views on politics that we find in the treatise named *Politics* – views that presupposed the 'Eudemian' theories of *eudaimonia* and the moral virtues, and were presented with references back to the *Eudemian Ethics*. Some time after that, presumably in the second of his two periods of teaching in Athens, towards the end of his life, he reworked and revised his views on ethics, placing them now explicitly into the framework of an expanded conception of the scope of political philosophy. (There are other reasons than the ones I have given for thinking that the *Eudemian Ethics* was composed before the *Nicomachean*.) It is to this later, *Nicomachean*, conception of ethics that generations of students, in modern as well as earlier times, have devoted their attention in coming to grips with Aristotle's moral philosophy. Though there is a great deal of interest also in the *Eudemian Ethics* (and the *Magna moralia* as well), I will follow tradition in limiting my discussion of Aristotle's ethical theory below to his views in the *NE*.[16]

The central concept and the central topic of the *NE* is *eudaimonia*, a Greek word that is traditionally translated as 'happiness' (sometimes instead as 'flourishing'). However, in Aristotle's usage this word is used most fundamentally as the name of a certain activity, something that human beings under ideal conditions can engage in. By engaging in that activity, a life is made a *eudaimōn*, or 'happy' or 'flourishing' one. So the term does not denote a whole good life, or some condition of it (its 'happiness' or character as 'flourishing'), but refers rather to that activity, focused on centrally in the way a life is led, that makes it fulfilled and 'happy'. The major question for Aristotle, and for his interpreters, is to specify which activity this is. Early in Book I (ch. 5) Aristotle mentions three lives, constructed round three conceptions of what this best activity is: the lives respectively of (sensual) pleasure, virtuous action on behalf of the community (the 'political' life), and philosophical study and 'contemplation'. When in I 7 he comes to give a preliminary sketch of *eudaimonia* he identifies it with 'activity of the soul deriving from virtue (human excellence), and if there is more than one virtue, from the best and most final (or endlike) of them' (1098a 16–18) over a finished lifetime. This activity, whatever exactly Aristotle has in mind, is the one that fulfils our nature as human beings and therefore constitutes our final or ultimate good. The vagueness of this specification has, however, left commentators in the lurch, since it seems to permit any of the following, very different developments. (a) *Eudaimonia* is constant activity (over a finished lifetime) deriving from the moral virtues (justice, courage, temperance and the rest), together with the very different excellent or virtuous activity consisting in refined philosophical understanding of the basic nature of the world and its fundamental ordering principles – all of these moral and intellectual excellences being taken together as the best and most final virtue. (b) *Eudaimonia* is activity deriving from perfect philosophical understanding, where, however, that is regarded as an added completion or ornament on top of the moral virtues. (c) *Eudaimonia* is (simply, with no addition) activity of perfected philosophical understanding of the world and its most basic principles.

NE ii–v deal with moral virtue in general and the specific virtues. Aristotle enumerates these as *courage, temperance* (control of the impulse for sensual pleasure), *liberality* (the right use of one's money and other material resources for the benefit of others), *magnificence* (extraordinary wealth well used), *'greatness of soul'* (the virtue of public heroes, displayed in receiving and responding to public honours, or seeking them), *proper pride, good temper* (control of the impulse to anger), the virtues of social intercourse (dignified *pleasantness* in dealings with others, *proper modesty, good taste*), and *justice*. In general Aristotle treats these virtues as having each not a single but two opposed vices (justice is a partial exception): good temper, for example, is a 'mean' or intermediate condition, lying between the vices of irascibility (an excessive tendency to anger) and what one could call 'inirascibility', the corresponding deficiency. The virtuous agent's virtuous actions and feelings, in differing circumstances and on different occasions, also fall within a mean – they are the measured, proper response, neither too great nor too little, to any situation that arises. Aristotle makes it perfectly clear that in his view no human life could count as a happy, fulfilled or flourishing one that did not have moral virtue and morally virtuous activity as goals and pursuits fundamental to the way it was lived. He explains at length (viii–ix) the value and importance of true friendship in any good human life – the mutual concern of each person for his or her friends and for their material, spiritual and intellectual needs, for their friends' own sake. And he discusses the nature and value of pleasure in two separate mini-treatises, vii 11–14 and x 1–5. It is only at the end of the treatise, in x 6–8, that Aristotle returns to the original, fundamental question, an answer to which was sketched in i 7–9: which activity is *eudaimonia*?

Though again his language leaves open other interpretations, which scholars in recent decades have developed with ingenuity and considerable interest, the most straightforward interpretation is clear: that *eudaimonia* actually consists in perfected, excellent activity of philosophical understanding of the world and its basic principles, i.e. the full, active understanding of god as absolutely first cause and principle of everything that there is – this activity being successfully made the *single*, overall organizing goal of one's life, standing above all other goals, concerns and pursuits. This is option (c) above. Thus, on this most natural interpretation, Aristotle holds that the happiest life for any human being is one in which the supreme value of this activity of 'contemplation' is both recognized and given a dominant position in all the agent's choices, decisions, and indeed (implicitly at any rate) in all the actions that make up his life (everything that he or she does intentionally, voluntarily). It seems, then, that Aristotle returns here in x 7–8 to the three lives mentioned in I 5 (the contemplative and political lives, plus the life of sensual pleasure), and declares that the contemplative life is the best human life, because its defining goal is, given our natures and natural capacities, our final and ultimate good. He ranks, however, as 'secondarily happy' what he calls 'the life of the rest of virtue' (x 8, 1178a 9), i.e. the life of moral virtue – the life that treats morally good activity, with its embeddedness in the social and political affairs of the community, as its single, overall organizing goal (thus overlooking or neglecting the superior value of philosophy and philosophical understanding). Though he does not call it that here (but see 1177b 12, 1178a 6–7), Aristotle seems to be ranking the political life of Book I as a worthy, good, happy life, too – but only 'secondarily' so. The life of pleasure has been implicitly eliminated earlier, since it rests on demonstrable mistakes about the nature as well as the value of pleasure: once pleasure is properly conceived, it turns out that both of the two happy lives are also extremely pleasant ones, much preferable simply in terms of pleasure to a life treating sensual indulgence as the highest good.

Interpreters have resisted accepting this straightforward interpretation, because it has seemed to them that people leading the contemplative life would inevitably neglect their ethical duties and interests, so as to indulge themselves instead in the pleasures of philosophical study, just as they plainly do downgrade the value of moral virtue and its social and political context – and it seems clearly inconsistent with the whole tenor of his discussion of the moral virtues to suppose that Aristotle meant to endorse the highest value of such an immoral, or amoral, life. However, how sound is this inference that people who know and make real in their lives the supreme value of the highest and fullest philosophical understanding of the world will inevitably in pursuit of that as their ultimate good find themselves neglecting at least some of the requirements of morality? In fact, perhaps Aristotle conceives the pursuit of philosophical understanding as ruling the best life in such a way that also the moral virtues and their activities are positively endorsed as being fundamental goods. Perhaps he thinks that the very same features of excellent contemplation that make it the supreme value also are found, instantiated in some lesser way, in moral actions. If so a contemplative might be expected, instead of relaxing his moral commitments, to have a deeper and fuller understanding of the true value of moral action than even the best 'political' person could do, while nonetheless retaining just as firm (indeed, a firmer) commitment to living his social and political life in such a way as to be a fully courageous, just, temperate, good-tempered, public-spirited citizen. If that interpretation can be sustained, then we can accept the straightforward interpretation of Aristotle's account of *eudaimonia* in Book x without undermining in any way his commitment to the overriding value in the social and political sphere of the moral virtues and the moral life.

NOTES

1 The *Sophistical Refutations* completes the project of the *Topics* and is sometimes treated as *Top.* IX.

2 Although this has long been the standard English title of this work, it is in no sense a history. It is in fact Aristotle's collected 'Researches on Animals'. Book x is probably not by Aristotle; cf. p. 331 below.

3 This is a later compilation but may contain Problems contributed by Aristotle himself.

4 The *Nicomachean Ethics* and *Eudemian Ethics* share three books: *NE* V–VII = *EE* IV–VI.

5 The text is not from Aristotle's hand, but seems to contain Aristotelian materials independent of the other two ethical treatises.

6 Many scholars attribute this work not to Aristotle himself but to some student(s) writing under his supervision.

7 These and the fragments of Aristotle's other lost works are most conveniently available in Barnes [70], see Bibliography.

8 For good reasons, it is fundamental to modern systems of mathematical logic that an argument from any proposition as premiss to that

same proposition as conclusion is treated as valid. Such an argument does not count for Aristotle as a *syllogismos*. (Nothing is 'collected (or 'calculated') together', which is the ordinary meaning of the verb from which this Greek noun derives, in reaching such a 'conclusion'.)

9 These are the exceptions: *AeB* implies *BeA* – that no dogs are horses implies that no horses are dogs; *BiA* implies *AiB* – that some dogs are females implies that some females are dogs; and *BaA* implies *AiB* – that all dogs are animals implies that some animals are dogs. Aristotle recognizes and makes separate use of these exceptions, under the rules of 'conversion' which he uses in his proofs of the validity of inferences in the three figures (see below).

10 Aristotle calls the term common to the two premisses (i.e. the one that does *not* occur in the conclusion) the 'middle term' of the deduction; the predicate of the conclusion the 'major term'; and the subject of the conclusion the 'minor term'.

11 In the table below I follow the traditional practice, begun by Aristotle himself, of using the letters A, B, and C for the terms of a first-figure deduction, M, N, and X for those in the second figure, and P, R, and S for the third.

12 In addition to the ones that Aristotle officially considers, a pair of premisses belonging to the first figure might have for its proposed conclusion the major term as subject and the minor as predicate, instead of the other way about (as in the moods recorded below). And indeed, there are five valid forms of this type (with medieval logicians, but not Aristotle, these constitute a separate set of valid moods of the 'fourth figure'). In fact, at one place or another in the *Pr.An.* Aristotle does recognize arguments of all these five forms as valid. Theophrastus provides the systematic treatment of these forms of argument that Aristotle omits, treating them as 'indirect' first-figure forms.

13 On this notion of 'form' see pp. 142–3. Inasmuch as *On the Soul* develops and discusses this notion of a thing's soul as its form (especially in chapters 1–3 of Book II), the work makes important contributions to Aristotle's metaphysical theories, as well as providing the grounding for his scientific studies of animals and animal life.

14 It is customary to refer to the books of the *Metaphysics* not, as with the rest of Aristotle's works, using Roman or Arabic numerals, but rather (or in addition) the letters of the Greek alphabet. (The Greeks used the letters of their alphabet as numerals.) The reason for this is that the work as traditionally constituted has a second, quite short, introductory book. This second introduction was traditionally counted using the same letter as the first book (the first letter of the Greek alphabet, Alpha) but now in lower-case: 'little alpha', it was called. That causes

confusion when the third book in the series is given the normal Greek letter for 2, viz. Beta. So in referring to the books of the *Metaphysics* I use the names of the Greek letters: Alpha (A) = I, little alpha (α) = II, Beta (B) = III, Gamma (Γ) = IV, Delta (Δ) = V, Epsilon (E) = VI, Zeta (Z) = VII, Eta (H) = VIII, Theta (Θ) = IX, I Iota (I) = X, Kappa (K) = XI, Lambda (Λ) = XII, Mu (M) = XIII, Nu (N) = XIV.

15   Books Delta and Kappa are generally agreed to be only loosely connected to the rest. Delta is a sort of philosophical lexicon, with discussions of various concepts of central use in metaphysical studies, and Kappa consists of summaries of earlier parts of the *Metaphysics* and some parts of the *Physics*. No scholar seriously doubts the Aristotelian authorship of Delta, but most scholars regard Kappa as spurious.

16   The relation of the *Magna moralia* to the other two ethical treatises, or rather to the lectures from which they derived, is much disputed. Many scholars have thought *MM* is simply derivative from the other two works, done up by some not entirely competent student of Aristotle's in the generation after his death. A better and more philosophically alert account of the evidence yields the view that they derive, for the most part, from a third set of lectures, whether given before or after the 'Eudemian' ones, written up by a student or associate of Aristotle's working from notes taken on their delivery – but that the 'editor' also takes account sometimes of views we now find in the *NE*. Comparing the treatments of topics common to *EE* and *MM* with those in *NE* is almost always illuminating.

6 Hellenistic philosophy

INTRODUCTION

The 'Hellenistic' age is a politically defined one, bounded at its beginning by the demise of Alexander the Great's empire (on his death in 323 BC) and at its end by Augustus' inauguration of the Roman empire, notionally in 27 BC. These three centuries were a time of major geo-political upheaval in the Greek-speaking world, due first to the growing power of eastern kingdoms and later to that of Rome.

In one way or another, philosophical developments kept pace with these political ones. At the start of the new age, Alexander's death was almost immediately followed by that of Aristotle (322), who in earlier days had been his personal tutor. In Alexander's later years, by contrast, he had been accompanied on his eastern campaign by Pyrrho, around twenty years Aristotle's junior and the philosopher whose name was to become synonymous with scepticism (later known as 'Pyrrhonism'). Pyrrho was as much the voice of the newly emerging age as Aristotle had been of the old.

Again in the closing years of the Hellenistic period, the new upheavals which philosophy underwent (see pp. 249–50) were closely tied to the growing dominance of Rome as a philosophical centre. In the Roman imperial era which followed, philosophy would typically be the preserve of political figures like Seneca and Marcus Aurelius (see chapter 7), or of professional teachers working in relative isolation in the provinces. This marks a sharp contrast with the Hellenistic age, in which nearly all the major players had been the heads of the official philosophical schools at Athens (see illustration, p. 10): the Stoa, the Epicurean Garden, and the Academy. (Aristotle's school, the Lyceum or Peripatos, also survived through all or most of the age, but had a very quiet time; cf. chapter 5, p. 130 above.)

These Hellenistic philosophies differed from their predecessors especially in the new centrality they gave to the quest for happiness. While happiness had been a concern of most fourth-century BC philosophy too, in the new era the search for personal salvation became more dominant, more insistent, more impatient. The impression is of customers queuing up for emotional therapy in the philosophy schools and expecting a quick cure. Although the major schools did not make this urgent pressure an excuse for abandoning the more theoretical parts of philosophy, they did insist that these parts ultimately find their justification only in the moral goal to which they are subservient. Their practical focus on the production of happiness became an enduring legacy to Rome. Disinterested speculation was in the Hellenistic age largely left to specialists in the mathematical sciences, now detached from the philosophy schools and functioning autonomously (see chapter 10).

PYRRHO

Pyrrho of Elis (c.365–c.275) falls chronologically between Aristotle and the founders of the new schools, but resembles neither. If anything, he was more of a Socrates, writing nothing but influencing others by his unique conduct, his charisma and his legend.

Aristotle had set out to acquire and disseminate a vast range of knowledge, while showing minimal concern to demonstrate that such knowledge is in fact accessible to the human mind. The founders of the major Hellenistic doctrinal schools by contrast put enormous emphasis on establishing the 'criterion of truth' – the guarantee that knowledge can be acquired. It would be a natural guess that in between Aristotle and the major Hellenistic schools there had been a thinker who challenged the human mind's capacity to know. Pyrrho is the perfect candidate.

Although the later 'Pyrrhonist' movement (see pp. 179–82 below) is descended from Pyrrho only at one or more removes, and although his importance lay largely in his personal example, there is every reason to suppose that he offered theoretical justifications for his rejection of the aspiration to know. Indeed, he seems to have maintained that a life devoid of beliefs is not only possible but actually the only way to be happy.

The biographical tradition portrays Pyrrho as indifferent to his own safety, not going out of his way to avoid vehicles, precipices or dogs, and placing no reliance on his senses. This picture of a reckless Pyrrho was rejected by the later Pyrrhonists, such as Aenesidemus (pp. 179–80 below). The truth may be that the displays of indifference to external dangers were put on for purposes of instructing his friends or followers, and were not repeated when he could not rely on others to rescue him (he did, after all, live to ninety!). A further series of anecdotes is different again, portraying Pyrrho living a quiet and fairly conventional life in the countryside. The co-existence of these differing traditions is partly explained by an anecdote where Pyrrho, on fleeing a savage dog, remarks 'It is difficult to strip oneself completely of being human': Pyrrhonian detachment is an ideal sometimes too difficult even for Pyrrho himself.

This same double image of Pyrrho may account for the later emergence of rival sceptical tendencies, with some regarding the true Pyrrhonist goal as 'insensibility' (apatheia), others as 'gentleness' (praotēs); and again with some favouring a 'rustic' scepticism which eschews beliefs of all kinds and passively bases everyday action on mere appearances, others an 'urbane' version which excludes none but philosophical beliefs.

Most of our information on Pyrrho himself stems ultimately from his pupil Timon of Phlius (c.315–c.225 BC), a flamboyant character and energetic writer who associated with Pyrrho for many years and is largely responsible for creating his master's legend. In his satirical poem Silloi Timon lambasts nearly all philosophers other than Pyrrho, although partially sparing those who to some extent prefigured Pyrrho's own outlook. In another poem, Indalmoi ('Images'), he asks his master the secret of his imperturbable serenity, and exalts him as an incomparable guide for living.

A further passage of Timon, reported by Eusebius (Evangelical Preparation XIV 18.2–4), is agreed to be the key testimony:

Pyrrho left nothing in writing, but his pupil Timon says that whoever wants to be happy must consider these three questions. (1) How are things by nature? (2) What attitude should we adopt towards them? (3) What benefit will result for those who have this attitude? (1) Regarding things, Timon says that Pyrrho declared them equally indifferent, unstable and unresolved, and that for this reason neither our sensations nor our opinions are true or false. Therefore (2) for this reason we should not put our trust in these one bit, but we should be unopinionated, uncommitted and unwavering, saying of each thing that it no more is [this or that] than it is not, or both is and is not, or neither is nor is not. (3) The benefit for those who actually adopt this attitude, says Timon, will be first speechlessness, then freedom from disturbance.

It is impossible here to discuss the many interpretative debates that surround this text. We may simply note certain salient features which distinguish Pyrrho, as presented here, from later versions of scepticism. Notably he starts, not from a critique of our cognitive faculties, but from a claim about the nature of the world: 'things are equally indifferent, unstable and unresolved'. That this premiss itself resulted from reflection on cultural relativities is suggested by another source (Diogenes Laertius IX 61):

He would maintain that nothing is honourable or base, or just or unjust, and that likewise in all cases nothing is [this or that] in truth; and that convention and habit are the basis of everything that people do; for each thing is no more this than that.

Evidence like this favours the interpretation that the differentiation which Pyrrho denied was above all one between *values*, rather than just between perceptible or physical properties. His scepticism may thus appear to have been more moral than epistemological in orientation.

If the above features seem to distinguish early from late Pyrrhonism, the eventual benefits described under (3), 'speechlessness' (i.e. non-assertiveness) and a resultant 'freedom from disturbance' or 'tranquillity' (*ataraxia*), were to remain vital desiderata for later Pyrrhonists too. Here Pyrrho's personal example became, and remained, an inspiration to his followers. Timon saw it as godlike:

This, Pyrrho, my heart yearns to hear, how you, though human, act most easily and calmly, never taking thought and consistently undisturbed, heedless of the whirling motions and sweet voice of wisdom. You alone lead the way for mankind, like the god who drives around the whole earth as he revolves, showing the blazing disk of his well-rounded sphere.

(Fragment 61A–D)

EPICURUS

Epicurus became as much a godlike figurehead to his own followers as Pyrrho was to his. The Latin poet Lucretius in the first century BC hailed him as a divine saviour, and two centuries later a certain Diogenes, in the small Asian town of Oenoanda, celebrated and advertised his philosophy by inscribing an entire colonnade with Epicurean writings.

Life. Born in 341, Epicurus presented himself as marking a new beginning in philosophy, emphasizing for example that he had learnt nothing from his own philosophical teachers – a Platonist and a Democritean – but was 'self-taught'. Despite this formal pose, there can be no doubt that his philosophy is a product of the atomist tradition founded by Democritus (see chapter 2, pp. 65–7).

After setting up schools in outlying regions of the Aegean, Epicurus moved to Athens in 306 and set up his main school, which was to become famous as the 'Garden', where he taught till his death in 270. Characteristically of the new age, the Garden was not a research centre such as the schools of Plato and Aristotle had primarily been, but a doctrinally focused community. It was frequented by children and adults, young and old, men and women. This close-knit community as a matter of policy abstained from anything beyond the minimum of involvement in civic affairs, instead cultivating its own internal friendship as the basis of social value. Parallel to civic isolation ran a rejection of conventional education, based as this was on such subjects of study as poetry and rhetoric; Epicurus also excluded the mathematical sciences, which Plato's school had made fundamental to a philosophical training. The only disciplines welcomed were those capable of curing human malaise, and these were all contained within Epicurus' philosophy.

Philosophy. All Epicurus' writings were geared, directly or indirectly, to this same therapeutic end. Most of the 300 scrolls from his pen are now lost, but we possess, in addition to small papyrus fragments of his magnum opus *On Nature*, three epitomes: the *Letter to Herodotus*, on physics, the *Letter to Pythocles*, on meteorological phenomena, and the *Letter to Menoeceus*, on ethics. We also have a collection of his maxims, the *Key Doctrines* (*Kyriai doxai*), whose first four, which were jointly known in an even more condensed form as the *Tetrapharmakos* or 'fourfold remedy', read in full as follows:

1   That being [i.e. god] which is blessed and imperishable neither suffers nor inflicts trouble, and therefore is affected neither by anger nor by favour. For all such things are marks of weakness.
2   Death is nothing to us. For what has been dissolved has no sensation, and what has no sensation is nothing to us.
3   The removal of all pain is the limit of the magnitude of pleasures. Wherever pleasure is present, as long as it is there, pain or distress or their combination is absent.
4   Pain does not last continuously in the flesh: when acute it is there for a very short time, while the pain which just exceeds the pleasure in the flesh does not persist for many days; and chronic illnesses contain an excess of pleasure in the flesh over pain.

It is not intellectual curiosity, but the dependence of our happiness on these same four attainments – not fearing god (1) or death (2), and knowing the limits of both pleasure (3) and pain (4) – that legitimizes Epicurus' philosophical enterprise. As he puts it in another maxim (*Key Doctrines* 11),

If we were not upset by the worries that celestial phenomena and death might matter to us, and also by failure to appreciate the limits of pains and desires, we would have no need for the science of nature.

Epicurus' pursuit of knowledge often seems more elaborate than this strictly utilitarian programme would warrant, and elsewhere he remarks explicitly that the pleasure of doing philosophy is intrinsic to the activity, not a mere after-effect. Nevertheless, the structure of his programme is such that physics, albeit a discrete branch of philosophy, is ultimately subservient to ethics. We will turn to these two sub-disciplines shortly, but first we must examine the third, theory of knowledge, which Epicurus called 'canonic' and outlined in a now lost work called the *Kanōn*.

Canonic. Democritus, Epicurus' principal forerunner in the atomist tradition, had admitted to severe methodological difficulties. If, as he held, atoms and void are the only fundamental entities, while all that the senses can access is qualities, such as colours, which lack objective reality, the data of the senses cannot suffice to confirm atomism; nor therefore, given its dependence on the senses, can reason. It was the need to break out of any such vicious circle, and to resist any other form of scepticism that might threaten, that led to the requirement, acknowledged by the Hellenistic doctrinal schools from Epicurus on, to name a 'criterion of truth' – an absolute starting-point on which truth claims could be securely founded. This criterion was also often called, like the title of Epicurus' treatise, a *kanōn* – a carpenter's straight stick against which the straightness of other lines can be tested.

Epicurus is reported to have nominated three such criteria: sensations, preconceptions (*prolēpseis*) and feelings, defending the first with the provocative dictum 'All sensations are true.' It was already well recognized that the data of sensations may conflict: the same thing may appear differently when perceived from different viewpoints, in different conditions, with different senses, by different subjects, etc. How then can all these sensations be true? Because, Epicurus replies, the impression of conflict arises from our failure to distinguish the sensation itself from the interpretative judgement that we superimpose on it. In itself, the sensation is the passive, mechanical and irrational recording of data by a sense. It is only when we interpret, indeed over-interpret, a sensation that it can be thought false, for example if we illegitimately assume the bent shape we perceive when we look at an oar in water to be the shape of the oar itself. In reality the falsehood lies in the interpretation, never in the sensory event itself. Taken for what it essentially is, a representational event reflecting its own causal history in the external world, the sensation is a self-certifying item of evidence, and, used with due caution, a proper starting point for inferential judgements.

The second nominated criterion, *prolēpseis*, is variously translated 'preconceptions', 'anticipations' etc., none of which is adequate. First introduced by Epicurus, the term came to play a key part in all Hellenistic systems. A *prolēpsis* is a universal notion of some kind of thing, and it earns its criterial status from the fact that, analogously to sensations, it is naturally and unreflectively generated in us, usually by repeated sense-perceptions. It is thanks to our naturally acquired stock of these, which amounts to our natural latent grasp of key concepts, that we are able to launch inquiries, focus our minds on the objects of those inquiries, and express ourselves in language. (Plato had argued that 'recollection' of the soul's prenatal acquaintance with the Forms is what makes such acts possible, see p. 116; in the Hellenistic age, reliance on natural *prolēpseis* became the empiricist's alternative to this.) Early on in his *Letter to Herodotus* (37–8), Epicurus emphasizes the role of our *prolēpseis* (he does not so name them, but the reference is clear) as an indispensable starting point for a philosophical inquiry.

An important example (though not necessarily a *typical* example, because its causal origins are both unusual and problematic) is the *prolēpsis* of god: if we consult existing notions of god, stripping away all cultural accretions, we will find their shared and irreducible core to be the idea of a blessed and immortal being. This then serves as a criterion against which we can judge a further characteristic often attributed to the gods (both by various religions and by philosophers such as the Stoics), their government of the world; since further conceptual analysis shows this activity to be incompatible with blessedness, and since blessedness is part of the *prolēpsis* of god, we must infer that gods do not engage in world government.

Like *prolēpseis*, sense-perceptions too are regularly invoked as a criterion against which opinions can be judged true or false. Opinions about simple empirical facts are subject to direct verification – called 'confirmation' (*epimartyrēsis*) – by the senses, failing which they must be rejected as false. But the opinions on which physics typically focuses concern microscopic or otherwise inaccessible entities (e.g. atoms, heavenly bodies, other worlds), and are therefore not candidates for direct confirmation; instead, they are to be accepted as true if and only if they receive 'no disconfirmation' (*ouk antimartyrēsis*) from the senses. Take a causal thesis about events at the atomic level, purporting to explain some phenomenon. Most competing explanatory theses – e.g. ones based on analysis of bodies not into atoms but into the traditional four elements earth, air, fire and water – will turn out to be disconfirmed by some sensory datum. That is to say, they will turn out to be *incompatible*, if not with the actual phenomenon that is being explained, at any rate with some analogous or otherwise relevant causal process which has been directly observed. If only one thesis survives this test – and Epicurus believes that the fundamental tenets of atomism are theses of this kind – it must unequivocally be accepted as true. But what if two or more theses survive the test, as often happens with the explanation of very distant phenomena such as those in the heavens? It would be arbitrary to favour any one of them, so all must be accepted equally. If at times the Epicureans seem to mean by this that all are actually *true*, not just possible, their formal justification is that over the entire infinity of worlds and time there is no distinction between the possible and the actual. However, Epicurus' own main emphasis lies not on this problematic notion of truth, but on his insistence that, provided we exclude all inappropriate types of explanation for a celestial phenomenon, especially explanations of a religious kind, and retain only the properly naturalistic ones which conform to our direct experience of how matter behaves, it is not all that important to go on and choose between this latter set of explanations.

Physics. Epicurus starts by establishing the permanence of the universe and its primary contents. Nothing (1) comes into being out of nothing or (2) perishes into nothing. These theses are not proclaimed, as by earlier thinkers, to be conceptually self-certifying truths, but are inferred from the observed fixity of natural processes. However, the next two principles *are* purely conceptual: the universe, being the sum total of what there is, cannot (3) grow through addition or (4) shrink through subtraction, because there could be nowhere else for the extra bits to come from or escape to.

Within that totality, nevertheless, change does occur, through *redistribution* of the primary occupants. These are interactive bodies, occupying and moving through an infinite 'void', which is itself conceived as a space whose parts are sometimes altogether unoccupied, sometimes co-extensive with occupying body. It is the insistence that motion depends on unoccupied portions of space – 'void' in its strictest sense – that represents Epicurus' opposition to the main rival physical systems (including the Stoic one), and his reversion to the atomism of Democritus.

The occupants of this void are 'atoms', physically indivisible portions of pure body, which differ from one another in shape and size. Their indivisibility makes them imperishable, and in fact at the level of individual atoms there is neither coming-to-be nor perishing: atoms are permanent and internally changeless. It is compounds of atoms that are transient. Atoms' innumerable, though finite, differences in shape and size enable them to account for the vast, though finite, spectrum of phenomena. Sensible properties like colour and odour have no existence at the atomic level, but are generated by microscopic arrangements of appropriate kinds of atom, which in themselves are distinguished by shape, size and weight but by no other properties. With an impressive degree of explanatory economy, the mechanical motions of these infinitely many atoms in an infinite void are argued to be sufficient to account for our world and everything in it, as well as for countless other postulated worlds at other locations and times.

The most important message of this physical model is the exclusion of divine intervention. Accident on a sufficiently large scale accounts not just for the emergence of some viable worlds, but also, within a single world like ours, for the emergence of viable life forms, ourselves included, and again, in the course of human history, for the original invention of all cultural institutions. At no point need god be invoked as a cause – and fortunately so, since, as we saw above, the activity of world government would be contrary to divine nature. This discovery that we are free of divine oversight is a vital benefit of studying physics, and eliminates the greatest fears that the world inspires in us.

Along with this reassurance, physics also teaches us the true nature of death. The soul (*psychē*), our animating force, must be itself an amalgam of atoms to possess the causal powers it evidently has, and it follows that, like any compound, it will eventually disintegrate – at the time when our body starts to do so in fact. This discovery too, once its implications have been thought through, will liberate us from fear – the fear that our future death will be a transition to a state of deprivation or even torture. Death is mere non-existence, which when present cannot distress us: being dead will be no worse than it was, centuries ago, not yet to have been born.

Ethics. As we saw in the opening two *Key Doctrines*, Epicurean ethics follows directly on from physics and starts with these two insights: neither god nor death holds any terrors for us. But the third and fourth of the Doctrines are the key to positive planning of our lives. These are the principles of managing pleasure and pain, and pleasure is proclaimed by Epicurus as the goal of all human (and animal) action. Just as in epistemology every doctrinal philosopher was expected to nominate the 'criterion of truth', so too in ethics the 'end' or 'goal' (*telos*) had to be named, and Epicurus' choice makes him the most prominent ancient exponent of hedonism.

Unlike Aristotle, who looked to the mature adult as the best judge of what is good, Epicurus appeals to the new-born infant, still blissfully free of whatever value system its family and culture will in due course impose on it, and therefore the true voice of nature's own values. And, so Epicurus argues, what guides the new-born from the first is visibly the pursuit of pleasant feelings and the avoidance of painful ones.

What Epicurus' ethics offers to add to our innate drive for pleasure is advice on how to maximize its attainment, a task which most people hopelessly bungle. Unlike the Cyrenaics, a contemporary hedonist school (famous also for its epistemological thesis that we have cognitive access to nothing but our own inner states), Epicurus insists that a static condition of painless sensation is already in itself a pleasure, rather than a merely neutral state. Indeed, this kind of 'static' pleasure is as pleasant as the experiences more commonly recognized as pleasures – positive and welcome but usually short-lived sensory stimulations, such as those involved in eating and drinking, which Epicurus places in the sub-class of 'kinetic' pleasures. Discovering that static pleasures are just as pleasant as kinetic ones, as well as longer-lasting and more dependable, is the first step towards redesigning our method of pleasure management. It means that not being hungry or thirsty, and being confident that this will continue, contribute more to our enjoyment of life than the actual kinetic pleasures of eating and drinking do, despite the fact that these latter fulfil desires which are 'both natural and necessary'. Even luxurious eating and drinking – the fulfilment of what Epicurus classes as 'natural but non-necessary' desires – do not actually increase the net total of pleasure. Indeed, exclusive concentration on such pleasures, which in the hands of the Cyrenaics had earned hedonism a bad name, is actually counterproductive to the maximization of pleasure. For however welcome they may be when they occur, an excess of them threatens to increase our reliance on their continued availability, and thus to make us more vulnerable to misfortune, and correspondingly less tranquil. The life-style both preached and practised by the Epicureans was therefore one of simple frugality, punctuated with just occasional feasts and other indulgences. The modern use of 'epicure' for *bon vivant* could scarcely be more misleading.

Despite the importance of properly regulating bodily pleasure, it is mental pleasure that counts most, because with our minds we can not only enjoy what is present but also relive past pleasures (presumably kinetic ones) and anticipate future ones. Properly used, these mental enjoyments can help us cheerfully endure intense but short-term bodily pain. But the most valuable pleasure of all is a 'static' mental one, tranquillity, or 'freedom from disturbance' (*ataraxia*), and it results from (a) ridding ourselves of the fears of god and death, (b) maximizing our independence of fortune by minimizing our needs, and (c) knowing how bodily pain, if it comes our way, can be endured. The supreme importance of *ataraxia* was Epicurus' legacy from Pyrrho, whom he much admired on the personal level, although his recipe for its attainment is no doubt quite un-Pyrrhonian.

Correspondingly, mental pains are the worst. The unjust are bad calculators: any short-term bodily pleasure gained from their wrong-doing will be outweighed by their long-term anxiety at the prospect of being found out. Indeed, the traditional virtues – justice, moderation, courage and wisdom – are, properly understood, the correct means to the maximization of pleasure, their value thus being instrumental rather than, as Plato and Aristotle had held, intrinsic to them.

Responsibility. Epicurus' inclusion of a class of desires that are 'natural but non-necessary' symbolizes his recognition of a hiatus between nature and necessity, a theme which comes to the fore in his treatment of determinism. His philosophical heritage from Democritus attributed all causation – psychological causation included – to the movements of atoms, movements necessitated by purely physical properties like weight and trajectory. To Epicurus' eye, this threatened to by-pass our own self-evident responsibility for our actions, robbing us of both the credit and the blame for them. Famously, he responded by introducing a minimal degree of *un*-necessitated movement in atoms, a tiny 'swerve' or 'deviation' (*parenklisis*, but better known by its Latin translation *clinamen*) from their trajectory at no fixed place or time, too small to generate macroscopic chaos but sufficient to leave the future undetermined.

How the swerve can account for our self-determination – rather than just make us disastrously unpredictable – is a notorious problem for interpreters, and unfortunately we do not have Epicurus' own account to help us solve it. Some of the evidence suggests that his main response to determinism lay in treating the self as an intrinsically autonomous source of actions, irreducible to a mechanical structure of atoms. If so, the swerve may have played an ancillary role, helping for example to account for the initial emergence of this autonomous self by making it causally independent of all its physical antecedents. (This, if correct, would be intriguingly parallel to a second reported function of the swerve: to initiate the series of atomic collisions that lead to the formation of a new world.) It seems equally plausible that the swerve continues to play a part in the behaviour and further development of the self. Is it in fact the swerve that, by ensuring our psychological flexibility and adaptability, opens us to benefits of the moral education offered by a philosophical school?

THE STOICS

The system. The Stoic school's foundation, around 300 BC, postdates that of the Garden by just a few years, and its founder, Zeno of Citium (born 334), died less than a decade after Epicurus. This chronological mirror-effect symbolizes the relation of the two doctrinal schools that were to dominate the Hellenistic era: with a little simplification, one could set out their two systems in polar opposition:

Epicureanism	Stoicism
methodology	
rejects dialectic	based on dialectic
physics	
Democritean	Heraclitean
anti-teleological	teleological
atomist	continuist
mechanistic	pantheistic
multiple worlds	single world
denies divine intervention	asserts divine providence
ethics	
hedonism	virtue ethics
politically minimalist	politically maximalist

There are certain features – typical of the period – that the two schools have in common: a degree of intra-school orthodoxy, the creation of a structured and comprehensive philosophical *system*, and the subordination, at least in principle, of theoretical inquiry to the practical goal of happiness. Even here, however, some distinctions are appropriate.

As regards orthodoxy, the Epicurean tradition was perceived as a very tight-knit one, based on the cult of the founder, whose writings were minutely studied and even memorized. By contrast, the Stoics were not (after the first years, at any rate) called 'Zenonians', instead taking their title from the place in Athens – the Painted Stoa (or 'colonnade') – where they gathered. And this different mode of self-definition corresponds to a greater degree of doctrinal flexibility and divergence than is found in the Garden.

Again when it comes to the structures of the two systems, a difference is evident. In the Epicurean system, a distinction is made between first principles and the consequences derived from them, these latter sometimes even being, as we have seen (pp. 158–9), left indeterminate. By contrast, the Stoic system prides itself on being an organic whole, so interwoven that, whichever thread you pull, the entire rope will follow.

Yet another asymmetry between the two schools lies in their respective places in the culture of the ancient world. Epicureanism, for all its success in outlying communities and its recruitment of charismatic individuals – at Rome, for example, not just Lucretius but another leading poet, Horace, and Cicero's friend Atticus – remained culturally marginalized. The only anti-Socratic school, suspected of atheism, pilloried for its hedonism, it was far from respectable. When in 155 BC the city of Athens sent a delegation to Rome, it chose three philosophers to represent it, and this celebrated occasion marks the true arrival of philosophy in the Roman world. But the philosophers chosen were a Stoic, an Academic and an Aristotelian: apparently there was no question of adding an Epicurean.

Stoicism, on the other hand, acquired a respectability which completely belies its origin. Zeno's first influence had been Cynicism, an informal philosophical movement famous for challenging and even outraging social and moral norms. (Its founder had been Diogenes of Sinope in the middle part of the fourth century, and the model set by his life-style had earned it the title 'Cynic', literally 'canine'.) Yet in the end Zeno was officially honoured by the Athenians on the grounds that he (in the words of the inscription they erected) 'lived the life of a good man, and exhorted those young men who came to join him to virtue and self-discipline and encouraged them towards what is best, setting up as a model his own life, which was one in accordance with all the teachings on which he discoursed'. Stoicism was a creed that easily adapted itself to a wide diversity of individuals and their circumstances, ranging from Roman emperors down to slaves. So widespread was its influence that its terminology and methodology became the common currency even of those who opposed its teachings.

The school. The Stoic school's long history is conventionally divided into three phases: 'early', 'middle', and 'imperial' or 'Roman' Stoicism – this last, the Stoicism of the Roman empire, falling outside the chronological bounds of Hellenistic philosophy proper. Early Stoicism is in effect the school's Athenian phase, running from its foundation down to the late second century BC: the age in which Stoicism was dominated by the school's metropolitan headquarters at Athens, under the headship first of Zeno (died 262), then of his successors Cleanthes (died 232) and Chrysippus (died 206), followed by a series of relatively minor school heads. Zeno had himself studied under the Cynic Crates; under Stilpo of the Megarian (more correctly 'Megaric') school, a largely ethical movement with a reputation for philosophical paradox, formally considered Socratic; and in Plato's old school the Academy. He also sat at the feet of the brilliant logician Diodorus Cronus. All these influences became vital ingredients in his newly constructed philosophy. His writings, however, were often laconic, and disputes about their correct interpretation became a frequent focus for his two successors. Cleanthes was above all Zeno's loyal follower and mouthpiece, although noted for the more strongly religious bent that his work took. Chrysippus, in his turn, so rigorously and voluminously developed the system as to be regarded by posterity as its re-founder, if not as its true founder.

Starting with Panaetius (died 110), and more so with his eminent pupil Posidonius, the school's critical mass was to drift away from Athens to other centres, particularly Rhodes and Rome. Panaetius and Posidonius are the main figures of 'middle Stoicism'. Finally, the roll-call of writers whose work represents Roman Stoicism for us eloquently testifies to its breadth of appeal: Seneca (AD 1–65), adviser to the emperor Nero; Epictetus (55–135), an emancipated slave who taught at Nicopolis, in a quiet corner of mainland Greece; and last but not least Marcus Aurelius (121–180), the emperor himself.

These will be more fully covered in the chapter on Roman Philosophy (pp. 203–8).

Of the literally thousands of Stoic books written in the early and middle phases of the school, none has come down to us intact, if one excepts Cleanthes' short *Hymn to Zeus*. What we know of them comes from numerous secondary citations, paraphrases (often hostile), and more or less systematic synopses. The chief sources are, in chronological order: Cicero's philosophical dialogues (mainly written in 45–44 BC); the anti-Stoic works of Plutarch (first to second century AD); the Sceptic Sextus Empiricus and the medical writer Galen (both second century AD); and the philosophical biographer Diogenes Laertius (second to third century AD), whose *Lives of the Philosophers* includes a whole book (VII) on Stoicism. By contrast, entire works by the Roman Stoics – largely on ethical themes, and less technical than earlier Stoic writing – have come down to us.

The Stoic system mirrors the Epicurean in its tripartition: into 'logic', 'physics' and 'ethics'. These are strictly speaking parts not of philosophy as such, ideally conceived as a seamless whole, but of 'philosophical discourse', which is inevitably fragmented so that its parts may be delivered in some linear sequence. The summary below must follow the latter expedient. The question of which order to adopt was controversial; by starting with logic, we will at least in this regard be siding with the preference of, among other Stoics, Chrysippus himself.

Logic. From the scholarship of recent decades, Chrysippus has emerged as among the greatest of pioneering logicians. However, Stoic 'logic' (*logikon*) is not limited to what is called by that name today, but is the study of discourse and reasoning (both called *logos* in Greek) from all points of view, including what we earlier encountered as the 'criterion of truth'. It is with this last, in fact, that we may begin.

Stoicism's success as a doctrinal system rests on the conviction that we possess a firm starting point, the criterion of truth. Their name for it is *phantasia kataleptikē*, often translated the 'cognitive impression'. Generically, an impression (*phantasia*) is a passive appearance, the way things strike us, especially via the senses, regardless of whether or not we take the appearance to be true. That further act of taking the impression to be true is called 'assent' (*synkatathesis*), and it is for this assent, rather than the initial impression, that we can be held responsible. Intellectual progress relies on our learning to grant our assent only to a certain species of impression, the 'cognitive' ones which, as it were, certify their own reliability. A cognitive impression is one that not only accurately portrays the object from which it is causally derived, but does so with a self-evident clarity which rules out the possibility of the subject's mistaking the object's identity. This latter proviso originated as a response to attacks by Zeno's Academic critic Arcesilaus (see below, pp. 176–8), who had cited examples, such as identical twins, in order to allege that even the clearest of impressions are fallible. It continued to be debated over a period of well over a century. In their defence, the Stoics could at least appeal to their own metaphysical principle, independently defended, that every being possesses a uniquely identifying lifelong 'peculiar quality'.

The receipt of cognitive impressions, and the resultant state of 'cognition' (*katalēpsis*), is just the beginning of the road to understanding. At the end of that road lies 'knowledge' or 'science' (*epistēmē*), whose possessor has integrated an entire set of cognitions into a rationally articulated and self-supporting structure, invulnerable to counter-argument. Only the semi-mythical sage (see further below) is credited with knowledge in this strict sense.

The typically sensory origin of cognitive impressions may make the Stoics sound like radical empiricists, but an equally strong streak of rationalism runs through their epistemology. In rational beings such as we are, impressions are themselves properly called 'rational' (*logikai*; perhaps also 'discursive'), because they are naturally captured by us in language; and it is these articulated, or articulable, impressions – at any rate the cognitive ones amongst them – that in time coalesce into concepts that, as a set, constitute adult rationality. This essentially rational structure of human experience is what places 'logic', the study of rational discourse or *logos*, at the heart of Stoic methodology. The Stoics distinguished two kinds of *logos*: externally uttered discourse (*logos prophorikos*) and internal discourse (*logos endiathetos*), this latter being identical with reason itself. The study of external discourse comprises such disciplines as rhetoric and grammar, the latter a discipline whose origin and development were largely due to the Stoics.

Logic in the narrower modern sense of this term is often identified by the Stoics with 'dialectic', a discipline whose origins stretched back through Aristotle and Plato to the model of method set by Socrates. Dialectic still for the Stoics sometimes reflects the oral question-and-answer format that such an origin suggests, but more often serves as the study of the formal rules governing truth and validity in arguments. (For Stoic logic in its broader historical context, see chapter 1.) Its focus is not 'signifiers', i.e. words and sentences, which the Stoics take to be corporeal in that as utterances they are physical events of some kind, but the 'signified'. These latter are the incorporeal contents expressed by language – especially by whole sentences – for which the Stoics' widely discussed alternative term is *lekta*, things 'said' or 'sayable'. Within this group, the key work in logic is devoted largely to one species, those *lekta* capable of truth and falsity – that is, propositions (*axiōmata*).

Whole propositions, rather than the single terms typical of Aristotelian logic (see pp. 132–6), are the basic units of Stoic logic. This brings with it a special concern for the connectives that link propositions: 'and', 'or' and 'if'. (The exact sense of the connective 'if' – that is, the criterion for a sound conditional – was the subject of a lengthy debate which had started before the advent of Stoicism with Zeno's teacher Diodorus Cronus and Philo, his fellow-student at Diodorus' classes.) Based on these connectives plus the negation sign ('not'), the Stoics arrived at five irreducible syllogistic forms, whose axiomatic status was conveyed by the label *anapodeiktoi* – 'indemonstrable' or, perhaps better, 'unproved' arguments:

1   If the first, the second; but the first; therefore the second.
2   If the first, the second; but not the second; therefore not the first.
3   Not both the first and the second; but the first; therefore not the second.
4   Either the first or the second; but the first; therefore not the second.
5   Either the first or the second; but not the second; therefore the first.

These five are held by the Stoics to be the forms which all valid arguments display or to which they are ultimately reducible by a set of four rules (*themata*).

A good deal of the Stoics' detailed work in logic was concerned with the solution of puzzles. Of these, the two most famous are the Liar Paradox (Is 'I am lying' true or false?) and the Sorites or 'Heap' paradox (How many grains make a heap?). This latter, which demands the precise point on a scale at which a given predicate starts, or ceases, to belong to a subject, was used by the Stoics' Academic critics to challenge some of the school's most basic conceptual distinctions, and seeking a solution to it became a particular priority for Chrysippus.

Physics. Like logic, 'physics' – the second part of the Stoic system – differs in scope from its modern counterpart. Above all else, Stoic physics is a grand vision of the world as a perfect unity, a divine living being governed by its own omnipresent and providential reason. It leaves to other specialists the detailed study of individual phenomena, processes and structures, and concentrates on the broad principles.

Perhaps the most surprising principle is its identification of being with corporeality. Only bodies have the power to act and be acted upon, a power without which nothing could strictly 'be' – constitute part of the furniture of the world. If then there *are* such things as virtue and other qualities, which act causally on bodies, as they evidently do, they must themselves be bodies. Justice, for example, is properly analysed as the soul in such and such a condition, where the soul itself is corporeal, being a portion of *pneuma* (see below). Thanks to analyses along these lines, only a very restricted residue of incorporeal items is admitted, in fact just four, of which one is the *lekta* already sketched above. The other three are place, void and time.

Place, as that three-dimensional extension which a body occupies, cannot itself be identified either with the occupying body – when the body moves, after all, it will leave the place behind – or with any other body. Void too is a three-dimensional extension, but unoccupied by any body, and its incorporeality is self-evident. According to Stoicism, there is no void in the world – which unlike the Epicurean world is completely filled with body – but only externally to it. Lacking any internal void, the world has a perfect cohesion which protects it from dispersal into the surrounding void. But eventually it will break up, at the end of each world phase (see below), and when it does so what it will expand into is the surrounding void.

Time, finally, was defined by Zeno as 'the interval of motion'. A simple illustration would be comparing a faster and a slower object travelling the same journey: the *spatial* co-ordinates of the journeys do not differ, so it must be in some other 'interval' or 'dimension' that the journeys do differ; and that interval is time. Chrysippus further specified that time is the interval of the *world's* motion, not thereby contradicting Zeno, but moving the focus from this or that part of time to time taken as a whole.

Leaving aside these special cases where incorporeality is conceded, the Stoic world is populated with bodies, which thanks to their corporeal status interact causally. Even at the lowest level of analysis, the world's two ultimate constitutive principles are bodies. These are a passive principle, called 'matter' (*hylē*), whose nature it is to be acted upon; and an active principle, variously called 'reason' (*logos* again) and 'god', which interpenetrates it and, by acting on it, shapes it into the four phenomenal elements, earth, water, air and fire, out of which in turn all more complex entities are formed. Matter and god are theoretical constructs, each of them representing one half of the official hallmark of body, its capacity to act or be acted upon. Matter, as the purely passive partner, is in itself a completely indeterminate entity, properly called 'prime matter'. (Such a view of matter has often been attributed to Aristotle, but its credentials as a Stoic concept are much stronger.)

The active principle, god, is in many Stoic contexts represented or replaced by an empirically more familiar entity, fire. Following in the tradition of Heraclitus (above pp. 59–61), Stoicism attaches special powers to a cosmic 'fire' which combines the creative functions of light and warmth – this latter including that of the warm 'breath' or *pneuma* (which in its Latinized form became our word 'spirit') that served as the vitalizing force of the Stoic world. God is sometimes defined as a 'creative fire that proceeds methodically to the world's coming-to-be'.

Fire's dominance of cosmic processes, including the very coming-to-be of the world, is intimately linked to the Stoics' conviction – which for once allies them with Epicurus and separates them from Aristotle – that the world comes to be and in due course ends. Each world phase culminates in a state of total fieriness known as the *ekpyrōsis*. Because this fieriness is the purest form of the intelligent immanent deity, the destructive connotations of 'conflagration', the usually favoured translation of *ekpyrōsis*, may mislead. The *ekpyrōsis* is an ideally good state of the world's stuff, and in it the deity concentrates on planning and setting up the next world-phase in a never-ending cosmic cycle. It is this last feature, intelligent world-government, that above all sets Stoic physics in stark contrast with Epicureanism.

The cosmic cycle brings with it a notorious paradox. The deity, being supremely wise, has no reason to do things differently from one world to the next. So successive worlds are indistinguishable from each other, even in their details. The present chapter has been written in the identical words infinitely many times in previous worlds, and will be again in infinitely many future worlds. In embracing this strange conceit, the Stoics may well have been attracted by its moral implications: don't dream of what you could do, or might have been able to do, 'in another life', because another life would be just the same as this one. There is nothing new under a sun which, even itself, is not new.

The power of the cosmic fire, or more particularly of the *pneuma* (usually analysed as an amalgam of air and fire), to control the entire world depends in part on the Stoic theory of total mixture. Matter is continuous and infinitely divisible, not atomic, and contains no void. Consequently two substances can interpenetrate each other entirely, a fact which makes it possible for the *pneuma* to be literally everywhere. It is the varying 'tension' of the *pneuma* in them that lends bodies their cohesion and endows them with their qualities. Minimally, an object has a 'tenor' (*hexis*) – its own particular coherence as a single discrete entity. But in a plant, the dominant *pneuma* is more than this, and is called its 'nature' (*physis*), the kind of coherence which it bestows being that of a living entity. Third and last, in an animal the controlling *pneuma* is called 'soul' (*psychē*), because it endows its possessor with that very special kind of unity and cohesion which animate beings alone possess. This is the route by which the Stoics arrive at the corporeality of soul, a doctrine which, as we have already seen, contributes to their analysis of all authentic 'beings', even the virtues, as bodies.

In addition to its explanatory role in constituting individual beings, *pneuma* has a diachronic function. Viewed from a universal perspective as an omnipresent power, it governs the entire world and its history in a rigidly determined causal progression, called 'fate', making the Stoics leading advocates of determinism (contrast Epicurus' position, pp. 162–3 above). In a celebrated image, Zeno and Chrysippus compared a human being to a dog tied to a cart: it may follow the cart willingly or unwillingly, but follow it it will. This immediately suggests an ethical problem that Stoicism's critics did not hesitate to raise, the 'Lazy Argument'. If the entire future history of the world is scripted in advance, they asked, why take preventive actions? For example, when you are ill it is already fated either that you will recover or that you won't. Given that you cannot change the destined outcome, why not save yourself the money and effort of calling the doctor? Chrysippus replied that outcomes are not fated in some absolute way, but are 'co-fated' along with such factors as our own decisions to act or not to act. Understanding how our own decisions and actions are causally related to the overarching network of fate is the key to seeing how individual responsibility is in fact compatible with determinism.

This last idea was developed with an elaborate classification of different kinds of cause. Fate does cause everything that happens, but does so by playing a causal role analogous to giving a drum the initial push that starts it rolling. It is the drum's shape that is primarily responsible for its rolling. Likewise it is our rational self that is primarily responsible for our acts. Fate's causal role is limited to an initial prompt, by means of the 'impressions' (*phantasiai*) of external facts and objects which unavoidably impinge on our consciousness. How we respond, however predictable in the light of our own past history and present character, is 'in our power': the responsibility for it is our own.

Ethics. The ethical system, founded on the twin principles of nature and reason, sets out to be both more authentically naturalist than Epicurus, and more integrally rationalist than Aristotle. It starts, like all ancient ethical systems, from the postulation of an 'end' (*telos*). That this end can be equated with 'happiness' (*eudaimonia*) was common ground, but the specific prescription for what it consists in was a question that divided school from school, and even Stoic from Stoic. Zeno specified it as either 'living in agreement' (*homologoumenōs zēn*) or, more precisely, 'living in agreement with nature'.

The less complete-sounding version has the advantage of emphasizing the importance of internal harmony, and etymologically the word for 'in agreement' has a component of *logos*, 'reason', which conveys that the 'agreement' in question is a rational one. Lack of internal conflict is certainly a vital part of the Stoic conception. But it is important at this stage to stress that there is no question of a conflict, as there was for Plato (above, pp. 121–2), between distinct rational and irrational components of the soul. The soul – or at least its 'directive' part (the *hēgemonikon*), which is the only relevant one for ethics – is entirely rational. Its supposedly 'irrational' states, the 'passions', are at root errors of evaluative judgement, and since they are in origin rationally chosen the appropriate therapy is one which holds the agent culpable for them and seeks not to moderate them (as in the Aristotelian tradition) but to eradicate them altogether. The therapy of the passions is a major focus of Stoic ethics.

The fuller formulation of the end as 'living in agreement with nature' became the object of repeated attempts by Zeno's successors to unpick its meaning. For example, was the 'nature' in question human nature or cosmic nature? Since it was, either way, an essentially rational nature, there was in the last analysis no conflict between the two views, and Chrysippus in fact decided that both kinds of nature were covered. The more substantive question was what it takes for developing human beings to align themselves with rational nature. And in this the Stoics worked out a scheme radically opposed to that of Epicurus (above, p. 161). Where Epicurus had pointed to pleasure and pain-avoidance as the natural aims of the new-born infant, the Stoics recognized the emergence of a very different kind of 'affinity'. *Oikeiōsis*, the Greek name for 'affinity', also variously rendered 'appropriation', 'familiarization', etc., most literally means 'making (something) one's own'. It became a term of art in Stoic and Stoic-influenced ethical theories. Creatures' first natural affinities are for themselves and their own 'constitution', for their survival and development, and for their own offspring. Pleasure may accompany their striving towards these goals, but even when it does not – as when a toddler persists in trying to walk, despite the pain of falling over, in order to develop its own nature – the striving remains unabated. In the case of rational beings such as we are, with maturation the affinities extend beyond ourselves to our family, friends, and fellow-citizens, and, ultimately, the entire community of rational beings, human and divine.

This same process of *oikeiōsis* makes us learn to place values, positive or negative, on environmental items according to their contribution to or obstruction of our natural aims. Somehow, from these primitive choices and avoidances – conformity with nature in a very humble sense – the Stoics invite us to progress to an elevated moral understanding. Very roughly, the progression is viewed as follows. Our natural choices lead us to develop a concept of the 'value' (*axia*) of the things chosen, and to learn the rule-like 'proper functions' (*kathēkonta*) which enhance our success in acting according to nature. As we perform these functions with increasing regularity and consistency, we begin to see that their individual value is altogether outclassed by that of the harmony or 'agreement' (*homologia*, cognate with *homologoumenōs*, 'in agreement') that obtains between them. It is in this harmony we first get a glimpse of 'the good', a term which the Stoics reserve exclusively for its moral use. Only moral virtue – itself understood as a perfected state of the intellect – confers genuine goodness on anything.

Other things conventionally called 'good' and 'bad', such as health and illness, are in reality indifferent, and are therefore reclassified as respectively 'preferred' (*proēgmena*) and 'dispreferred' (*apoproēgmena*). Progression from conventional values, founded on these preferences, to a Stoic ethical outlook, in which the real 'good' eclipses them, is the key to moral enlightenment. A helpful way to see this progression is as one in which a concentration on the *matter* of deliberate choice is supplanted by one on its *form*. The initial objects of choice are items as humble as food, drink and shelter, and what counts is actually obtaining them, for the sake of survival. But the agent's interest becomes increasingly focused on the regularity and rational coherence of the set of choices, and that rational coherence is an object whose attainment can be ensured independently of any matching success in obtaining the external items themselves. For this reason, while conventional 'goods' are often beyond our control, the true 'good', whose attainment amounts to happiness, is invulnerable to fortune.

Things which are conventionally valued, such as wealth and reputation, do not, even if obtained, contribute to happiness. For this reason the Cynics had counselled against pursuing them, and had therefore behaved in ways calculated to outrage civic norms. The Stoic position is subtly different from its Cynic origins. These objects, recommended by nature, *are* worth pursuing. The reason is as sketched above: what matters is not their attainment, but the

rationally conceived pursuit of the things which are naturally preferable. Hence a Stoic sage on the one hand behaves very much like any
conventional citizen, but on the other is driven by an utterly different set of valuations. It does not matter to him at all if the naturally
preferred objects which he seeks do not eventuate. He seeks them
only with a kind of provisionality known as 'reservation' (*hypex-
airesis*), well illustrated by Chrysippus' words (quoted by Epictetus,
Discourses II 6.9):

> As long as the future is uncertain to me I always hold to those things which
> are better adapted to obtaining the things in accordance with nature; for god
> himself has made me disposed to select these. But if I actually knew that I
> was fated now to be ill, I would even have an impulse to be ill. For my foot
> too, if it had intelligence, would have an impulse to get muddy.

This idealized 'sage', the central figure in most Stoic moral theorizing, was a theoretical or semi-mythical construct, since the Stoics
were hard put to it to name any actual person – themselves included –
who had ever become one. Yet only the sage is good and happy, and
even such conventional aspirations as to be free, rich, a king etc.
are in reality (i.e. once these terms are properly understood) attained
only by him. Worse, all we non-sages have the opposite predicates:
we are bad, miserable, slaves, poor etc. And this is just as true even
if we have advanced a long way towards the standard set by the sage.
As the Stoics grimly remark, if you are drowning, you drown just
as effectively whether you are inches from the surface or far below
it. Nevertheless, enormous importance is attached to encouraging
'progress' (*prokopē*) towards sagehood, and vast stretches of Stoic ethical writing were designed to facilitate exactly that. The last word
can be left with Chrysippus (quoted by Stobaeus v 906.18–907.5):

> One who progresses to the furthest point performs all proper functions with-
> out exception and omits none. However, his life is not yet happy. Happiness
> supervenes on it when these intermediate actions acquire the additional
> properties of firmness and tenor and their own particular fixity.

SCEPTICISM AND ITS VARIETIES

The name 'Sceptics' was introduced as an alternative school title
for the neo-Pyrrhonists only after the end of the Hellenistic age.
When, in this chapter, the word and its cognates are spelt without the

initial capital, they function as an informal label generalizing over philosophers and movements with often very different ideas. The two schools in question are the Academics and the Pyrrhonists. We have already early in this chapter encountered Pyrrho, historically the first sceptically inclined philosopher of the age. Our next topic is the sceptical Academy. (The use of the capitalized term, 'Sceptics', for this school, although widespread in modern studies, is seriously misleading.)

Arcesilaus. Plato's own work had manifested an increasing tendency towards systematic doctrine, and following his death in 347 BC his successors in the school he founded, the Academy, continued the process – notably his immediate successor Speusippus and *his* successor Xenocrates. After a very quiet period in the late fourth and early third centuries under the headship of a certain Polemon, the school underwent a revolution in the 260s BC when it elected as its head Arcesilaus. For Arcesilaus' brand of Platonism rested, not on the development of Plato's supposed doctrines, but on a return to the Socratic spirit of his more open-ended dialogues, the ones that typically ended in a failure to find what they were seeking and in the defeat of those interlocutors who thought they could do better. That tendency had recurred in even what is now thought to be a relatively late dialogue by Plato, the *Theaetetus*, where all attempts to define knowledge meet this same fate. Small wonder, then, that Arcesilaus was able to present the systematic renunciation of knowledge as Plato's true legacy.

Arcesilaus' school came to be known as the New Academy (or sometimes, to allow for further subsequent developments, the 'Middle' Academy). For all its Platonic credentials, it was seen as something of a hybrid. The contemporary Stoic Ariston of Chios, in a spoof Homeric line, described Arcesilaus as a philosophical chimaera, 'Plato in front, Pyrrho behind, Diodorus in the middle' – this last being a reference to the virtuoso dialectician Diodorus Cronus (above, pp. 165, 168), perceived as inspiring Arcesilaus' philosophical methods. In addition to these possible influences, Arcesilaus' move is naturally interpreted as a reaction to the arrival on the scene of so highly doctrinal a philosophy as Stoicism. Arcesilaus, who died in 241 BC, was some twenty years younger than Zeno, and is reported to have engaged in extensive debate with both him and his school.

Cicero, himself a follower of the New Academy (see below, pp. 197–203), offers an admirable digest of Arcesilaus' philosophy (*Academica* 1 44–6):

It was with Zeno, so we have heard, that Arcesilaus began his entire struggle, not out of obstinacy or desire for victory – in my opinion at least – but because of the obscurity of the things which had brought Socrates to an admission of ignorance; and before him already Democritus, Anaxagoras, Empedocles, and almost all the ancients, who said that nothing could be grasped or cognized or known, saying that the senses are restricted, the mind weak, the course of life short, and that (to quote Democritus) truth has been submerged in an abyss, with everything in the grip of opinions and conventions, nothing left for truth and everything in turn wrapped in darkness.

So Arcesilaus was in the practice of denying that anything could be known, even the one thing Socrates had left for himself, the knowledge that he knew nothing: such was the extent of the obscurity in which everything lurked, on his assessment, and there was nothing which could be discerned or understood. For these reasons, he said, no one should maintain or assert anything or give it the acceptance of assent, but one should always curb one's rashness and restrain it from every slip; for it would be extraordinary rashness to accept something either false or incognitive, and nothing was more dishonourable than for assent and acceptance to run ahead of cognition and grasp. He used to act consistently with this philosophy, and by arguing against everyone's opinions he drew most people away from their own, so that when reasons of equal weight were found on opposite sides on the same subject the easier course was to withhold assent from either side.

They call this Academy new, though I think it is old if we count Plato as one of the old Academy. In his books nothing is asserted and there is much argument pro and contra, everything is investigated and nothing is stated as certain.

What we have here seen to be Arcesilaus' modification to the position of Socrates, refusing to make firm pronouncements even about *not* knowing anything, represents one of the special concerns of Hellenistic scepticism, namely its own internal consistency.

Arcesilaus' denial of knowledge is worded in a way that reflects his confrontation with Zeno and with the latter's theory of the 'cognitive impression' (above pp. 166–7). The policy of 'withholding assent', technically called *epochē*, is presented in our sources as Arcesilaus' response to (a) Zeno's own advice against ever assenting to non-cognitive impressions, equated with indulging in mere fallible 'opinion', combined with (b) his failure, in debate with Zeno, to learn of any conceivable circumstances in which an impression *could* be cognitive, i.e. self-certifying.

But his scepticism was not just an inter-school debating tactic. We learn that his own didactic practice was to encourage his students to put forward views of their own, then to convince them in debate that an equally strong case could be constructed for the opposing position, while allowing them to defend their side of the debate as best they could. One result was meant to be a reduced trust in anyone's authority, and a greater reliance on the power of argument itself. Despite a certain common ground between the two of them, Arcesilaus' dialectically conducted and intellectually motivated campaign for the withholding of assent, pursued in direct rivalry with leading Athenian schools, stands in strong contract to Pyrrho's predominantly moral recipe for personal happiness in the form of tranquillity.

Carneades. The other towering figure of the New Academy is Carneades, who was school head in the mid second century BC (retired 137, died 129). In 155 it was he who joined the celebrated embassy to Rome (p. 164 above), and he scandalized the Romans when, following a speech in which he praised justice, he returned the next day to deliver a second speech denouncing justice. He wrote nothing (thereby emulating Socrates, Pyrrho and Arcesilaus), but his arguments were voluminously catalogued by his disciple and amanuensis Clitomachus. Even to his own followers his methodology and aims were much less clear and more elusive than those of Arcesilaus had been. Although hailed by Clitomachus as a champion of *epochē*, he sometimes appeared to advocate a form of fallibilism – accepting those impressions which were 'convincing' while acknowledging their fallibility. And where Arcesilaus had combined (a) Zeno's assertion that the sage never assents to non-cognitive impressions with (b) the argument that no impression is cognitive, to generate the conclusion that one should never assent, Carneades instead combined (b) with (c) Zeno's assertion that the sage does assent to some impressions, to produce the quite different conclusion that one should assent to some non-cognitive impressions, i.e. hold mere opinions. To what extent either or both of Arcesilaus and Carneades may have here been arguing in the *ad hominem* mode typical of dialectic we cannot be sure. But both this argument and Carneades' approval of 'convincing' impressions led some of his followers to father on him a fallibilist philosophy which was doctrinal in content (see p. 243 below). And thus it was that, in the hands of Carneades' successors, notably Philo of Larissa (c.161–c.84 BC; see further, chapter 7, p. 198 below), the Academy of the early first century BC retreated from its strongly sceptical stance, incurring from one contemporary critic the description 'Stoics fighting Stoics'.

Neo-Pyrrhonism. That critic was Aenesidemus, who, after Pyrrho, Arcesilaus and Carneades, is the fourth and last outstanding innovator in the history of ancient scepticism. Although his philosophical background and date are a matter of some controversy, there is no doubt that his revival in the first century BC of Pyrrhonism was to a large extent his reaction against the recent dilution of scepticism in the Academy (of which he had probably himself been a member). Aenesidemus proclaimed Pyrrho and his (alleged) line of heirs, including himself, to be the true voice of scepticism.

None of Aenesidemus' works has come down to us, but they constituted an important part of the background to the surviving writings of a later neo-Pyrrhonist, Sextus Empiricus (second century AD). These latter are *Outlines of Pyrrhonism* (abbreviated *PH*), and *Against the Professors* (*Adversus Mathematicos*, abbreviated *Adv. Math.* or *M*). Aenesidemus' most monumental achievement was his Ten Modes (more fully, the Ten Modes of Suspension of Judgement), which he synthesized and organized out of a vast body of material, much of it bequeathed by the tradition. The Modes combine to show why we could never acquire cognitive access to how things are in their own right:

1 Different creatures perceive things differently, and there is no ground for preferring one *species'* impressions to another's.
2 Even if we preferred one species, the human one, different humans perceive things differently, and there is no ground for preferring one *human's* impressions to another's.
3 Even if we preferred one human's impressions, the five senses often conflict with each other, and there is no ground for preferring one *sense* to another.

4 Even if we preferred one sense, the same sense can perceive things differently in different conditions, and there is no ground for preferring one set of *conditions* to another.

5 *Positions, distances etc.* affect how we perceive things.

6 Our impressions are contaminated by *accretions* from the environment or our own body-chemistry.

7 The same objects make different impressions according to their *quantity and arrangement*.

8 All things are, in one way or another, *relative*.

9 Things strike us differently depending on whether they are *familiar* or not.

10 How things appear is often *culturally* determined.

In all these respects a thing may appear in two or more conflicting ways, and, being ourselves in no position to adjudicate the conflict, we are obliged to suspend judgement as to what they are like in themselves. The same result, suspension of judgement, was meant to follow from what we are told were numerous attacks by Aenesidemus on the doctrinal positions put forward in all the main philosophical sub-disciplines. According to Aenesidemus such an acknowledgement of one's own ignorance is the way to 'philosophize according to Pyrrho'; indeed, suspension of judgement in itself is the end, and constitutes happiness. If Aenesidemus, perhaps influenced by Timon's interpretation of Pyrrho, was here offering a more intellectualized and less emotive notion of happiness than on Pyrrho's original model of 'tranquillity', that no doubt reflects his scepticism's immediate background in Academic dialectic.

In this regard at least, the scepticism of Sextus, writing two centuries later, represents to some extent a reversion to Pyrrho, for Sextus presents tranquillity (*ataraxia*) as the end, and *epochē* as no more than the means to it. In a celebrated image, the sceptic (or rather, Sceptic, since this term, literally 'inquirer', was by his day competing with 'Pyrrhonist' as the school's title) is compared by Sextus to the painter Apelles, who, after repeated failures to paint the froth round a horse's nostrils, gave up and hurled his sponge at the painting, thus creating exactly the effect he had been aiming for all along. Likewise the Sceptic is someone who, in the interests of attaining tranquillity, started by trying to resolve all the philosophical disputes that disquieted him; but it was only when he gave up in despair and decided to suspend judgement that he discovered, to his surprise, that he had thereby inadvertently attained his goal, peace of mind.

Beyond such shifts of ethical focus, the Scepticism espoused by Sextus is likely to differ in some methodological aspects from that of Aenesidemus, although the difficult question of the *nature* of such changes cannot be addressed here. Certainly in the intervening two centuries other members of the school developed its methodology, notably Agrippa (of uncertain date), whose Five Modes complement, rather than replace, the Ten Modes of Aenesidemus. They are (1) disagreement (*diaphōnia*), (2) infinite regress, (3) relativity, (4) assumption, and (5) circularity. An example using all but one of these is the following argument of Sextus (*PH* II 19–20), which starts from the existing lack of consensus as to whether there is or is not a criterion of truth:

This *disagreement* they will either pronounce resoluble or irresoluble. If they pronounce it irresoluble, they will admit without further ado that we should suspend judgement. If on the other hand it is resolved, let them say by what criterion it is going to be adjudicated, when we neither have an agreed criterion, nor have any idea whether one exists, but are inquiring into exactly that. Besides, in order that the disagreement that has arisen over the criterion should be resolved, we need to have an agreed criterion through which we will be able to adjudicate it. And in order that we should have an agreed criterion, the disagreement about the criterion needs to be resolved first. In this way the argument falls into the mode of *circularity* and the discovery of the criterion is blocked off. For we do not permit them to select a criterion by *assumption*; and if they want to adjudicate the criterion by a criterion we set them off on an *infinite regress*.

Although his life postdates the Hellenistic age (as probably does Agrippa's), Sextus Empiricus is today the major surviving voice of the late Hellenistic neo-Pyrrhonist movement. In his philosophical critiques, the range of his attacks reflects the state of philosophical debate during the Hellenistic period much more than the philosophical developments of his own era. For instance, he is well informed about early Stoicism, but ignores the so-called Imperial Stoa. He is deeply interested, for obvious reasons, in the successive phases of the 'New Academy', but knows nothing about the movement, contemporary with him, now known as 'Middle Platonism' (see below,

p. 243). And he speaks very little of Aristotle and his school, which, significantly, had had a low profile during the Hellenistic period, seeming to ignore completely the revival of interest in Aristotelianism and the beginnings of the Aristotle commentary tradition, which had been gathering pace since the mid first century BC. It is therefore not unreasonable to treat him, as is commonly done, under the heading of Hellenistic philosophy.

In recent decades Sextus has been increasingly respected as a creative philosopher, working to build Pyrrhonism into a stronger, more coherent and more sophisticated philosophical stance. Particular attention has focused on his answers to two recurrent charges made against Pyrrhonist scepticism: that it is theoretically inconsistent, and that it makes practical life impossible. The Sextan Sceptic on the one hand avoids all *dogma* – a word used to designate not all belief, but any doctrinal view on a disputed issue – and on the other hand non-committally acquiesces in passive 'appearances' (*phainomena*). Whether this is a policy that aims to avoid all belief, and, if it is, whether it succeeds in doing so, are questions that continue to be hotly debated by historians of ancient philosophy.

AFTERWORD

The Hellenistic philosophers were until recent decades seriously undervalued. This attitude was due in part to the content of their teaching – Epicurus, for instance, was seen by some as offering a shocking synthesis of crude materialism, hedonism and crypto-atheism – in part to the popularizing form in which it was often presented. In the case of Stoicism, accidents of survival must take a share of the blame: while the school's ethics was elaborately documented in our Roman sources, the system's more technical details had largely perished with the loss of the early Stoa's writings, and had to be laboriously reassembled. Factors like these combined to give the Hellenistic era a long-standing reputation for one of philosophical decline, overshadowed by the recent glories of Plato and Aristotle.

Much might be said about why and how the Hellenistic philosophers have, since the mid twentieth century, largely recovered the high standing they enjoyed in their own day, attracting renewed interest and respect. This philosophical rehabilitation has worked primarily in favour of Stoicism. Stoic logic has been a major player in the story. After having been despised as pedantic and formal for centuries, particularly during the nineteenth century, it came to be recognized, whether for good or bad reasons, as a worthy forerunner to a range of modern theories in logic, semantics and philosophy of language. In the mid twentieth century, Stoic physics came to be admiringly compared to some anti-mechanistic trends of modern physics. And in more recent decades, Stoic ethics – in particular the theories and practices of the Imperial Stoa – has been revisited in depth, and has even acquired a fashionable currency in some circles.

But this renewal of attention to Stoicism has also derivatively benefited the other Hellenistic schools, and even pre- and post-Hellenistic philosophies. When reading some recent synoptic accounts of ancient philosophy, one might gain a highly Stoicized picture of the Greek philosophical world, stressing for example the intimate interdependence of intellectual theory and spiritual practice. For anyone who continues to recognize ancient philosophy as the best entry-route to the study of philosophy itself, Hellenistic philosophy has a strong claim to be the ideal starting point.[1]

NOTE

1   The initial draft of this chapter was written by David Sedley, using Jacques Brunschwig's existing writings on Hellenistic philosophy as the main basis. It was then adjusted and finalized through extended discussion between the two.

7   Roman philosophy

INTRODUCTION

The title of this chapter would have struck most Romans at the time of Cicero as provocative if not downright inapt. Philosophy had entered Rome as a Greek importation, and those who taught it mainly stemmed from Greece or from still further east of Italy. Romans who wished to study philosophy generally travelled to Athens or to other Greek-speaking centres. Early in the principate of Augustus (27 BC–AD 14), Quintus Sextius founded a school that combined Stoic ethics with such principles of Pythagoreanism as abstention from meat. But, apart from this short-lived and unremarkable sect, there were no exclusively Roman schools of philosophy, as distinct from the long-established Academics, Peripatetics, Epicureans and Stoics. The Cynic movement, which gained Roman adherents in the early Empire, did not count as a formal institution, and it too was originally Greek, looking back to Diogenes whom the Stoics had appropriated along with Socrates. There was no home-grown option of any consequence, and therefore no Roman philosophy as such.

Yet, with the benefit of hindsight, that verdict will hardly stand. On many thinkers from the early Renaissance to the middle of the eighteenth century, the influence of Cicero and Seneca was enormous, outstripping in its general diffusion the impact of even Plato and Aristotle (see further, chapter 12). Montaigne's essays constantly reflect his reading of Seneca's *Moral Letters to Lucilius*. Locke, like many others, drew heavily on Cicero's *On Duties* (*De officiis*) for his political thought. Hume modelled his celebrated *Dialogues Concerning Natural Religion* on Cicero's *On the Nature of the Gods* (*De natura deorum*). Another seminal text, especially for the neo-Epicureans of the seventeenth century, was Lucretius' didactic poem *On the Nature of Things* (*De rerum natura*). These books are a sample of the potent legacy of Rome in philosophy. They owed their striking afterlife to the fact that they were written in accessible Latin and not in Greek.

Prior to Lucretius and Cicero, there had been no philosophical writing of consequence in the Latin vernacular. This explains Lucretius' complaint in his poem about the 'poverty' of the Latin language for rendering the obscure details of Epicurean physics. Cicero, writing a few years later, frequently finds it necessary to coin Latin words for the Greek terms he needs to convey to his readers. Hence we have, as English derivatives from Cicero's Latin, such words as 'quality' (*poiotēs*). The Latin that he and Lucretius inherited was ill-suited to expressing the nuances of philosophical Greek. Yet, thanks to their remarkable initiative, Latin was launched on the way to becoming the superb instrument for scientific discourse that it would be for Copernicus, Galileo, Descartes and Newton. Indeed, a large part of our English philosophical terminology, although ultimately derived from Greek, is most directly taken from classical and mediaeval Latinizations of Greek terms, e.g. 'virtue', 'substance', 'essence', 'element', 'principle', 'matter', 'form', 'potentiality', 'accident', 'efficient cause', 'final cause', etc. (cf. glossary, pp. 373–85, for details of these and others).

What gives substance to this chapter's title includes not only the production of influential works in Latin but also the roles that philosophy played in Roman culture from the late Republic onwards. Although few Romans cultivated and wrote philosophy at a high level, their number is counterbalanced by the many whom it touched and influenced vicariously. The great Augustan poets Horace and Virgil, both of whom had studied philosophy, include Stoic and Epicurean themes in their verse. In the early Imperial period, Stoicism figures strongly in the satires of Persius, Lucan's epic *On the Civil War*, and the astronomical poem of Manilius. Tacitus, Pliny the Younger and Quintilian are eminent writers whose education involved some exposure to philosophy, and that is still more evident in the erudite conversations reported in the *Attic Nights* of Aulus Gellius. Augustus, the first Roman emperor, had already found it politic to have a court philosopher, and two centuries later the Stoic Marcus Aurelius would sit on the imperial throne. From the third century AD the Latin works of Christian apologists such as Tertullian and Lactantius, though officially hostile to pagan philosophy, help to carry the tradition forward. With them and with Augustine, a century later, we reach figures too massive to be surveyed for their own sake in this chapter; but their contributions to Christian theology are also the afterlife of Roman philosophy.

It is difficult to think of a society where members of the upper class were more generally aware of philosophy than seems to have been the case in Imperial Rome. For some of them, indeed, that awareness will have been quite superficial and scarcely positive, but every senator or knight would have known the difference between the values of a Stoic and those of an Epicurean. The novelist Petronius makes the point amusingly when his comic freedman character Trimalchio tells the guests at his gargantuan dinner-party that his epitaph is to say: 'He left 30 million sesterces and never listened to a philosopher' (*Satiricon* 71.12).

Two hundred years earlier, philosophers in Rome had been viewed by the authorities as a disturbing novelty. When the Academic Carneades had visited the city in 155 BC as an ambassador and made a big splash with public lectures arguing for and against natural justice (above p. 178), the Elder Cato had persuaded the Senate to send him and two other philosopher ambassadors on their way before they had time to subvert the youth of Rome. How do we account for the change from suspicion of philosophy to its diffusion among many of the Roman elite?

Any answer to this question must allow for the special interests of individuals, but among the generic factors the following are especially important: access to Greek philosophers in and outside Italy; availability of Greek philosophical texts; requirements of higher education in the areas of rhetoric and grammar; the poverty of Roman religion as a context for ethics and spirituality; and above all perhaps, the civil wars that brought the Republican era to an end, leaving the Senate a rubber stamp of imperial autocracy rather than a satisfying arena for intellectual debate and self-definition. A brief review of all these factors is in order before we turn to a survey of the principal contributors and trends.

Starting with the Stoic Panaetius in the later years of the second century BC, eminent Greek philosophers spent time in Rome. During Cicero's youth these included the Academics Philo and Antiochus and the Stoic Posidonius. Cicero and the Younger Cato each gave permanent housing to a Stoic philosopher. Cicero, Atticus, Varro, Brutus and Horace studied in Athens with philosophers who included Cratippus, the leading Peripatetic of the time. In the middle years of the first century BC the Epicurean Philodemus, under the patronage of Calpurnius Piso, taught in the Naples area, as did another Epicurean, Siro, who numbered Virgil and probably Horace among his students. The table of names, incomplete though it is, shows how many of the most intellectually able Romans were taking advantage of a philosophical training.

Major Roman philosophical writers

name	biographical	allegiance	main surviving writings of philosophical import
Lucretius	unknown; c.95–50 BC	Epicurean	On the Nature of Things = De rerum natura (DRN) (didactic poem)
Cicero (full name Marcus Tullius Cicero)	Roman orator and statesman; 106–43 BC	Academic	Republic = De republica Laws = De legibus Stoic Paradoxes = Paradoxa Stoicorum Academica (Ac.; Book I sometimes called Varro, Book II Lucullus) On Ends = De finibus bonorum et malorum Tusculan Disputations = Tusculanae disputationes On the Nature of the Gods = De natura deorum (ND, DND) Timaeus (incomplete Latin trans. of Plato's dialogue) On Old Age = Cato maior, de senectute On Divination = De divinatione On Fate = De fato

(cont.)

(*cont.*)

name	biographical	allegiance	main surviving writings of philosophical import
			Topics = Topica *On Friendship = Laelius,* *de amicitia* *On Duties = De officiis*
Varro	Scholar, 116–27 BC	Antiochean	*On the Latin Language =* *De lingua Latina*

Seneca (the younger)	Roman statesman and scholar;
	C.AD 1–65
		Stoic	Consolations
			  (various)
			On Anger = De ira
			On the Shortness of
			  Life = De brevitate
			  vitae
			On Steadfastness = De
			  constantia sapientis
			On Tranquillity = De
			  tranquillitate animi
			Pumpkinification of the
			  Divine Claudius =
			  Apocolocyntosis
			On Providence = De
			  providentia
			On Mercy = De clementia
			On the Happy Life = De
			  vita beata
			On Leisure = De otio
			On Favours = De
			  beneficiis
			Natural Questions =
			  Naturales quaestiones
			Moral Letters to
			  Lucilius = Ad Lucilium
			  epistulae morales

Musonius Rufus	Roman knight and teacher; born C.AD 20	Stoic	*Discourses* (in Greek)

name	biographical	allegiance	main surviving writings of philosophical import
Cornutus	Teacher of philosophy and rhetoric; born c.AD 20	Stoic	*Compendium of Greek Theology* (in Greek)
Epictetus	Slave at Rome; after emancipation, taught at Nicopolis in Greece; c.AD 55–135	Stoic	*Discourses = Dissertationes* (in Greek) *Handbook = Enchiridion* (in Greek)
Marcus Aurelius	AD 121–80; Roman emperor 161–80	Stoic	*Meditations* (in Greek)
Apuleius	Orator, philosopher and novelist (*The Golden Ass*); born c.AD 125	Platonist	*On Plato and his Doctrine = De Platone et eius doctrina* *On the God of Socrates = De deo Socratis* *On Interpretation = De interpretatione*
Tertullian	Cleric and theologian; born c.AD 160	Christian	*On the Soul = De anima*
Lactantius	Rhetorician and Christian apologist; c.AD 240–320	Christian	*On God's Creation = De opificio Dei* *Divine Institutes = Divinae institutiones* *On the Anger of God = De vitae Dei*
Calcidius	unknown; fourth century AD	Platonist; possibly Christian	commentary on Plato's *Timaeus*

(cont.)

(cont.)

name	biographical	allegiance	main surviving writings of philosophical import
Marius Victorinus	fourth century AD	Platonist and Christian	commentary on Cicero's rhetoric
Augustine	Bishop and theologian; AD 354–430	Christian	*Against the Academics = Contra Academicos* *On Dialectic = De dialectica* *On Free Will = De libero arbitrio voluntatis* *On the Teacher = De magistro* *Confessions = Confessiones* *City of God = De civitate Dei*
Macrobius	Unknown; fifth century AD	Platonist	commentary on Cicero, *Scipio's Dream*
Martianus Capella	Roman administrator; fifth century AD	Platonist	*The Marriage of Philology and Mercury = De nuptiis Philologiae et Mercurii*
Boethius	Roman administrator; AD 480–524	Christian and Platonist	commentaries on Porphyry's *Isagoge*, on Aristotle's *Categories*, on Aristotle's *De interpretatione*, on Aristotle's *Prior Analytics*, and on Cicero's *Topics* *On Hypothetical Syllogisms = De hypotheticis syllogismis* *On Division = De divisione*

name	biographical	allegiance	main surviving writings of philosophical import
			On the Categorical Syllogism = *De syllogismo categorico* *Introduction to Categorical Syllogisms* = *Introductio ad syllogismos categoricos* *Consolation of Philosophy* = *De consolatione philosophiae*

Note. This chart includes, in addition to the main Roman pagan philosophers, a few major Christian writers who consciously wrote in the (mainly Ciceronian) tradition of Latin philosophy. The variant Latin and English titles listed are not meant to be exhaustive, but sufficient to enable readers to recognize both full and abbreviated references to works. Works are all in Latin except where Greek is indicated. They are listed in chronological order so far as this can be established.

The philosophical curriculum was divided into the three fields of physics (inquiry into the nature of the world), ethics, and logic, the last of which included language, grammar, and rhetoric. Philosophy, as famously construed by Plato, was antithetical to merely persuasive speech, and throughout antiquity rhetoricians were sharply distinguished from philosophers. But rhetoric was too deeply entrenched in Greco-Roman culture for philosophical teachers to ignore, while rhetoricians needed the training in argument that philosophers were excellently equipped to provide. Cicero's Academic teacher Philo was especially renowned for his work in rhetorical theory. As a budding jurist, Cicero, like other ambitious Romans, had strongly practical as well as theoretical motivations for studying techniques of *pro* and *contra* argumentation under such a teacher.

Besides rhetoric, there was a need for training in grammar. Basic grammar was a subject for elementary instruction, but at a higher level it had been the object of notable research by Stoic philosophers, whose work was being carried forward by specialist grammarians. In this sphere, as with rhetoric, Greek philosophy infiltrated higher education. Varro's most famous work was his study of the Latin language, and in composing this great series of books, although himself a follower of Antiochus rather than a Stoic, he was strongly influenced, like all later grammarians, by Stoic phonology and classification of the parts of speech.

Cicero recognizes the difference between philosophy and rhetoric, but he constantly insists on the desirability of combining them, to the mutual advantage of each. That theme, which is one of his distinctive contributions, strongly influences his manner of writing philosophy. What applies to Cicero is also pertinent to Roman philosophy more generally. Seneca's writings and even the *Meditations* of Marcus Aurelius (composed in Greek) are highly rhetorical, sententious, and artfully constructed. These writers could hardly have insulated their composition of philosophy from their rhetorical training, but their liking for striking discourse, as distinct from unimpassioned and technical prose, is also symptomatic of another feature of Roman philosophy – its strongly ethical and practical tenor.

Whether we take Lucretius at the beginning of our period or the Christian Boethius at the end, philosophy composed in Latin and philosophy written by Romans in Greek tend to be urgent in tone and therapeutic in desired effect. These tendencies, which presuppose the *per se* value of philosophy, are not Roman in origin. Its promise to cure mental ailments and re-orient values goes right back to Socrates and Plato. But that goal had been given particular emphasis by Stoics and Epicureans, who offered their systems as comprehensive philosophies of life; these two schools were the liveliest and most influential during the later Roman Republic and early Empire. Elaborate theory, of course, was the underpinning of both systems. That was fully understood and well reflected by the leading Romans who wrote about them. But they were living at a time when all philosophy, as taught by Greeks, was characterized by school allegiance and authority rather than conceptual innovation or purely open-ended inquiry. The big developments in philosophy, associated with the emergence of Neoplatonism and Aristotelian commentary (chapter 9 below), postdate the figures we primarily think of as Roman philosophers. They are creative chiefly in the way they write about their Greek inheritance, in what they select from it, and in the educational mantle they assume.

Lucretius, at the beginning of his poem, looks to Epicureanism as the antidote to the strife and competition that were wrecking the Roman Republic. Cicero in the *De officiis* turns to Stoicism for the moral re-armament he thinks the state needs in the aftermath of the civil wars. Two years earlier in 46 BC, Cato, the most famous Roman Stoic of this period, had committed suicide rather than submit to the Caesarians against whom he had resolutely fought. These troubled times, which are reflected in the poems of Virgil and Horace, were a significant influence on the Roman turn to philosophy. As long as the main fabric of the Republic was intact, leading Romans had chiefly defined themselves by reference to family tradition and the renown that civic and military service could promote. With the state in complete disarray and no ethical or emotional support to be derived from official religion, we begin to find a more reflective and ascetic mentality, that would become still more prominent in the Empire.

What I have just described is a set of conditions conducive to philosophy at Rome rather than an impossibly tidy characterization of Roman philosophers as such. Yet, the conditions and the characterization are sufficiently close to facilitate a broad sense of what was Roman about Roman philosophy. In contrast with their Greek mentors and school authorities, the Romans I have been mentioning were not professional teachers. By a further contrast, with the possible exception of Lucretius, they all came from the upper echelons of society. Three of them, Cicero, Seneca and Marcus Aurelius, had remarkable political careers, and the retirement that gave Cicero and Seneca the opportunity to concentrate full-time on philosophy was forced upon them. The political activism and experience of these men add a significant dimension to their philosophical works, not only where they discuss society directly but also in their allusions to Roman events or persons and in their refraction of Stoic or other philosophical concepts through an explicitly Roman lens.

Cicero wanted his burst of philosophical work at the end of his life to be construed as a patriotic service. By presenting the doctrines of the Greek schools in a series of Latin books, he gave his countrymen a cornucopia of philosophical literature that they had previously lacked. Lucretius dedicated his poem to Gaius Memmius, a politically active nobleman. Seneca, though less overtly political than Cicero, wrote the *On Mercy* for Nero as advice to the young emperor at the beginning of his reign. Whether discussing anger or tranquillity or instructing Lucilius in the *Moral Letters*, Seneca also presents himself as a severe critic of Roman luxury, cruelty and moral decline. Marcus Aurelius probably wrote his *Meditations* simply for himself, but while being a totally committed Stoic he cannot fail to make us also think of Plato's ideal of a philosopher ruler (pp. 111–12 above).

Having reviewed a broad context for Roman philosophy, we can now look more closely at the leading figures and their distinctive contributions, focusing on the four writers whose work I have already emphasized – Lucretius, Cicero, Seneca and Marcus Aurelius. Each of these is too idiosyncratic to provide material for any linear history of Roman philosophy; yet that fact itself tells us a lot about what Romans made of their Greek philosophical inheritance.

LUCRETIUS

The *De rerum natura* is an astonishing work. As a poetic rendering of Epicurus' philosophy, it seems to spring out of nowhere. Lucretius was writing just at the time when an Epicurean school was flourishing at Herculaneum under the leadership of Philodemus, but he shows no clear trace of that teacher's influence. He bases his exposition on the master-work of Epicurus himself – his thirty-seven books *On Nature*. Yet, rather than imitate Epicurus' dry prose, Lucretius transforms his doctrines into a hexameter poem, modelled on the philosophical verse of Empedocles, which rivals Virgil's *Aeneid* in scale and literary genius.

If Lucretius had been Greek, his synthesis of Empedocles and Epicurus would be quite strange, but in his Roman time and place it was an inspired decision. He opts for the medium of verse as (in his own famous image) honey placed on the rim of a cup of bitter medicine, and in typically Roman fashion he adopts an illustrious Greek literary model. Virgil in the next generation boldly presents himself as the Roman Homer, while Cicero no less boldly apes Plato by calling his first philosophical works *Republic* and *Laws*. Epicurus was not an illustrious literary name, but Empedocles had achieved that status through his cosmological poem, also entitled *On Nature*. Around the time of Lucretius Empedocles had already been adapted into Latin, as we learn from Cicero, who contrasts Sallustius' *Empedoclea* unfavourably with the brilliance of Lucretius' poem.

We today credit Lucretius with a philosophical intelligence that no other Roman, including Cicero or Seneca, surpassed. In Rome itself, however, his choice of genre labelled him a poet rather than a philosopher. This explains the otherwise remarkable omission of Lucretius' name from all of Cicero's philosophical corpus.

Because Epicurus' original work is today extremely fragmentary, the *De rerum natura* is often our fullest source for the founder's thought. Lucretius includes fundamental topics such as the atomic 'swerve', the evolution of society, and the anthropology of religion about which we learn nothing from Epicurus himself. No detail is too recondite for Lucretius to reproduce and elaborate. He is amazingly resourceful in his efforts to turn Epicurus' technical Greek into elegant Latin. His arguments generally have a logical structure even when, as so often, he embellishes them with striking images, wordplay and other poetic devices. Like all Epicureans, he looks back to Epicurus as his unique authority; he has no interest in doctrinal innovation or substantive deviation from the texts he takes to be canonical. Yet, while Lucretius has rightly been called a 'fundamentalist' Epicurean, his work is immensely creative not only in its poetic form but also in its rhetorical and emotional power and social relevance.

Epicurus had elaborated his atomistic cosmology as the only effective antidote to fear of divine control and fear of death. He had also developed theories about cognition, mental experience, values, and social practices, tracing failure to live contentedly to false beliefs about nature and the cultivation of unnecessary desires. All of this is in Lucretius, but he deals most expansively with Epicurean physical theory and psychology, especially the mortality of the soul. He presents these doctrines, in true Epicurean fashion, as the foundation of the philosophy's liberating prescription for an untroubled life. But in regularly personifying 'nature' as a wondrous creative agent, Lucretius uses metaphors that could lead the unwary to think he has abandoned the austerely mechanistic physics of Epicurus himself.

Rather than expound the technicalities of Epicurean ethics, he tends to confine his explicitly moral teaching to the prefaces and conclusions of his six books. These sections include his most powerful poetry and rhetoric, and they are also the most clearly original parts of his work. There we find his indictment of religious superstition, exemplified by Agamemnon's brutal sacrifice of Iphigeneia;

his contrast between Epicurean tranquillity and the competitive rat-race emblematic of Roman society; his eulogy of Epicurus as the unique saviour of mankind; his lengthy satire of persons who cling to life from irrational fear of death; his mordant disquisition on sexual desire; his ridicule of mythology; and his horrific portrait, drawn from Thucydides, of those who died in the Athenian plague at the beginning of the Peloponnesian War. The last of these passages, which is an extraordinary way to conclude the poem, makes it plausible to suppose that Lucretius has not left his work completely as he intended; and there are other reasons for thinking that the poem lacks final revision.

To what extent, apart from his virtuoso use of Latin, has Lucretius Romanized his Epicurean source? The places and proper names he mentions are largely Greek, and in such contexts he peppers his verse with Greek words, honouring the culture of Epicurus. He leaves his readers in no doubt that the author of their salvation, like philosophy itself, is Greek through and through. But Lucretius does incorporate Rome, not only in the opening of his poem, with its invocation of Venus, 'mother of Aeneas and his race', and the prayer for her to turn Mars away from civil war, but also in allusions to Scipio, the conqueror of Carthage, and to Ennius, a great poetic predecessor. Epicurus along with his intellectual and philanthropic eminence is also presented as the ideal Roman father, supplying in his pages 'paternal precepts'. Lucretius makes fear of death the principal cause of 'greed, and the blind passion for honours, which compel unhappy men to transgress the limits of law... and with exceeding effort to climb the pinnacle of power' (III 59–63). He charges social and political competitiveness, so antithetical to the Epicurean ideal, with responsibility for Rome's current disasters.

The quietism that Lucretius advocated could not sit well with most members of the Roman elite. They had been raised on an ideology that placed a premium on military achievement and political renown. Lucretius' poem, however, coming at the collapse of the Roman Republic, was a remarkable challenge to traditional Roman values. Cicero, though he admired Lucretius, had no sympathy for Epicureanism. Yet, both men shared the belief that philosophy of some kind was necessary to explain and alleviate the predicament of Roman politics.

CICERO

For many reasons Cicero has to be the central figure of this chapter. His voluminous philosophical writings range over most of the topics and thinkers that were talking points during the period when he wrote. He was acquainted, as we have seen, with leading Greek philosophers, and many of his Roman friends shared his philosophical interests. If he had been a professional teacher or scholar, his actual output would be thoroughly notable. In fact, although his interest in philosophy was constant, he devoted only a few years of his remarkably energetic life to full-time study and composition. Legal work and politics largely occupied his time except for the two years of Caesar's dictatorship when he was in retirement. In that short period (46–44 BC), Cicero wrote well over thirty books. The series began with *Hortensius*, a dialogue so eloquently recommending the study of philosophy that it inspired Augustine to turn to the New Testament as the source of wisdom. The *Hortensius* survives only in a few quotations, but we still possess the complete text of most of Cicero's philosophical works. These include topically organized surveys of the philosophical schools of his day, works of rhetorical theory, essays on old age and on friendship, partial translations of two Platonic dialogues, and finally his most influential work *On Duties* (*De officiis*). While he was completing this last set of books, he was also returning to the political arena, with the series of Philippic orations directed against Marc Antony.

Cicero's status as a world-historical figure owes much to his extraordinary combination of rhetoric, politics, and philosophy. While his contributions to philosophy are our subject here, even a summary assessment of them needs to be prefaced by recognizing that Cicero never detaches himself from his identity as an exceptionally accomplished orator and participant in the Roman public arena. Over the last five hundred years his reputation as a thinker has fluctuated hugely. It reached its highest point during the Renaissance and Enlightenment. More recently, however, Cicero has frequently been regarded as an edifying windbag, technically deficient and valuable largely as a source for the lost works of Hellenistic philosophy. Now, after years of neglect and depreciation, his philosophical writings are again being studied intensely. His achievement has begun to be recognized in terms of the criteria appropriate to his Roman time and place. Although he makes no claim to be a thinker with a fresh set of theories or methodologies, his philosophical output is creative in numerous ways, and it is marked throughout by his powerful personality.

In what follows I shall comment first on Cicero's philosophical allegiances and priorities; next, I shall survey the projects he undertook as a Roman author of philosophy; finally, I shall offer a brief assessment of his philosophical achievement.

Philosophical allegiances and priorities. As we have seen, Cicero in his youth had first-hand acquaintance with leading philosophers. He possessed a fine library, which probably contained the whole Platonic corpus and representative texts of other schools, including some of Aristotle's lost dialogues. Although he knew little of Aristotle's technical writings, which were returning to circulation only at the end of his life, he frequently invokes Aristotle, especially as a model for the *pro* and *contra* methodology that he himself advocates as constituting the basic affinity between rhetoric and philosophical argument. He must have drawn heavily on previously published Greek works for his accounts of Stoicism, Epicureanism and Academic philosophy, but the *De officiis* is unique in the explicitly stated dependence of its first two books on a work by the Stoic Panaetius.

Cicero constantly praises Plato as the pre-eminent philosopher, and registers this allegiance by calling himself an Academic. With this label, however, Cicero also aligns himself with the tradition of scepticism that had marked the Academy from Arcesilaus down to Philo of Larissa (pp. 176–9 above). His own *Academica* is our best source for this complex phase of the Academy's history. From it we learn that Cicero, as a young man, became a Philonian sceptic: that is to say, someone who, while disclaiming any access to objective certainty practises *pro* and *contra* argumentation with a view to arriving at verisimilitude or approximation to truth. This procedure is evident in many of the works Cicero wrote at the end of his life, but not in all of them and not in his earlier *Republic* (*De republica*) and *Laws* (*De legibus*). How do we explain the discrepancy?

The notion of Plato as a rigorous sceptic was always one-sided. Cicero's other Academic teacher Antiochus rejected it completely (chapter 9, p. 243 below). In direct opposition to Philo, he renounced scepticism in favour of the Stoic theory of knowledge. More notably and influentially, he interpreted Plato, and the Peripatetics too, as offering a unitary philosophy that had largely been incorporated into Stoicism. Such a claim, though also one-sided, was far from being the woolly eclecticism historians have often judged it to be. If we adopt a large perspective for reviewing Epicureanism, scepticism and Stoicism, and then ask about their relationship to Plato and Aristotle, we are bound to find Stoicism far and away the closest congener; and so far as Plato is concerned, his cosmology, theology, ethics and political theory actually were prime influences on the Stoic tradition.

Cicero does not espouse Antiochus' Stoic epistemology. But this other Academic, more moderate than the Stoics in his ethics, was probably the strongest contemporary influence on Cicero's moral thought. His Philonian scepticism is entirely compatible with choosing theories that, on examination, he finds the most plausible or probable. This dual allegiance to Philo and, with qualification, to Antiochus, is a highly intelligent interpretation of the Academic tradition. It allows Cicero to draw heavily on Plato and Stoicism, in advocating positions he strongly supports, while preserving an exploratory rather than dogmatic style, and reserving the right to criticize Stoics and even Plato on occasion.

Although Cicero's scepticism is more than a literary ploy, its significance for his philosophical mentality should not be over-emphasized. Outside the *Academica* neither he nor his spokesmen are concerned with questions of epistemology. He offers us many contexts where he or those who seem to speak for him affirm strong beliefs in such doctrines as the immortality of the soul, divine providence, natural justice, and the divinity of human reason. His position on all these points is unequivocally opposed to Epicureanism. Cicero is sometimes called a Stoic, and while that description is officially incorrect it is to Stoicism that he turns for the *De officiis*. In other works too, especially *On Friendship* and *On Old Age*, the Stoic ethical imprint is unmistakable, as is also the case with the doctrine of natural law in *Laws*.

With or without the mediation of Antiochus, Cicero's temperament and political commitments turned him strongly against Epicureanism. He disliked the rigidity and technical refinements of Stoicism, but he strongly approved that philosophy's focus upon rationality, social obligation and control of the passions. These cardinal features of Stoicism chimed well with his nostalgia for the Roman rectitude he found largely absent from his own times. All in all, it is perhaps best to call Cicero a Platonist. Not only does that fit his hybrid support for Philo and Antiochus; it also acknowledges his constant evocations of Plato, and his close reading and translations of that great predecessor.

Philosophical works. Cicero began to write philosophy only in the last decade of his life. His political career seemed to be largely over, but he had been so involved in public life that when he turned to large-scale composition politics was his obvious first choice as subject. In the *De republica* and the *De legibus*, modelling his dialogue style and his titles on the largest of Plato's works, he set down his reflections on government and announced himself as the Roman Plato. Notwithstanding this acknowledgement and specifically Platonic injections, Cicero's two works are Roman through and through.

In the *De republica*, the main spokesman is the great soldier and statesman Scipio Africanus. Criticizing Plato's utopianism, Scipio favours a mixed constitution, with an elected meritocracy and a judicial system that emphasizes the equality of all in law. In effect, Cicero is defending the mature Roman constitution. Rather than design an ideal state, Cicero emphasizes pragmatism and the value of checks and balances established over a long period of trial and error, as reflected in Rome's early struggles and eventual success. Questions are raised concerning the naturalness and necessity of justice for a successful community. The work is too fragmentary to show how these were settled, but we can assume from what Cicero writes elsewhere that the argument for a universal and natural law prevailed.

That theme is developed, with the help of Stoicism, in the *De legibus*. There, Cicero makes himself the main speaker. He describes law as:

the highest reason, situated in nature, which commands what ought to be done and forbids the opposite. The very same reason, when it has been established and perfected in the human mind, is law.   (1 18)

Connections are then drawn between perfected reason, wisdom, natural justice and the divinely directed commonwealth of gods and humans. (We can be certain that Cicero fully subscribed to this Stoic system of ideas because he returns to it elsewhere, especially in his political testament, the *De officiis*.)

In comparison with Plato or Aristotle, these two Ciceronian works
are lightweight on theory. What chiefly gives them substance is their
wealth of historical examples. As modern readers, we probably find
Cicero's efforts to validate his political and legal ideals by reference
to the paradigm of Rome misguided, but this patriotism is essential
to his conception of his role as a pioneer Roman philosopher.

He adopted that role most insistently in the last two years of his
life. His motivations were in large part personal, but there is no reason to doubt his sincerity when he writes:

Philosophy [at Rome] has lain dormant up to now, lacking any illumination
in Latin. If I, when I was busy, have been of some service to my fellow
citizens, I should also, in my leisure, try to help them by casting light on
philosophy and advocating it.   (*Tusculan Disputations* I 5)

He goes on to remark that such Latin works as are available are
shoddily and incompetently written. What Roman philosophy needs,
in other words, is an author with Cicero's eloquence and expertise.
He formed and executed the plan of composing a series of books
that would not only defend his allegiance to Academic scepticism
(*Academica*) but also survey the competing theories in ethics (*On
Ends* (*De finibus*)) and theology (*On the Nature of the Gods* (*De
natura deorum*)). He supplemented this ambitious agenda by writing
on divination and on fate, and by advocating the therapeutic value
of philosophy (*Tusculan Disputations*). Within the same period he
also wrote shorter works on oratory and the moralizing dialogues on
friendship and old age.

These works did not cover every topic of contemporary philosophy because logic and cosmology are treated only sporadically. But
they provide us, as they provided Cicero's Roman readers, with a
remarkably full account of the subject we call Hellenistic philosophy. We are almost entirely dependent on him for our knowledge of
Philo and Antiochus. His treatment of Stoic ethics is fundamental.
We need Cicero much less for Epicureanism, but his bias against that
philosophy is an important historical counterweight to the eulogies
of Lucretius.

Cicero's final essay in philosophy, the *De officiis*, falls outside his
encyclopaedic agenda. Addressed to his son, the work is not a dialogue but a study of the conduct and moral dispositions incumbent
on the Roman citizen Cicero hopes that his son will strive to be.
Although Cicero draws his main theory from the Stoic Panaetius, he

devotes his third book to a question that Panaetius (he tells us) omitted: 'Can moral excellence conflict with expediency?' In arguing that it cannot, Cicero aligns himself with the Platonic and Stoic tradition, but his numerous allusions to his own career and his constant attacks on Romans (notably Caesar) who have ruined the Republic make this work his most personal and passionate contribution to philosophy. By grounding traditional Roman values in Stoic theory, and by also invoking history and his own experience, Cicero offers a moral and political philosophy in this work that is essentially Roman.

Philosophical achievement. The works I have outlined, though hardly original in philosophical theory, are much more than a survey of second-hand doctrines. With their cast of characters and carefully chosen settings, Cicero's dialogues seek to be models of urbane discussion. In this imitation of Plato, he obviously falls short; but he succeeds as well or better than his own imitators Berkeley and Hume. In particular, he conveys the sense that philosophical talk is what matters, as distinct from the dry rehearsal of doctrines we find in the Greek doxographical literature. He Romanized philosophy not only by the material he disseminated in Latin and his constant allusions to Roman history and literature, but also by exhibiting debates between Roman participants. His own persona can vary between open-minded inquirer and utterly committed exponent of what he takes to be moral and political certainties. If we find that variety a blemish, we shall have to charge Plato with the same fault.

Because we frequently read Cicero simply as a source of information on other philosophers, it is tempting to castigate him for his omissions and to complain about his fulsome style and non-philosophical digressions. Such criticism requires Cicero to be someone who suits modern interests rather than the remarkable Roman intellectual that he was.

When no more than nineteen or twenty years old, he wrote the work on rhetoric called *De inventione*. At the end of his life he dismissed it as a crude piece of juvenilia, and it is rarely mentioned today. In fact, it is a precocious work, showing Cicero's capacity in basic logic, which was an integral part of rhetorical theory. In his introduction the young Cicero states the position, maintained throughout his life, that underwrites his complex career as statesman, orator

and philosopher. It will serve better than anything else as a concluding comment.

After long reflection, reason itself has led me to the following conviction
above all: philosophy without eloquence is of little help to communities,
but eloquence without philosophy is generally harmful. Therefore if anyone, neglecting reason and duty, which are the most correct and honourable
pursuits, devotes himself to a rhetorical training, he grows into something
useless to himself and damaging to his country. He, on the other hand, who
arms himself with eloquence, not to attack his country's interests but to
fight for them, will be in my opinion a man most useful both to his own and
to public concerns and a most loyal citizen.

SENECA

Cicero's youthful comments provide an intriguing, though shaky,
bridge between his Roman philosophy and Seneca's. Both men were
masters of eloquence, became consuls, and influenced public policy. But the hundred years that separate their births saw Roman
government change from senatorial rotation of offices to imperial
autocracy. A Ciceronian career in politics was not open to Seneca,
but it would hardly have suited his more reclusive temperament.
Though his father was a famous rhetorician, the young Seneca preferred philosophy, under the guidance of teachers who gave him his
life-long allegiance to Stoicism. It was only at the age of fifty that
Seneca became a public figure, first as tutor to Nero and then as
the young emperor's political adviser. In AD 62, when Seneca retired
from imperial duties, he began writing the *Moral Letters to Lucilius*,
his greatest work. Three years later Nero forced him to commit
suicide.

By comparison with Cicero, Seneca's philosophical contributions
are much narrower in scope but they are correspondingly more sustained. The two authors also differ strongly in methodology and
style. Even within the *Natural Questions* – his lengthy investigation of such phenomena as comets, winds and earthquakes – Seneca,
like Lucretius, incorporates moralizing prefaces and conclusions.
Throughout he writes as someone completely committed to the
main principles of Stoicism in ethics, cosmology and theology. He
allows himself the right to criticize certain Stoic doctrines, and
to adjudicate between Stoics with different views. He also draws

positively on ethical maxims of Epicurus and on Platonic theology. When dealing with a controversial topic, such as the circumstantial propriety of anger, he may present both sides of the question before refuting the anti-Stoic position. If a recondite doctrine interests him, he has the conceptual and linguistic resources to explore it rigorously. But the main purpose of his philosophical writings is the creative application of a Stoic framework to the practical concerns of his addressees and himself.

Seneca had a powerful mind. Would his natural bent for philosophy have generated more varied work if he had been Cicero's contemporary? While the question is scarcely answerable, the two men's philosophical background as well as their temperaments and political contexts differed sharply. Cicero was deeply shaped by his Academic teachers, but for Seneca the Academy is no longer a live option. Unaware of the current revival of scepticism, under the name of Pyrrho (pp. 179–82 above), he sees no need to justify the truths of Stoicism. All the contemporary philosophers who directly influenced him were Stoics or Cynics. Through reading he was obviously aware of a wider body of philosophical literature, but in the circles where he moved Stoicism had become the dominant philosophy, as it was not for Cicero.

In the writings of Seneca, Stoicism is internalized in ways that make his presentation of that philosophy quite different from Cicero's and anticipatory of Marcus Aurelius' introverted *Meditations*. Even in the *Tusculan Disputations*, where Cicero's treatment of mental malaise most closely foreshadows Seneca, the author remains rather detached from his material. Cicero does not give the impression that he is anxious about his own moral progress. In Seneca, by contrast, Stoic philosophy becomes a constant, monitoring voice.

Every day I plead my case in the presence of myself. . . . I scrutinize my entire day, and I go over my acts and my words. I hide nothing from myself, I omit nothing.

Why should I be afraid of my mistakes, when I can say: 'See that you don't do that again. I pardon you this time. In that discussion you spoke too fiercely. Next time don't consort with inexperienced people. . . . You admonished that person more candidly than you should have done; and so you annoyed him instead of correcting him.'   (*On Anger* III 36.3–4)

Stoicism underscored this 'care of the self', as Michel Foucault has well called it, by a series of doctrines that are central to Seneca's interests. They include the ideal of the perfectly rational sage; the concept of progress towards that strenuous ideal; the analysis of passions as correctable errors of judgement; the 'indifference' of external contingencies for a person's genuine well-being; and intentions, not outcomes, as the only proper object of moral appraisal. All these doctrines were taken to be mandated by the divinity whose omnipresent providence is supremely manifested in giving rationality and potential excellence to persons. What Seneca chiefly does for Stoicism is to give life to these ideas by applying them to his own or other people's every-day experience and by furnishing them with his brilliant rhetorical skills.

The centrality of this applied Stoicism for Seneca's philosophy can be recognized from a review of the titles of his so-called 'dialogues' – works we would call essays because they rarely involve different speakers. Besides control of anger, their themes cover providence, firmness of character, happiness, tranquillity and the shortness of life. Seneca also wrote three 'consolations', two addressed to persons who had suffered bereavement, and the third to his mother during his own youthful exile. More than any other writer, Seneca is responsible for our use of the word 'philosophical' to signify a resolute and unimpassioned response to life's vicissitudes.

His dialogues also include works that deal directly with the Roman social and political context. Like Cicero, he defends his absorption in philosophy against the charge that the leisure it involves is incompatible with patriotism. In retirement from Nero's court, as Seneca probably was when he wrote *On Leisure* (*De otio*), he insists that he can still serve humanity in general by his inquiries into ethics and cosmology. Roman society was largely held together by an ideology of reciprocity. In *On Favours* (*De beneficiis*) Seneca explores the exchange of gifts and favours at great length, offering a subtle exploration of questions concerning the true nature and value of benefits and the criteria for determining gratitude.

A consistent theme throughout his work is disgust at cruelty. Gladiatorial contests, the slaughter of animals at the games, and horrific punishments inspire some of his most powerful rhetoric. In *On Mercy* (*De clementia*), addressed to Nero at the start of his reign, Seneca urges the young emperor to regard mercy as a ruler's pre-eminent virtue, while treating pity (which the Stoics officially regarded as a mental ailment) and severity as equally reprehensible. This work, as the prototype of 'advice to princes' literature, helps to explain Seneca's popularity during the Renaissance (pp. 336–7 below).

Seneca turned to epistolography as the genre for his best and latest work in philosophy. In 124 letters, ranging in length from one to as many as twenty pages, he addresses Gaius Lucilius, a friend with the rank of knight, and an administrator of various Roman provinces. The correspondence, though plainly intended for publication, seems to be genuine. Seneca sometimes responds to questions Lucilius has put to him. He treats his friend both as a philosophical partner seeking instruction and encouragement, and also as a confidant with whom he can converse on any topic. The philosophical level becomes more technical in the later letters where Seneca includes expositions of Stoic doctrines in psychology and metaphysics as well as ethics; but he largely passes over logic and epistemology.

While the letters maintain an authentic aura of topicality and self-revelation, they are as studiedly rhetorical as any of Seneca's other compositions. Their characteristic starting-points – a journey, a health problem, a book, the time of year – are largely vehicles enabling Seneca to launch into virtuoso reflections on the therapeutic value of Stoicism, and advice to Lucilius and himself on how to avoid the mistakes to which most people are prone. The following passage is representative:

Philosophy is not a popular craft; nor is it designed for parading. It is concerned with things not words. It is not taken up as a pleasant diversion for the day, or as a relief from boredom. It shapes and builds the mind; it organizes life, directs behaviour, shows what one should do and not do, sits at the helm and keeps one on an even keel through turbulent waves. Without it no one can live fearlessly or safely. Every hour countless things occur that demand a policy that needs to be sought from philosophy.

(*Moral Letters* 16.3)

The *Moral Letters* are Seneca's witness to the value of Stoicism as a challenging and supportive belief system for every hour. There, still more strikingly than in Cicero's works, we find the characteristically Roman deployment of rhetoric at the service of philosophy.

LATER DEVELOPMENTS

For the Roman elite during the first century of the Christian era Stoicism remained the dominant philosophy. Prominent Stoics included Musonius Rufus, whose lectures at Rome, delivered in Greek, were attended by the emancipated Phrygian slave Epictetus. Both men, along with others, were exiled when tyrannical emperors decided that philosophical freedom of speech required suppression. There was no officially Stoic opposition to the principate, but some prominent Romans who were also Stoics became icons of Republican nostalgia by refusing to subordinate their liberty to imperial demands.

Epictetus, on leaving Rome, established a Stoic school at Nicopolis in western Greece. His pupils included Arrian, later a prominent writer and public figure, who recorded Epictetus' teaching in a manner that strikingly and designedly echoes the Socrates of Plato and Xenophon. Like Socrates, Epictetus engages his interlocutors in brilliantly challenging dialogue. His most distinctive contribution to the Stoic tradition is his constant insistence that volition, as distinct from the body and external things, is the only domain in which persons can achieve freedom and happiness. Because Epictetus was not a Roman by origin, I mention him only cursorily here; but his importance and influence as a Stoic and Socratic philosopher are second to none.

Under the more enlightened regimes of Trajan and Hadrian, threats to philosophers abated. In AD 177 philosophy received an extraordinary boost when Marcus Aurelius, as emperor, established at Athens four chairs of philosophy, in Platonism, Aristotelianism, Stoicism and Epicureanism, endowing each with a large salary. The first two of these schools were experiencing so strong a revival that they would soon eclipse the latter pair as live options.

Marcus himself, though a Stoic through and through, registers the diffused influence of Platonism in his *Meditations*. Like Epictetus, whose Stoic *Discourses* greatly influenced him, Marcus tends to treat body and soul in the strongly dualistic manner of Plato's *Phaedo*. This 'spiritualizing' tendency, which is a general feature of philosophy in the second century AD, foreshadows the Platonism of Plotinus. It also helped to make pagan philosophy adaptable, within limits, to Christian theology.

The *Meditations* of Marcus, though written in Greek, are a re-markable instance of philosophy at work in the life of a great Roman figure. For him, like Seneca, Stoicism is a practice of self-government and self-scrutiny; but whereas Seneca publicized his Stoic regimen, Marcus appears to have written solely 'to himself', which is the title appended to his text. A reluctant emperor, not born into that office, Marcus uses Stoicism as a way of reflecting on his strenuous duties, boosting his morale, and urging himself to find comfort in being foreordained to play his part in the providentially organized universe. He urges himself to 'welcome all that happens, even if it seems harsh, because it leads to the health of the universe' (5.8).

With Marcus, just as with Seneca, we find a creative use of Stoicism. Although Roman Stoics were dependent on the Greek tra-dition for the doctrines of their philosophy, they made it their own by distinctive emphases and literary style. Marcus, for instance, is espe-cially interesting for his reflections on the passage of time and on the present moment as all that any person can be said to have. His focus on temporality makes his philosophical outlook both contemplative and a spur to resolute action.

Lucretius, Cicero, Seneca and Marcus Aurelius are the writers who best exemplify Roman philosophy, as distinct from philosophy composed by persons living under Roman rule or composed by early Christian writers. From this mass of further material I select a few figures whose work deserves much lengthier treatment than this chapter can provide.

The renewal of interest in Platonism is reflected in Latin works transmitted under the name of Apuleius. *On Plato and his Doctrine* is a handbook exposition, covering cosmology and metaphysics in Book I (largely a summary of the *Timaeus*), and ethics in Book II. The other philosophical works attributed to Apuleius are also symp-tomatic of intellectual interests at their probable date of composition (late second century AD): a book on demonology, a translation and adaptation of the pseudo-Aristotelian cosmological treatise *On the World* (*De mundo*), and an introduction to logic. This last is the ear-liest text to describe the famous 'Square of opposition', as a way of exhibiting the relation between the four basic Aristotelian types of proposition.

What we can infer from these works is a Latin readership in-terested in acquiring a background in the philosophies that were beginning to supersede Stoicism and Epicureanism. Special attention to Plato's *Timaeus* was not new because Cicero had written an incomplete translation of the work. In spite of its extraordinary difficulty, the *Timaeus* was viewed (not unreasonably) as the most compendious guide to Plato's philosophy from the author's own pen, and its theological focus suited the taste of the period. Probably from the fourth century AD, we have an incomplete Latin translation of the work, with commentary, written by Calcidius. This was an important vehicle for transmitting knowledge of Plato to the Middle Ages. Calcidius, who may have been a Christian, comments on Plato in terms that give us one of our best sources for Stoic physics. Long after Stoicism ceased to be a living system, it continued to influence the language and concepts of philosophy, both pagan and Christian.

Other Latin Platonists include Marius Victorinus, Macrobius, Martianus Capella, and Boethius. Victorinus commented on Cicero's rhetorical writings from a Neoplatonic perspective. His lost works included translations of Plotinus that influenced Augustine. Macrobius wrote a Neoplatonic commentary on 'Scipio's dream', the other-worldly vision with which Cicero ends his *De republica*, modelled on the myth of Er in Plato's *Republic*. In Martianus' *The Marriage of Philology and Mercury* we have an instance of the late-antique passion for allegorical interpretation and numerical symbolism. The author tells a narrative concerning traditional gods and personified abstractions, but these are to be understood as a figurative way of explaining the hypostases of Neoplatonism (see p. 267 below).

Much more significant philosophically is the work of the Christian Platonist Boethius. When in prison at the end of his life, he wrote his most famous work, *The Consolation of Philosophy*. Combining prose and verse, he imagines himself conversing with Philosophy, who asks him to withdraw his thoughts of happiness from fortune and locate them completely in God as the chief good. (Here too we see the continuing influence of Stoicism.) In addition to theological treatises, Boethius wrote copiously on Aristotelian logic, and he also published numerous commentaries on Aristotle and Porphyry. As a Latin author, he probably did more than any other single figure to transmit Platonism and Aristotelianism to the countries of western Europe during the Middle Ages.

Writing in the early sixth century AD, Boethius shows no signs of needing to justify his philosophical interests, as a Christian. Three centuries earlier, the new religion found powerful defenders in Tertullian and Lactantius whose works inaugurate the tradition of Latin theology. As zealous converts, they take Christianity to be the only true philosophy, but while neither of them favours any official synthesis with pagan thought both writers, implicitly and explicitly, appropriate numerous ideas from the Greco-Roman philosophical tradition. Tertullian in his work *On the Soul* draws heavily on Stoicism, aligning himself against Plato with the Stoics' identification of the soul with 'breath' and also with that school's doctrine that the soul originates at birth. Lactantius is strongly indebted to Cicero, especially Cicero's work *On the Nature of the Gods*, and he also quotes many passages from Cicero's *De republica* which are missing from the only surviving manuscript of that work. Although Lactantius takes issue with Cicero's *De officiis*, finding that work deficient in its reticence concerning Christian charity, he judges Cicero, in spite of his ignorance of Scripture, to have hit upon many truths. Both Tertullian and Lactantius express their approval of Seneca, who was believed to have corresponded with St Paul.

With Augustine, writing a century later than these early Christian apologists, we arrive at a thinker whose intellectual brilliance and literary output overshadow everyone else discussed in this survey. Yet, 'Roman philosopher', though obviously inadequate to categorize Augustine completely, is a fitting description of this gigantic figure, especially in the early stages of his literary work.

His tortuous route towards conversion began when he read the exhortation to philosophy composed by Cicero in his lost work *Hortensius*. Failing to find in the Bible or the Manichaeans the wisdom that that work inspired him to pursue, Augustine turned to Cicero's *Academica*; but instead of endorsing scepticism, he was drawn back to Christianity and composed the dialogue *Against the Academics*, as a rebuttal of Cicero's conclusion that certitude is not attainable. Near the end of his life Augustine retracted the qualified praise he had bestowed on Plato and the Academics in this book, but the philosophy he learnt from reading Cicero, especially Stoicism, is a pervasive presence in much of his voluminous work.

8   Philosophy and literature

INTRODUCTION

Greek and Roman philosophy developed in a close and frequently adversarial relationship to various literary genres, especially epic and lyric poetry and tragic and comic drama. Moreover, philosophers themselves used some of these genres and created still others (such as the philosophical dialogue, the philosophical epistle); the literary form of philosophical texts is frequently an essential ingredient in their philosophical expression. Philosophers thought in subtle ways about what literary genres themselves express about human life and what is important in it; their contest with the tragedians and other authors was thus fought both on the level of content and on the level of form or style itself. At the same time, literary authors made their own claims to tell the truth about important human matters, going in some cases deliberately against the theories of philosophers. This being the case, the topic of philosophy's relation to literature in ancient Greece and Rome is as vast as the subject of philosophy itself, and cannot be treated exhaustively. Two key texts for understanding the interplay between literature and philosophy in the entire tradition are Plato's *Republic* (his account of his ideal city) and Aristotle's *Poetics*.

CONCEPTUAL PROBLEMS: THE GREEKS AND THE 'AESTHETIC'

Before we can approach even pieces of this topic, we need to begin with an understanding of why our intuitive modern ways of framing it are so likely to mislead. The modern university, in Europe and North America, sharply segments philosophy from literature, presenting them as distinct humanistic disciplines. Our broader cultural understandings contain, by and large, that same split. In Athens of the fifth century BC, where this account will begin its detailed treatment, there was no general category of 'literature'; there was no general category of 'philosophy', and thus, obviously, no understanding of philosophy as a field of inquiry or expression distinct from literature. Plato began to forge that understanding, in conflict with the poets; what he describes as a 'contest of long standing between the poets and the philosophers' is one to the forging of whose conceptual categories he contributed in a major way. But Plato himself understood his own art to involve a literary, even a mimetic, dimension; and his ideal city contained art, in the form of hymns to the gods and praises of good men.

Moreover, an equally serious difficulty for us as we approach the texts, there was no general category of the aesthetic, as distinct from the ethical and political. Certainly there was no doctrine of aesthetic detachment, no notion that the arts ought to be seen as separate from the urgent practical questions of every-day life. Our symphony halls, proscenium stages, and museums all encourage the idea that the arts are a separate domain of life, to be contemplated with detachment. In ancient Greece, by contrast, theatre, epic and lyric poetry, music, and the other arts were thoroughly woven into the fabric of daily life, especially religious life. Spectators were encouraged to expect that what they would hear and see would contribute to their thought about what both individuals and the city should do. Literature was thus ethical in the largest sense of that term, that is, bearing on the question how human beings should live.

Such ways of approaching literary texts are of course not altogether foreign to our contemporary habits. Some forms of theatre do ask the spectator to be active and reflective rather than passive. (The Epic Theatre of Bertolt Brecht has affinities with some aspects of ancient Greek theatre.) Nor have novels typically been read with an aspiration to detach oneself from the emotions they solicit. Indeed, many of the greatest novelists, such as Dickens and Dostoyevsky, have understood their works as contributions to their society's reflection about its future. Especially close to the Greeks, perhaps, is Ralph Ellison, for whom the novel is a 'raft of perception, hope, and entertainment' on which citizens of a troubled democracy may attempt to 'negotiate some of the snags and whirlpools' they encounter on the way to their democratic goals. Despite such parallels, however, we must work hard to suspend modern preconceptions if we are to understand how Plato and the tragic poets came to be, not colleagues peacefully working away in adjacent departments, but bitter rivals for the souls of the city's youth.

Another liability is our tendency to think of literature as a genre distinct from both music and 'fine art' (painting and sculpture). For the Greeks of this period, all poetry had some type of musical accompaniment, and almost all music had a text set to it. Usually text and melody/rhythm were very closely linked. The single word *mousikē* stood for both elements; in order to refer to music without text, one had to say *psilē* (bare) *mousikē*. Even as late as the first century BC, this interweaving is taken for granted, and debates are carried on about how weighty the emotional contribution of each element is. This is hard enough for us, but what makes things still more mysterious is the fact that our knowledge of ancient Greek music is exiguous. Despite increasingly refined attempts to reconstruct ancient instruments and to make sense of what ancient 'modes' actually were like (with the aid of recent papyrus finds), we still lack a good appreciation of what Plato is really talking about when he comments on the emotional effects of various musical 'modes' in the *Republic*. We do not even know for sure whether 'modes' were modes in the mediaeval/modern sense, or more like melodies on which variations were made. With metre/rhythm, we are on slightly firmer ground, since we may assume that text and music are usually closely linked, and we do have a pretty good understanding of Greek and Latin metrics; nonetheless, there are problems here too, since our own reconstructions of ancient metre suffer from our difficulty, as speakers of a language that has stress accent and no pitch accent, and in which metre is based more on stress than on vowel quantity, in imagining and reconstructing the interweaving of quantity with pitch accent in Greek, which had both of these, but no stress accent.

We have a corresponding difficulty, both conceptual and practical, with the visual elements of ancient theatre. Both Plato and Aristotle understood that drama has an important visual aspect, which is part of its impact on the emotions and understanding of the spectator. Once again, we must work against at least some of our modern habits to recover this sense of the complex theatrical work, although of course the idea of a unified artwork in ancient Greece has by now been celebrated and 'reinvented' by Wagner, Nietzsche and others. More seriously problematic is our relative ignorance of what the performances really looked like. Despite some vase paintings depicting performances, our knowledge of costume and scenery is very incomplete, and our knowledge of dance elements virtually nil. At the same time, we typically read ancient Greek dramas from a book, as if they *were* books, and this habit distances us even further from the experience of the Greeks, which must have been highly kinetic and multi-sensory. Nor did Greeks typically read dramatic works from books at all. The literacy rate in ancient Athens is very much disputed, but it hardly matters, for dramas were not frequently copied or circulated (not 'never', as is shown by the fact that Dionysus in Aristophanes' *Frogs* has a text of Euripides with him); they were also not given repeat performances until a much later period.

GENRES: THE EARLY BACKGROUND

If ancient Athens does not contain these cherished modern categories and distinctions, what does it contain? We find various genres of both poetic and prose writing, each with its characteristic forms of expression and each with its set of tasks and expectations. Oldest of all are the poems of Homer and Hesiod, which in some ways provide the starting point for most later poetry. Homer's epics the *Iliad* and *Odyssey* were closely linked by Athenians of the fifth and fourth centuries with tragic drama, despite their metrical and other formal differences. Plato treats Homer as, basically, one among the tragic poets, though he is well aware of the distinction between direct representation and narration. These poems provided later tragic drama with many of its plots and much of its sensibility, as suspense is constructed out of the vulnerability of human lives to manifold disasters.

By contrast, Hesiod's poems *Works and Days* and *Theogony*, are didactic and aetiological rather than primarily narrative; they become in many ways the background against which a tradition of natural science or nature-philosophy begins to emerge in the sixth century BC. This is the place where modern interpreters typically locate the emergence of philosophy, and these are the people who are typically taught as 'the Presocratics'. The Greeks called them *physikoi* or *physiologoi*, 'nature-men' and 'nature-explainers', because they centrally used the idea of *physis*, nature, and understood natural processes as unfolding from within the nature of things, rather than as manipulated by anthropomorphic deities. Some members of this tradition – Parmenides (early fifth century BC) and Empedocles (mid fifth century BC) above all – wrote in epic metre, closely modelling their style on Hesiod; but they understood the world in a different way, replacing the gods of traditional religion with orderly universal principles. In this company, too, later Greek thinkers classified some who wrote in prose, such as Anaximander (sixth century BC), Heraclitus (early fifth century) and Anaxagoras (late fifth century). Prose had been established from an early date as the typical choice for historical and geographical inquiry, and, later, medical science. No doubt we would understand the literary choices of the *physiologoi* better if we knew more about their local cultures: for they lived in widely scattered parts of the Greek-speaking world.

In the fifth century, however, epic verse, though culturally central, was not a living genre at Athens; its use even by the Italian *physiologoi* came to a stop in the middle of the century with Empedocles. The living genres within which people searched for wisdom were prose narrative, in the case of medicine and history, and lyric and dramatic poetry, in the case of matters ethical, religious, emotional, and political. (Of course fifth-century histories such as those of Herodotus and Thucydides also contain major contributions to ethical and political thought.)

Lyric poetry has a long history; different lyric genres evidently addressed different human predicaments. The intricate lyric metres of Sappho, for example, in the sixth century BC, seem to focus on the vicissitudes of erotic emotion (although she also wrote in epic metre, subverting the traditional values of the epic, casting aspersions on masculine aggressiveness in favour of the values of love and friendship). Other lyric works were dramatically performed by choruses, especially at Sparta. In the fifth century, the victory odes of Pindar and Bacchylides constitute a distinctive lyric genre that reflects on human excellence. Taking their start in each case from an athletic victory, they ruminate in complex and meandering ways about mythic examples of virtue and the dangers life contains for the person who is attempting to be outstanding, whether in sports or in other aspects of life. They assert the beauty of human achievement while acknowledging that it is extremely transient and fragile.

Already in this background sketch we may see some hints of an emerging split between philosophers and (other) poets, in the sense that the tradition of the *physiologoi* subverts much of traditional religion in favour of an appeal to rational principle. That split continues through the fifth century, in the form of parallel, and sometimes hostile, developments of science, on the one hand, and traditional civic religion, on the other. Both Anaxagoras and Socrates were accused of impiety for apparently preferring reason to the gods of the city, although, as we shall see, Socrates' link to this tradition is in part constructed by his adversaries. But the most heated contests between poetry and philosophy took place on the terrain of ethical and political value; although Homer and Pindar were certainly among Plato's targets, the principal contestants were the tragic poets and Plato, their complex adversary.

TRAGIC DRAMA: THE GOOD PERSON CAN BE HARMED

Tragic dramas were performed at sacred religious festivals attended by virtually all citizens and many non-citizens (since women, although not citizens, were very probably in the audience). All activity ceased, and the city came together to spend the whole day watching dramatic works. Actors and playwrights were leading citizens, and the competitions were adjudicated by the audience. When we go to the theatre, we typically sit in the dark, looking straight ahead, encouraged to be oblivious of the presence of our fellow spectators. Athenian spectators, sitting together in the light of day, looked across the stage at the faces of their fellow citizens on the other side of the semi-circular theatre. These physical circumstances further encouraged the idea that responding to a tragedy was a serious business, closely connected to thought about central political values and, especially, tensions or problems within them. Dramas were standardly assessed on the basis of their ethical content, and political debate frequently appealed to tragic examples as sources of ethical and political insight. To say this, however, is not to say that the festivals were deliberative in a detached or unemotional way: strong emotional responses were encouraged and often recorded in descriptions of the performances. Deliberation took place in and through such responses, rather than despite them.

We have only a small fraction of the tragic dramas of the fifth century, but this sample, combined with accounts of lost works by other authors, gives us enough to form a view of Plato's target. Our term 'tragedy' suggests to us a play with a grim ending. The Greek term had no such connotation, and many tragedies end happily. (The word *tragōidia* seems to mean 'goat song,' though whether reference is made to the sacrifice of a goat in some early stage of the festival, or to goat-like 'bleating' voices of adolescent males who may have constituted some of the choruses, or to something else, we cannot say.) What the surviving works do share, however, is a sense of the exposure of human strivings to events the striving person does not control – in short, the denial of a proposition on whose truth Socrates insisted his audience should rely, that 'a good man does not suffer anything bad either in life or in death' (Plato, *Apology* 41d).

The plot of a tragic drama, as Aristotle noted, tends to revolve around a reversal, or *peripeteia*, in the fortunes of a hero (or heroine), who is typically a good person, 'better rather than worse', though not perfect or divine, and who is usually also well endowed by fortune to start with, of good birth and rank. Typically the reversal threatens to plunge the person, or does plunge the person, into extreme misery and suffering. At the last minute catastrophe may be averted (a plot form Aristotle particularly likes); or a hero brought low by catastrophe may possibly be raised up again, as in Sophocles' *Philoctetes*, where the unjustly abandoned hero, who has endured isolation and excruciating pain on a lonely island, will be restored to health and companionship. But in such cases no less than others it is clearly demonstrated that the strivings even of the virtuous are exposed to disaster.

Sometimes the disaster is the work of the gods, or of natural forces utterly beyond human control. Sometimes it is, instead, the work of human malice or aggressiveness, as in the many plays that deal with the horrors of war and the sufferings of defeated women and children. Thus the plays do not as a group encourage the thought that human beings are powerless in the face of forces they do not control: often their contribution to deliberation may be precisely to show human beings what sufferings they inflict on others in ways that they can control – as when Euripides presented the *Trojan Women*, a play depicting the sufferings of the enslaved women of the defeated city, shortly after the citizens of Athens had voted to put all the adult male citizens of a rebellious colony to death, and to enslave the women and children. And sometimes, indeed, it is emphasized that political life is all about the judicious, and indeed judicial, management of powerful forces that used to tear families apart through private vengeance, as in Aeschylus' celebration of Athenian law in the final play, *Eumenides*, of his *Oresteia* trilogy, concerning the cycle of revenge that mars the house of Atreus and its eventual resolution. But even in these cases it is made clear that the minute people care about striving and achievement, indeed even friendship and political activity, in an uncertain world, they open themselves to disaster on a large scale.

Aristotle thus perceptively urges that tragedy is itself philosophical because it shows 'things such as might happen' in a human life (*Poetics* ch. 9). Unlike history, which, he says, simply sets down what in fact has happened, whether it is typical or not, tragedy explores general forms of human possibility. He also suggests that the pleasure spectators take in watching such dreadful events can best be understood as a pleasure of increased understanding.

These claims are further illuminated by Aristotle's perceptive accounts of the two emotions central to the experience of tragedy, pity and fear. (Here we must combine his analysis in the *Rhetoric* with his scantier remarks in the *Poetics*.) Aristotle is not innovating here: he records a traditional understanding of these emotions that can be found as far back as Homer's *Iliad*, and that is central to the plot structures of many, if not most, tragedies. Pity (the word standardly used to translate the relevant Greek words, though 'compassion' might be a better English term) is a painful emotion directed at another person's pain or suffering. The emotion is painful, but it also involves three thoughts. First is a thought about *size*: in our pity, we see the other person's suffering as serious or large. Second is a thought about *fault*: when we pity, we see the event as hitting the person from outside, so to speak. Although the person may have contributed in some way to the disaster (and Aristotle actually prefers plots in which a mistake in action (*hamartia*), blameworthy or not, is a key part of the causal nexus), in order to pity we must hold that the suffering is out of all proportion, at least, to what the person deserves. The person is seen as undeserving of such great misfortune. Third is a thought about *similar possibilities*. We do not pity, Aristotle holds, if we think that we are utterly immune to the sort of disaster the person we witness is facing. Aristotle calls this state of mind an 'overweening disposition' (*hybristikē diathesis*). (Rousseau expanded this thought in *Emile*, arguing that kings do not pity the sufferings of their subjects, since they 'count on never being human beings'.) Thus when we pity a tragic hero, we are saying something about ourselves and our own possibilities.

Fear, similarly, involves both pain and thought: the thought that serious misfortunes are impending, and that we are not fully in control of warding them off. Like pity, then, fear involves the idea that elements of human life that are important for a person's well-being lie beyond that person's control. (Once again, these may be elements that are in principle uncontrollable, such as the gods, or fate, or they may just be other human beings, or aspects of the world, such as disease, that we might control, but do not.) Aristotle says that we fear for the tragic hero, seeing him as someone similar to ourselves; so our fear involves, as does our pity, a thought about our own possibilities.

How might tragic pity and fear enhance ethical understanding? If pity requires fellow-feeling, we will not have pity at all if we really do think ourselves exempt from the common lot of human beings. But often people recognize their vulnerability in an inconstant or flickering way. For such people, tragedy can make vivid the awareness of life's possibilities, cutting through self-protective stratagems. It can also make us aware that people who are unlike us, or distant from us, suffer in ways similar to our ways, perhaps as a result of policies such as we ourselves have chosen: thus the *Trojan Women* might be expected to awaken in an Athenian male not only a recognition of the equal and similar sufferings of women, but also a moral concern about the policies of enslaving (and raping) women of a conquered city. Obviously enough, such recognitions have to live side by side with the rest of a person's experience, and thus they may prove short-lived. What one might plausibly claim, however, is that these dramatic experiences, in and of themselves, contain elements of ethical understanding. One would assert this only if one believes that human life is in fact exposed to disaster, that elements salient for well-being do in fact lie outside the control of the human agent.

That sort of revelation or 'clearing up' of the inner landscape is one possible meaning of the disputed Aristotelian concept of *katharsis*, and it makes sense of Aristotle's notoriously obscure claim that *katharsis* is accomplished through pity and fear. Aristotle's definition of tragedy says that tragedy accomplishes, through pity and fear, 'the *katharsis* of experiences of that kind' (*Poetics* 1449b27–8). He offers elucidation of every other element of the definition elsewhere in the work, but nowhere, apparently, a further elucidation of the concept of *katharsis*. Because the work is incomplete, it is possible that some pertinent discussion is missing; it is also possible that the discussions of understanding as the goal of our interest in all representation, in chapter 4, and of the philosophical function of tragedy, in chapter 9, are at least a part of the needed elucidation. All that is clear is that *katharsis* and its relatives typically mean 'clearing up' or 'cleaning up', often by the removal of some obstacle (the dirt from a horse's coat, the chaff from the wheat). The idea of medical purgation, which cleans up the body by removing obstacles, is one *application* of the general idea of cleaning up, but it is not the meaning of the word; moreover, such ideas of purging are not found in Aristotle's biological writings, nor is his analysis of the emotions at all based on such physiological ideas. It is also clear that Plato, Aristotle's common target, held in the *Phaedo* that the soul achieves a clearing up (using the *katharsis* word-family repeatedly) only when it separates intellect from the confusion of the passions (see below, p. 229). No interpretation of the *Poetics* should lay much weight on this disputed term; but it seems that the interpretation that links it with emotion-based illumination or understanding has as much going for it as any. At any rate, such ideas are present elsewhere in the work.

Whether or not we approach tragedy through the categories offered by Aristotle, we should grant his essential point: that tragedies explore, in a wide variety of ways, what one might call the gap between being good and living well, between a reasonably good human character and the fullness of human flourishing, or *eudaimonia*. At this point we might distinguish four different varieties of tragedy, depending on how the gap between the hero's goodness and his fortune opens up.

First, we have what we might call *tragedies of impeded action*. Here good people do not get to live well because they simply are prevented from doing the things they used to do, or that they want to do. In Euripides' *Trojan Women*, for example, we see good women put into a situation of extreme powerlessness, in which, stripped of citizenship, friends, family ties, resources, they can no longer choose the actions in which their goodness was formerly expressed. All that remains is for them to speak, and mourn their disaster. Sophocles' *Philoctetes* has a more complex plot, but at least a part of its structure revolves around pity for the deprivations of political action, of friendship, of normal movement, of conversation with other human beings, involved in Philoctetes' lonely, pain-filled existence.

Second, there are *tragedies of involuntary action*. Here circumstances beyond the person's control bring it about that the person makes a terrible error, doing something that he did not intend to do. Oedipus aims at living well, and he makes the best choices he can. But ignorance for which he is not to blame brings it about that he commits horrible acts. Aristotle is fond of this plot, though he prefers it when the catastrophe is avoided by a revelation at the last minute (before the person kills his relative, for example).

The *Oresteia* (especially its first play, *Agamemnon*) and Sophocles' *Antigone* belong to a different pattern, which we might call the *tragedy of ethical dilemma*. Here luck steps in a different way: not by frustrating action altogether, but by producing a contingent conflict of two important obligations, in such a way that no innocent course is available. Agamemnon cannot both honour the gods and preserve his daughter Iphigeneia's life. Creon and Antigone both appear unaware that the sphere of civic obligation clashes with the sphere of family religious obligation, but, as Hegel said, the audience could be expected to see that clash clearly. In such cases, as Hegel also noted, a challenge is implicitly posed: how might this tragic conflict have been avoided? The *Oresteia* supplies its own answer in the final play: by civic institutions that honour the gods of the family and that also support public institutions of justice. The *Antigone* gestures toward a similar answer, and Pericles boasted that Athens did in fact honour the 'unwritten laws' of religious obligation as a part of its conception of civic virtue. Thus tragedies, far from encouraging resignation and pessimism, frequently challenge their audience to constructive political action.

Aeschylus and Sophocles typically portray their heroes as retaining nobility in misfortune – although Philoctetes does display an obsession with revenge that is rightly criticized by the other characters. In Euripides tragedy at times cuts deeper, and we see what we might call the *tragedy of eroded character*. Among the women of the *Trojan Women*, most retain good character, but Cassandra is driven mad by rape, and this loss of rationality, sad and grotesque rather than noble, is one of the most appalling spectacles the play offers. Euripides' *Hecuba* depicts a once-noble queen whose best friend betrays her trust, murdering her child. This betrayal causes her to lose all trust in human beings, and to devote herself henceforth to projects of revenge. Becoming in character the 'dog' that the play's ending prophesies she will become in fact (dogs, known for eating carrion, symbolized total lack of moral awareness), she even offers to prostitute her remaining child in return for aid in her schemes. The prophesied metamorphosis is probably a deliberate inversion of the ending of the *Oresteia*. There the revenge goddesses, through a pledge of trust, become citizens of Athens, and are changed from dogs, hunting their prey, into human women with kindly intentions. Here a woman with kindly intentions, losing the ability to trust, is changed into a dog, hunting her prey. Both transformations show the vulnerability of the civic virtue that is thus transformed. What is done can also be undone. Such tragedies remind us that our political and other human actions do not stop at the surface of the person, damaging only what is superficial but leaving nobility to 'shine through' (as Aristotle puts it). Sometimes, at any rate, they damage what is deepest in the heart and mind.

Many accounts of Greek tragedy's ethical significance have been offered by philosophers who value it. For Hegel, tragedies, showing the clash of one sphere of right with another, prompt the transcending of these conflicts through human freedom and its gradual unfolding. For Schopenhauer, tragedies, showing our utter powerlessness before a world we do not control, induce us to give up our attachments to this world and to pursue a state of pessimistic contemplation. For Nietzsche, the fact that tragedies affirm the worth of human nobility even in the face of the worst the universe can do constitutes an affirmation of life in a world in which no divine justice can be found: they are thus instructive for human beings grappling with the loss of faith. (One strength of Nietzsche's interpretation is that he does not forget that tragedies are multidimensional performances: he gives both dance and music an important place in his idea of tragic affirmation.) For Bernard Williams, closer to Schopenhauer than to either Hegel or (this reading of) Nietzsche, tragedies tell us unequivocally that there is no 'good news' to be had about human life, and thus puncture the optimistic pretensions of most of the tradition of moral philosophy. I think that there is some truth in each view, and of course we should not expect to find a unified view of life among three such different playwrights, or even within the work of any. But Hegel's idea that tragedies pose a challenge to political thought certainly has much truth to it, not only concerning plays of the *Antigone* type, but also concerning the plays about war, rape, lying, and other 'all too human' calamities. (We should insist, however, that the Greeks themselves were perfectly capable of reflecting in a very sophisticated way about what might be required in order to overcome the tragic problem. Hegel's idea that understanding had to emerge over two millennia is utterly unnecessary.)

Nietzsche's emphasis on the affirmation of continued engagement with life in a world of suffering and chance is also very important. Even if some tragedies can be avoided by better human thought, and even if tragedies do repeatedly challenge us to that better thought (about war, rape, deceit, loneliness and illness), the aspiration to manage the entire world of chance by human arts expresses a *hybristikē diathesis* that tragic poetry rightly criticizes.

THE COMIC POET AND THE TRAGIC POET

The other form of dramatic art that was of special importance to fifth-century Athens was comedy. The Socrates of Plato's *Symposium* is represented as insisting that comedy and tragedy could be the work of one and the same individual, and there is an important sense in which this is true, the same Platonic objections applying, *mutatis mutandis*, to both. The 'Old Comedy' of which Aristophanes is the great practitioner is like tragedy in its concern with contemporary political topics such as war and peace. Typically the comic hero, whether a rural farmer or a citizen's wife, is depicted as a resourceful canny subverter of the venality, pomposity, and corruption of other types in the city, including famous politicians and generals. In this way, albeit with a light touch, comedy contributes to civic deliberation.

More deeply, comedy, like tragedy, depicts a universe in which human beings are not in control of the most important things. Their most ambitious plans are frequently brought low – whether

by human corruption or, even more frequently, by the sheer surprisingness and neediness of the human body. The humour of Old
Comedy is frankly and insistently bodily, both scatological and sexual. Frequently the humour derives from the fact that someone who
wants to do something very grand is held up by the ridiculous behaviour of his own body. Men who would like to focus on fighting the
Spartans are walking around with large erect phalluses because their
wives deny them sex and they cannot live without it. A father who
wants to train with the philosophers finds that instead of learning
his lesson he is farting because he ate a lot of bean soup. This is not
tragedy, but it has important analogies with tragedy. The grandiose
aspiration to self-sufficiency is repeatedly punctured, and the only
ones who fare well are those who are not grandiose in the first place –
Dicaeopolis, who farts while he waits for the Assembly to begin its
business, Lysistrata, who knows the power women's sexuality can
exert over male scheming. (Perhaps the most revealingly comparable modern text is James Joyce's *Ulysses*, which similarly skewers
aspirations to self-sufficiency, whether contemplative or political,
through the comedy of the body.)

PLATO'S CHALLENGE: THE SELF-SUFFICIENCY OF THE GOOD PERSON

But for Socrates, we recall, a good person cannot be harmed. And this
conviction (whether or not it should be directly imputed to the historical Socrates) led Plato to conduct an all-out assault on tragic and
Homeric poetry, as damaging to the moral education of the young.
Socrates' own relation to literary traditions is complex. Although
Aristophanes' representation of him, in his comedy *Clouds*, as a
physiologos hanging in a basket and studying the air is surely inaccurate, the play's suggestion that Socrates intends to replace traditional
religion with new gods of reason was mentioned by Socrates himself,
in Plato's *Apology*, as one of the most influential sources of the prej-
udice against him. Much could be said about the extent to which this
accusation is true, though no account of Socrates' religious views is
free from controversy. Probably Socrates shared at least part of the
agenda of the *physiologoi*, and thus their assault on traditional myth
and poetry, in the sense that he did want citizens to live on the basis of rational principles that they themselves found and articulated,

rather than on the basis of authority and tradition. This led him to develop forms of interaction that focused on argumentation and cross-examination, rather than on the emotive powers of rhetoric and verse. As we shall see at pages xx–xx, this focus leads Plato to construct the philosophical dialogue as a distinctive literary form in which the ideals peculiar to Socratic inquiry can be expressed, a form that represents a radical break from traditional poetry.

Let us, however, focus on Plato's *Republic* and its assault on the content and form of tragic poetry. And let us suppose that we believe, with Plato's Socrates in that dialogue, that virtue requires knowledge and is centrally structured around knowledge, and that virtue, so conceived, is sufficient for the flourishing life. The good person is seen as completely self-sufficient for good living: the inner mental life is the important thing and accidents out in the world do not matter to him at all. In the light of that understanding of the world, what would we think about the traditional tragic plots? First and most obviously, they contain a lot of statements that are false, and they put these false statements about value into the mouths of characters whom the young are encouraged to emulate. Second, and more deeply, the entire structure of interest through which they captivate their audience is itself false. We follow such plots with eager attention because *we* believe that what happens to city, family and friends matters deeply, and the plot itself reinforces those commitments. The plays solicit emotions of pity and fear that form the core of their engagement with an audience, and these emotions themselves have falsehood built into them, in the form of the thought that significant damage can come to people through no fault of their own, and beyond their control.

In *Republic* Books II and III, Socrates' argument begins from the assumption that the stories we tell the young are very important in shaping their malleable young souls; he focuses on the danger that the soul will accept false beliefs. Myths about divine and heroic figures are taken to be influential through a kind of admiring identification. Therefore, Socrates forbids literature showing the gods causing undeserved suffering: thus one major occasion for pity is ruled out from the start, and Socrates simply asserts that if the gods hurt someone that must be shown as a just punishment. Furthermore, both gods and heroes must be represented as entirely self-sufficient, in need of nothing from the world. Heroes cannot be shown fearing death or grieving over the deaths of loved ones, lamenting and calling out for pity. For the good man does not believe that the death of a friend or a son or brother is a terrible thing. Speeches of lamentation are permitted only if they are assigned to inferior men and women, so that young citizens will 'have an aversion to behaving in a similar way' (388a). Numerous passages from Homer are stricken on these grounds. In general, furthermore, literature is required to show that even among non-heroic humans, the just live well, the unjust badly. Plato's accompanying censorship of musical forms is difficult to follow for reasons already given, but it clearly reinforces the campaign against intense concern with changing events in the world.

Republic x takes an even stronger stance against tragic poetry, ruling out all *mimēsis* (representation or enactment), with the exception of hymns to the gods and praises of good men. Once again, the ethical objection raised against tragedy is that it shows good people encountering reversals in fortune and grieving as if these had great significance. Again, the unseemly behaviour of the tragic hero is contrasted with the self-sufficient calm demeanour of the truly good man, who recognizes that 'nothing among human things is worth much seriousness' (604b). Here pity is central to the analysis. Socrates points out that tragic poetry leads to fellow-feeling, and 'nourishes the element of pity in us, making it strong' (606b). This makes it more difficult, he alleges, to achieve a calm demeanour in our own sufferings. The right response to such works is not enthusiasm, but disgust. Socrates remarks that it is difficult to represent the truly good person in a way that excites interest in the theatre.

Plato's assault on literature is above all moral. His remarks in Book x about its derivative status, two removes from reality, should be understood in this context. Just as a represented bed cannot even fulfil the functions of an actual bed, far less of an ideal bed (a Platonic Form of bed, that is), so too, the artist's representation of a just person or a just action cannot even do what an actual just person or action in the world does, being made without real inner understanding of the essence of justice; far less does it display the inner essence of justice that must be learned by ascending to contemplation of the Forms. So the complaint about epistemological status is an aspect of the moral complaint: artists have a deformed understanding of justice because they focus on how people really carry on in the world, and aim at pleasing the audience by giving a pleasing representation of that world, all this without any deeper or more critical understanding of the nature of the virtues.

Plato's assault on the arts is usually found heinous by modern readers because it betrays no sense that people have a right to free speech, nor (a distinct point) any sense that the freedom of the artist might possibly be an important source of benefit to society. Although these thoughts are familiar to us in a modern formulation, they were not alien to ancient Athens, where the topic of freedom of expression was often discussed, and where comic playwrights, especially, asserted it as a precious critical value. To such concerns Plato's implicit reply is that the danger is too great: when young souls are being ruined, we cannot pause to be concerned with the speech of artists. His position has a close relationship to arguments on topics such as pornographic art and racist and sexist speech that are current today. If one really believes that literary works powerfully mould the soul and create a pernicious social climate, one will at least take such arguments seriously, even if one thinks that other serious values tell against any restriction. Despite the affection most Americans commonly have for the First Amendment, its real meaning and reach are deeply contested, and almost nobody is really a thoroughgoing absolutist about the freedom of speech. We accept without much question restrictions on false advertising, perjury, misleading medical advice, threats and bribes, and a whole host of other forms of speech. Moreover, I am talking now only about legal restrictions. Virtually all parents and teachers of the young exercise a whole host of more informal restrictions.

We should admit, then, that our own understanding of what is too dangerous to allow in the hands of the young is evolving and incomplete, and we should argue seriously with Plato, rather than dismissing or condescending to his contentions. As we argue, we should carefully distinguish objections based on the overriding value of free speech from objections based upon the content of his moral values. We find it easy to defend the tragic poets in part because most of us think that they are telling the truth and Plato is wrong in his praise of self-sufficiency. But suppose the would-be censor is right: what then?

Plato pursues his engagement with the artists in other dialogues as well. In the *Ion* he offers an account of poetic inspiration that has frequently been alluded to in the history of aesthetic theory, although he ultimately casts doubt, as in the *Republic*, on the poets' claim to have any genuine understanding of their subject-matter. The *Phaedrus*, to be discussed further in the next section, seems to take a more generous line with the poets, or at least with poetic and erotic elements of language, when used with understanding by a philosopher. The *Laws* contains prescriptions that are in some ways similar to those of the *Republic*, although possibly more liberal. It contains the famous, albeit mysterious, claim that the ideal city itself is the 'truest tragedy'. This very probably means that the city tells the truth about those matters of value concerning which tragedy gives a false and erroneous account: it is that *mimēsis* of the life of the good and serene person that the *Republic* would admit in place of existing tragedies. Once again, we should remember that 'tragedy' does not mean 'play with an unhappy ending'. It designates a serious mimetic work, in a certain high style. Nonetheless, the statement, so interpreted, remains shocking, for it replaces existing tragedy's focus on reversal with the praise of self-sufficiency and serenity.

PLATO'S ANTI-TRAGIC THEATRE

Plato is also one of the most distinguished writers of prose literature in the ancient Greek language, and his dialogues have been generally understood as highly literary. How does this fact comport with his evident hostility to existing poetry? We should remember, first of all, that we typically find Plato a literary philosopher because we compare him with subsequent works of prose philosophy that seem dry, and that in some cases (e.g. Descartes and Spinoza) self-consciously express the philosopher's emulation of the natural sciences. But in the ancient Greek world there were no such dry prose treatises of philosophy. As we have seen, there were the poetic (and prose) works of *physiologoi*, and there were the ethical investigations of the poets. (Even after Plato's time, the surviving writings of Aristotle cannot be assessed stylistically, because they are thought to be lectures or lecture notes, and we also know that Aristotle published dialogues that were renowned for their stylistic eloquence.) There were prose scientific treatises and histories, and there was poetic drama. Plato's works include the first surviving examples of prose drama in Greek, along with the roughly contemporary philosophical dialogues of Xenophon, some of which concern Socrates;

there is some evidence that other thinkers wrote prose dialogues in which Socrates was a central figure. Plato's dialogues ought to be seen as they no doubt would have been received by their audience: as rivals to the tradition of tragic drama.

Let us, then, try to imagine how a person accustomed to Athenian tragedy would react to these works. And let us recall that Socrates, in the *Republic*, remarked that it was very difficult to keep the attention of an audience while depicting the 'wise and serene character, always consistent with itself' (604e). Plato's dialogues do, however, represent such a figure, a Socrates who cares little for the prospect of his own death, and who pursues his philosophical search regardless of his external circumstances.

Plato's *Phaedo*, which depicts the death of Socrates, begins with a story that has all the ingredients of tragic action: a good and just man has been unjustly condemned and is soon to die. The interlocutors initially view the story this way, and remark that they expected to feel pity. They did not, however, because Socrates' attitude toward his reversal strongly discouraged that response. Xanthippe, Socrates' wife, is sent away because she is weeping; Apollodorus is sternly admonished for his 'womanish' grief. We might say that here, as Socrates recommends in *Republic* III, Plato has ascribed lamentation to a woman and an inferior man; and the effect of this strategy is indeed, as Socrates said there, to mark these as inappropriate responses, which people should be ashamed to emulate. Socrates the *Phaedo*'s non-tragic hero, by contrast, treats death as something that does not really affect him. He calmly pursues the search for understanding; and the 'drama' of the work becomes the drama of unfolding argument, to be apprehended by the intellect alone. This intellect, Socrates here informs us, reasons best when it manages to avoid the influence of unhelpful emotions and desires, achieving a state in which, impediments removed, it can see 'cleanly' or 'clearly' (*katharōs*, 65c, 69c; see remarks on Aristotelian *katharsis*, p. 220 above). Plato's depiction of Socrates' death has proved deeply inspiring over the ages. Seneca clearly modelled his own death scene on this literary example, and he is probably not the only Stoic thinker to do so.

We see here the core of a new form of philosophical literature and a new paradigm of heroism. Plato succeeds in making this 'wise and serene' figure compelling in part because of his remarkable character

portraiture, and in part because of the compelling power of the arguments Socrates presents. (I bracket here the controversy over what
parts of Plato's portrait may be imputed to the historical Socrates,
focusing simply on the figure of Socrates *in* the dialogues.) Plato's remarkable combination of portraiture and argument, combined with
his justly admired prose style and his keen wit, have made literary monuments of quite a few of the dialogues, including *Euphy-
phro, Charmides, Laches, Lysis, Gorgias, Protagoras, Symposium,*
and *Phaedrus*. These qualities make Plato still an author whom students new to philosophy find especially engaging.

There is, however, an inherent tension between these two sources
of literary interest in the dialogues. What Socrates demands of his followers, and Plato of his readers, is a focus on the search for truth, and
on the progress of the argument. But what very often results from an
engagement with these 'literary' dialogues is a focus on the example
of Socrates the unique individual man. The portrait of Socrates can
hook people into the study of philosophy in a way that few pieces of
philosophical writing can, but some readers become fascinated with
Socrates as a unique individual, and care about that portrait more
than about the difficult arguments. Plato was well aware of this paradox. Indeed he depicted it in the *Symposium*, where he shows quite
a few characters who are more focused on remembering this or that
saying of Socrates than on pursuing truth and understanding.

In the light of these difficulties, it is not altogether surprising that
Plato, as he investigated highly complex philosophical questions,
some of them far removed from the ethical topics that were probably the focus of the historical Socrates, gradually does less with the
dramatic elements of the figure of Socrates and spends more time
simply unfolding the arguments. Thus, in works such as *Republic*,
and especially in the dialogues usually regarded as later (including
Parmenides, Theaetetus, Sophist, Philebus, Statesman, and *Laws*),
the dialogue form is used in a less dramatic way, and long stretches
of abstract argument are set forth – still, especially in the *Republic*,
with brilliant use of language, image and myth, but without as much
dramatic interaction.

Does Plato ever allow his enthusiasm for drama to lead him to
permit the views of the character Socrates to be seriously contested?
Typically Socrates' interlocutors, while both varied and intriguing,
exemplify various levels and types of resistance to philosophical

inquiry, and to its underlying belief in the self-sufficiency of goodness. Characters such as Critias (in the *Charmides*) and Callicles (in the *Gorgias*) display some of the false values of the Athenian democracy, its excessive concern with status and power; the generals Laches and Nicias (in the *Laches*) show the sluggishness of even good people when they need to give an account of their beliefs; Euthyphro and Meno (in the dialogues named after them) show the arrogance of false pretenders to expertise. Is there any dialogue in which a more serious challenge to the views and methods of Socrates is put forward, a challenge that we are urged to view with sympathy? The sophist Protagoras (in the *Protagoras*) does better than most interlocutors. He is portrayed as a serious thinker about democratic values who does have a conception of virtue to offer that might, at any rate, be seriously defended (it has a lot in common with Aristotle's ethical views), although he himself does not do a good job of defending it.

But it is in the *Symposium* that we may find a more thoroughgoing curiosity about whether Socrates' approach to life can possibly be adequate to the complexities of erotic love. Socrates does express (through the speech he says he heard from the wise Diotima) some compelling ideas about the ascent of love to the contemplation of the ideal Form of beauty, ideas that were to have great importance in the entire history of western philosophy and art, decisively influencing thinkers as otherwise diverse as Plotinus and Shelley. But, as is not the case in other dialogues, his speech occupies just one relatively brief stretch of the dialogue, and other interlocutors are given both ample space and a serious case to make for their own views.

Among the speeches in praise of love that this stylistically diverse and brilliant work contains, only one (Agathon's) is clearly ridiculous, and only one other (Eryximachus') has regularly been found to be without much serious interest. The speeches of Phaedrus and Pausanias are usually at least appreciated as good examples of educated Greek thought about same-sex love and its civic benefits, useful for reconstructing the history of this topic; but readers, early and late, frequently also sympathize with the views these men express about the capacities of high-minded lovers for sacrifice and the pursuit of excellence. And two speakers who explicitly refuse to join the chorus of admiration for Socrates' speech deliver especially tough challenges to his view that love has as its ultimate object the abstract Form of the beautiful. Aristophanes' speech (written with a deep understanding of the values inherent in Aristophanic comedy) depicts love as the search to be reunited with one's lost 'other half'. Its myth of human beings as overweening creatures who were cut in two in punishment for their impious ambitions, and who must now run around searching for the other part of themselves, expresses something important about the nature of desire and love that finds no place in Socrates' vision of the world: the sheer contingency and surprisingness of erotic love, the sense one has that love is essential to one's own completeness, but that it is a matter of chance whether the right person manages to turn up, and stay around. Aristophanes' lovers see the person they love not as a vehicle for an abstract quality, but as unique and irreplaceable. The literary qualities of his speech, both comic and tragic, further convey the view of a world not totally controlled by reason.

The final speech in the dialogue, moreover, is given not to Socrates, but to Alcibiades, who enters, drunk and crowned with violets, toward the dialogue's end. Instead of praising love, he praises Socrates. His disorderly and impassioned account presents a remarkable and moving portrait that could not have been made by anyone who sees the world as Socrates requires, as just a 'wide sea of beauty'. He is obviously a character bound for ruin, and the ruin of others, and is selected deliberately by Plato with his bad end in mind; but he also is (as by all accounts he was) an immensely compelling figure who cannot quite be dismissed, and whose challenge to ideal love in the name of a love of real individuals lingers unresolved at the dialogue's close. The work as a whole shows us that Plato never fully departed from the universe of tragic theatre, with its focus on individuals and their sometimes unfortunate loves.

In *Republic* x, Socrates remarks that a person who is in love, if he believes that love is not good for him, will continually rehearse to himself all the arguments against love as a 'counter-charm' against its spell. Similarly, he continues, the lover of poetry should continually rehearse to himself the arguments against poetry – unless and until a defender of poetry should convince him 'in prose without metre, and show that it is not only delightful, but also beneficial to orderly government and all of human life' (607d–608b). These remarks seem self-referential, in the sense that Plato, clearly a lover of poetry, does continually rehearse the arguments against it, and against the sort of erotic love that is so frequently its theme.

If that is so, we might see his *Phaedrus*, written after *Republic* and *Symposium*, as a highly qualified but genuine apologia for both erotic love and poetry. Clearly it is the work in which Plato's own prose style becomes most poetic, and in which he offers the most generous appraisal both of erotic love and of the inspired language of the lover. The very setting of the dialogue, in the countryside outside the city-walls, is significant: for Socrates never really did go outside the city-walls (as he tells us elsewhere). So we are presented with a fiction about Socrates, and with a Socrates who praises personal love in a way that departs from the aloof attitude of the character depicted in all other dialogues.

After giving two speeches (one a remarkable imitation of the style of the Athenian orator Lysias) in which he does indeed rehearse arguments against passionate love and in favour of a type of sexualized friendship – which was not uncommonly seen as a goal of a same-sex relationship – Socrates declares that he has been impious and owes the gods a recantation. His statement that *erōs* (sexual love) is a god (242e) is most surprising to anyone who recalls Socrates' condemnation of *erōs* in the *Republic* as a dangerous tyrant. The ensuing famous and highly lyrical speech of recantation depicts erotic love between men as a key source of both motivation and insight. Socrates suggests that without the physical presence of the beloved and the psychological ferment to which it gives rise, the soul's wings will remain dry and parched. The pair of lovers are depicted as remaining in a long-term relationship that contains passion on both sides, although its physical expression is carefully limited in the most ideal case. They never abandon their focus on the individual in favour of a progress toward the abstract Form, as the *Symposium* seems to urge; instead, they pursue their search for understanding within the context of devotion to an individual. With this apparently enhanced appreciation of the personal in love goes what seems to be a new appreciation of the inspired language of love poetry. Socrates ascribes his recantation-speech to the poet Stesichorus, 'Son of Reverent, from Desire' (244a) – thus linking – shockingly to one familiar with the austerity of the *Republic* – piety, poetry and passion. And the best life is described as that of 'a person who will be a lover of wisdom or a lover of beauty or some follower of the Muses and a lover' (248d). 'Madness' or inspiration is praised as essential to the greatest benefits. Although Socrates remains determined not to let a poet such as Homer teach the young unless he can answer questions about his work (278c) – and although, in this sense, the only love poet of whom Plato seems fully to approve is himself – the work surely does contain love poetry (in prose) of a very high order, which has had a tremendous influence, of both style and content, on almost every subsequent writer about love in the western philosophical and literary traditions.

ARISTOTLE'S ETHICS: A SPACE FOR TRAGEDY

Aristotle's account of tragedy, and of the tragic emotions, has already played a role in this chapter as a guide to the ethical values inherent in tragedy. And indeed Aristotle's interest in tragedy is no mere detached stylistic interest; it expresses a view of life that suffuses his ethical writings. For Aristotle, unlike Plato, holds that the good person can indeed come to grief through factors beyond his control. Although he resists the Euripidean idea that good character might itself be undermined by bad fortune, he does allow that *eudaimonia*, or human flourishing, requires more than good character. Thus the good person remains in need of things outside himself if he is to attain to, and retain, human flourishing.

In the *Nicomachean Ethics*, Aristotle strongly rejects the view that good character is all that is required for *eudaimonia*. Activity is also required. But then the world begins to play a role: for in order to act well one needs resources. Aristotle recognizes that people of good character will typically be able to use life's materials better than others, and thus will manage to act well in circumstances that would frustrate lesser people, just as a good general will make the best use out of the troops he has been given. Nor will a good person do really *bad* things under pressure of misfortune. But if he encounters the luck of Priam, that is, 'big and numerous' misfortunes prolonged over a period of time, he can be 'dislodged' from *eudaimonia*, and, if that happens, he will not get it back again 'in a short time, but, if ever, in a long and complete time, if, in that time, he gets hold of big and fine things' (1101a8–14). Aristotle concludes that a person has *eudaimonia* 'if and only if that person is active according to complete excellence and is sufficiently equipped with the external goods not for some chance period of time, but for a complete life' (1101a14–15).

Aristotle's distinguished pupil Theophrastus made a significant contribution to literary history with his *Characters*, portraits of unpleasant types of people, which have had importance for the history of comedy.

HELLENISTIC CONTINUATIONS

The Hellenistic period (beginning in the late fourth century BC) saw a very rich development of relationships between philosophy and literature in both Greece and Rome (up through the early centuries AD), as both the Epicurean and the Stoic schools took a keen interest in poetry as a vehicle for philosophy, and also developed new philosophical genres. Epicurus himself seems to have little interest in poetry; with such statements as 'I have spat upon the beautiful (*kalon*) and all who gaze upon it in an empty fashion,' he expressed contempt for elite culture, preferring, it seems, to cultivate forms of writing that were open to people of all backgrounds and classes.

In the first century BC, the Roman poet Lucretius turned Epicurus' philosophy into a great epic poem, *De rerum natura* (*On the Nature of Things*): see chapter 7. Lucretius' poetry is very powerful, and at times shocking. His descriptions of the sadism of sexual love and the depredations of aggression have been found difficult by some readers. And his attacks on the gods and on providence are part of a long tradition of religious scepticism that has been controversial wherever it has been present. So the story grew up (recorded by St Jerome) that Lucretius went mad from drinking a love potion, and wrote the poem in the lucid intervals of this madness. That is a convenient way of avoiding the challenge of the poem's critique of traditional values. But Lucretius' poetry is extremely controlled and tightly argued, and the vivid poetic depictions of human violence serve appropriately a therapeutic function, convincing the reader of the seriousness of the diseases of the soul that Epicurus proposes to treat.

It has been traditional to teach Lucretius as if the poetry and the philosophy were basically separate elements that could be studied apart. But Lucretius draws attention to his role as poet-philosopher, and argues for the value of poetry in presenting Epicurus' difficult doctrines: his verse is the honey around the cup that will enable readers to accept such initially bitter, but ultimately liberating, doctrines as the mortality of the soul and the badness of love.

The Stoic school also took a keen interest in literature. Cleanthes, the second great leader of the Stoa, wrote a Hymn to Zeus that survives, and Seneca reports him as arguing that poetry can express philosophical meaning in a sharper and more focused way than prose. Cleanthes compares the focusing power of poetry to the way the shape of a trumpet forces the breath into a focused and loud-sounding form. Subsequent Stoics both wrote literary works of various kinds and made educational use of existing works of literature.

In many ways, the Stoics' attitude to literature resembles Plato's, because their ethical doctrines also stress the self-sufficiency of the good person, the irrelevance of chance events for happiness. Taking Socrates as their model of the good life, they argue that the good person will meet adversity without fear or disturbance, caring little for external things. They both employ such examples in their teaching and try to present their own lives as examples of struggle toward that goal. At the same time, they conduct a stern critique of existing literature. Unlike Plato, they do not seek to remove or ban it: for they hold that it can be a useful vehicle for recognizing the variety of forms taken by human vice and excess. Instead the teacher must encourage the young to cultivate a stance of critical detachment from the work – like, it is said, Odysseus tied to the mast so that he will hear the Sirens' song but not be destroyed by it.

Tragedy, as we might expect, is a constant stalking horse of Stoic philosophy. Thus Epictetus (first century AD) defines tragedy as what happens 'when chance events befall fools' (*Discourses* II 26.31), and argues that the purpose of a good life should be:

to study how to remove from one's own life mournings and lamentations, and such expressions as 'Alas' and 'Wretched that I am' and misfortune and ill fortune... For what else are tragedies but the sufferings of people who have been wonder-struck by external things, displayed in the usual metre?

(*Discourses* I 4.23–30)

In an imaginary conversation with Euripides' heroine Medea, who murdered her children to get revenge on a husband who deserted her, Epictetus attempts to convince her that she had a lot going for her, but made just one big mistake: falling in love with her husband. 'Stop wanting your husband,' he tells her, 'and there is not one of the things you want that will fail to happen.' Against these bad examples, Stoic philosophers set a variety of good examples: Socrates, the Roman hero Cato, and, at times, themselves.

The self-presentation of the philosopher becomes a crucial element in the literary forms preferred by Roman Stoics, whose works, unlike those of their Greek predecessors, survive whole. Both Seneca (first century AD) and Epictetus use a type of dialogue in which the philosopher is always present – although, in both cases, the label 'dialogue' is somewhat misleading because the interlocutor is minimally present. Seneca also further develops the form of the philosophical epistle, in a manner that makes much use of his own (possibly fictive) experiences; the replies of the addressee are represented only in his own imagined responses. Although the correspondence has sometimes been read as a set of letters to a real person, there is no evidence at all that any of the letters was ever sent, and the whole work is best read as a construct expressing a certain picture of philosophical education, and engaging the reader in the process of philosophical therapy. The interlocutor Lucilius is gradually led, with many backslidings, toward the extirpation of passion and a devotion to virtue alone.

Stoics also wrote in existing literary genres. Seneca wrote tragedies that have exercised enormous influence on literary history, particularly through an Elizabethan translation that changed the course of English literature. These works, probably written for public reading rather than staged performance, are highly rhetorical, lurid in their depiction of physical suffering and crimes such as incest and the eating of one's own children, and extreme in the range of passions they contain. Their relation to the philosophical works is hard to pin down. Clearly they do show in graphic form the horrible excesses of passion and the ease with which a good person can be led into horrible vice once she makes the error of valuing just one external person (for quite a few of the tragedies concern women who are disappointed in love). But there is something about the plays that eludes easy reconciliation with the prose writings: at times they appear to depict the passion for external things as heroic, the life of serene goodness as sluggish and small. It is perhaps difficult to write in the tragic genre without slipping into such attitudes, and we might say that the form has simply taken over. But we also might see Seneca as more conflicted about Stoic norms than the prose works suggest.

Seneca's one other surviving literary work, the *Apocolocyntosis Divi Claudi* (*Pumpkinification of the Divine Claudius*) lends weight to this conjecture. If Stoic tragedy is already problematic, Stoic comedy would appear to be a contradiction in terms, since the Stoic attitude of measured preparedness for all of life's events allows no room for the surprise that is essential to humour. But the *Apocolocyntosis* is the funniest work that survives from imperial Rome. A scathing political satire, it depicts the death and attempted deification of the emperor Claudius, who is ultimately sent to an ignominious occupation in hell. Its in-group knowingness, its no-holds-barred pillorying of the bodily and mental defects of the late emperor, and its general sense of comic freedom from restraint (except during those passages that offer fawning praise of the new emperor Nero) all seem more like Aristophanes than like the Seneca we otherwise know. The work reinforces the picture of a man who was not fully at peace with Stoic norms.

Stoic norms also had a profound influence on poets who did not write works of philosophy. The ideas of Stoicism were broadly disseminated at Rome in the first century BC and the first two centuries AD, and entered deeply into the ways poets had of seeing the world, much in the way that the ideas of Christianity did in other eras. (We can see the extent of this influence, for example, in the letters of Cicero, who expects his addressees to get jokes that presuppose quite a detailed knowledge of philosophy, even if, like his wife Terentia, they are not particularly well educated.) Lucan, Seneca's relative and contemporary, is the most obvious example of a Stoic poet; his *Pharsalia* has Cato as its hero, and explores Stoic themes throughout. But Virgil's *Aeneid*, completed early in the first century AD, also shows serious Stoic influence, and younger contemporary poets such as Ovid and Propertius are quite familiar with its normative idea of therapy for passion. Horace is the exception: an Epicurean, of a rather more gentle sort than Lucretius, he develops Epicurean ideas of calm pleasure and contemplative serenity.

Cicero, neither a Stoic nor an Epicurean, was both a major philosophical thinker and one of the literary giants of ancient Rome, at the end of the Roman Republic (first century BC). His philosophical dialogues offer extensive debates on most of the major philosophical themes and give a detailed account of the positions of different schools on these topics (see chapter 7). Written with an eloquence

and grace that is quite amazing – considering the speed of their composition, and the fact that for much of that time he was also writing
major political speeches and also moving around from place to place
to avoid the assassins who eventually caught up with him in 44 BC –
Cicero's philosophical dialogues are concerned less with detailed
characterization and more with exposition than are Plato's; they had
a great influence on later writers of dialogue in the western philosophical tradition, including Berkeley and Hume. Cicero also prided
himself on his poetic compositions, which focused on his own political achievements; a few extracts survive in self-quotations in his
other works.

Cicero was not only one of history's great orators, he was also
one of its most influential theorists of rhetoric and literary style. In
works such as *De oratore*, *Brutus* and *Orator*, he sets the study of
rhetoric and style on a course that it has followed more or less to the
present day, forging or further articulating the conceptual categories
in terms of which speeches and related texts are analysed.

Cicero also wrote epistles, many of which were intended for
publication as a record of his political and intellectual career. A
large number survive: a very complete, though one-sided, correspondence (probably not intended for publication) with his lifelong friend
Atticus, a wealthy Epicurean who remained aloof from politics as
Epicurus recommended; and a wide range of letters, sometimes with
answers from their addressees, to and from his wife, daughter, and
other relatives, leading politicians, and a wide range of other friends
and acquaintances. These letters vary greatly in style: the more public ones are frequently rhetorical and highly crafted; the letters to
Atticus are compressed, full of jokes and private references, a moving testimonial to a friendship of unwavering love and loyalty. Many
of the letters concern philosophical matters, and one can see in both
Cicero's and his correspondents' texts the extent to which philosophical thinking shaped the way the events of life were seen and
the norms towards which people aspired. In this sense they may
be compared with Seneca's more deliberately crafted philosophical
epistles.

At the same time, the letters also show in a fascinating way the
limitations of philosophy in face of the events of life. Repeatedly,
in interpreting people and events around him, Cicero finds himself
recommending (or criticizing the want of) *humanitas*, which seems

to mean a delicate concern for the particularities of person and situation. (There is a fascinating example of this in the rather biased account he sends to Atticus of the bad behaviour of Atticus' sister Pomponia toward her husband Quintus, Cicero's none-too-admirable brother. This very funny letter also shows that bad marriages have changed little over the ages.) *Humanitas* is a human value Cicero derives from his experience, but he does not appear to find it in any of the philosophers he studies (although he might have found something like it in Aristotle).

Even more remarkable is the clash between philosophy and experience over the issue of death. Cicero's philosophical works take the strict Stoic line on death: it is never appropriate to fear it or to grieve when someone one loves has died. He reports as admirable a bereaved father's statement: 'I was already aware that I had begotten a mortal.' Cicero's daughter Tullia was the great love of his life. He clearly delights in her more than he ever does in either of his wives, and only Atticus holds a correspondingly intimate place in his affections. She had three marriages, the first two unhappy; she died in childbirth during the third. Shortly before her death, Cicero writes to a bereaved friend recommending the usual Stoic thoughts about death. Her death devastates him. When, after some months, Atticus suggests that he might return to work, he angrily responds that he could not do that, and, moreover, he does not think that he ought to. Much of his time before death was spent trying to build a shrine for her.

We can see from this correspondence, as we do in the works of Seneca, the deep seriousness with which Romans typically approached philosophy. Even when they could not altogether follow it, they felt its challenge; even when it did not encompass all their experience of life, it never quit the scene.

The traditions that have been described here continued onward. Later authors such as Lucian, the younger Pliny, Dio Chrysostom, and the epic poet Statius employ Stoic concepts in literary works of various kinds. Christian writers reflect on the norms and terms of the debate and fashion distinctively Christian versions of classical literary and philosophical-literary forms. Neoplatonist philosophers, above all Plotinus in the third century AD, develop Platonic ideas about beauty and the ascent of love into a fully new aesthetic theory.

Meanwhile, the important work *On the Sublime*, probably written during the first century AD, by an author whose name is usually given as Longinus, inaugurates a distinctive strand of theorizing about literature that was to prove of major importance in the later Western tradition. In the space of a single chapter, it has not been possible to cover these and other developments. Nevertheless, the range and richness of the subject should be evident enough; though frequently ignored on account of the modern segmentation of the disciplines, it remains one of the most exciting areas of ancient Greek and Roman thought.

FRANS A. J. DE HAAS[1]

9   Late ancient philosophy

INTRODUCTION

This chapter covers a fascinating stretch in the history of ancient Greek philosophy, ranging from the dawn of the Roman empire in the first century BC until the Arab conquest of Alexandria in AD 640. It is well known that in this period most of the ancient legacy to Byzantine, mediaeval and Renaissance philosophy received its definitive shape. However, in the transmission of this legacy to later centuries much of the depth, detail and motivation of late ancient philosophy was lost. Only in recent decades has the period begun to receive the attention it deserves. Within the confines of the present chapter we shall bring together a selection of the first – often tentative – conclusions in this rapidly advancing area of ancient philosophy.

First a few words on labels and periods. There is some justice in speaking of late ancient philosophy as *Imperial* philosophy. Nearly all philosophers mentioned in this chapter lived and worked in the Roman empire (western, eastern, or both), and some of them even owed their position to emperors. However, none of the philosophers discussed here wrote in Latin – even if they taught at Rome. (Latin writers on philosophy were covered in chapter 7.) They testify that Greek continued to be an important language for philosophy throughout the Roman empire.

For reasons that will become clear I propose to divide the history of late ancient philosophy into two main periods, viz. a period of *establishing the universal truth*, from the end of the Hellenistic era in the first century BC until Plotinus in the second half of the third century AD, followed by a period of *exploring the universal truth*,

from the immediate successors of Plotinus until the Arab conquest
of Alexandria in AD 640. A brief Who's Who of the main figures to be
discussed may serve as a background. It will be followed (pp. 246–9)
by a chart tabulating the main surviving late ancient commentaries
and their authors.

First period. This runs from Philo of Larissa to Plotinus. Philo of
Larissa (c.161–c.84 BC), head of the sceptical Academy of Athens (see
above, chapter 6, p. 179), and his pupil Antiochus of Ascalon (c.130–
68 BC) mark an important shift from Hellenistic to late ancient philosophy. Philo late in life claimed that Plato had not been a sceptic
after all, and that Academics were sceptical about the Stoic definition
of knowledge, not about knowledge as such. Antiochus rose to the
occasion and defended the Stoic definition of knowledge as well as
the general convergence of Stoic, Old Academic and Peripatetic doctrine. To this trend of convergence the Platonist Numenius (second
century AD) contributed by regarding pure Platonism as perfectly in
agreement with Pythagoreanism, and by seeking support from Greek
and Oriental religious practice. Alcinous (second century AD) is the
author of a famous *Handbook of Platonism* for teachers in philosophy, briefly outlining the main characteristics of his brand of so-
called Middle Platonism which combines Platonic, Peripatetic and
Stoic doctrine. Plutarch of Chaeroneia (c.AD 45 to after 120), prolific
moral philosopher, famous biographer of Greek and Roman politicians, and a Delphic priest, wrote critiques of Epicurean and Stoic
doctrine, while incorporating Pythagorean, Peripatetic and Stoic
thought into his ethico-political views; his religious writings preserve useful material on Greek and Egyptian religion. The main representative of the Peripatetic tradition is Alexander of Aphrodisias
(fl. c. AD 200), appointed Professor of Aristotelian Philosophy on behalf of the emperors Severus and Caracalla (whether in the chair at
Athens – for which see pp. 207 above and 251 below – or at Rome is
unclear). His impact on the development of philosophy can hardly be
overestimated: in later centuries he was to be known as the commentator *par excellence* for his numerous commentaries on Aristotle,
and his own *On the Soul* and *On Fate*. He was read in the class-
room of Plotinus, who probably drew on him to a greater extent than
we will ever be able to tell; and when later Platonists show themselves critical of Aristotle's arguments, they can often be shown to

attack Alexander's interpretation of Aristotle rather than Aristotle himself. The physician Galen (late second century AD, see pp. 295–8, chapter 10), whose logic, epistemology and physics bear a distinctive Peripatetic stamp, chose to disagree with Alexander on, for instance, issues of dynamics and psychology.

The cornerstone of late ancient philosophy is Plotinus (AD 205–70). In a brilliant synthesis of earlier philosophy he develops the concept of a universal truth into a comprehensive system transcending the former schools. Plotinus is regarded as the founder of what is now called Neoplatonism, although he himself was convinced that he was only expounding Plato (no *Neo-*), and although his pupil Porphyry (AD 232–309) rightly signalled that Plotinus incorporated most of Aristotle's metaphysics, to mention just the most important source (no *–platonism* strictly speaking). Plotinus set up a school in Rome, and was well acquainted with emperor Gallienus and his wife, as well as politicians, doctors and literary men from all parts of the Mediterranean. In his fifties he began to write down his teaching in treatises which Porphyry edited into six *Enneads* (sets of nine) some thirty years after Plotinus' death. Even where later Neoplatonists dissented from Plotinus in important ways, their achievements can be understood as deepening, correcting, and extending *his* vision of the universal truth.

Second period. This runs from Porphyry (AD 232–309) to Stephanus (fl. 610); only a few philosophers can be mentioned here. Porphyry developed Plotinus' philosophy, adding a strong interest in religious practice and allegorical interpretation as sources of wisdom, and fiercely attacking Christianity. Porphyry's pupil Iamblichus of Chalcis (250–325) opened a school in Apamea (Syria) where he worked on the full and explicit integration of Neoplatonism with Pythagoreanism, and made important changes to the theory of soul (see further, p. 265 below). He also decided the canon of Platonic dialogues to be read in the philosophical curriculum (see pp. 255–6 below). Themistius (fl. 340–85), a well-known orator and politician, ran a philosophical school in Constantinople. For his own convenience he wrote influential paraphrases of Aristotelian works which show not only Platonic interests but also an independent mind, especially in his paraphrase of *On the Soul*.

In Athens Neoplatonism reached new heights with Syrianus (died 437), who innovated in metaphysics and vehemently opposed

Aristotle's criticisms of Platonism and Pythagoreanism. His pupil Proclus (411–85) is most famous for his systematization of Neoplatonism in the 211 propositions of his *Elements of Theology*, which had Euclid's *Elements of Geometry* as its model of presentation. He also wrought a full integration of Neoplatonic metaphysics with Greek pagan religion, attributing to gods, demons and heroes their place in his *Platonic Theology*. His influence extends through the Middle Ages to the Renaissance revival of Neoplatonism. Damascius (fl. c.529) deepened the Neoplatonic understanding of Plato's *Parmenides*. His pupil Simplicius (writing after 529) left us extensive commentaries on Aristotle which not only testify to the broad learning of later Neoplatonism but have also preserved numerous fragments and testimonies concerning the Presocratics, the Stoics and the early commentary tradition.

In Alexandria Platonism was represented by one of the few female philosophers of antiquity, Hypatia (fl. 370–85), of whom little is known apart from her death at the hands of the Christian mob. Ammonius son of Hermias (c.435–526) heads a series of Alexandrian Neoplatonists, among whom the Christian Philoponus (c.490–570) stands out for his criticism of Aristotle and Proclus, and for his innovations in physics. After Olympiodorus, David and Elias (all second half of the sixth century), who left commentaries on both Plato and Aristotle, Stephanus (fl. c.610) was acting head of the school when the emperor Heraclius invited him to the Chair of Philosophy in Constantinople shortly after 610. With him the teaching of philosophy moved to the Byzantine empire.

No doubt the most important historical process contemporary with the period of late ancient philosophy is the rise of Christianity. Especially after the reign of Constantine (306–37), who converted to Christianity (AD 312), pagan and Christian philosophers and theologians found themselves in opposite camps. The emperor Theodosius even declared Christianity the state religion of the empire. Legislation by Theodosius (379–95) and Justinian (527–65) increasingly hampered the teaching of pagan philosophy. In 529 Damascius, then head of the Academy at Athens, and some of his pupils including Simplicius, took off to the Persian king Chosroes. They soon returned to find better luck within the empire. Only the Alexandrian school starting with Ammonius son of Hermias seems to have found a practical mode of co-operation with Christian students and church officials, allowing Philoponus, a Christian, to put his mark on philosophy before Christian scholarchs like David, Elias, and Stephanus took over. Despite many interesting debates and many cases of cross-pollination between the two camps, this chapter will be almost exclusively confined to pagan philosophy.

Late ancient philosophical commentaries

In a volume of this size and scope there is no possibility of listing all philosophical commentaries from late antiquity. Nevertheless the table gives a good sense of what now survives, whole or in substantial part, including many of the works which are accessible to non-specialist readers.

commentator	date	author	commentary on
Anon.	between 50 BC and AD 150	Plato	*Theaetetus*
Aspasius	fl. 100–30	Aristotle	*Nicomachean Ethics* I–IV, parts of VII–VIII
Anon.	end 2CAD	Aristotle	*Nicomachean Ethics* II–V
Alexander of Aphrodisias	fl. c.200	Aristotle Aristotle Aristotle Aristotle Aristotle	*Topics* *Prior Analytics* I *On Sensation* *Metaphysics* Alpha–Delta *Meteorology*
Calcidius	c.256–357	Plato	*Timaeus*
Porphyry	232–309	Ptolemy Aristotle	*Harmonics* *Categories*
(?) Porphyry	232–309	Plato	*Parmenides*
Themistius	c.317–88	Aristotle Aristotle Aristotle Aristotle Aristotle	*Posterior Analytics* *Physics* *On the Heavens* *On the Soul* *Metaphysics* Lambda

commentator	date	author	commentary on
Iamblichus	died 325	pseudo-Pythagoras	*Carmina aurea*
		Nicomachus	*Introduction to Arithmetic*
Dexippus	4C	Aristotle	*Categories*
Syrianus	died 437	Aristotle	*Metaphysics* Beta, Gamma, Delta, Lambda, Mu
Hermias	5C	Plato	*Phaedrus*
Proclus	411–85	pseudo-Pythagoras	*Carmina aurea*
		Plato	*Alcibiades*
		Plato	*Cratylus*
		Euclid	*Elements* I
		Ptolemy	*Tetrabiblos*
		Ptolemy	*[Introduction to Ptolemy's Tetrabiblos]*
		Plato	*Republic*
		Plato	*Timaeus* 17a–44d
		Plato	*Parmenides*
Hierocles	5C	pseudo-Pythagoras	*Golden Verses*
Ammonius	435/45–517/26	Porphyry	*Isagoge*
		Aristotle	*Categories*
		Aristotle	*De interpretatione*
		Aristotle	*Prior Analytics* I
Asclepius	6C	Nicomachus	*Introduction to Arithmetic*
		Aristotle	*Metaphysics* Alpha–Zeta
Philoponus	490–570	Nicomachus	*Introduction to Arithmetic*

(*cont.*)

(cont.)

commentator	date	author	commentary on
		Aristotle	*Posterior Analytics* I
		Aristotle	*Prior Analytics*
		Aristotle	*Categories*
		Aristotle	*On the Soul*
		Aristotle	*On Coming-to-be and Passing Away*
		Aristotle	*Meteorology* I
		Aristotle	*Physics* I–IV, with excerpts of V–VIII
pseudo-Philoponus	6C	Aristotle	*Posterior Analytics* II
		Aristotle	*On the Soul* III
Boethius	c.480–524	Aristotle	*Categories*
		Aristotle	*De interpretatione*
Damascius	462 to after 538	Plato	*Phaedo* (2 redactions)
		Plato	*Philebus*
		Plato	*Parmenides*
Simplicius	fl. 530	Epictetus	*Handbook*
		Aristotle	*Categories*
		Aristotle	*On the Soul* I–II
		Aristotle	*On the Heavens*
		Aristotle	*Physics*
pseudo-Simplicius (Stephanus?)	6C	Aristotle	*On the Soul* III
Priscianus Lydus	6C	Theophrastus	*On Sensation, Solutions to Chosroes*
Olympiodorus	6C	Aristotle	*Categories*
		Aristotle	*Meteorology*
		Plato	*Phaedo*
		Plato	*Alcibiades*
		Plato	*Gorgias*

commentator	date	author	commentary on
Elias	6C	Porphyry	*Isagoge*
David	6C	Porphyry Aristotle	*Isagoge* *Categories*
Anonymus	6C	Aristotle	*De interpretatione* *16a30–24b7*
Stephanus	6/7C	Aristotle Aristotle	*De interpretatione* *Rhetoric*
Anon.	?	Aristotle	*Posterior* *Analytics* II

The commentators on Aristotle are standardly cited by page and line number in the multi-volume H. Diels (ed.), *Commentaria in Aristotelem Graeca* (= 'The Greek Commentaries on Aristototle'; Berlin 1882–1909). A large number have now been translated into English: for details, see Bibliography [144].

THE PROJECT OF PHILOSOPHY

In the period of establishing the universal truth, the more or less clear-cut divisions between the Hellenistic schools (see chapter 6) were gradually replaced by complex shifts of position between the existing schools, as well as revivals of Aristotelianism and Pythagoreanism. This complex development was due to an equally complex combination of factors, none of which would probably have been sufficient on its own. Let us first describe briefly the philosophical landscape in the first century BC.

Only three schools were philosophically fertile: the Stoa, the Epicurean Garden, and the sceptical Academy. By that time the Lyceum had already dwindled; many of Aristotle's esoteric writings had apparently disappeared, and later Peripatetics hardly participated in the ongoing debates of the other schools. In the mean time generations of Stoics and sceptics had exerted themselves in ever more ingenious technical debates about the criterion (if any) of truth. At the same time they competed in their contempt for the Epicurean alternatives in these areas. No final breakthrough was forthcoming as long as the traditional boundaries between the schools persisted.

Yet, a new division of the territory was already discernible. After all, the three main philosophical issues in the first century BC concerned, in logic, the choice between scepticism and reliable knowledge; in physics the choice between mechanical atomism on the one hand, and teleology and a material continuum on the other; and in ethics the choice between pleasure and virtue. Sceptics and Epicureans faced the Old Academics, Peripatetics and Stoics alike. A new merger of the latter three would soon eclipse both sceptics and Epicureans. But first Plato and the Old Academy had to become respectable again, and the interest in Aristotle and the Peripatos had to be rekindled.

Historical circumstances put an end to the Athenian centres of philosophical orthodoxy, thus providing room for change: in 88/87 BC Mithridates seized power in Athens; in the following year the Roman general Sulla besieged, captured and ruined the city. Among the many that fled the war we find Philo of Larissa, then head of the Academy. Afterwards the Academy of Athens was not heard of for more than a century. Nor do the Athenian Stoa and Garden seem to have survived the onslaught. The authoritative tradition of their founders was broken, and other centres of philosophical activity rose all over the Mediterranean (Alexandria, Rome, Pergamon, Rhodes).

Sulla's capture of Athens was beneficial to the Peripatetics: without realizing the value of his booty, the Roman general took with him to Rome a library containing Aristotle's works. In the first century AD a version of these manuscripts became available in a philosophically sensible order, starting with the so-called logical works later dubbed the Organon (*Categories, De interpretatione, Prior and Posterior Analytics, Sophistical Refutations, Topics*). Although some of Aristotle's works had been known throughout the Hellenistic era (e.g. the *Rhetoric* and the *Topics*), the re-emergence of this set of texts caused a veritable revival of interest in Aristotle and gave new edge to many existing discussions. Through the later Platonic commentaries on e.g. the *Categories* and *On the Soul* we are familiar with a series of early critics and defenders of Aristotelian doctrines testifying to the lively discussions from the first century BC onwards. These critics formulated a respectable number of textual and doctrinal problems which more benevolent commentators would have to solve. Even if the critics' aim was largely destructive, they gave fresh impulses to philosophy. The problem-oriented approach to Aristotle's text – which had its Platonic counterpart in, for example, Plutarch's *Platonic Questions* – is reflected most clearly in the format of works like the physical and ethical *Quaestiones* by Alexander of Aphrodisias and his circle, and Porphyry's *Question-and-Answer Commentary on the Categories.* Much later it is still part of the fabric of the elaborate sixth-century Neoplatonic commentaries on Aristotle by Simplicius and Philoponus.

Given the revivals of Aristotelianism and Platonism it is no surprise that when the Stoic emperor Marcus Aurelius (see pp. 207–8 above) decided to appoint professors of philosophy at Athens (AD 176) he established four chairs: Platonism, Aristotelianism, Epicureanism and Stoicism.

With these four schools in office again, we need to ask for the main reason why philosophers increasingly combined doctrines from different origins. The vexed issue of the criterion of truth was surpassed by the growing belief in a universal truth from which all human wisdom had drawn from times immemorial. The Stoics' etymological exegesis of what they regarded as the primitive and diffuse philosophizing of the ancients was being developed into an art. Nevertheless some philosophers resisted the process of convergence. A notable example is Alexander of Aphrodisias who quarrelled with both Platonism and Stoicism in his attempts to develop Peripatetic answers to questions Aristotle had not dealt with in any detail.

From the first century AD onwards most philosophers came to treat the history of philosophy as a series of attempts at unfolding and exploring this single truth. It was believed to be contained in religious theory and practice within the Greek world (Greek mythology, oracles, Homer, Orphism, Pythagoreanism), as well as in the Egyptian mysteries, and in revelations of the Persians, Assyrians and the Indian Magi, to name the most important.

Obviously some early philosophers would have succeeded in elucidating the veritable truth better than others. As it happened, apart from the Academy two of the three other influential schools could easily be shown to derive from Plato: Aristotle had been Plato's pupil, and the Stoic founding father Zeno of Citium had been taught by, among others, Polemon, one of Plato's successors. Therefore this development tended to favour Platonism as having the best claim to the truth, especially when Plato's biography was posthumously enriched with travels to distant countries which allowed him to incorporate ancient Pythagorean, Egyptian, and other kinds of wisdom, including the books of Moses. Platonism never collapsed into Pythagoreanism or Egyptian mysticism because Pythagorean and Egyptian writings were considered far more obscure than Plato's dialogues. On the other hand, a full understanding of Plato's dialogues required the study of these ancient doctrines. Hence we find an increasing number of Platonist commentaries on for example Pythagorean texts, as well as the appearance of pseudo-Pythagorean treatises to cover for theories, such as the Aristotelian ten categories, which Platonic commentators also managed to find in Plato. The so-called *Chaldaean Oracles*, which are the revelations ascribed to a father and son Julian, two Chaldaean magi living in the second century AD, describe a version of second-century Platonism. The *Chaldaean Oracles* were to play an important role in later Neoplatonic theology.

Pythagoreanism deserves special mention since it pervaded so much of late ancient philosophy in wedlock with Platonism. The Platonist Numenius (second century AD) used the Pythagoreans' fidelity to their master and their unity of mind to scorn the dissension between Platonist schools. Nevertheless, he believed, Plato's doctrine had remained intact, bearing the sign of veritable truth. Freed from later Academic adulterations, and clearly set apart from Aristotle and the Stoics, the pure Platonism that emerges proves to be pure Pythagoreanism! For Numenius the difference between Pythagoras and Plato is one of style and emphasis rather than doctrine. The Platonist Nicomachus of Gerasa (second century AD) wrote an *Introduction to Arithmetic* which was inspired by Pythagorean number theory. In Iamblichus' *On Pythagoreanism* Nicomachus' work finds its place alongside chapters on the physical, ethical and theological applications of arithmetic. In Plato's *Republic* the study of mathematics had a protreptic function in relation to ethics, politics and metaphysics, since it prepared the soul for knowledge of intelligible objects. In Iamblichus the study of Pythagorean arithmetic has the same function. Finally, Porphyry promoted the Pythagorean lifestyle in his *On Abstinence*, and it is telling that aspects of his description of the true philosopher can be found in his *Life of Plotinus*.

In the previous sections it has been pointed out that the development of philosophy in late antiquity came to focus on the authoritative texts of Plato, Aristotle, the Stoics, and the Pythagorean tradition, as well as on non-philosophical writings such as revelations and oracles. This focus on texts of such diverse character explains the increase of the number of philosophical commentaries in late antiquity. It will be convenient to list a number of factors which contributed to the popularity of the genre:

(a) In the absence of an oral tradition and an acting successor of the founders of the schools the self-definition of philosophers came to depend more on the study of the school texts.

(b) In early commentaries there is considerable attention to lexicographical explanations which had become necessary because vulgarized (*koinē*) Greek had replaced the classical Greek of the more ancient authors. Even lexica of Platonic terminology were assembled. More serious problems of vocabulary and grammar were to be expected when the rather idiosyncratic Pythagorean and revelatory texts were studied. In later commentaries it turns out that the myths in Plato's dialogues as well as the dialogues themselves were in need of different well-defined modes of interpretation.

(c) Against the Academics a non-sceptical reading of Plato and the Old Academy had to be established explicitly.

(d) Throughout the commentary tradition there is a clear awareness of the problems of diverging manuscript traditions and the ensuing discussion of different readings. On the other side there is evidence of philosophically inspired tampering with texts.

(e) In order to safeguard internal consistency problematic works of relevant authors had to be proven spurious, and more congenial ones proven authentic.

(f) Texts of Pythagorean, Peripatetic and Stoic origin had to be interpreted in such a way that they more or less agreed with the tenets of Platonism, or could be construed as imperfect representations or foreshadowings of such tenets.

(g) As soon as the unity of Greek philosophy was established the commentary provided a convenient locus for the criticism of rival commentators and the careful (and unobtrusive) development of new insights which tacitly received the seal of orthodoxy because they arose from the study of an authoritative text. To this purpose the commentary tradition could be manipulated by selectively drawing on different strands of the tradition.

(h) Neoplatonic commentators tend to regard the study of authoritative texts, but also of inspired commentaries on such texts by e.g. Iamblichus, as itself a spiritual exercise which contributes to the progress of specific parts of their souls towards union with the first cause, the One. Hence the writing of commentaries requires divine inspiration, and is similar in this respect to the writing of hymns to the gods.

For all the impact this new conception of the project of philosophy had on the self-image of the schools, the format of much of their literary production, and their actual convergence, it never reduced philosophy to a reconstruction and defence of one's philosophical lineage. Appeals to authority never stood on their own: serious argument regarding the philosophical issues remained mandatory. After all, it was a sincere quest for philosophical truth that led to this conception in the first place. And if the result looks like 'eclecticism' or 'syncretism' to us, these designations seem less apt insofar as they suggest that philosophers were busy selecting convenient morsels of doctrine for a construction of their own, or losing themselves in a blessed confusion of different creeds. On the contrary, once the *fact* of the unity of truth had dawned upon them, and the genealogy of relevant traditions had been worked out, it was only natural to continue exploring each of these traditions for their contribution to the understanding of that single truth. This was the project that dominated the second half of our period when the question of authority was no longer in need of discussion.

For these very reasons philosophy in late antiquity had a remarkable capacity for innovation. Major developments in ethics, logic, physics, psychology and metaphysics will be briefly illustrated below. These were the product of the acumen of trained professional philosophers who possessed an impressive familiarity with all previous philosophical and religious thought. They were sufficiently critical to spot the loopholes in their masters' thought and sufficiently creative to mend them in more than a single way. In their hands the format of the philosophical commentary which they often (not always) preferred was no more and no less than a vehicle for doing philosophy, and never a straightjacket.

The order by which I shall present different areas of late ancient philosophy in the remainder of this chapter is derived from
the order of the philosophical curriculum after Plotinus, viz. ethics
and politics, logic, physics, psychology, and metaphysics or theology. This is the order which Porphyry imposed on Plotinus' treatises in his edition of the *Enneads*, as well as the order of Proclus'
philosophical training as described in Marinus' *Life of Proclus*, to
mention just two examples. In the later Platonic curriculum the
study of Plato's pupil Aristotle came to serve as an introduction
to Platonic philosophy. A capable commentator had to show that
the same truth shines through Aristotle's on the whole too mun-
dane dealings with logic, physics, psychology and metaphysics, the
more so since the aim of his philosophy was considered to be nothing less than the Neoplatonic 'One'. Especially in logic and physics,
Aristotle's works provided a level of sophistication not found in any
Platonic or Pythagorean text. The biological treatises, a major part
of our Aristotelian corpus, were discarded as irrelevant to philosophy proper. The order of topics listed above was used to determine
the order of both the Aristotelian and Platonic courses. Each work
of Aristotle was prefaced by a standard set of questions; a slightly
different set of questions was used as an introduction to each work
of Plato. Perhaps the most important question concerned the aim
(*skopos*) of the work to be commented on, since the answer to this
question determined both its position in the curriculum and the perspective from which it was interpreted.

A full sixth-century course of philosophy might consist of the
following texts, to be read under the guidance of a teacher. First the
novices were subjected to a reading of the Pythagorean *Golden Verses*
or Epictetus' Stoic *Handbook* in order to prepare their souls for philosophy proper. The teachers had recourse to these non-technical
works because Aristotle's ethical treatises could not be mastered
without previous logical training. The ethical preparation was followed by a general introduction to philosophy and its parts, and by
Porphyry's *Isagoge* ('Introduction'), prefaced by an introduction of its
own. After a biography of Aristotle the student would proceed with
Aristotle's *Categories, De interpretatione, Prior Analytics, Topics,
Posterior Analytics, Sophistical Refutations,* and perhaps *Rhetoric*
and *Poetics*. Then followed the technical treatises on ethics and politics: *Nicomachean Ethics, Economics, Politics*; physics: *Physics, On*

Coming-to-be and Passing Away, On the Heavens, and *Meteorology,*
leading up to *On the Soul,* perhaps accompanied by some of the
Parva naturalia (the collective name for the short treatises on sen-
sation, memory, etc., see p. 128 above); and finally the *Metaphysics.*
The Platonic course was prefaced by a biography of Plato, and again
took the student through ethics (*Alcibiades, Gorgias, Phaedo*), logic
(*Cratylus, Theaetetus*), and physics (*Sophist, Statesman*) to theol-
ogy (*Phaedrus, Symposium*), culminating in the Good (*Philebus*).
The course was rounded off by comprehensive pictures of physics
(*Timaeus*) and theology (*Parmenides*).

ETHICS AND POLITICS

In Alcinous' *Handbook of Platonism* 27–34 we find the ingredients of
much of late ancient ethics. The good for man consists in the knowledge and contemplation of the primal Good, which Alcinous equates
with Divine Intellect. Hence happiness is to be found in the goods
of the soul alone. The purpose of life is 'likeness to god' (based on
Plato, *Theaetetus* 176a–b and *Phaedrus* 248a), but Alcinous indicates
that this must be the god *in* the heavens (i.e. the Demiurge), not the
god *above* the heavens (Intellect) whose transcendence should not be
compromised by human efforts. In progressing towards this goal, natural aptitude, training and teaching combine with the purification
and preparation instilled by music and the mathematical disciplines
to achieve the four cardinal virtues – courage, self-control, justice
and prudence. These virtues are mutually dependent: because of the
rule of reason involved in each, a person cannot possess one without
the others. They are summits which do not allow of variation, as well
as 'means' (cf. Aristotle's doctrine of the mean, p. 146 above) insofar
as they result from a moderation of the emotions (*metriopatheia*),
not their extirpation (*apatheia*).

Plotinus *Enneads* 1 2, which reads as a commentary on *Theaetetus* 176a–b, further explores the hierarchy of virtues which was to
be developed more explicitly in Porphyry *Sentences* 32. This hierarchy comprises civic or political virtues, followed by purificatory,
theoretical and paradigmatic virtues. Each of these kinds of virtue
is a manifestation of all four cardinal virtues as they are modelled
in Intellect (no longer the Demiurge as in Alcinous) and mirrored at
lower levels of the human soul respectively, thus determining different kinds of life of the human being as a whole. Thus at each

level these virtues can be regarded as images of god (Intellect) in the human rational soul. Interestingly, the realization of such an image at any level is not only part of a person's progress towards 'likeness to god' but at the same time part of the fulfilment of this goal, and a persisting condition of his or her soul. Eventually, the virtue of prudence brings with it the communion between gods and men foreseen in the myth in Plato's *Phaedrus*. Iamblichus associates Plato's *Alcibiades* with the initial stage of self-knowledge, *Gorgias* with political virtues, and the *Phaedo* with purificatory virtues, thus determining the position of these dialogues in his curriculum. Porphyry intended his *On Abstinence* for more advanced students already longing for the theoretical virtues. On the whole, Neoplatonic rationalism tends to favour *apatheia* as the final goal, although the notion of progress allows an initial stage of overcoming irrational emotions by *metriopatheia*. In the case of Simplicius' commentary on Epictetus' *Handbook*, which has its place before the philosophical curriculum proper, this leads to the complication that a Stoic work prescribing *apatheia* has to be interpreted as advocating Neoplatonic *metriopatheia*. The acute awareness of a student's progress through ever higher virtuous states of his soul is the explanation of striking differences in e.g. metaphysical sophistication between commentaries on (Aristotelian) works early in the curriculum, and (Platonic) works read at a more advanced educational stage. It makes sense to provide more sophistication only when the student's soul has reached the appropriate stage.

Although many Neoplatonic writings dwell at the highest stages of intellectual knowledge, Neoplatonists allot political virtue a definite role, if only because Plato clearly required fully educated philosophers to guide the less fortunate. This tenet is recalled at the end of Plotinus' *Enneads*, in a passage which contains an exhortation to disseminate goodness in the same way as the One disseminates itself. Hence it is not surprising that Plotinus is reported to have attempted the foundation of Platonopolis, a city to be governed by the laws of Plato, in Campania. Moreover love of the Good, which leads to contemplation, at the same time produces love of man (*philanthrōpia*), a concept which owes much of its content to Aristotle's account of friendship as well as the Stoic doctrine of universal kinship (*oikeiōsis*, pp. 173–4 above). Therefore philosophers have the obligation to help other human beings become godlike. At the same time, their activity is itself godlike and constitutive of their own virtue because it participates in god's providential activity. Becoming godlike thus requires *both* contemplative *and* socio-political activity. So in the end the goal of achieving likeness to god introduced by Plato as the proper escape of the soul from its incarnated existence necessitates socio-political activity.

LOGIC

The contribution of late antiquity to logic mostly consists of systematization and harmonization between the achievements of Peripatetic and Stoic logicians and the methodology displayed in Plato's dialogues. Logic was conceived as a discipline which embraced such diverse methods as demonstration, dialectic and sophistical argument. Thus in a section called the 'study of reason' Alcinous deals with Platonic dialectic and Aristotelian syllogistic in consecutive chapters, in which he illustrates syllogistic theory by means of examples drawn from Platonic dialogues. Peripatetics like Alexander of Aphrodisias point out that the aim of logic resides in the realization of the parts of philosophy proper for which it serves as an instrument (*organon*). For a Platonist like Plotinus dialectic, which embraces the methods of analysis, synthesis, division and definition, is a means of exploring the intelligible realm. Therefore he favours a distinction between dialectic, the noblest part of philosophy, and formal logic, or the petty rules of discussion which can only be of a preliminary character. The Neoplatonic commentators on the *Analytics* follow a tradition already present in Alexander's discussion of the issue when they claim that logic is both a part and an instrument of philosophy: are not hammer and anvil both products and instruments of the smith's art? In effect they shift the perspective from the opposition between Peripatetic/Stoic logic and Platonic dialectic to the distinction between formal logic and its application in philosophy, or in more general terms the distinction between logical form and matter. Ammonius and Philoponus read this distinction back into Plato and the Academy, so that we find them using different concepts of logic and dialectic on a par.

The commentators on Aristotle's logical works imposed the familiar division of logic into the domains of terms (*Categories*), propositions (*De interpretatione*), and inferences (*Prior and Posterior*

Analytics, Topics, Sophistical Refutations). They tried to set out the existing body of logic in a more systematic fashion, e.g. by applying a rigorous division of syllogisms on the basis of the relation between the premises. In this framework the basic role of the first-figure syllogism (pp. 135–6 above) became an important issue: does this 'perfect' syllogism guarantee the validity of the other syllogistic modes (as Alexander believed), or does each mode itself guarantee its own validity (as was held by the Neoplatonists, who were thus free to explore non-Peripatetic kinds of formal logic). One example of a late ancient extension to Aristotle's logic is the so-called tek-meriodic proof from effect to cause. On a slim basis of Aristotelian texts on inferences from signs and a number of hints in Themistius, Philoponus and Simplicius developed a kind of proof which they considered especially appropriate in physics. After all, physics aims at an understanding of the sensible realm (the effect) by referring it to its intelligible causes which have a higher status in the Platonic hierarchy of being. This type of inference was equated with Aristotle's approach to a problem by proceeding from 'what is better known to us' to 'what is better known by nature', or from an as-yet diffuse whole as it presents itself to the senses, to its constituent elements grasped by reason.

Since the *Categories* came to be placed at the beginning of the logic course, some of its reception pertains to logic rather than metaphysics – if a division between these parts of philosophy applies at all in such a context. A famous example is the concept of genus. In Aristotle genus is one of the predicables and describes the relation between subject and predicate when the latter is a non-convertible predicate belonging in the essence of the former (e.g. *animal* belongs in the essence of *human being* although *human being* does not belong in the essence of *animal*). Aristotle subscribed to the Academic rule that a predicate which is applied to subjects that differ in priority among each other is not a genus (e.g. *number* is not the genus of the natural numbers 1, 2, 3 etc.). In his treatise *On the Genera of Being* Plotinus turned this rule against an important interpretation of Aristotle's categories which regarded categories as highest genera. Plotinus points out that in *Categories* 5 Aristotle applies the term 'substance' to both primary and secondary substances, and in *Metaphysics* Zeta 3 to all of form, matter and the composite of both: two instances of hierarchical series. Hence, judging from Aristotle's own naming practice, the categories are not genera technically speaking. If so, they turn out to be useless for Plotinus' own project of establishing the genera of true being; to fill the gap he turns to the five 'greatest genera' of Plato's *Sophist* (Being, Sameness, Difference, Motion and Rest; above, chapter 4, p. 124 note 13). Together this quintet constitutes the timeless being of Intellect.

Does Plotinus' conclusion forfeit all divisions of sensible being, even though Plato, especially in the *Philebus*, instructed us to attempt such divisions? Surely not. The five intelligible genera produce lower kinds on the level of the sensible realm which Plotinus allows us to call genera of the sensible realm, though they are no longer highest genera nor genera in the traditional sense. For these lower genera imitate the productive nature of their causes and turn out to be both cause and (therefore) predicate of their effects. Against this background Plotinus carefully and critically explores the significance of the categories of substance, quantity, quality and relation, along with a newly crafted category of motion, as means of describing the sensible realm. Plotinus envisages the possibility that in the end these five 'categories' might well reduce to the Platonic duality of independent versus relative being.

In Porphyry's influential introduction to Aristotelian philosophy, the *Isagoge*, we find this kind of genus hailed as the notion of genus philosophers are interested in. In the famous Tree of Porphyry, a division of substance through animal and human being down to the particulars Socrates and Plato, the highest genus of substance is not only the predicate of each member of this hierarchical series but also its cause. Because the *Isagoge* served as an introduction to the Aristotelian curriculum which started with the *Categories*, its un-Aristotelian notion of genus influenced the interpretation of the *Categories* in late antiquity. And because the *Isagoge* precedes the *Categories* in most mediaeval manuscripts, Aristotle's work has often down to this day been read through Porphyry's spectacles. The widely discussed problem of universals received its shape from a tantalizing passage in the *Isagoge* in which Porphyry notes that he will *not* discuss it since it is beyond the scope of his work.

In his commentaries on the *Categories* Porphyry restricted the applicability of the work to the sensible realm (as Plotinus had done), and drew arguments from the Peripatetic tradition to rescue all ten items from Plotinus' criticism as genera of *names*, indicating genera of *being* only indirectly. In the later commentary tradition the aim of the *Categories* was generally regarded as being an exhaustive division of the kinds of simple *names* (*phōnai*) signifying simple *things* (*pragmata*) via simple *concepts* (*noēmata*). This is the basis of late ancient semantics; from its Latin version in Boethius' translations and commentaries sprang the mediaeval logic of terms (see p. 209 above and p. 324 below).

PHYSICS

From the extensive late ancient debates on physics we shall here single out three issues which have continued to draw interest in later times: (a) the nature of matter, (b) the correct number of the elements and the concept of their mixture, and finally (c) the birth of impetus theory.

Matter. According to Aristotle, matter and form constitute two principles necessary to explain the change that is characteristic of the objects of physics. Following indications in Aristotle's anything but clear discussions of these principles, Alexander of Aphrodisias developed the theory in important ways. He claimed that the changes of fire, air, water, and earth into each other require a common substrate which does not possess any of the qualities that characterize the elements, including corporeality. This means he conceives of elemental change as an exchange of forms in a permanent substrate. This incorporeal formless matter, later called prime matter, cannot exist without the form of one of the elements, and no elemental form can exist without prime matter. To later authors Alexander's notion of prime matter suggested identification with both the Receptacle of Plato's *Timaeus* (p. 109 above), which receives the images of the Forms without changing itself, and with Stoic matter, which was also defined as devoid of qualification (p. 170 above). In Plotinus and Proclus (for whose differences on the question, see p. 269 below) we find this kind of matter as the bottom level of the sensible realm. In addition Neoplatonists draw on a reading of Aristotle *Metaphysics* Zeta 3 when they insist against the Stoa that matter fails even to possess the three dimensions which define corporeality. From the same text Proclus derives the conclusion that three-dimensionality must be a separate level between prime matter and the elements, one which is unqualified but not formless.

Later Neoplatonists wondered whether a matter devoid of any determination can play a causal role at all. Simplicius and Philoponus in particular explored the possibility that the level of three-dimensional matter, or rather three-dimensionality without quantitative limits, is all we need to explain elemental changes. In this way the elemental form is responsible for the quantitative limits displayed in e.g. the natural limits of expansion (a given volume of water will always evaporate into a proportionally equal volume of air), while at the same time matter can be held responsible for the three-dimensional extension and divisibility incorporeal forms suffer in the sensible realm. Simplicius keeps prime matter for metaphysical reasons, whereas Philoponus is alone in drawing the conclusion that incorporeal prime matter is useless for physical explanations – a conclusion he exploits to attack one of Proclus' arguments in favour of the eternity of the world. Philoponus' theory of the three-dimensional prime matter of natural bodies sits well with his notion of place as a static three-dimensional extension which is always filled with bodies without exerting any influence on them. This notion of place had its rival in Iamblichus' theory of place as a cohesive power of the universe as a whole and of each thing in it, a mould which makes possible the very existence of the universe and moves with it. Drawing on his teacher Damascius, Simplicius expounds this doctrine at some length in his *Physics* commentary, especially the digression in it known as the 'Corollary on place'.

Elements and mixture. The fate of Aristotle's 'aether' (above, p. 139 and below, p. 280) is testimony to the converging tendencies of late antiquity. While Alexander has no doubts about the existence and properties of Aristotle's fifth element, Platonists vacillate between rejecting it and assimilating it to the aether mentioned by Plato at *Phaedo* 111b or even to the fifth regular solid for which Alcinous and Plutarch refer us to *Phaedo* 110b6. A further alternative was to assimilate aether to the Stoic creative fire. At the other end of the spectrum, Philoponus rejects the existence of aether and tries to subvert each and every argument put forward in defence of its existence in Aristotle's *On the Heavens*. The remaining fragments of this critique are quoted and indignantly rebutted by Simplicius' commentary on this latter work, in which Simplicius' sole aim is to preserve the immutability and eternity of the heavens which he saw as jeopardized by Philoponus' attacks.

With respect to Aristotle's concept of mixture, late ancient philosophers display a remarkable variety of positions which can still be discerned in mediaeval and Renaissance discussions of the issue. Aristotle believed that the four elements mix to form higher-order materials like blood and bone by achieving a new balance between the four qualities hot, cold, moist and dry that characterize them. Without further elucidation he claims that each ingredient remains potentially in a mixture because in principle each ingredient can be recovered from the mixture. Alexander's *On Mixture*, a sustained polemic against the Stoics, specifies that when a mixture is analysed into its constituents these will reappear specifically, though not numerically, the same as before. Alexander also specifies that recovery is possible because in the mixture both the forms and the qualities of the elements have been preserved in an imperfect state of their actuality, which can easily be restored to its previous state of perfection. In Philoponus' commentary on *On Coming-to-be and Passing Away*, this view is regarded as a proper interpretation of Aristotle's intentions. Nevertheless Philoponus himself holds that only the qualities, not the forms, of the elements are preserved in this imperfect state. For if the maximum degree of heat is an essential characteristic of fire, the slightest reduction of heat must be equivalent to the extinction of fire.

Proclus and Simplicius, on the other hand, reject the notion of mixture entirely in the wake of their abhorrence of Stoic materialism. Never will bodies constitute a new unity; only their incorporeal qualities interact to create what is no more than the impression of a new unity. Simplicius draws the vivid picture of a set of torches, the flames of which seemingly unite into a single flame, but prove to have been separated all the time when their sticks, which never formed a unity, are drawn apart. In the same way threads of different colour woven together make the impression of a new colour, although they never change. On his view mixture is one of the delusions so characteristic of the world of seeming and becoming.

Impetus theory. A set of problems in Aristotle's dynamics is our last port of call in this section. Aristotle embraced a theory of contact causality: each thing moved is moved by something in contact with it. This position had a number of consequences. In the void motion was impossible, and this was in fact one of Aristotle's reasons for rejecting the existence of void. Furthermore, projectile motion stood out as a problem: how can the javelin continue to move after leaving the hand of the thrower? Aristotle's most famous suggestion was an estafette among pockets of air rushing in behind the javelin to push it forward. But why then does projectile motion come to an end?

Philoponus is famous for having dealt with these issues in terms of the late Neoplatonic notion of the transmission of power. This theory rests on the notion of *dynamis* as meaning both 'power' and 'potentiality', the former active and characteristic above all of intelligible causes, the latter passive and characteristic of the lower levels of reality on which they exert their influence. In virtue of their creative 'power' intelligible causes bring about their effects by acting on substrates which have a specific 'potentiality' to receive this influence. In the case of projectile motion, or so Philoponus suggests, the thrower implants into the javelin a limited power which enables the javelin to move until the power expires. In his *On the Creation of the World* (*De opificio mundi*), a Christian defence of creation, Philoponus unifies dynamics by extending this mechanism to the heavens, in which God implanted the power to move at the moment of their creation, as he implanted the natural motions in the elements, and souls in living beings.

Along the same lines motion in a void can be defended. Given the rule that a limited body can receive only limited power there is no reason to fear a movement of unlimited duration or speed in the absence of a medium, as Aristotle suspected. The only role the medium plays is that of an additional obstacle to the motion. It has no part to play in the transmission of force, for the actual motion depends primarily on the power or inclination inherent in the moving object.

PSYCHOLOGY

The history of philosophical psychology in late antiquity is perhaps the best example of how Platonists refined their understanding of a limited set of Platonic concepts by means of Aristotelian distinctions. A major addition to Plato's bipartite and tripartite divisions of

the soul (pp. 111–13 above) became Aristotle's *phantasia* (often translated 'imagination'), storage room for perceptions and working area
for the intellect. Here Platonists located the process of the recollection of Forms: the *phantasia* was conceived as the common ground
where perceptions from the outside and projections from the innate
logoi in the divine rational part of the soul are compared in order to
be recognized for what they are. In this way, too, the process of induction produces universals in the mind that can serve as trustworthy
starting-points for true scientific argument.

Late ancient epistemology depends largely on the ontological position of the human soul. On this score Plotinus found himself opposed
by all later philosophers. He believed that the rational part of the soul
never fully descends from the intelligible realm. Our lack of knowledge of the Forms is not due to a true lapse from Intellect but to
our being unaware that part of our soul is still functioning on that
level. Hence 'recollection' (p. 116 above) is described as a movement
of the self (or 'the we' as he calls it) towards a proper recognition of
what it still is – this interiorization is at the same time the project of
Plotinian ethics. From Iamblichus onwards Neoplatonists no longer
believed that the rational soul still resides in Intellect. Hence, when
soul was established as a level of being separate from Intellect (see
further p. 269 below), it must have suffered a truly substantial change
which cannot be repaired by recollection. The result is a less optimistic view of the knowledge acquired by means of philosophy
and science: the best a human being can achieve is to uncover the
image of Intellect which is his or her own. Full comprehension of,
for instance, how the gods create the body, or its life, or how they
link them together is beyond us. Hence in Iamblichus and in later
Neoplatonism so-called theurgy can find a place as means of overcoming the fatal separation between the two realms. Theurgy, 'the
work of gods', is a rite conducted by human beings but empowered
by divine symbols, by which man is clothed in the shape of gods and
is raised up to be united with them. This short cut to the realm of
the divine complements the hardships of rational philosophy as one
way among many that bring the soul into contact with the intelligible realm.

Aristotle's tantalizing chapters on the intellect (*On the Soul*
III 4–5) inspired Alexander and Themistius to innovative and remarkably influential theories. Aristotle decreed that soul displays

a distinction between the productive intellect 'which makes every-thing', and the material intellect 'which becomes everything', the former of which is somehow associated with divine immortality. In his own *On the Soul* Alexander presents a tripartite division of intellect: (a) the potential or material intellect, which all human beings possess at birth; (b) the dispositional intellect which not only possesses the capacity to abstract its objects from sense perceptions but also considers them already contained within itself. Not all humans fully reach this level of actualization. The cause of this actuality is (c) the active intellect, itself a pure form, and supremely intelligible. Alexander famously identifies this intellect with the First Cause, the Unmoved Mover of *Metaphysics* Lambda. Therefore the active intellect is the cause of both the being and the intelligibility of all objects of thought, although much remains unclear about its mode of causation. Moreover, there is only a single divine active intellect for all human beings. In Arabic and mediaeval philosophy this line of thought was to be hotly debated.

Alexander rejects any kind of immortality of the individual soul – a consequence of his Aristotelian view that the human soul is nothing but the form of the human body and has to perish with it. This 'hylomorphic' (as it is now called) conception of soul and body dominated the Peripatetic tradition after Alexander, whereas before Alexander interpreters of Aristotle had rather identified the *pneuma* ('breath'), not the human body as a whole, as the instrument of the soul. This dependence of soul on body can be rephrased in terms of the soul's supervenience on the body, in much the same way as the form of the mixture supervenes on a suitable blend of elements.

Themistius rejected the view that Aristotle's productive intellect is to be identified with god, who is thus protected from association with human thought. Themistius describes how the productive intellect, a 'second god', is eternally associated with a single potential intellect in a relation of form and matter. This composite intellect is separate from the human body, although the potential intellect is more closely related to the human soul, and the productive intellect is sometimes identified as 'we'. Below this couple resides the passive or common intellect which is perishable, and responsible for memory, emotion and discursive reasoning. Since only this latter intellect is a firm part of the human soul there is no room in Themistius for personal immortality; nor is there any hint that an intellectual life is in any way godlike for a human being: true intellective activity transcends the human level.

METAPHYSICS

The major characteristics and the development of the elaborate metaphysical systems of late antiquity can perhaps be best explained by starting from Plotinus. He develops a system of three so-called hypostases or levels of existence, viz. the One, Intellect, and Soul. Plato's *Republic* 509b 'the Good is beyond being' inspired Plotinus to the conclusion that the principle of being, the One which he identified with the Good, must be above being and devoid of all qualifications we commonly ascribe to beings. From the plenitude of the One emanates, as the radiation of its perfection, the level of Being, viz. the divine Intellect which embraces all Forms in a single unified act of thought. This act of unification by self-contemplation is Intellect's way of returning to its source, the One. From Intellect Soul emanates because in an act of recklessness Intellect does not contemplate itself but 'gazes outwards'. The discursive reasoning of Soul and its interest in what is other than itself create prime matter and the sensible world which are below Being. Since Soul governs the universe and involves all particular souls that govern parts of the universe such as plants, animals and human beings, the sensible world is not a hypostasis of its own. In short: Soul's desire to belong to itself has led to self-alienation. Yet Soul and all souls strive to return to their source, Intellect, by focusing on their rational part and discovering that it never left Intellect. By taking part in Intellect's return to *its* source, the One, 'we', viz. the rational part of our soul, can return to the first principle in an act of so-called *ekstasis* ('ecstasy'), which transcends the rational thought that was necessary to reach the realm of Intellect. Plotinus' system is essentially dynamic because emanation (*prohodos*) and return (*epistrophē*) are both required to constitute fully the hypostases of Intellect and Soul. Since the three hypostases are eternal, there is no beginning or end to this process. Generation and corruption, as well as discursive thought, are mere signs of weakness on the part of lower beings to be explained by a lack of unity which is ultimately due to their loss of orientation towards the One.

This system is a brilliant synthesis of elements from different philosophical currents that can be discerned before Plotinus. For instance, in Alcinous we find the tenet that the Forms are the perfect and eternal thoughts of god, which is an older Academic view already embraced in some form or other by Antiochus and the Jewish Platonist Philo of Alexandria (first century AD). In Alcinous' case god is both the Platonic Good and an Intellect engaged in self-contemplation, modelled on Aristotle's god. Its ineffability can be approached by negations, by analogy, or by tracing beauty to its source (as in Plato's *Symposium*). Alcinous' set of principles is completed by Matter. This triadic system competed with the dualism of the One and Indefinite Dyad familiar from Plato's so-called unwritten doctrines, and ubiquitous in the reception of Plato's philosophy from the Old Academy onwards. A third competitor was Pythagorean monism, in which a single principle called the One, Henad, or Monad, performed two functions: it was the primary cause, while at the same time serving as a constituent of lower realms together with the Dyad. Plotinus defends his three hypostases headed by a single One by identifying them with the first three hypotheses of Plato's *Parmenides*, i.e. the first One, the second One or One-Many (Intellect), and the third One or One-and-Many (Soul). A similar reading of the *Parmenides* along Pythagorean lines foreshadowing this development can be traced back as far as the first century AD.

After Plotinus the position of the One is further enhanced. Syrianus and Proclus develop a system of so-called henads, the roots of which are perhaps to be found in Iamblichus. Their aim is to guarantee the absolute transcendence of the One without losing the explanation of unity and unification by which lower levels may return to their sources. For unlike the One henads can be participated in; they exist both self-subsistently and as immanent in their participants. In Proclus the henads are unities located directly below the One, but before the Monad and Indefinite Dyad, or Limit and Unlimited, which combine to produce all lower levels of intelligible and sensible being. The self-subsistent henads are gods each heading their own chain of connected beings, a chain which reaches to the lowest levels of the sensible world. An extended example of a chain given by Proclus (*On Plato's Parmenides* 903) is the Form of the Moon which is said to appear at the divine level as the 'one' and the 'good' of the Form because all things are divinized by the light of truth; it appears at the angelic level in its intellectual phase, and on the demonic level in living beings that image that Form in thought and are intellectual, imitating it in living rather than thinking; among animals the Egyptian Apis-bull and the moon-fish are its manifestations; and finally there is the so-called moon stone which is believed to wax and wane with the moon. Thus the entire universe is divinized, and no part devoid of divine providence. In Proclus' *Platonic Theology* these and other gods are identified with Olympian gods and demons familiar from Greek religion, thus giving them the philosophical underpinnings they needed so badly to survive the increasing pressure of Christianity. Damascius, again musing on the *Parmenides*, made further progress in drawing the ultimate consequences of a strict concept of the One, stressing above all its ineffability.

Further consideration of the structure of the intelligible realm and further study of the *Parmenides* led to a novel conception of emanation and a multiplication of hypostases. Proclus' influential *Elements of Theology* aims at providing the basic rules of causation from which such a system can be deduced. One of these rules is that every higher cause operates prior to its consequents and extends its power further down the hierarchy than a lower cause. This means that the highest cause, the One, is solely responsible for the existence of prime matter; Intellect, together with the One, extends its influence as far as the presence of Forms, down to unqualified body; Soul extends only to living bodies. Emanation is no longer a strict top-down process but a process in which the higher more general causes generate the substrates on which the lower more specific causes operate. The difference with Plotinus is perhaps most notable in the case of matter: for Plotinus matter is the cause of evil because it distracts the soul; for Proclus matter is the effect of the One, and therefore good, so that evil only has oblique subsistence as the by-product of the declining powers of higher causes at lower levels.

The multiplication of hypostases rests on the concept of mediation which guarantees the continuity of the procession: between two terms in the hierarchy a third may exist which mediates between the two (cf. Plato, *Timaeus* 31b–c for the principle that Proclus is following here). Such triadic structures are supported by universal triads such as Remaining–Procession–Return, of which Being–Life–Intellect (already found in Porphyry) is a prime example.

Each principle resides at its own level of existence and remains undiminished while by the power of its very being, or life, it produces a lower level in the procession. At the same time this lower level strives to return to its source, which in rational souls takes the form of an act of thought. When such triads are applied time and again to all conceivable distinctions found in Platonic and Aristotelian writings as well as Pythagorean and religious sources, the number of hypostases increases without end – or *almost* without end, for all late ancient metaphysics continues to pay heed to Plato's advice in the *Philebus* and patiently divides unity step by step before yielding to infinity. In Proclus' terms: 'every plurality partakes in some way of unity'.

NOTE

1   The author wishes to thank Keimpe Algra, Han Baltussen, Tony Long, Jaap Mansfeld, Douwe Runia, Richard Sorabji, and the editor of this volume for their expert advice on earlier drafts of the present chapter.

10 Philosophy and science

THE BEGINNINGS OF PHYSICAL SCIENCE

The earliest literary survivals from the Greek world, the epic poems of Homer and Hesiod, contain, *inter alia*, accounts of natural phenomena and of the origins of the universe. But the latter are speculative mythology, while the former invariably impute large-scale natural phenomena to supernatural forces: Zeus coruscates miscreants with thunderbolts; Poseidon shakes the earth in anger; Apollo visits plagues upon the impious. There is no attempt to explain events in naturalistic terms (that is, as the natural result of natural forces and the intrinsic properties of things), and no effort to reduce the apparent diversity of phenomena to a small set of explanatory concepts in terms of which they are to be accounted for.

The Greeks themselves considered that with Thales (fl. c.585 BC) there emerged a wholly new way of looking at things, one characterized by Aristotle as the search for the *archai*, or basic 'principles' of things. According to tradition, Thales, the first of the so-called Presocratics, made water his *archē*. Water was fundamental to the world and its processes, perhaps, as Aristotle says, because of the observation that moisture is necessary for life and that 'heat comes from moisture'; moreover, the earth 'rests on water', a feature which accounts both for its general stability, and also (probably) for the occasional earthquake. Thales also claimed that magnets possess souls, presumably because they have that power to induce motion which is characteristic of animate life.

This is science of a sort: explanatory principles of great generality are postulated, but in such a way as to be at least consistent with experience, and perhaps more; and Thales' speculations express the

concern for taxonomical precision, along with the occasionally surprising result which flows from it, which is one of the hallmarks of
science. However, whether, and for what reasons, ancient physical
speculation really merits the designation 'science', and if so which
parts of it, is a vexed scholarly issue; the ancients never developed a
scientific method as such, and were both sparing and haphazard in
their use of experiment.

Thales' pupil Anaximander (early to mid sixth century BC) rejected
the idea that any one familiar stuff was basic, preferring to postulate
a theoretical substrate, the *apeiron* or 'indefinite', out of which the
familiar substances were generated and transmuted, in accordance
with a conservation principle, which explains why this world is only
one among many which follow each other in an infinite cycle. And
in a remarkable conceptual leap, he held that the earth remains at
rest not because it is supported by anything (such as Thales' water),
but simply because it lies at equilibrium in the centre of a spherical
universe, having no reason to move one way rather than another
(above, p. 49).

Anaximenes (mid sixth century BC) abandoned the hypothesis of
the *apeiron*, generating the physical world out of a familiar substance, air (singled out because it is 'closest to the incorporeal'), by
processes of rarefaction and condensation (above, chapter 2, p. 50).
Indeed he apparently conceived of heat and cold not as fundamental
properties (or substances) in their own right, as other Greek thinkers
were to do, but as supervenient upon these various states of condensation and rarefaction, the whole system being imbued with an
eternal principle of dynamic motion, again ascribed to the air.

The earth is not immobile at the centre because of indifference,
but rides on air 'like a lid'. Anaximenes liked analogies. Some may be
read as supplying genuine physical explanations: just as old houses
may collapse at the slightest provocation, and hence without discernible cause, so too may the ricketier parts of the earth, causing
earthquakes. Others suggest relevant similarities of structure: lightning is caused by the tearing of the clouds, just as oars tearing the
sea produce a flash.

GOD, FLUX AND KNOWLEDGE

These last two explanations are also important for another reason: for they exemplify the Presocratic rejection of the epic poets'

supernatural accounts large-scale physical events, a rejection the Hippocratics were to extend into the realm of medicine and the understanding of disease: pp. 276–7 below). The Presocratics do not reject theology – Thales supposed that the world was full of gods, and Anaximenes described his basic air as divine – but their divinities were not the jealous, interfering, quarrelsome gods of Homer. Aristotle (*Physics* III 4) says that all of the early thinkers were inclined to regard their *archē*, that out of which everything was ultimately generated and into which it was resolved, as being divine; divinity, then, becomes an attribute of what is constant, unchanging and fundamental in the world, as it was to be for the Hippocratic doctors.

Heraclitus (fl. c.500 BC) was a byword even in antiquity for obscurity: but sense may be sucked from some of his sentences. Things are cyclical in nature ('beginning and end are common', KRS 290),[1] and the elements intertransmute in the Anaximandrian manner ('cold things grow hot, the hot cools, the wet dries, the parched moistens', 22 B 126 DK), in accord with similar divine conservation principles. Fire is fundamental, however; it is the material of the soul and of dynamism in general; we become sentient by absorbing divine fire into which everything is ultimately resolved.

For Heraclitus, motion and change are constant components of everything: 'Everything flows'; moreover, everything is a dynamic compound of opposites; indeed, the very fluidity is responsible for what unity things possess: 'Things which have a natural circular motion are preserved and stay together because of it; if indeed, as Heraclitus says, the barley-drink separates if it is not stirred' (22 B 125 DK). These opaque theses are metaphysical as much as physical; but they may have had an empirical origin. Later atomists and others argued for the constancy of sub-perceptual change by noting that constant wear rubs down plough-shares and dripping water erodes stone; Heraclitus may well have done something similar.

At all events, he emphasized the importance of reasoning in forming a properly sophisticated picture of the world. His older contemporary Xenophanes (above, chapter 2, pp. 42–5 and 56–8), presumably in response to the plurality of incompatible fundamental theories on the Presocratic market, sounds the first note of scepticism in western philosophy (quoted above, pp. 56–7, and below, p. 306). Only god (a non-anthropomorphic intellectual god, remote from human affairs) can know everything. But Xenophanes is not a sceptic – he allows that with diligent application we may progress in discovery. Heraclitus too derides most ordinary claims to knowledge; but this is because people too readily give uncritical credence to the immediate evidence of their senses, not because knowledge of the world cannot be won. The world is not created by the gods, but it is divinely organized, by a force which Heraclitus calls 'thunderbolt' (i.e. Zeus: KRS 220). Heraclitus' physical philosophy thus has a teleological cast; but it also presents a world that is structured, albeit with a structure remote from the phenomenal appearances of things.

That idea of a world radically different from the way it appears at first sight was shared by Democritus (late fifth to early fourth century), one of the originators of ancient atomism. Atomism was developed partly in response to Parmenides and his followers, who argued that all change was illusory, since change entails that things are generated out of what is not; but what is not is nothing, which cannot even be referred to, much less function as a causal principle; whatever exists is eternal and unchanging. This prohibition on generation extends to all change. The atomists countered by arguing that there was such a thing as what is not – void or emptiness; it can be referred to, and it can be causally significant (there could be no motion, they thought, without it). Physical objects are built up out of microscopic component atoms which are eternal and unbreakable (Parmenidean objects in fact); there is thus no real generation, and certainly no creation *ex nihilo*.

Everything else is mere 'convention' (above, chapter 2, p. 67). In modern terms, Democritus is an eliminative materialist. His physics is radically different from the phenomena it seeks to explain. This poses a problem in epistemology: if the real world is so unlike the world of the senses, how can we reason from the latter to the former? In a fragment from a dialogue between reason and the senses, Democritus has the senses upbraid the intellect: 'Wretched mind, do you take your evidence from us and then seek to overthrow us? Our overthrow is your downfall' (KRS 552). But he evidently thought that reason had a decent rejoinder, for he is reported to have agreed with Anaxagoras' dictum that 'appearances are a glimpse of what is unseen' (KRS 510). The reports of the senses cannot be accepted as literally true: but they provide the explananda that science seeks to explain. Hence a scientific picture of the world must be able to explain how it is that the senses can give the appearances that they do, even if, strictly speaking, they are false.

It is not clear whether Democritus clearly formulated this solution, which lies at the heart of all subsequent scientific epistemology. But Democritean atomism presents the world for the first time with a notion of how science can show us that the microstructure of things may be radically different from the way the appearances would initially lead us to believe. On the other hand, the ancient atomists could not entirely divorce themselves from ordinary empirical conceptions: the properties they ascribe to the atoms (solidity, resistance, weight) are familiar sensible properties of ordinary objects. Their world is still rooted much more directly in the categories of experience than the world of modern particle physics, where even particles are not really particles; but Greek atomism clearly points down the road that will ultimately lead to the modern vision of a fundamental reality almost unimaginably unlike the phenomenal world we ordinarily inhabit.

THEORETICAL AND PRACTICAL MEDICINE

The question how to justify theoretical claims in philosophy and science remains at the forefront of speculative inquiry; and the issue of the proper relations between empirical evidence and theoretical reason comes to dominate methodological debate in the sciences. Such concerns also animated the jurisprudence that developed in the fractious liberty of the Greek city-states, pre-eminently Athens; and related issues of how to argue persuasively on any given topic engendered the circus of travelling teachers of persuasion we know as the sophists (see chapter 3).

The best evidence for such a debate in the fifth century BC is to be found in the multifarious medical writings that make up the Hippocratic Corpus. There are more than sixty texts in the collection that has come down to us under the name 'Hippocrates'; and they are widely different in style, subject-matter, and theoretical presuppositions, and were probably produced in a variety of different places over a period of about 200 years. Obviously, they cannot all be ascribed to the historical Hippocrates of Cos, and which texts (if any) should be was already a live 'Hippocratic Question' in antiquity.

Medicine and philosophy, empiricism and theory, had already combined in the person of Alcmaeon of Croton, a Pythagorean-influenced doctor of the early fifth century BC. He is said to have dissected an eye (although the truth of this report remains controversial); he held that the brain was the seat of consciousness and understanding, perhaps on the basis of anatomical investigation; and he developed a rudimentary empiricist theory of knowledge, which echoed Xenophanes' epistemological pessimism, while still believing that our ignorance is not entirely irremediable. He also formulated the view, later to dominate western medicine for two millennia and still popular in the East, that health consists in a balance of opposing properties.

The Hippocratic texts not only deal with practical matters of observation, diagnosis, prognosis and cure; they also engage with the theoretical issues which underlie them. They present, however, no unified orthodoxy. Some (in particular the *Epidemics*) offer concise accounts both of epidemic conditions and of particular cases with little or no theoretical speculation. Others (most notably *On Regimen* and *On Breaths*) seek to provide a comprehensive theoretical account of the fundamentals of human physiology, in terms of elements (fire and water for *Regimen*, air for *Breaths*). *Nature of Man*, on the other hand, argues for the necessity of understanding the humours (black and yellow bile, blood and phlegm), which its author takes to be 'obvious constituents' of the body, but against any reduction to the elements. He attacks monistic theories, such as that of *On Breaths* and the late Presocratic Diogenes of Apollonia (above, chapter 2, pp. 68–9) who both made air basic, on the grounds that if there were only one element there could be no differentiation among things, and no change.

On Ancient Medicine is even less theoretical, favouring a medicine based on directly observable properties and conditions (sweet, sour, salt, acid, etc.), decrying 'the invention of new-fangled hypotheses' as 'philosophizing in the manner of Empedocles' (on whom see chapter 2, pp. 69–72 above). The proper, dietetic approach to medicine and health has already been discovered empirically, and simply needs to be applied, refined and extended.

A further strand is added to the weave by texts like *On the Art*, a sophistic (although not sophistical) defence of medicine's claims to being a proper expertise (*technē*), against its various detractors. Medicine is difficult, but not impossible, provided that the hidden internal workings of the body can be grasped by the intellect (cf. Anaxagoras and Democritus, p. 274 above). A rationally grounded practice may deliver results on the basis of genuine understanding of its domain, and yet still fall short of one hundred per cent success for reasons which do not impugn its scientific standing. Patients fail to follow the appropriate regimen; and sometimes the disease is too well established for any measures to be successful against it (a point also made in *On Prognosis*), or is simply beyond the scope of the art. Proper doctors do better than charlatans or lay-people; and so medicine is more than merely a pseudo-science. The issue of how (if at all) to demarcate proper science from hocus pocus was to recur later in antiquity (see pp. 293–4); and it is central to modern philosophy of science.

Finally, a famous text, *The Sacred Disease*, argues against the view that epilepsy and related seizures are divine visitations; rather they are physical ailments with determinate physical causes, as can be seen both from the failure of the magical practitioners to alleviate it, and by physiological observation: epilepsy, our writer thinks, is most likely to strike those of a phlegmatic disposition (in the original humoral sense: they suffer from an excess of the cold and the wet in the form of phlegm; the writer also supposes the disease to be hereditary).

The drive to explain events in terms of regular physical causes as opposed to divine intervention is as characteristic of the Hippocratic temper as it is of the Presocratics; and it is central to the practice of science. Moreover, the Hippocratic texts (in particular *Epidemics*) distinguish crucially between the external occasion for some pathological effect, and the particular internal dispositions of the patient upon which the occasions operate. Depending on their different temperaments (the particular balance of their humours), different patients may react quite differently to the same external influences. This sophisticated approach allows causation to be a regular, perhaps even deterministic force, while being compatible with the evident variation in the effects (see pp. 295–6 below).

MATHEMATICS AND THE WORLD

We have followed the development of bold, general attempts to explain the world and its workings in naturalistic terms, as well as the various attempts of scientists to answer objections, both metaphysical and epistemological, to the coherence and possibility of their enterprise. What is noticeable, in the material presented so far, is the lack of application of any mathematical concepts to such speculations. Only Empedocles sought to account for things (the constitution of compound materials such as bone and blood) in terms of precise ratios of elementary constituents; and these attempts seem jejune and unmotivated by any discernible empirical considerations.

Ancient science is often castigated for being insufficiently quantitative or mathematical in its approach; but a clear exception is the number-dominated physical speculation of the Pythagoreans. Pythagoras himself is a shadowy figure, more mystic than mathematician (above, chapter 2, pp. 51–6). But later followers elaborated a 'Pythagorean' view of the world which was enormously influential, captivating intellects as diverse as Plato and Kepler. This philosophy is a complex product of the fifth and fourth centuries BC, and Aristotle dismisses it as mere number-mysticism. But its crucial impulse came less from *a priori* rationalism than from an astounding empirical discovery, namely the mathematical basis of musical harmony. Pluck a string of half a given length and you will sound a note an octave higher, and the same ratio is maintained in pipes, blocks and vessels of water. Similarly, the ratio 2:3 produces a pitch a perfect fifth higher; and 3:4 a perfect fourth. Harmony is an acoustic phenomenon; but it exhibits mathematical regularity, and (in the form of harmonic resonance) physical properties. Intoxicated with this discovery, so the story goes, the Pythagoreans proceeded to impose numerical ratios on everything else, mostly of thoroughly fantastical nature (2 was the number of female, 3 of male – hence 5 was the number of marriage).

They also created a 'table of opposites' (as did Alcmaeon): limit and unlimited, odd and even, one and many, right and left, male and female, resting and moving, straight and curved, light and dark, good and bad, square and oblong. That is a pretty heterogeneous bunch; and it is presumably not an accident that there are ten pairs, ten being the perfect Pythagorean number (the sum of 1, 2, 3, and 4, the components of the harmonic ratios). But they represent an attempt to mix geometrical, arithmetical, physical and biological materials in one categorization; and the fifth-century Pythagorean Philolaus made the first opposition central to his account of the structure of the world: things are products of the unlimited (matter) and limiters (imposing form).

As a piece of general metaphysics, the theory is opaque and of doubtful scientific value. But it did give rise to genuine science, in the form of mathematical harmonics; and it was responsible for the curious musical view, which persisted until the Renaissance, that the only real concords were the octave, fourth and fifth.

However Plato was sufficiently impressed with it to make mathematics fundamental to his ontology. His *Timaeus* (above, chapter 4, pp. 108–10) offers a complex, if fanciful, account of how the four elements stand to one another in different mathematical ratios. The elements are geometrically structured parcels of matter, fire in the form of the pyramid, earth the cube, water the icosahedron, air the octohedron. The fact that they are ultimately composed of triangular faces accounts, Plato thinks, for the intertransmutability of the elements, a view derived from Anaximander, Anaximenes and Heraclitus, with the significant innovation that earth can never become one of the other elements, since its faces are composed of right-angled isosceles triangles, as opposed to the others, whose fundamental triangles are right-angled triangles with sides $1, 2, \sqrt{5}$, which can be combined to form equilateral triangles.

Plato also distinguishes different types of the elements, with different properties, according to the sizes of the triangles which make them up, and whether the masses are made of uniform- or non-uniform-sized corpuscles. Then he discusses the origins and material bases for the various properties of things such as heat, hardness, heaviness, lightness, roughness and smoothness, and such perceptual properties as sweet, bitter, salt and acid, and the various smells and colours. All of these things, Plato says in summary, have come to be in accordance with two causes, 'the divine and the necessary' (68e–69a): the latter are the limitations imposed on creative possibility by the nature of the possible materials, while the former is the intention of the Creator or 'Demiurge' (literally 'craftsman', for the world is the rational product of rational, benevolent design) to fashion the best possible result out of those materials.

In what remains of the dialogue, Plato applies these teleological principles to animal, and specifically human, physiology; and their conjunction yields some interesting results. For instance, we could not have been made both intelligent and longer lived, since intelligence cannot be induced in anything other than soft and perishable material, and nor, if it is to be sensitive, can it be encased in a heavy covering of flesh and bone.

What is noticeable about this is how far removed it is from any empirical basis. The four elements are supposed to be (in some sense) ordinary stuffs – but no attempt is made to justify the choice of these over any others (indeed such attempts are few and far between in Greek science). On the other hand, although the physiology is in many ways fanciful, not least in its assignment of the three-part Platonic soul (see above, chapter 4, pp. 121–2) to the brain (intellect), the heart (emotion), and the belly (appetite), it betrays an informed awareness of the state of anatomical and physiological understanding of the time.

ARISTOTELIAN ELEMENTS

Aristotle's element-theory is altogether less fantastical. His universe is finite in extent, indeed necessarily so, since he argues that there can be no actualized infinity, numerical, spatial or material. Observation of the fixed stars confirms the universe's sphericity, which in turn determines the physical nature of its component parts. *On the Heavens* I 2–4 argues that the elements should be differentiated by their distinct intrinsic propensities for motion and rest, nature itself being defined as 'a principle of motion and rest' (*Physics* II 1). There are in a sphere only three privileged directions, towards, away from, and around the centre, which supply the candidates for genuinely simple (in the sense of undeviating) motion. Hence the elements may be expected to move naturally with one, and only one, of these simple motions.

Thus there are three natural, elemental motions: rising for light objects, falling for heavy objects, and revolution for the eternal matter of the heavenly bodies. In this way, Aristotle argues for the necessity of there being an extra celestial element quite distinct from the others, and not subject to transmutation; he calls it 'aether'. This thesis is not based solely on *a priori* considerations: it is an empirical fact that light things rise, heavy ones fall, and the heavens revolve. His element-theory is an attempt to construct an empirically responsive account of the basic structure of things on the basis of an economical stock of explanatory postulates: its success or failure depends ultimately on its coherence, its explanatory power, its economy, and its empirical adequacy; and it makes use of mathematics (geometry) not in Plato's vague, semi-mystical manner, but in an empirically grounded way.

Elsewhere in *On the Heavens* and *Physics*, Aristotle develops these ideas. The elements, if removed from their natural places (earth in the centre, surrounded by concentric rings of water, air and fire), will seek to return to them by the shortest possible routes (thus Aristotle's theory anticipates the modern physical principle of least action: see further p. 290); the greater the quantity of displaced stuff, the faster it will go; and its speed will also depend upon the medium through which it passes.

Moreover, in *Meteorology* IV 4 and *On Coming-to-be and Passing Away* II, Aristotle further analyses the elements as combinations of the four primary qualities, hot, cold, wet and dry (fire is hot and dry, earth cold and dry, water cold and wet, air hot and wet). The qualities had already figured in the Hippocratic treatises (although not always positively: *Ancient Medicine* dismisses them as explanatorily useless); Aristotle refines the theory by making hot and cold fundamentally active and wet and dry fundamentally passive, a view to be taken over, with some further refinements, by the Stoics. These basic 'powers', as he calls them, are themselves the reductive basis for other properties such as brittleness, ductility and malleability.

Earlier sections of *Meteorology* seek to account for a wide variety of phenomena, some but not all of them meteorological in our sense. He treats of meteors, the Aurora Borealis, comets, the Milky Way, rain, cloud, mist, dew, hoar-frost, snow, hail, winds, rivers, springs, climatic and coastal changes, the origin and saltiness of the sea, earthquakes and volcanoes, thunder and lightning, hurricanes, haloes, rainbows, and mock-suns. This apparently disparate collection of phenomena is unified by the fact that they have their origins in the behaviour of the elements intermediate between the earth and the heavens, namely water, air and the upper element, which Aristotle now prefers to call 'the inflammable' rather than fire, since fire is, as he says, a type of active chemico-physical change ('an excess of heat and a sort of boiling': *Meteor.* I 3). These phenomena are all the result of physical processes whose ultimate motor is the motion of the sun along the ecliptic and its diurnal orbit producing constantly changing local variations in heat and cold.

TELEOLOGY AND MECHANISM

Plato, as early as the *Phaedo*, attacked Presocratic materialist physics for ignoring the manifest order and purpose of things in favour of ascribing them to chance and necessity (which were invoked as explanatory devices by both Empedocles and the atomists). Proper explanations should explain *why* things are the way they are, not merely give some account of how they have come to be that way.

Such accounts are, Plato thinks, irreducibly teleological in form: in order to explain why some state of affairs has come about, we need to be able to show why things are *better* thus than they would be under any alternative arrangement. In the *Timaeus* the Creator, being himself good, made his creation as good as was materially possible (cf. pp. 279–80 above) by instantiating in matter the geometrical proportions to form the elements; and while material and mechanical factors matter to the process, they are secondary, the instrumental means by which the creator realizes his design of producing in the visible universe a material likeness of the eternal Forms. Mere mechanism cannot supply a suitably rich account of the world's evident structural organization. Such teleological principles may be discerned as early as Heraclitus; but Plato is the first to place them centre-stage in the drama of explanation, where they were to remain until the seventeenth century, when Galileo and Newton once again banished them from science.

Thus Plato staked out a firm position in what was to become the most important debate in ancient physics and cosmology: can the world and its occupants be accounted for simply in terms of mechanistic causes operating with no thought to the future, or must we suppose that goal-directedness is somehow written into the very fabric of the universe? On the side of mechanism, we find primarily the atomists, but also renegade Aristotelians like Strato of Lampsacus (died c.267 BC). In favour of some form of teleology are ranged Plato, Aristotle, the Stoics, later Platonists, Galen and the Neoplatonists.

Plato also grasps a distinction crucial to meeting Parmenides' challenge: while generation involves a process between opposite states, it is not the case that one opposite *causes* the other; rather something is brought from one condition into its opposite condition as a result of something which is already in that opposite condition. In this Plato anticipates Aristotle's more detailed account; and both of them make form fundamental.

But Plato and Aristotle part company in the ontological arena. Aristotle has no time for Plato's independently existing hypostasized Forms: form for him is something that only exists in suitably qualified objects, although it is something which one (suitably qualified) object may induce in another: that, indeed, is the paradigm of both natural and artistic generation. Nor has Aristotle's world any creator, intelligent and benevolent or otherwise: it has no need of one, since it has always existed. Hence, although it is structured, no designer structured it.

Aristotle resolves this apparent paradox by making form an irreducible structural principle of things, and by insisting that, even if the world is neither created nor organized by a divine intelligence, it is still teleological in nature. The biosphere consists of processes which are directed towards the end of maturation, even though no intelligence ever so directed them. This teleological drive is a basic and irreducible feature of the way the world is: no random agglomeration of material components could ever generate the world of regular and repeatable structure that we inhabit. This applies just as much in the sphere of elemental dynamics as it does in biology; heavy objects seek to rest as close as possible to the centre of the universe, light ones tend to the periphery, while the matter of the heavenly bodies seeks to maintain its eternal rotation. We cannot hope to give a complete account of the world if we ignore its fundamental goal-directedness. But equally the world is also a world of physical processes which occur for antecedent causal reasons. Stags shed their antlers because it is in their interests to do so; but these also fall off because they become too heavy.

Aristotle sketches an account of how form, information, is transferred from one animal to its offspring in the act of generation. The male semen bears, in the form of internal 'movements', the capacity for structuring the matter provided by the female menses; here he rejects the view of the Hippocratics, taken up by later theorists such as Galen, that the female too contributes form. Quite how this is supposed to work is never made clear. But the theory is interesting as an example of the rigour with which Aristotle seeks to marry his fundamental metaphysical categories (of matter and form, potentiality and actuality) to an account of the physical processes of animal conception and development which is responsive to empirical concerns.

Generation of Animals also involves detailed analysis of careful observation and acute criticisms of other theories, notably that of pangenesis, the idea that semen consists of a mixture of parts taken from all over the body (propounded in the Hippocratic *On Semen*). Acquired characteristics are not, he thinks (in contrast with the Hippocratic *Airs, Waters, Places*), generally inherited; while resemblance is a matter of morphology, not just of having the appropriate matter. Thus the crucial *explanandum* is the transmission and generation of form, which requires the postulation of a particular capacity for so doing. Here again, the theories of the atomists (among others) are found wanting – they cannot explain the regularity of animal generation.

Sexual dimorphism (which he knows not to be universal, and also realizes is exhibited in some plants) exhibits a difference of function: the male is 'that which generates in another' while the female 'generates within itself' (he tries to show, in line with his teleological commitments, why this separation is a good thing). Males are hotter than females, and it is this heat which accounts for their ability to transmit form; by contrast, females can nurture and nourish, but not produce and transmit it. This view, argued for at length in the first two books of *Generation of Animals* (along with a detailed discussion of the differences in reproductive economy among different animals), although partly observationally based, rests largely on theoretical considerations.

Semen is extremely dynamic, with the capacity to coagulate the menses as rennet sets milk: it is the efficient cause to the menses' matter. It contains *pneuma*, a vitally informed air (see further p. 295). The 'movements' it transmits serve to begin the formation of the embryo, because they contain its form in potentiality. The heart, which Aristotle thinks is the basis of all animal activity, at any rate in creatures which have it, is the first organ to be produced, and then directs further organogenesis. In *History of Animals* VI 3, he claims to have observed this in a series of observations made on chicken-embryos at various stages of development.

OBSERVATION AND EXPERIMENT

This introduces another central issue: how far was ancient science responsive to empirical observation? And how far (if at all) did it actively seek out critical data by way of experiment, or at the very least controlled observation?

The Hippocratics frequently appeal to evidence, sometimes in the form of data directly relevant to the matter at hand (the incidence and diffusion of disease, for example), sometimes by way of analogical observations. *Airs, Waters, Places* seeks to categorize different types of water (epidemic diseases are due to bad water or air, or unhealthy locations: hence the title) by their varying degrees of lightness and sweetness; it maintains (correctly) that the sun draws off only pure water, pointing to the fact that people are sweatier under their clothes, because the sun draws off the moisture from the exposed skin. Elsewhere, *Ancient Medicine* notes that fluids naturally turn from sweet to sour outside the body, and infers that something similar will take place, with implications for pathology, inside it; while *Sacred Disease*, arguing that winds are crucial pathogenic factors, remarks that 'jars of wine...in the cellar containing wine or any other fluid are affected by the south wind and change their appearance' (ch. 16). None of these are very impressive. Even when the observations are correct, they hardly serve to support the conclusions drawn from them.

Things improve somewhat with Aristotle. He understood the importance of gathering large quantities of data, and while the quality of the observations and reports is variable, some of it is detailed and careful, and the conclusions drawn appropriately cautious. After a lengthy description of the habits of bees, he concludes that they reproduce asexually; but he admits that this is only provisional:

As far as theory and the apparent facts about them go, this seems to be how things stand with regard to the generation of bees. But the facts have not been sufficiently ascertained, and if ever they are then perception must be believed rather than theories, and theories only so long as they show themselves in agreement with the phenomena.

(*Generation of Animals* III 10, 760b28–33)

The sentiment is admirable; and in many cases his theories are indeed developed in the light of data, some of it recalcitrant. He believes (falsely but not unreasonably) that some animals are spontaneously generated, and tries to account for that from within the framework of his general theory. He knew that some fishes are externally viviparous, and observed the hectocotylization of one tentacle of the octopus, guessing it to be a reproductive adaptation, neither of which was discussed again until the nineteenth century.

But Aristotle often falls short of his own high methodological standards. At *Generation of Animals* I 16, he claims to have seen insects copulating by means of the female inserting something into the male; and he supposes (obscurely) that this supports his account of generation. Numerous other instances of faulty observation and overconfident inference, not to mention bizarre 'experiments', could be cited.

Moreover, the teleological commitment has disadvantages as well as advantages. On the positive side, it encourages the search for function in organic structures where none is immediately apparent, and is also responsible for the sophisticated account of useless structures as 'residues', necessary but functionless consequences of other processes which are themselves teleologically demanded. On the negative side, it sometimes forces Aristotle into extraordinary contortions. In discussing the windpipe and oesophagus, he notes that the fact that food has to pass over the former to get to the latter, entailing the need for the epiglottis to prevent choking, might seem to be a sub-optimal arrangement. But the heart must be located at the front upper part of the body (because it is a superior organ, and this is the most noble position; and because it is the source of motion and perception, and these are located in a forwards direction); and the lungs need to be around it (since their function is to regulate its heat); so the oesophagus has to go down the back; so there needs to be an epiglottis (*Part of Animals* III 3). This argument exemplifies both the strengths and the weaknesses of his teleological biology.

THE STRUCTURE OF ARISTOTELIAN SCIENCE

Aristotle was the first person to reflect in depth on what it is for something to be a science (*epistēmē*), an organized body of knowledge. In *Posterior Analytics* [*Post. An.*] he elaborates an account of an axiomatic system, in which axioms, which derive partly from real definitions[2] of the denizens of the domain, yield, by the deductive logic of his *Prior Analytics*, necessarily true theorems, generally in universal affirmative form: all As are Bs; all Bs are Cs; so all As are Cs (see chapter 5, pp. 133–6 above) The axioms must be 'true, primary, immediate, more intelligible than, prior to and explanatory of the conclusion' (*Post. An.* 1 2).

The last condition is crucial: the 'middle term' of a properly scientific syllogism explains why the predicate holds of the subject in the conclusion. Thus men are mortal because they are animals, and animals are mortal; and this can be arranged as a syllogism with 'animal' as the middle term (A = man, B = animal, C = mortal). Thus not every sound syllogism is explanatory (let B = mammal). Moreover the same material may yield two or more valid inferences, only one of which is explanatory of its conclusion. Aristotle considers the case of the non-twinkling of the planets: they do not twinkle because they are near, rather than the other way around, although since the class of near objects and that of non-twinklers are co-extensive a sound argument can be constructed in either direction ('everything near doesn't twinkle; planets are near', vs 'all non-twinklers are near; planets don't twinkle'). This is both sound and important; for it shows, contrary to some modern orthodoxies, that not all sound deductions of particular cases from covering generalizations are equally explanatory.

Two other features of Aristotle's view of science merit brief comment. First, while he clearly believes that the premisses of science must be general, they need not be universal and exceptionless. His science allows sentences qualified by 'for the most part' (e.g. 'most men have beards'). These are not merely provisional, to be replaced in a completed science by qualified universal ones; for Aristotle holds, for metaphysical reasons, that no such replacement may be possible, not because the world is necessarily causally indeterministic, but because the particular failures to comply will be differently caused in many cases: there need be no one reason why they do so.

Finally, there is the commitment to empiricism. If science is about finding the causes of things, still it must start from the phenomena, the systematization and organization of which will ultimately make patent, or so Aristotle optimistically thinks, the axioms required to ground a fully explanatory science:

For this reason, it is the business of experience to supply the first principles
(*archai*) in each case; I mean for example in the case of astronomical science
(*epistēmē*) it is the business of astronomical experience (for only when the
phenomena had been grasped sufficiently in this manner were the astronomical demonstrations discovered): and the same goes for any other art (*technē*)
or science at all.   (*Prior Analytics* I 30, 46a17–22)

AXIOMATICS AND THE SCIENCES

That model of science as an axiomatized structure owes much to contemporary advances in geometry, whose most famous (albeit slightly
later) fruit is Euclid. Geometry was an old Greek obsession. Thales
is credited (by late and unreliable sources) with discovering certain
theorems and with practical expertise in mensuration, while the
Pythagoreans have always been associated with hard advances in
serious geometry as well as with numerological speculation. Indeed,
it is likely that it was the striking success of the geometers of Plato's
circle in bringing rigour and order into the science that convinced
Aristotle that the demonstrative pattern was appropriate for all
mature sciences.

There were axiomatic geometries being developed in Aristotle's
own time, although we know little or nothing about their actual
details. Nonetheless, they will have been forerunners of the great
system expounded by Euclid in the thirteen books of the *Elements*
a generation or so after Aristotle's death (Euclid's dates and history
are very uncertain), which was to become the basis of all geometrical
science – and until very recently of the teaching of it. Euclid's text
is organized with exemplary rigour. Beginning each section with a
list of definitions (e.g. 'a point is that which is partless': *Elements* I,
Def. I), he adds a set of postulates, propositions which are essential to
the system but not necessarily provable within it, such as 'a straight
line can be drawn between any two points' (I, Post. 2); 'a circle can
be drawn with any centre and any diameter' (I, Post. 3); and most
famously of all, the parallel postulate (I, Post. 5), which states (in
its common modern, although not Euclidian, form, that of Playfair's
axiom) that only one line may be drawn through a point on a plane
adjacent to a given line which is parallel with that line. Attempts to
prove the postulate began in the ancient world (notably by Ptolemy
and Proclus) and continued through the Middle Ages to modern
times, until it was finally shown in the nineteenth century that it

was consistently deniable, and that by denying it one could create alternative geometries. On the basis of these definitions and postulates, plus a few more general 'common notions' (such as 'equals subtracted from equals leave equal remainders'; called 'common' because they apply to all magnitudes and not merely geometrical ones: 1, cn. 3), a brilliant sequence of geometrical deductions are made, which establish the science as one of unparalleled rigour, elegance and consistency. Elsewhere in the *Elements*, Euclid develops with great acuity a theory of proportion (Book 5); subjects the incommensurable magnitudes (irrational numbers) first discovered by the Pythagoreans to rigorous analysis (Book 10); develops the method of exhaustion for determining the relations between the areas of circles and regular polygons (Book 12); and makes some pioneering steps in stereometry (Book 13).

The model of science as an axiomatized structure proved seductive throughout the rest of antiquity. Aristotle himself never tried to exhibit his sciences in the form he himself recommended for them (although later commentators amused themselves by presenting his arguments in his canonical forms); but parts of his *oeuvre*, e.g. *On the Heavens* I 2–4 on the elements, clearly show him trying to extract plausible general principles with which to deduce phenomenal effects; and

> we consider that we have given an adequate demonstrative account of things unavailable to sensation when our account is consistent with what is possible.   (*Meteorology* I 7, 344a5–7)

Furthermore, in spite of his insistence that sciences should be self-contained, he recognizes that certain of them in particular owe direct and undeniable debts to geometry and arithmetic, notably optics, astronomy and musical theory. Indeed, Euclid himself composed an *Optics*, which is arranged axiomatically, as well as a lost treatise on music.

Other areas of applied science were influenced by axiomatics and the mathematical sciences. The pseudo-Aristotelian *Mechanics* correctly reduces the properties of the lever to arithmetic and geometry. The greatest ancient practitioner of mechanics and hydrostatics, Archimedes (c.287–212 BC), was also a considerable abstract geometer. But his most famous and important achievement (apart from constructing ingenious siege-engines for the tyrant of Syracuse; his tyrants, like those of Leonardo and Galileo, preferred their science applied) is significant precisely for its abandonment of qualitative physics in favour of precise measurement. Set to find a way of telling whether a golden crown was made of adulterated metal, Archimedes hit upon the solution as he leapt into the bath, thereby discovering one aspect of the hydrostatic theory of displacement. He immersed the crown in a full container, and measured the amount of water displaced; then he immersed an equal weight of pure gold, and discovered that it displaced measurably less. The adulterator was caught; and Archimedes made his great contribution to the history of quantitative hydrostatics, as well as a minor one to that of nudism.

Hero of Alexandria (dates very uncertain: perhaps first century AD), a mathematician and inventor, is also worth a brief notice. He is best remembered now for his ingenious mechanical devices, some of them involving steam power. But he also reflected on physics, and the introduction to his surviving *Pneumatics* perhaps betrays the influence of Strato (see below, p. 294). His *Catoptrics* ('On Reflection') discusses the scattering of light from less than perfect surfaces, and attributes the fact that the angle of reflection equals that of incidence to the Aristotelian principle that 'nature does nothing in vain', thus anticipating the principle of least action.

But in general applied mechanics was not much developed in the ancient world; and what little there was (in the form of cranes, mill-machinery, etc.) had little or no impact on philosophy.

ASTRONOMY

The one major science to have reached a high degree of development in the ancient world that we have not yet discussed is astronomy. The Homeric poems presuppose an astronomy, or perhaps rather a cosmology: the earth is flat, surrounded by the River of Ocean, around which the sun sails from the west to the east at night. Thales is reported to have written a *Nautical Astronomy*, but that is unlikely. Anaximander's and Anaximenes' speculations about the structures constituting and ordering the heavenly bodies have been considered in an earlier chapter (see chapter 2, pp. 48–50 above). For Heraclitus, the heavenly bodies are hollow bowls filled with fire, eclipses and phases of the moon being caused when the bowl turns its back towards us. Xenophanes is reported to have thought that the sun moved in a straight line to infinity, and hence that there was a new one every day.

All of this is speculative, and most of it is false. Nor is it really astronomy. But two sonorous lines of Parmenides show that genuine astronomy had arrived in the Greek world; of the moon, he writes:

Night-shining, wandering about the earth, an alien light,
Always gazing towards the rays of the sun.   (28 B 14, 15 DK)

Plato's universe is geocentric, although it is left to Aristotle to supply arguments for the centrality and sphericity of the earth (earth falls towards the centre where it congregates in a sphere; the shadow cast on the moon during a lunar eclipse is always convex; there is no observable stellar parallax), arguments that were taken up and expanded by Ptolemy (c.AD 100–175) in his great work the *Syntaxis*.

But Plato himself was said to have issued a challenge to the mathematicians in his Academy, to find a mathematical model to account for and predict the motions of the heavenly bodies, including their latitudinal variations and the retrogradations of the planets, and the variation in lengths of the seasons (Anaximander is credited with determining the solstices and equinoxes). In one of history's great intellectual achievements, the geometer Eudoxus managed, in the mid fourth century BC, to produce a model of the motions of the sun, moon and planets (later refined and complicated by Callippus) which succeeded remarkably (apart from the case of Mars) in accounting for their motions, by postulating that each of them moved on the innermost of a set of nested rotating spheres, whose poles were set at a variety of angles, the resulting motion being a superposition of the spherical motions.

But while Eudoxus and Callippus had sought to provide a purely instrumental, predictive model, Aristotle (*Metaphysics* Lambda 8) tried to give it a physical interpretation. That is, he conceived of the heavens as actually constructed of spheres, suitably oriented to each other, each moving with its own natural elemental motion. This required the postulation of additional spheres, to counteract each inner set and thus restore the diurnal motion of the outer sphere of the fixed stars, although, as he says, he will leave the details to the mathematicians, a remark which betokens the increasing specialization of intellectual activity in his day.

Brilliant though it was, Eudoxus' theory was, mathematically speaking, an intellectual dead-end. It was superseded by the new model of Hipparchus (c.180–120 BC), a superb observational astronomer who corrected many of the errors in Eudoxus' almanac, and discovered the precession of the equinoxes, which he calculated to within 10 per cent of the correct value. But his enduring contribution to astronomy was the development of the epicyclic system, which dominated astronomical modelling until the time of Copernicus. The earth was located in the centre still; but the planets were carried on a small circle, or epicycle, whose centre was itself carried on a larger orbit (the deferent) around the earth. By suitable arrangements of epicycles, Hipparchus found he could produce a predictive model of unprecedented accuracy.

But a predictive model was all it was; there was no attempt actually to represent the physical architecture of the heavens. And when a century earlier, Aristarchus of Samos (c.310–230 BC) first proposed the heliocentric theory, it was as a mathematical hypothesis only (it was left to his shadowy successor Seleucus to treat it as a physical fact); even so, he risked prosecution for impiety. Aristarchus also developed a method for measuring *The Sizes and Distances of the Sun and Moon*, his treatise upon which has survived. His method is perfectly sound in theory, although vitiated by observational inaccuracies, and is important in that it seeks to do more than simply predict appearances: it tries to determine the actual magnitudes of the objects in physical space. Likewise, his younger contemporary Eratosthenes sought to measure the earth's circumference by noting the different elevation of the sun at different latitudes at the same time, and did so with surprising accuracy, compared with Aristotle, whose estimate in *On the Heavens* II 14 had been out by a factor of at least 50 per cent.

In the second century AD Ptolemy developed Hipparchus' system with unparalleled rigour and observational accuracy; but he too, at any rate in the *Syntaxis*, treats it purely as a calculating device. Nonetheless, as the opening of the work shows, he thought of himself as a philosopher (he wrote a short work of epistemology, *On the Criterion*), and not a mere mathematician; while in the *Planetary Hypotheses*, which partially survives in an Arabic translation, he tried to give the model a physical realization. Thus another modern concern in the philosophy of science, the dispute between realist and instrumentalist interpretations of the metaphysical status of scientific models, was anticipated in antiquity.

ASTROLOGY

So, while there was a progressive divergence of mathematical astronomy from philosophy, the two were never entirely divorced. And
both astronomers and philosophers were keenly interested in astrology, as they would continue to be until the seventeenth century.
The Hellenistic period saw a resurgence of divination of all types, but
astrology, with its pretensions to mathematical rigour, was the queen
of the divinatory sciences. The Stoics favoured the possibility of divination, on the grounds that the future was causally determined, and
hence in principle knowable, while divine providence was likely to
make such useful knowledge available to humans sufficiently wise
to decode it. Later Platonists, too, accepted the likelihood of predictive astrology.

But the avatars of divination did not have things all their own way.
The Academic sceptic Carneades (second century BC; see pp. 178–9
above) produced a series of influential arguments against it which
became part of the sceptical tradition: horoscopes are either too vague
to be testable; or if testable they turn out false; nor is it clear that
it is in our interest to know the future. Similar considerations are
rehearsed in Cicero's *On Divination*; on the other side, its proponents
claim that its rate of successful prediction is no worse than that of
medicine, an accepted science.

But even Ptolemy supported at least the theoretical possibility of
astrology, writing his *Tetrabiblos* in defence of it. The sun and the
moon clearly have physical influences on the world, as well as on
the life-cycles of animals; why should there not be subtler influences
emanating from the planets? He allows that astrologers often err, but
that reflects on them not on the art itself. Planetary influences are
not the only determining effects of human fate – other things apply
as well, and astrology can never offer particular predictions of events,
only outlines of individuals' characters: hence Carneades' objection,
that twins share horoscopes but may have very different fates, is
blunted.

These debates also prefigure modern concerns: how to distinguish
science from pseudo-science; what counts as an acceptable (or more
to the point an unacceptable) empirical success-rate; how far a lack
of success can be put down to poor practice as opposed to inherent

defects in the 'science' itself; and the extent to which statistics (albeit of a very rudimentary and imprecise kind) can be arbiters in such cases.

HELLENISTIC PHYSICS

The fundamental divide between teleologists and mechanists persisted throughout the ancient world. The Stoics were enthusiastic champions of a creationist teleology. Epicurus and his followers were heirs to the atomistic tradition, and took over (with some refinements) from Democritus his mechanistic and discontinuous physics, as well as his tolerance for an infinity of space and matter. Aristotle's pupil and successor Theophrastus restricted the scope of natural teleology; his successor Strato abandoned it altogether. Strato also allowed for the existence of void (which Aristotle had argued against at length), insisted that all bodies, air and fire included, had weight, and rejected the aether: he was an Aristotelian in little more than name.

The physical theories and methodologies of the Stoic and Epicurean schools have been described earlier (see chapter 6). In general they show little sign of the empirical research characteristic of Aristotle's school, and officially physics was considered by both schools subordinate to ethics. There were, however, one or two exceptions to this relative neglect of natural science, in particular the Stoic Posidonius (early first century BC), who was described by one critic as 'Aristotelizing'. He certainly wrote on a wide variety of mathematical and scientific disciplines, including the topics of Aristotelian meteorology, and investigated the tides, suggesting that they were due to lunar influence.

MEDICINE

Plato thought that the brain was the seat of intelligence (p. 280). Aristotle, on the other hand, located thought as well as emotion in the heart; and so did the Stoics. Alcmaeon had favoured the brain (pp. 275-6), as had the Hippocratics. Yet Praxagoras, active at the end of the fourth century BC, plumped for the heart, perhaps because he thought that the nerves (which he may have been the first properly to distinguish from tendons) were the thinned-out ends of the arteries.

The view is also found in the third-century BC treatise *On the Heart*, in spite of its relatively sophisticated understanding of the heart's ventricular structure.

That the Stoics could continue to believe this after the isolation of the motor and sensory nervous systems by Herophilus (fl. c.260 BC) scandalized Galen (AD 129–c.215),[3] the greatest doctor of later antiquity and a considerable philosopher as well. Dissection clearly shows that the nerves ramify from the brain; and experiments involving neural sections and ligatures (performed in public by Galen to great acclaim, or so he tells us) equally clearly establish that control flows from the brain. In numerous passages in his *On the Doctrines of Hippocrates and Plato*, Galen stresses that philosophical accounts of the soul must at least be consistent with the latest advances in neurophysiology; and on several occasions he accuses the Stoics, in particular Chrysippus, of simple ignorance and incompetence in such matters.

Herophilus' great advances, and those of his contemporary Erasistratus, were probably made with the aid of experimentation on live human subjects. Herophilus' cautious attitude towards causal theorizing emphasized the importance of the phenomena, suggesting that a comprehensive understanding of the deep structure of things may be unattainable. Yet he probably adopted a form of the humoral theory first elaborated in the Hippocratic *Nature of Man*, and certainly spoke of four primary 'powers' in the body.

Erasistratus rejected humoral theory, supposing that most illnesses were caused by the transfusion of excess blood from the veins into the arteries (which, he believed, under normal circumstances contained only *pneuma*). This *pneuma* is not precisely that of the Stoics (above, pp. 170–1); and *pneuma*, which originally simply means 'wind', had a long and various medical history. The Hippocratic *On Breaths* differentiates the *pneuma*, which is internal to the body, from the external 'air'; and Praxagoras too had made *pneuma* central to his physiology. It was, however, generally thought to be carried by the arterial system (even by doctors such as Galen who realized that the arteries normally contain blood).

Erasistratus also refused to allow that external occasions for illness really were causes, on the grounds that such occasions did not affect everybody in the same way, while similar causes should produce similar effects. Galen argued against this in *On Antecedent*

Causes: such external factors (e.g. excessive heat or cold) are not the *sole* cause of the maladies associated with them; but they are part of the overall cause, in concert with the patients' particular dispositions. Thus Galen marries his commitment to Hippocratic humoral theory with a sophisticated philosophical analysis of causation.

Medicine also intersects with philosophy in the field of epistemology. Diocles of Carystus (fl. c.300 BC) objected to certain styles of aetiologizing on the grounds that they were neither necessary nor attainable. Herophilus emphasized the difficulty of drawing secure theoretical inferences. These sceptical tendencies were deepened by the medical Empiricists. Medical Empiricism had a long history; and it came in stronger and weaker forms. But crucially it rejected the idea that science required, or could provide, an understanding of the underlying structures of things; all that doctors need are theorems, based on repeated experience and the reports of others, relating evident signs and symptoms to tested remedies. By contrast, their opponents, compendiously known as 'Dogmatists', believed that skilled physicians both could and should infer from the phenomena to their underlying causes.

Galen sided with the Dogmatists: he believed that with intelligence and application the scientist could indeed uncover the deep nature of things; there was no need to settle for instrumental hypotheses and constant phenomenal conjunctions. But the task was difficult, and Galen insists, against some of his more sanguine contemporaries, that the deliverances of reason (*logos*) must be constantly checked against experience (*peira*), which also suggests the hypotheses to be tested. Some things are evident to reason, others to the senses; with a judicious marriage of the two, the scientist can indeed make real progress. But reason needs to be rigorously trained in logic; and the senses honed to the highest pitch of sensitivity. Galen cherished a vision of medicine as an Aristotelian axiomatic science; but in a modern jargon, reason only supplies the context of justification, while the phenomena provide that of discovery.

Moreover, in Galen's view, relevant phenomena should be actively sought out, by detailed observation and experimentation. He tried to show that it was not necessary for the air supply to be replenished, by having a slave-boy breathe into and out of the same bladder for a whole day. He also thought he could show that the pulsative force was carried in the arterial coats by exposing an artery, opening it, inserting a thin reed, and then ligating the arterial coat tightly around the reed: the artery below the cut, he says, does not pulse. Both of these experiments are well conceived but clearly poorly carried out. On the other hand, the systematic sectioning and ligature of the nerves and the spinal cord mentioned above are brilliant in both conception and execution. And whatever the failings of his actual experimental practice, Galen should surely be commended for seeing its theoretical importance with a clarity not to be realized again until the Renaissance.

For Galen, the world which is revealed by such careful reasoning from the results of observation and experiment was self-evidently the product of design. Galen is an unequivocal supporter of the *Timaeus* type of teleology: the production and management of the world by an immanent, benevolent divinity. He describes his *On the Function of the Parts* (*UP*) as a Hymn to Nature; and its whole purpose is to exhibit nature's beneficence, by way of a detailed account of the complexity and adaptiveness of animal structures, following, as he says, but going beyond the example of Aristotle's *Parts of Animals*. Throughout *UP* he derides such doctors as Erasistratus and Asclepiades for refusing to see the providential hand of teleology in the world.

This marriage of theoretical commitment to practical observation may be seen at work in the short text on *The Formation of the Foetus*, where he denies, against Aristotle (see p. 284), that the heart is the first organ formed (he opts for the liver, the seat of his Platonic nutritive soul). He observes the network of blood-vessels in the amniotic sac, and how they are connected to the womb, and reasons that blood from the mother provides the initial nutrition for the embryo (he notes that blood coagulated in water resembles liver-tissue) – but the question still arises of how its construction is overseen. He rejects the Epicurean supposition of pure random action producing such a finished product, as well as the Aristotelian idea (see p. 284) that the heart takes over from the semen and directs the operation itself. He admits uncertainty, but thinks it unreasonable to suppose that the initial directive force disappears, preferring to believe that the whole operation is under the guidance of soul of some kind, a thesis suggested by the systematic generation of a vast number of individual parts and functions, all linked into an overall economy of activity.

At the end of *The Formation of the Foetus*, Galen admits to uncertainty over the nature and properties of the soul; but that there is
such a thing is clear, and it is equally clear that there is a creator god.
Galen is prepared to admit that there are limits to what he can know
about god, the soul, and other knotty problems. But the method of
discovery is secure (gather data, make logical inferences from them),
as is the fundamental belief in the teleological (providential) organization of things.

THE END OF ANTIQUITY

Galen was a man of his time. For all his rationalism, he was deeply
religious, and quite prepared to believe prescriptions sent him in
divinely inspired dreams. The intellectual spirit of the age tended
towards syncretism (see chapter 9), and Galen, in his adoption of a
synthetic teleology which owed its fine structural detail to Aristotle
but the general providential framework to Plato, and in his zeal to
represent his twin intellectual idols, Hippocrates in medicine and
Plato in philosophy, as being at one on all important issues, exemplifies that temper.

Nevertheless, he never wavered in his commitment to a rigorous,
empirically informed science. The succeeding centuries saw the rise
of both Christianity and Neoplatonism, both more given to spirituality than science. For whatever reason, both scepticism itself
and the sceptical tenor in thought which had given rise to medical Empiricism fell into disuse, and science produced no figures of
the stature of Ptolemy or Galen. But three figures who tried to keep
scientific philosophy alive deserve brief mention.

First, Iamblichus (see chapter 9): he was in many ways a typical
mystical Neoplatonist, composing an *On the Mysteries* in defence
of the practice of theurgy, the attempt to achieve spiritual union
with the divine. But in his *On the General Mathematical Science*,
he outlines a compelling vision of the proper relation between mathematics and the physical sciences: the former establishes the limits
of the possible for the latter; mathematical notions can be applied to
physical objects, and physical objects in turn can be seen, in the regularity of their behaviour, to embody mathematical ideas. None of
these suggestions would be followed up scientifically for more than
a millennium, any more than his equally prescient rejection of the

Aristotelian idea that the transmission of causal influence requires contact.

A second great Neoplatonist, Proclus (fifth century AD), wrote an *Outline of Astronomical Hypotheses* which was designed to show that none of the predominant astronomical models, of Aristarchus, Hipparchus and Ptolemy, could account for the actual mechanics of the heavens, since they are inconsistent with his (modified) Aristotelian physics. They may serve as useful (if inaccurate) calculative devices; but if we are to account for the actual physics of the heavens we must suppose with the Platonists that they are ensouled self-movers.

The third name is that of Philoponus, the sixth-century AD Christian Neoplatonist. His brilliant critique of the Aristotelian theory of projectile motion, and his corresponding development of the impetus theory, have been described earlier (see chapter 9). When Aristotelianism revived in the late Middle Ages, the inadequacies of Aristotle's account of projectile motion were soon felt, by Buridan among others; and, although he rejected the theory of impressed impetus too, when Galileo finally came to undermine the baroque structure of Renaissance Aristotelian physics, he did so acknowledging the force of Philoponus' destructive arguments. In science as well as in philosophy, Philoponus is one of the last of the ancients – and the first of the moderns.

NOTES

1   References flagged 'KRS' are to Kirk, Raven, Schofield, see Bibliography [10], while 'DK' refers to Diels–Kranz, see chapter 2 note 4, p. 72 above.
2   In Locke's terminology: a real, as opposed to a nominal, definition actually spells out the structure of the item it defines.
3   Galen is standardly cited by volume, page and line number of the global edition by C. G. Kuhn, *Galeni Opera*, 20 vols. in 22 (Leipzig 1821–33). However, individual works are frequently cited by reference to more modern editions.

11 Philosophy and religion

ANCIENTS AND MODERNS

While ancient philosophy continues to live on, and indeed to flourish, in the modern discipline of philosophy, the religions of ancient Greece and Rome have left very little discernible trace upon the religions of the modern world. It was only because, and only to the extent that, the pagan religions of Greek and Roman antiquity were radically transformed, almost beyond recognition, into the vast, eclectic world religion of Christianity, that anything of them at all managed to survive the fall of the classical world. The result is that, while the Christian Church shrewdly adapted its practices to the traditional conditions of the mass pagan world it found itself in and while the Christian Fathers elaborated a brilliant theoretical synthesis of certain elements of pagan intellectual culture with Judaeo-Christian theology, religion in the modern world is so different from what it was in antiquity that it requires considerable effort to appreciate ancient religiosity without a feeling of bewilderment, repulsion or superiority. For modern religious sentiment, there may well seem to be something rather disturbing in that most basic and widespread of Greek religious rituals, the public ceremonial in which a large domestic animal is presented, ornamented, slaughtered to the accompaniment of the screams of women, flayed, dismembered, cooked, and eaten by the community – to say nothing of the often apparently quite bizarre local cults, for example at Athens, where the Stenia festival was devoted largely to the exchange of verbal abuse between the sexes, or at Lesbos, where every year the local girls competed in a beauty contest at the sanctuary of Zeus, Hera and Dionysus.

Matters seem different in the case of philosophy. The practice of theoretical inquiry into the fundamental conditions of the worlds around us and within us which is pursued in university departments of philosophy in almost all countries bears an easily recognizable similarity to the work of the ancient Greek and Roman philosophers. What is more, the modern discipline is the direct descendant of the ancient activity and can hardly be imagined even having come into existence, let alone having taken on its present-day form, without it.

It is the discontinuity between ancient and modern religion that makes it difficult for us to understand ancient religion, but it is the very continuity between ancient and modern philosophy that poses traps for understanding ancient philosophy, for, as we shall see later, the ways in which philosophy was practised in antiquity shared many of the most prominent features of religion.

The fundamental feature of ancient classical religions which makes them so different from modern western ones is that they were polytheistic. This meant, first, that a certain amount of contradiction was built ineradicably into the religious system: different gods represented irreducibly competing views of what was right, and situations inevitably arose all too frequently in which a human being could not satisfy one god's demands without slighting another's. Greek myth never tires of illustrating the impossibility of giving all the gods without exception what they think they deserve – in other terms, the impossibility of living a life which is perfect in all regards, self-consistent and fully harmonious, and does not violate some fatal prescription. But, second, the plurality of gods also meant that the ancients were inclined to view such contradictions with a greater degree of tolerance (which does not mean with enthusiasm) than we would be likely to feel. Within the internal dynamics of any particular ancient religion, the existence of competing religious views tended to be accepted as an irremediable (and often painful) fact of life; the drastic opposition, familiar to us, between orthodoxy and heresy was generally quite lacking. Third, the same high threshold for tolerance of contradiction functioned externally to make the ancients eclectic and assimilative with regard to foreign religions. Where the boundaries between right and wrong in one's own religion were far from clear, it made little sense to insist upon the importance of such boundaries between religions – indeed, the ancients were fascinated by foreign religions and were usually eager to identify similarities or to adopt cults.

The existence of many gods meant obviously that no one god could have unlimited power (what would the others have said?). As early as Homer and Hesiod there is a tendency to single out one god, Zeus, as the most important one, and to attribute pre-eminent power to him; but monotheism, the idea that there really is only one god, was not a genuine option for the most part in ancient culture, and most such passages point instead towards something more like henotheism, belief in one supreme god transcending or subsuming all other ones. The gods were thought to be more powerful, more beautiful, and above all more happy than human beings, but they too had their insuperable limitations. They depended in some way upon human worship – for one thing, it was often thought that they were nourished by the sacrifices that humans made to them – and they could become quite nasty, and even petty, if they were offended. Even if they did not die ('the immortals' is one standard way to refer to the gods in Greek), they were nonetheless all born, as humans are, and hence they entered at a certain point in cosmic history onto the stage of a natural world which was already there before they were and which they themselves had no role in creating. Furthermore, they were almost never thought to be omniscient, omnipotent or omnipresent. That is why, when the ancients prayed, they did so, unlike Christians or Jews or Moslems, by standing up with their arms outstretched to the heavens and speaking aloud: like small children or shipwrecked sailors, they were trying to attract the attention of distant and more powerful beings who could help them if they chose to but who could also, in their blissful self-absorption, simply fail even to take the slightest notice of them and their problems.

Ancient religion, like so much of the rest of ancient culture, was thoroughly local and geographically heterogeneous in character. In a world where communications were time-consuming and travel cumbersome, there was great curiosity about how other peoples organized their lives but no sense that any one such organization was the only right and possible one. It is perhaps only from the perspective of the resolutely monotheistic Jewish and Christian religions that the hodgepodge of varieties of Greek and Roman religious experience could possibly ever have come to seem all to form part of the same category, to be 'pagan' – etymologically meaning 'from the (backward) countryside', as contrasted with the already converted city. Not only did the Greek or Roman pantheon comprise a plurality of gods, but, what is more, each such god was worshipped in numerous temples in many cities and regions in cults which differed from one another in matters small and great, both at any one time and during the course of historical development. Was Aphrodite a goddess of love, or of the sea? Did Dionysus have a beard or not? Was the Zeus whose tomb the Cretans pointed to the 'same' god worshipped as deathless in the rest of Greece? No modern religion could remain indifferent to such local variations: for the ancients they were a matter for curiosity or for amusement, but never for outrage. In antiquity, there was no Church, no single institutional hierarchy, no divinely revealed holy scripture, which could authorize a definitive distinction between right and wrong in such matters: even Delphi, despite its prestige, had nothing like the authority of the Vatican, for in the end it was only one cult of Apollo, it never had more than a limited and very local political power, and for the most part it did not promulgate theological systems but only responded to specific questions with more or less ambiguous oracles. Very various kinds of religion were practised by the very same people at a variety of levels – individually; within the narrower and larger family; within various kinds of professional and non-professional, temporary and more permanent associations; within narrower and larger political organizations.

By and large, the ancients were simply not bothered by the fact that other people did things differently from themselves. The crucial consideration was that, within the confines of the relevant group, one performed scrupulously precisely what tradition enjoined one to do and what all the other members of the same group did and saw one another doing. Indeed, ancient religion, on the whole, tended to be regarded in its essence as being a practical activity performed visibly within these relevant groups rather than as consisting in an individual disposition available above all to introspection. Ancient piety was not so much a matter of a particular kind of subjective feeling, the emotion of belief, the tremor of awe, but rather the performance of the required rituals considered to be valid within the terms of one's community: the Greek phrase *nomizein tous theous* is often translated as 'to believe in the gods' but usually means instead 'to indicate that one acknowledges the gods of the city by performing their rituals'. And it was just as hard to exist outside such religions as it was to exist outside the political communities whose structure was inextricably tangled up with them, for every city-state (*polis*) comprised a highly complex organization of multiple, locally specific cults. Hence the ancient gods may not have been omnipresent, but ancient religion was: few indeed were the activities the ancients engaged upon which were not in some way linked to their worship of the gods, from eating meat and drinking wine to founding cities and waging war. That is why, just as monotheism was not a viable cultural option in antiquity, so too, symmetrically, atheism was virtually unknown: ancient lists of those philosophers who denied altogether the very existence of the gods never manage to come up with more than a handful of names. Diagoras and the Cyrenaic philosopher Theodorus are the only ones who turn up on more than a few such lists; Euhemerus and Protagoras are also occasionally (and, at least in the latter case, quite wrongly) considered atheists. But what is usually meant in such cases is not a radical denial of the very existence of divinity, but instead a more or less sceptical attitude towards one or more of the traditional features of the gods as these were worshipped in the established myths and cults.

In all these regards, ancient religion is undeniably foreign to our modern experience. It was only, if at all, in the Greek mystery cults, such as Orphism, the Bacchic and Eleusinian mysteries, Hermeticism, and Gnosticism, and in the worship of Rome and of the emperor and his family under the Roman empire, that, in very different ways, ancient religion came to develop features closely comparable to certain key aspects of its modern counterparts: in the former case a promise of individual salvation in the after-life conditional upon the adept's learning precepts and/or following certain practices in this life, as well as an emphasis upon sublime doctrines, correctly interpreted, and convulsive emotionality, stimulated and shared; in the latter, the solaces of a universal cult which transcended local constraints, thereby providing all the members of a vast global community with an opportunity to celebrate values not only political, but also genuinely religious in nature.

With philosophy, matters seem to be different. After all, courses on Plato and Aristotle are taught in most university philosophy departments, and many contemporary philosophers still find the writings of the Greek and Roman philosophers no less worth interpreting and disagreeing with than those of their living colleagues. Yet the similarities, real as they are, can be misleading, for they do not tell the whole story. Contemporary philosophy is an academic, professional discipline, devoted to the elaboration, testing, and refinement of arguments and theories. Ancient philosophy was sometimes this too, but not often, and usually it was something else, and something more. Most ancient philosophers did not teach philosophy in official educational institutions but worked freelance, or in small, private groups of friends and disciples, and directed their publications not only to other professional philosophers but also to nonspecialist readers; although most ancient philosophers did put forth general views and attempt to support them by reasoned argument, in fact not all did so, and even when they did, this was not all that was thought to qualify them as philosophers. Ancient philosophy was also a way of life, an exercise in self-discipline, a process of self-transformation which expressed itself not only in the theories one propounded but also in the clothes one wore, the food one ate, and the way one behaved with regard to gods, animals and other men. The crucial test of a good philosopher, in many people's eyes, was not how well his doctrines resisted refutation, but how well he died. It is appropriate that Diogenes Laertius' handbook of ancient philosophy is entitled, *The Lives and Opinions of the Eminent Philosophers*, and combines historical reports and anecdotes concerning their biographies and personalities on the one hand with summaries of their doctrines and sayings on the other: for it was the interrelation of both components, the way of life and the mode of thought, that went to make up the quality of an ancient philosopher.

That is why, in order to understand the relation between ancient philosophy and ancient religion, it is necessary, but insufficient, to discuss the specific views that ancient philosophers held concerning religious matters; this will be the object of the following section. It will be necessary as well to consider at least some of the relations between the forms of ancient religious practice and the ways in which ancient philosophers lived: this will occupy the third and final section.

ANCIENT PHILOSOPHICAL THEOLOGY

At least since the Enlightenment, if not since the Reformation and Counter-Reformation, we have come to expect an adversarial relation between philosophy and religion: reason conflicting with faith, religion unmasked as superstition, philosophers persecuted as heretics. For those who seek ancient precursors for the modern project of enlightenment, it is not difficult to find ancient philosophers who can be made to serve as heroes and martyrs. After all, Lucretius' impassioned condemnation of Agamemnon's sacrifice of his daughter, 'so great was the evil that religion was capable of inspiring' ('tantum religio potuit suadere malorum', I 101) was to become one of the most often-cited verses of Latin poetry and a rallying cry of the eighteenth century. On the one hand, it was reported in antiquity that the philosophers Anaxagoras and Socrates, the sophist Protagoras, and the lyric poet Diagoras were all prosecuted for impiety in three separate trials at Athens in the last decades of the fifth century BC and the very beginning of the fourth; all four were said to have been condemned to death, and Socrates famously submitted to execution by hemlock, while the others had to flee into exile. On the other hand, the Presocratic Xenophanes (see pp. 56–7 above) already ridiculed the ingenuous anthropomorphism of Greek religion:

But if cattle and horses or lions had hands, or were able to draw with their hands and do the works that men can do, horses would draw the forms of the gods like horses, and cattle like cattle, and they would make their bodies such as they each had themselves.   (KRS 169)[1]

And in a number of his dialogues, such as the *Euthyphro*, the *Republic* and the *Laws*, Plato demonstrated by unremitting philosophical analysis the weaknesses of traditional notions of Greek piety, of the inherited myths about the gods and heroes, and of established views about the nature of the gods.

But it is only our own modern expectations that lead us to single out such episodes as paradigmatic and to charge them with a simplistic, epoch-making weight that, examined more closely and within their own context, they will hardly bear. Even the celebrated Lucretian tag quoted above is in fact an attack not on religion as such, but on false superstition, and Lucretius' poem advocates reverence for the gods, provided only that their nature is understood and respected. On the one hand, trials for impiety are the rare exception rather than the rule throughout Greek as well as Roman history: it would be quite unwise to generalize, beyond the desperate turmoil of democratic Athens during and immediately after its catastrophic defeat in the Peloponnesian War – the very same years in which these trials took place in Athens were in fact also ones in which a variety of new religious cults were introduced into the city from abroad – in the direction of any degree of concern on the part of the ancient state with investigating and punishing the religious convictions of its citizens, philosophical or otherwise. And on the other hand, neither Xenophanes nor Plato had any intention whatsoever of demonstrating the non-existence of divinity or of unmasking the falsity of religion *per se*. Both were concerned only to show the absurdity of certain features of established religion so as to replace them with more philosophically tenable substitutes. Xenophanes does not replace anthropomorphic gods with no gods whatsoever, but rather with a single, non-anthropomorphic, immobile, fully conscious and vastly powerful being: 'All of him sees, all thinks, and all hears' (KRS 172). In Plato's *Euthyphro*, Socrates' dismantling of the smug self-confidence of Euthyphro's conviction that he knows what piety is does not in fact result, in this dialogue, in the construction of a positive definition of what true piety would be; but the utter discomfiture of a putative expert on religious matters does seem to be designed to prove to the reader's satisfaction the radical deficiency of those traditional views on the subject which resulted, among other things, precisely in the condemnation of Socrates in his trial for impiety, with which Plato takes care to link his conversation with Euthyphro. And Plato is at pains, especially in Book x of his *Laws*, to indicate that the purpose of his critique of certain features of established religion is not at all to support any atheistic tendencies that might be current in his culture, but on the contrary to controvert these, by proposing views of religious matters which can stand up to sustained rational analysis and thereby satisfy even the most hardened sceptic.

In fact, the fundamental tendency of the vast majority of ancient Greek and Roman philosophers is not at all to debunk religion, but to reinforce religiosity. This they try to achieve in two basic ways: either by completing religion, by attempting to satisfy needs and answer questions which, because of the peculiar nature of the ancient religions, these did not seem to them to be able to supply themselves in a satisfactory manner; or by correcting religion, by modifying those features of traditional myths, cults and beliefs which most clearly violated what were seen to be the demands of reason or of morality, and thereby producing a more philosophically acceptable version of traditional religion. But just as the ancient philosophers did not envision destroying the established religions of Greece and Rome, so too they do not seem for the most part to have aimed at substituting their own philosophical version of religion for the traditional forms of worship cultivated by the majority of their fellows. Philosophical theology remained a matter internal to philosophy and neither in intent nor in consequence did it have any noticeable impact upon the cults of the city. Whatever was the original purpose of Varro's celebrated distinction between three types of theology – mythic (the fables told by the poets), political (the cults acknowledged as legitimate in all ancient cities), and natural (the doctrines elaborated by the philosophers) – in practice it served to establish a clear division of labour between three separate forms of religiosity, thereby immunizing not only the great poets of the past, Homer and Hesiod above all, but also the institutions of the city, in their political and religious complicity, against any corrosive impact which might otherwise have derived from philosophical speculation about the true nature of divinity.

The theoretical connections between philosophy and religion in the ancient world are not exhausted by the specific doctrines and arguments of the philosophers regarding religious matters strictly defined. The peculiar nature of Greek and Roman religion led ancient philosophers to reflect about a variety of matters which were not religious in the narrow sense, but concerning which the philosophers speculated in ways profoundly influenced by those religions. Hence, beyond the narrow confines of theology itself, the ancient philosophers may also be said to supplement religion in at least three domains: (a) cosmology, (b) eschatology and (c) morality.

(a) How did the world begin? What is the foundation upon which rests all that is? Such questions perplex many people, and they have been provided with authoritative answers by many religions, including those of a number of ancient Near Eastern cultures, as well as Judaism and Christianity: the beginning verses of Genesis, for example, locate the whole of the physical world within the volition of God, and thereby supply a foundation in permanence and meaningfulness for everything that might otherwise seem merely ephemeral and purposeless. But the religions of Greece and Rome tended not to address such issues: they were for the most part too local, too immediate, too human in their concerns to aspire to such transcendent dimensions. Only Hesiod (c.700 BC), in his *Theogony*, went beyond the few obscure hints to be found in Homer and a couple of scattered local legends, to attempt to provide a systematic account of the beginning of things; and in order to do so he seems to have had to have recourse to archaic Oriental myths.

(b) How will it all end? In particular, and more urgently (at least for most of us), what will become of us after our death? The religious practices which covered so many major and minor moments in the ancients' lives certainly took prominent provision for that most worrisome of transitions, from life to death: funeral procedures were carefully regulated, forms of private and public commemoration highly elaborated. But no religious institution established authoritatively whether there was an afterlife, and if so what its nature was. The testimony of the poets was sparse and contradictory; local practices and beliefs varied widely; for a culture obsessed by memory, just what hope one could have with regard to living on in some way beyond one's death, besides the temporary and unreliable commemoration of one's relatives and friends, was far from clear for most ordinary people (as contrasted with the ancient heroes or with present kings). Only the mystery cults offered a promise of immortality on the basis of initiatory knowledge: but not everyone had access to these, and the precise details of the knowledge they presupposed, like the conditions of the after-life they promised, were kept under the seal of a rigid secrecy.

(c) In the mean time, between the beginning and the end, in this life here, how should we conduct ourselves? Many of the ancient religions around the Mediterranean and the Near East provided detailed codes of rules designed to regulate the ways in which the members of their communities were supposed to interact with one another, reinforcing precepts and prohibitions by reference to an infallible justice and inescapable sanctions. The religions of Greece and Rome, in contrast, did certainly prescribe in considerable detail the ritual rules according to which piety to the gods, the heroes and the dead was to be expressed, but left radically underdetermined the question of the proper modes of moral behaviour. Indeed, in the traditional myths they provided examples of divine conduct which no human could take as a model without disastrous consequences – as Xenophanes put it, 'Homer and Hesiod have attributed to the gods everything that is a shame and reproach among men, stealing and committing adultery and deceiving each other' (KRS 166).

In all three of these areas, ancient philosophers seem from the beginning to have discovered a relative deficit on the part of ancient religion and to have recognized therein a particularly fruitful opportunity to fill gaps and to answer questions. But not only did philosophy supplement traditional religion: it also undertook to correct and improve it, by systematizing its intuitions, by reinforcing its justifications, by generalizing its applicabilities. This can be illustrated by a brief chronological survey of the views of some of the most important ancient philosophers concerning religious matters.

The early Presocratic philosophers, by the inaugural act of defining as 'divine' the permanent foundational principle of the natural world – whatever this is, be it Anaximander's 'unlimited', Anaximenes' 'air', Diogenes of Apollonia's 'air', or something else – indicate thereby what the features are of what according to them would alone truly count as a god: eternity, no longer mere immortality but uncreatedness as well; singleness, for otherwise limits would be set to its power and control; and orderliness, as the guarantor for the regularities noticeable throughout the cosmos. For these thinkers, the anthropomorphic, rambunctious gods of myth and the provincial, punctilious gods of local cult can only be matters of popular opinion; true philosophical wisdom directs itself to divinities worthier of study and veneration and recognizes divinity not only in Homer and in Delphi but everywhere, including the earth, the heavens, and the celestial bodies. According to Aristotle, 'Thales thought that all things are full of gods' (KRS 91). But in the course of the fifth century BC, the philosophers seem to become increasingly wary of identifying in too much detail the god they construct: for Heraclitus, god is the unknowable and unnameable unity behind all the tensions and contradictions we can see around us and in us; Parmenides and his followers identify what alone can count as true being as being perfect in all regards – unborn and imperishable, inalterable and immovable, single, continuous, and spherical – but they are usually reticent about calling this divine; and Socrates refused to characterize in any detail the divine sign, the *daimonion*, which he said prohibited him from performing certain actions, but nonetheless his insistence that he repeatedly heard its voice may well have been one reason he was prosecuted for introducing new gods. Only

Empedocles retains not just the language and verse of traditional inspired poetry but also the plurality of divine principles and, at least in name, some of the Olympian gods. In the latter part of that century, the sophistic movement rendered temporarily fashionable in intellectual circles certain forms of scepticism about traditional religiosity – notoriously, Protagoras began his treatise *On the Gods*, 'As to the gods, I have no means of knowing either that they do exist or that they do not exist. For there are many obstacles to knowing: the obscurity of the matter and the fact that man's life is short.'

It was Plato who seems, as far as we can tell, to have invented the term 'theology' (*theologia*); he uses it in the second book of his *Republic* to refer not to a branch of philosophy, but to the traditional tales told about the gods. And these he subjects to devastating criticism in the name of a brusquely programmatic, highly detailed set of arguments concerning what alone could count for him as a philosophically tenable conception of divinity. Plato moves decisively beyond the limits of Greek religion not so much by attributing power, knowledge, immortality, and bliss to god – for all this there was ample precedent – but above all by insisting, in the wake of Xenophanes yet far more drastically and systematically, that a god, to be a god, must be morally good. Plato's god can only be the source of the good, of all that is good and of nothing except what is good, and must be perfect in all regards: hence he cannot cause evil, or deceive men, or change his shape, and all the many traditional accounts which claim otherwise (indeed, virtually all the traditional accounts) must be censored as false and deleterious. On the contrary: Plato's god (or gods: in a number of passages Plato seems to admit the existence of multiple gods of different levels and capacities) is not only non-anthropomorphic, 'he' is entirely non-material: devoid of sensible materiality, with all its inherent imperfection, corruptibility, and caducity, divinity is pure thought, closely associated with the Forms, themselves divine, above all with the One and the Good and the Beautiful. The goal of the philosopher is to become as much like this god as a human possibly can: by devoting himself to the study of all that is divine, from the Forms to the rational regularities of the cosmic cycles, to reduce his own share in materiality and to train himself in the disciplines of the mind, above all in mathematics and dialectic. Plato's fullest exposition of his conception of divinity is found in the *Timaeus*, his account of the creation of the material world by a benevolent divine craftsman applying as far as possible the pattern of the Forms to recalcitrant matter; but Platonists have never been able to decide to what extent his account is metaphorical or literal, chronological or systematic, serious or ironic. Indeed, it is precisely the crucial importance Plato attaches to divinity and to its transcendent location beyond language and experience that leads him to speak of god above all in the language of enigma and of ambiguity: in myth, allusion, irony, and the discourse of the mysteries.

Like his teacher Plato, Aristotle too applies the term 'theologian' to the pre-philosophical utterances of the poets: on his view, these may well conceal a few philosophically interesting views concerning the cosmos, but even if they do they are so veiled in allegory and so sparse in content that they are worth merely registering by the historian of philosophy, not studying seriously – unlike the doctrines of the genuine philosophers, starting with Thales and concluding with Aristotle himself. But unlike Plato, Aristotle also uses the term 'theological science or philosophy' to describe the ultimate and supreme form of philosophical research, that which is superior even to mathematics and physics because it is directed to the study of the ultimate and supreme form of being, namely god; he also describes theology as 'first philosophy', since it is concerned with that kind of being which should come first in any systematic account of being. Thus for Aristotle philosophy may be said both to begin and to end as theology. Above all, Book Lambda of his *Metaphysics* makes an extraordinary attempt to provide a systematic deduction of the existence and characteristics of a supreme divinity on the basis of the existence and characteristics of the physical world: the only way to explain the eternal motion of the physical world, and in particular the perfectly regular and circular movement of the heavens, without incurring an infinite regress is to posit an ultimate cause of motion which is itself unmoved, eternal, non-spatial, and immaterial; since activity is more perfect than inaction, this principle must be incessantly engaged in doing something, which of course cannot be physical motion, but only the pure activity of contemplative thought, directed to its own thinking as the highest possible object, and which, since it completely achieves its end, must be consummately happy; and since this principle is at the same time the object of thought and desire for the whole cosmos, it moves the universe as its final cause. Aristotle's vision of god as the unmoved Prime Mover is one of the most influential contributions of Greek philosophy to western thought; but in other writings, Aristotle also admitted a plurality of gods to explain particular aspects of the physical universe, for example the various movements of the planets. Thus Aristotle's god is in the first instance of importance for ontology and physics. But it also has an ethical dimension, though in a very abstract sense: both the *Nicomachean* and the *Eudemian Ethics* conclude with slightly differing forms of the argument that the only way in which men can achieve the highest degree of happiness available to them is not to engage only in practical action but to cultivate what is divine within them, the mind, and by following the theoretical life to become immortal so far as this is possible for a human being. For Aristotle, as for Plato, one of the fundamental purposes of engaging in philosophy is, by studying god, to become as godlike as possible.

Plato's closest followers in the Academy, and Aristotle's in the Lyceum, elaborated critically their masters' views, in theology as in other matters: Speusippus seems to have retained from Plato as creator of the universe a divine craftsman transcending the world and associated with the mathematical entities, and Xenocrates developed a highly systematic account of the gods, introducing a hierarchy of many intermediate levels for lesser deities he termed 'demons' (*daimones*), and attempted by employing allegory, myth and other means to establish connections between these philosophical divinities, closely linked with the heavenly bodies, and the traditional gods of Greek myth and cults; while Theophrastus pointed to difficulties in Aristotle's doctrine of the Unmoved Mover (according to ancient reports, his own explanations for the movements of the heavens were various and inconsistent) and, in a wide-ranging ethnographic account of the historical development of religious practices from earliest times to the present, identified true piety not as the performance of ritual sacrifices in their own right but rather as the worshipper's pious attitude, which was expressed in them.

For all their many obvious differences, Epicureanism and Stoicism, the two greatest schools of Hellenistic philosophy, share three fundamental features in their theologies: they closely link the study of god with the study of physical nature; they retrospectively legitimate key aspects of traditional Greek religion; and they emphasize the psychological and ethical value of a correct understanding of divinity.

For Epicurus, physics, which includes theology since the gods exist as part of nature, serves the function of freeing men from their fear of such false terrors as divine intervention (which does not exist) and death (which is nothing to us). As for what exactly Epicurus' positive conception of divinity was, this has been controversial since antiquity, and Epicureans have often been labelled atheists by their philosophical opponents; but the evidence strongly suggests that Epicurus himself confidently asserted the existence of a plurality of anthropomorphic, imperishable, blissful deities in the form of incessant streams of images, innate in all men, representing an ideal of human perfection and happiness. Proper piety towards such happy gods – who are far too cheerful to be troubled by running this universe, but who otherwise can be easily reconciled with the traditional divinities of Greek religion – consists not in fear, but in reverent worship, including participation in the established civic cults and prayers. The tranquillity, detachment and bliss of the gods can be acquired by the sage too, if he studies and understands them, and in doing so he can himself become divine: the first of Epicurus' *Key Doctrines*, 'That which is blessed and imperishable neither suffers nor inflicts trouble, and therefore is affected neither by anger nor by favour. For all such things are marks of weakness,' leaves carefully ambiguous whether we are to understand its prime reference as being to the god or the philosopher – evidently, it is both. Against the background of the custom of deification of political rulers and other great men, theorized by Epicurus' contemporary Euhemerus and practised throughout the Hellenistic world, it is hardly surprising that Epicurus can suggest that his pupils will be deified, nor that he himself was worshipped as a god by his followers.

If, most basically, Epicureanism seeks to free men from unfounded dread, Stoicism seeks to bring them to an appreciation of the systematically ordered, living creativity which rationally organizes the universe as a whole as well as every single part of it. Stoic physics does not simply include theology, on the grounds that the gods are one part of nature among others; rather, since the leading Stoics, according to Diogenes Laertius (VII 148), say 'that the whole world and heaven are the substance of god', the study of the physical world in its vital and systematic rationality is tantamount to the study of god – physics, properly understood, culminates or is fulfilled in theology, or, as Chrysippus put it, 'what should come last in the physical theorems is theology. Hence the transmission of theology has been called "fulfilment" ' (Plutarch, *On Stoic Self-contradictions* 1035A). The Stoics define god as 'intelligent, a designing fire which methodically proceeds towards creation of the world', but, differently from Plato, they stress that divinity does not transcend a world it creates once and for all, but instead is immanent from beginning to end as a self-fulfilling, self-directed teleological principle within this world, for which it provides both a systematic orderliness as its structure and a meaningful life-history in the form of its providential evolution over time (hence the Stoics can sometimes equate god with nature, or with fate). Applied to the individual, the recognition that one is inevitably part of this divine structure and evolution must lead to the decision to live in accordance with it: thus ethics too attains its fulfilment as piety. This is a very ambitious and rather abstract view of god; but the Stoics' firm conviction that all elements within the universe, however trivial or repugnant they might seem to uninformed eyes, must be capable of being recognized to embody at least partially the consummate rationality which governs the whole, leads them to insist upon salvaging what they can of traditional Greek religiosity rather than discarding it wholesale: they devote an extraordinary effort of highly sophisticated allegorical interpretation to the ancient myths and the established cults so as to demonstrate that, rightly understood, they are identical with their own doctrines.

With the Neoplatonists, the link between physics and theology is finally and decisively severed. Once more, god is the ultimate source of all that is and the ultimate goal of all that moves and desires; but now the materiality of the physical cosmos is taken to be so irremediably corrupt and defective that, even though there is nothing that could be entirely devoid of even some small spark of his saving presence, the first and highest god, in his immaculate purity, must transcend all contamination with the natural world – unlike the many lower echelons of inferior divinities and demons, who were thought to have some degree of materiality mixed into their constitution and hence to be capable of mediating between the various hierarchical levels of an ever more baroque demonology. The goal of the Neoplatonist philosopher is to seek to return across these mediating instances to the ultimate source of his being and to cast off the shackles of materiality that bind him to ignorance and passion; in so doing, he attempts to approximate to godhood during his life in the body and he can nourish the hope of being finally rejoined to it afterwards. Whether this ultimate god was rationally intelligible for humans was a source of disagreement among various Platonists in later antiquity: thus Alcinous denied that the first god could be an object of predication or definition, but asserted that he could be grasped in thought by means of a process of abstraction, induction and analogy; while Plotinus located 'the One' consistently beyond reason, thought, volition, and being, assigning to lower, intelligible gods the status of being equivalent to the Forms, and Iamblichus claimed that human thought is too weak to grasp divinity on its own without the help of the gods. In consequence, theology was no longer considered to be the sole discipline which sought proximity to god, or rather the Neoplatonists tended to enlarge their concept of what counted as theology so as to encompass other practices besides rational proof and argument: holy writings, of the Jews, Chaldaeans, and Orphics, Homer and Plato (but not of the Gnostics or Christians, against whom the Neoplatonists polemicized vigorously, no doubt because these represented genuine rivals), were valued as ancient intimations of philosophical truth and were subjected to intricate allegorical exegesis in order to prove this (so already by Philo of Alexandria, an eclectic Jewish philosopher of the early first century AD); theurgy, a loose set of various magical practices designed to ensure divine assistance for the philosopher's project, became increasingly important in Neoplatonism starting with Iamblichus; increasingly, the goal of philosophy became identified not as knowledge of the divine but as a kind of mystical union with it.

Almost eleven centuries separate the Presocratic Thales' assertion, 'All things are full of gods', from the following passage from *The Elements of Theology* written by the Neoplatonist Proclus, who varies, interprets, distorts, and refunctionalizes that very same adage, one that by his time had become hoary and almost anonymous:

For all things are dependent from the gods, some being irradiated by one god, some by another, and the series extend downwards to the last orders of being. Some are linked with the gods immediately, others through a varying number of intermediate terms; but 'all things are full of gods', and from the gods each derives its natural attribute.   (Prop. 145)

During that whole millennium, ancient philosophical thought had found no form better than theology in which to reflect upon its own limits and aspirations. Reflecting on god, ancient man reflected himself.

ANCIENT PHILOSOPHY AS A RELIGIOUS WAY OF LIFE

But, as suggested in the first section of this chapter, the manifold connections between philosophy and religion in the ancient world are not exhausted by the ways, many and various as they were, in which philosophers chose as objects of conscious reflection god's relation to his world and man's relation to his gods. Philosophy was also intimately linked with religion as a form of social practice, as a recognizable way of life. In conclusion, I point briefly to two aspects of this linkage: the philosopher as a kind of holy man, and the philosophical school as a kind of religious community.

(a) Throughout all of antiquity, the *theios anēr*, the 'godly man' or 'holy man', was a familiar figure. The phrase first occurs in Hesiod's *Works and Days* (731); references recur regularly through the following centuries in all genres of Greek literature, among the philosophers especially in Plato and the Stoics; and they seem gradually to swell in an unbroken crescendo until they reach a deafening fortissimo in late antiquity, when it sometimes seems there were more 'godly men' around than ungodly ones. There were numerous varieties, depending upon time, place, kind, speaker, and other factors; yet certain features seem to have been largely invariant. In a world which tended to differentiate sharply between mortals and immortals, the godly man was a person of unsettling and hence fascinating ambiguity, ineluctably mortal, yet possessed of a special knowledge of matters divine, which could be expressed in the form of capabilities otherwise beyond the scope of ordinary mortals, ranging from legislation, monarchy, or wisdom, to bilocation, miracle cures, knowledge of the future, and action at a distance. In a society founded upon the political institutions of the city, he was usually an outsider, wandering through the countryside, arriving at the city so as to provide an astonishing display of his powers, and then vanishing again. In a culture profoundly sensitive to beauty and pleasure, he was an anchorite, unkempt and self-sufficient, poorly clad, usually vegetarian, and indifferent to the temptations of the flesh. We ourselves, according to our inclination, might describe these figures as miracle-workers or as charlatans; the ancients called them 'godly men', or, surprisingly often, 'philosophers'.

What is the relation between these 'godly men' and philosophers in our narrow sense? It is tempting to dismiss the former as a trivial phenomenon of popular culture, particularly widespread in what many consider the decadence of late antiquity, and to insist upon its differences with regard to the high-culture intellectual tradition of the great ancient philosophers. But to do so would be to project uncritically our own values onto the ancient world, and would make it impossible to understand a number of figures without whom no history of ancient philosophy could be complete – Empedocles, Pythagoras and Iamblichus, to name only a few. It is surely preferable to acknowledge the intricate connections between the two phenomena. On this view, the term *theios anēr* denotes a broad, diffuse and continuous stream of eccentric figures which accompanies what we might call the standard culture of antiquity, like its dark and necessary shadow, from beginning to end. At a certain point, let us say during the sixth century BC, a particular and much tinier rivulet, one which is dedicated as well to rational argument and investigation, separates out from this larger stream and goes on to define itself as philosophy and to develop its own traditions and conventions, but it is never entirely free of the influence from that larger context and eventually, especially after the third century AD, it tends more and more to be swallowed up once again by it. Put in these terms, the ancient philosopher is a specific variety of the ancient *theios anēr*, one who could (but did not have to) express his godliness in a more or less rational form of wisdom; and we will not understand him completely unless we bear his origin and context in mind.

These considerations make sense of many aspects of ancient philosophy which might otherwise seem bizarre. For doubtless we might be inclined to make light of the more supernatural details in the Neoplatonist hagiographic biographies of Pythagoras, Plotinus and Proclus (to say nothing of Philostratus' closely related account of the miracle-worker Apollonius of Tyana), and to disbelieve such reports as, for example, that Iamblichus (who is regularly termed *theios*) floated above the ground when he prayed or that a divine light illuminated Proclus' head during his lectures. But, whatever the historical veracity of such reports, they clearly belong to the same vast realm of social belief as ancient religion does, and it is just as captious and vain to question the one as the other: what matters is not whether or not such incidents actually happened, but that they could be credibly reported to have done so. And they begin long before the Neoplatonists, and are not restricted to shaman-type figures like Empedocles. Speusippus reported that his uncle Plato had been sired by Apollo himself: Ariston, the husband of Plato's mother Perictione, had tried in vain to force himself upon her, and upon desisting had seen a vision of the god; she had remained a virgin but had been impregnated by Apollo, and it was from him that the great philosopher had been born. One of Aristotle's students, Clearchus of Soli, reported that his master had met a Jewish sage in Asia Minor who had imparted a secret wisdom to him, and that he had once used a psychagogic rod to draw a sleeping boy's soul out of his body and had then had him report what he had experienced on his travels outside the body. Such examples could easily be multiplied, but the point should already be clear. The ancient philosopher, whatever else he was, was also a specific kind of religious figure: not only did he provide a philosophical interpretation of certain aspects of ancient religion, what is more his philosophy itself may be seen as having formed an aspect of ancient religion.

(b) One of the most obvious differences between the ancient philosophers and many of the other figures referred to by the ancients as 'holy men' is that the former tended to institutionalize the communities of their disciples in the form of more or less durable philosophical schools, whereas the latter usually did not succeed in leaving behind them lasting structures of followers who could revere their person and transmit their doctrines. Informal groups of disciples who followed a sage during his lifetime and honoured him for a little while after his death were a common phenomenon throughout the ancient world; but it was precisely the formalization of this relationship in the shape of recognizably structured and long-lasting philosophical schools, above all the Academy, Lyceum, Garden and Stoa, which guaranteed the survival of individual ancient philosophies and thereby, ultimately, of ancient philosophy as a whole.

How are these philosophical schools to be understood? The term 'school' can be misleading, for it might suggest that the philosophers simply applied to their own discipline educational institutions already existing in the world around them: yet in fact formal schools of the sort familiar to us existed hardly if at all in the pre-Hellenistic period and, when they did begin, slowly and with difficulty, to develop during and after the Hellenistic age, they were certainly at least as much influenced by the pedagogical programmes of the philosophers as the other way around. In 1881, Ulrich von Wilamowitz-Moellendorff suggested that the philosophical schools were nothing other than religious associations, known as *thiasoi*, centred at least formally upon a cult of the Muses. His proposal found favour for many years, but has recently been contested, and rightly so. To be sure, Plato did found such a cult in his Academy, and Aristotle's successor Theophrastus seems to have done the same in imitation of Plato; but apart from these two examples the evidence for such a strictly cultic activity in those same schools, directed to the divinities of the established Greek pantheon, is virtually non-existent, and furthermore it does not seem necessary, to understand their exact legal position within the system of contemporary legislation, to see them as anything other than just one more variant of the many clubs and voluntary associations that flourished throughout the Greek world.

But to say that the philosophical school was not a *thiasos* does not mean that it must have been altogether free of religious implications and values. Instead, it seems best to see this phenomenon as a version of the hero cults which were so prominent a feature of Greek religiosity. The heroes were mortals who had provided benefits of one sort or another to mankind and whose memory continued to be revered by groups of worshippers focused upon a specific cultic centre, usually the tomb. There was sometimes, particularly starting in the Hellenistic age, a fixed priesthood authorized in successive generations to perform specified rituals; there were often ceremonies recurring at regular intervals, and relics linked significantly to the life of the hero. The similarities of these features to standard aspects of the ancient philosophical school is striking. The philosophical school was founded by a living philosopher but it was only after his death that it was institutionalized as a lasting institution, usually by explicit provisions in his testament; it was highly localized, normally in the immediate vicinity of his place of death; often his library (not only the books he had read, but above all the manuscripts he had written) was bequeathed to his successor and provided a focus for the activity of his followers and a relic which guaranteed authenticity and continuing inspiration; a succession of directors of the school was instituted and maintained, in some cases for many generations; the school continued to be focused upon the reverent commemoration of the person of its founder – for example, the founder's birthday was customarily celebrated every year in a formal ritual which marked the high point of the school's activities. In all these regards, the philosophical school seems less like the transitory, prosaic, recreational, and most often commercially centred voluntary associations whose legal status it may well have shared, and more like an only partially secularized form of the long-lasting, idealistic, highly serious hero cult. Certainly, the worship of Epicurus within his school, and of a variety of precursors and scholars within Neoplatonism, makes good sense in this context – as does, more generally, the extremely strong tendency among the members of most of the ancient philosophical schools towards a dogmatic defence of what were taken to be the views of the school's founder rather than toward free inquiry and inner-directed polemic, and towards the justification of innovations as interpretations of founding texts.

In both these regards, the practice of ancient philosophy assumed the specific forms it did because it belonged, at least to a certain extent, to the wider context of ancient pagan religiosity; and in general it may be said that ancient philosophy was confined within the same limits as was that religiosity. Yet ancient philosophy has survived, and ancient religion has not. Why? As it happened, one ancient *theios anēr* did manage, without transforming the circle of his disciples into a formal philosophical school, to create an institution of belief that lived on long beyond his own death. He was not a Greek or Roman, but a Jew, and he was named Jesus. Jesus himself, of course, did not arise out of the traditions of Greco-Roman philosophy, but out of messianic movements within Judaism. Yet already the Gospel of John had begun by identifying Jesus as the *logos*, the rational discourse, which had been the central term of all of Greek philosophy; and the eventually triumphant institutionalization of Christianity as the religion of the Roman empire meant that his teachings came to be interpreted not only within a narrowly Jewish context, but also in terms of the dominant traditions of pagan philosophy, above all in those of Neoplatonism, the leading philosophical school in late antiquity. Church Fathers like Clement of Alexandria, Origen and Pseudo-Dionysius the Areopagite helped create a large-scale synthesis between Christian revelation and pagan philosophy which legitimated the former for their contemporaries and rescued the latter for us. But that is another story.

NOTE

1   For KRS citations, see p. 72 n. 1.

12 The legacy of ancient philosophy

INTRODUCTION

It has been claimed, with some justification, that the 'legacy of Greece to Western philosophy is Western philosophy'.[1] The Greeks, after all, not only defined the main areas of philosophical inquiry – metaphysics, logic, epistemology, ethics and so on – but also formulated the questions which that inquiry has always sought to answer. Yet it was in the period from the twelfth to the seventeenth century that Greek thinkers, together with their Roman interpreters and followers, exerted the most profound influence on later philosophy. During this long epoch, extending from the late Middle Ages through the Renaissance and into the start of the early modern era, everything which survives today of ancient philosophy, with the exception of a few works,[2] was recovered after the losses incurred in the aftermath of the Roman empire's collapse. Moreover, continuing the work of the Church Fathers, vigorous efforts were made, at different times and with varying degrees of success, to bring the major schools of pagan philosophy into line with Christianity. Once restored and reconciled with Christian theology, ancient philosophical traditions supplied the framework within which the philosophers operated and the foundation on which they built their own systems. In the seventeenth century, however, this situation started to change, with the gradual emergence of what we now think of as 'modern philosophy'. Not that interest in Greek and Roman thought disappeared. Far from it. But its impact on the course of philosophical development began to wane, as the legacy of ancient philosophy became increasingly the preserve of philologists and historians rather than philosophers.

THE LATE MIDDLE AGES

Latin was the language of philosophy in western Europe throughout the Middle Ages – indeed, it was not replaced by the vernacular until the seventeenth century. So while Roman philosophy, most of it written in Latin, could be directly assimilated, translation into Latin was a crucial stage in the revival of Greek philosophy. In the case of the Aristotelian corpus, the mediaeval phase of this process started with the *Organon*: renewed interest in logic during the twelfth century led to the recovery of Boethius' translations, only a few of which were previously in circulation, and the appearance of a new version of the *Posterior Analytics*. Before the close of the century, many other Aristotelian treatises had been translated into Latin, some directly from the Greek, others by way of Arabic intermediaries. And by the end of the thirteenth century, virtually all of Aristotle's extant works were available in Latin. A key figure in this undertaking was the Flemish Dominican William of Moerbeke, who produced Latin versions of several Aristotelian treatises from the Greek and revised a number of existing translations. Apart from the *Organon*, it was his versions which were studied and commented on right through the Middle Ages and for a large part of the Renaissance.

Given the difficulties presented by Aristotle's treatises, the existence of Latin versions – translated word-for-word in the mediaeval manner, with many Greek technical terms merely transliterated – was not sufficient to permit philosophers to understand and exploit them. Aids to their interpretation were also necessary. For this purpose, William of Moerbeke translated some of the ancient Greek commentaries on Aristotle. He saw his work on these texts as a valuable complement to his Aristotle versions, as he grudgingly acknowledged in the preface to his version of Simplicius' commentary on *On the Heavens* (*De caelo*): 'By dint of great bodily toil and much mental tedium, I offer this work to the Latin world, believing that I have contributed a great deal to Latin studies with this translation.'[3] The English philosopher and theologian, Robert Grosseteste, shared William's estimate of the importance of these works: his translation of the *Nicomachean Ethics*, completed around 1246–7 and still in use in the fifteenth century, was made in conjunction with a body of Greek commentaries dating from the second to the twelfth century.

Only a small portion of the Greek commentaries on Aristotle made it into Latin during the Middle Ages. In terms of impact on the Aristotelian tradition, they were overshadowed by the commentaries of the Muslim philosopher Ibn Rushd, known in the West as Averroes. His epitomes, paraphrases and detailed expositions, which were translated into Latin in the 1220s and 1230s, achieved canonical status for many mediaeval and Renaissance Aristotelians, for whom Averroes was 'the Commentator', just as Aristotle was 'the Philosopher'. Averroes won this position because he clarified many of the obscurities in Aristotle's thought. But he also put forward interpretations which highlighted the incompatibility of Peripatetic philosophy with Christian dogma, in particular regarding the sensitive issues of the eternity of the world and the immortality of individual souls.

Even before Averroes' commentaries began to circulate in Latin, the ecclesiastical authorities were well aware of the danger which Aristotelian philosophy presented to Christian orthodoxy. Yet despite repeated attempts on the part of the Church to prohibit or limit the study of Aristotle in the newly founded universities, especially at Paris and Oxford, by the middle of the thirteenth century Aristotelian treatises had come to dominate the philosophical curriculum. They would continue to do so until the seventeenth century. Aristotelianism could not have maintained this central position in the philosophical culture of the West without a fundamental accommodation of its doctrines to the tenets of Christianity. The thinker who deserves most credit for this enormous achievement was Thomas Aquinas, who managed to transform Aristotle from an enemy of Christianity to its staunchest ally. Baptized and translated into Latin, Aristotelian philosophy was free to develop in new directions during the fourteenth century, from the nominalism of William of Ockham and his followers to the complex mathematical physics devised by the philosophers of Merton College, Oxford.

When we look at the Platonic legacy in the late Middle Ages, a quite different story emerges. To begin with, rising interest in Platonism during the twelfth century did not stimulate a spate of new translations. Apart from the Latin versions of the *Meno* and *Phaedo* produced in southern Italy between 1154 and 1160, which had few readers, the only Platonic text to be translated before the fifteenth century was a substantial chunk of the *Parmenides* (126a–142a) included in William of Moerbeke's partial translation of Proclus' commentary on the dialogue. Far from searching out new works of Plato, the philosophers involved in the twelfth-century renaissance of Platonism concentrated narrowly on the portion of the *Timaeus* (17a–53b) which had been translated into Latin and commented on in the fourth century by Calcidius. William of Conches, Bernardus Silvestris and their colleagues in the cathedral schools of northern France, augmenting their meagre first-hand knowledge of Plato with material from Latin authors such as Boethius, Macrobius and Apuleius, sought to reconcile Platonic cosmology with the account of creation in Genesis. While Thomas Aquinas faced an uphill struggle in attempting to bring Aristotle within the Christian fold, these French thinkers could draw on the authority of the Church Fathers, above all Augustine, to support their belief in the closeness of Platonism to Christianity. Even so, it was possible to push this line of argument too far: among the doctrines for which Peter Abelard was condemned by the Council of Sens in 1140 was his alleged identification of the world soul of the *Timaeus* with the Holy Spirit.

As Aristotle moved to the centre of the philosophical scene during the thirteenth century, Plato was increasingly marginalized. The Aristotelian monopoly of the university curriculum, securely established by the middle of the century, meant that the *Timaeus* ceased to play a part in philosophical education. The failure of Platonism to gain a foothold in the universities was in large measure due to the fact that Aristotle's treatises, with their straightforward and systematic treatment of discrete bodies of knowledge, were much better suited to serve as textbooks than Plato's dialogues, which, apart from their allegory, irony and digressions – not to mention their unseemly sexual content – did not fit neatly within disciplinary boundaries.

As for Greek Neoplatonism, the mediaeval West knew it chiefly through the philosophy of Proclus. William of Moerbeke, in addition to his partial translation of Proclus' commentary on Plato's *Parmenides*, produced a Latin version of his *Elements of Theology*, a summary of Neoplatonic metaphysics in the form of Euclidean geometrical propositions. Access to the *Elements* enabled Thomas Aquinas to uncover the true identity of *The Book of Causes*, a Latin work translated from the Arabic which circulated under Aristotle's name and which was regarded as a supplement to his *Metaphysics*. Thanks to William's translation, Thomas recognized that it was in reality an Arabic reworking of the *Elements*. Otherwise, Proclus' treatise was not a great success. It inspired only one commentary, a massive exposition written between 1340 and 1361 by Berthold of Moosburg, a Dominican who taught at the University of Cologne. Proclus encountered a warm welcome in this unusual milieu, characterized by a strong current of Neoplatonism deriving from Albert the Great (who imbibed it partly from the *Book of Causes*) and a tradition of German religious mysticism, which combined to challenge the Aristotelianism that elsewhere reigned supreme.

Generally speaking, it was not through the medium of his own writings that Proclus' thought reached mediaeval readers. Instead, it came to them by way of a body of Greek texts written in the early sixth century by a Christian disciple of his, purporting to be Dionysius the Areopagite, St Paul's Athenian convert (Acts 17:34). These treatises, among the most influential forgeries of the Middle Ages, presented a Christianized version of late Neoplatonic theology and ontology, emphasizing divine transcendence and the hierarchical structure of reality. First translated into Latin in the ninth century, the Pseudo-Dionysian texts were commented on by a host of mediaeval thinkers, including Albert the Great, Thomas Aquinas and Robert Grosseteste, who also retranslated them into Latin.

Of the main Hellenistic schools of philosophy, it was Stoicism which played the largest role in mediaeval thought. Two factors help to account for this. First, a great deal of Stoic philosophy was conveyed in the works of Seneca and Cicero, two of the most popular Latin authors of the Middle Ages. Seneca, a professed Stoic, was best known for his ethical teachings. He was praised by twelfth-century authors such as John of Salisbury, familiar with *On Favours* (*De beneficiis*), *On Mercy* (*De clementia*) and *Moral Letters to Lucilius*, as 'a faithful guardian of virtue and enemy of vice'.[4] Cicero, though not a member of the sect, presented detailed expositions of its ethical doctrines in *On Ends* (*De finibus*) and *On Duties* (*De officiis*), its views on natural law in *De legibus* and its cosmology in *On the Nature of the Gods* (*De natura deorum*). While no new Greek sources of Stoicism became available in the Middle Ages, some information could be gleaned from Simplicius' commentary on Aristotle's *Categories* and Alexander of Aphrodisias' *On Fate*, both put into Latin by that most prolific of mediaeval translators, William of Moerbeke.

The second reason why it was relatively easy for mediaeval thinkers to take up Stoic ideas was that many of them, particularly in
the field of ethics, had already been adopted by the Church Fathers.
The *De officiis* of St Ambrose, for instance, was modelled on Cicero's
treatise of the same name, itself based on the writings of the
Greek Stoic Panaetius. The spurious correspondence between Seneca
and St Paul, accepted as genuine during the Middle Ages, gave a
further boost to the belief that much of Stoicism was compatible
with Christianity. Nevertheless, for all its advantages, Stoicism was
a pervasive presence rather than a powerful force in mediaeval
philosophy. Limited for the most part to ethics – little of Stoic
physics or logic was known at the time – Stoicism could not provide
a viable alternative to the comprehensive philosophical curriculum
of Aristotelianism.

The principal Latin sources of Epicureanism during the Middle
Ages were the same as those for Stoicism: Cicero, whose account
of the sect, especially in *De finibus* and *De natura deorum*, was
unflattering but informative; and Seneca, whose reservations about
Epicurean philosophy did not prevent him from painting a sympathetic portrait of its founder and repeating many of his choice sayings.
Transmitted in the works of these widely read authors, knowledge of
Epicureanism was not thin on the ground, even without Lucretius'
De rerum natura, only snippets of which circulated in various flori-
legia. For an ancient philosophical system to have any impact, however, it needed more than just availability. It also had to be perceived
as broadly in conformity with Christian theology – or at any rate
not blatantly in contradiction with it. On this score Epicurus' denial
of divine providence and of immortality, as well as his exaltation
of pleasure over virtue, created a vast gulf between his philosophy
and Christianity which would not be bridged until the seventeenth
century. Before then, Epicureanism remained a pariah among ancient
philosophies. John of Salisbury spoke for his contemporaries when he
said that Epicureans were engaged in a fruitless pursuit of pleasure,
unaware that the tranquillity they sought could only be obtained in
the next life through divine grace.[5]

Mediaeval philosophers had only limited access to ancient scepticism. Cicero's *Academica*, an essential source for our understanding of Academic scepticism, managed to escape the popularity of
his other works. Such knowledge as the Middle Ages possessed of

the Academic position more often came from Augustine's polemic against it in his *Contra academicos*, which combined information and condemnation in equal measure. Henry of Ghent, at the end of the thirteenth century, was unusual in knowing Cicero's treatise as well as Augustine's. Rarer still, he took the epistemological challenge posed by the sceptics seriously enough to begin his *Summa* by inquiring whether it was possible for humans to know anything, concluding, inevitably, that it was. All that can be said about the Pyrrhonian variety of scepticism is that a Latin translation of Sextus Empiricus' *Outlines of Pyrrhonism* is preserved in three manuscripts of the thirteenth and fourteenth centuries, one of which also contains a fragmentary Latin version of *Against the Professors*. Neither work, however, left any discernible trace on mediaeval philosophy.

The earliest Greek philosophers, referred to since the nineteenth century as 'Presocratics', were known to the Middle Ages principally through the writings of Aristotle, who portrayed them as thinkers engaged in the study of nature. Additional information could be found in Cicero, Macrobius and some of the Greek works available to mediaeval readers such as Simplicius' commentary on *De caelo*. Thales, Anaxagoras, Democritus, Parmenides, Zeno of Elea and Pythagoras, among others, featured in a collection of 131 potted biographies of philosophers compiled in the first half of the fourteenth century by the Englishman Walter Burley. One of his sources was apparently a lost twelfth-century Latin translation of Diogenes Laertius' *The Lives and Opinions of the Eminent Philosophers*. On the whole, mediaeval authors showed little interest in these philosophers either individually or as a group.

THE RENAISSANCE

The revival of ancient philosophy, already well under way in the late Middle Ages, continued apace during the Renaissance. Aristotelianism held on to its leading position throughout the period. But it faced powerful challenges from competing ancient philosophical traditions, above all Platonism and Stoicism, both of them bolstered by the recovery of new works from the Greek and by further endeavours to stress the harmony of their doctrines with Christian beliefs. Knowledge of Epicureanism and scepticism was considerably increased, but both systems remained in the philosophical hinterland.

The Presocratics, especially Pythagoras, acquired a higher profile and also began to develop a collective identity.

During the fifteenth and sixteenth centuries Aristotle continued to be the mainstay of the philosophy curriculum. In order to supply universities all over Europe with textbooks, the printing industry produced several thousand editions of Aristotle, the overwhelming majority in Latin translation. Though the mediaeval versions got into print, they competed against and were gradually replaced by translations produced in the Renaissance. Most of these were the work of 'humanists', so called on account of devotion to the *studia humanitatis*, the study of the written and material remains of antiquity. These connoisseurs of all things Classical despised the literal versions of the Middle Ages, which offended their sense of good Latin syntax, grammar and vocabulary. We now know, however, that many fifteenth-century humanist translations were essentially revisions of the mediaeval versions: errors were corrected against the Greek text; transliterated Greek terms were given proper Latin equivalents; the style was classicized, often in misguided imitation of Cicero; but the fundamental structure was retained. It is clear, for example, that the humanist Leonardo Bruni, who criticized mediaeval translators for their ignorance and incompetence, nevertheless used Grosseteste's version of the *Nicomachean Ethics* and William of Moerbeke's of the *Politics* as the basis for his own translations of these treatises. Bruni's version of the *Oeconomica* (thought to be a genuine work of Aristotle at the time) is an even more telling case in point: unable to find a Greek text of Book III – it has never been recovered – Bruni simply recast a mediaeval translation by turning it into Classical Latin.

Bruni and most other Italian humanists of the fifteenth century learned their Greek from the Byzantine scholars who came to Italy both before and after the fall of Constantinople in 1453. Some of these émigrés acquired sufficient fluency in Latin to make translations of their own. Cardinal Bessarion, an accomplished philosopher as well as a high-powered churchman (he nearly became pope), made a typically humanist translation of the *Metaphysics* by reworking William of Moerbeke's version – though this was unknown to Immanuel Bekker when he included Bessarion's translation in the Berlin Academy's authoritative 1831 edition of the *Opera* (whose page numbers we still use to cite the Greek text of Aristotle).

Bessarion's protégé, Theodore Gaza, took a radically different approach to translation. Convinced that the edition of Aristotle's writings put together in Rome in the first century BC, from which the entire manuscript tradition descended, was a botched job, Gaza had no qualms about departing in his translations from the transmitted Greek text, which he rearranged and even rewrote as he saw fit. This cavalier attitude can be seen in his translation of the *History of Animals*. He rejected the tenth book, missing in some Greek manuscripts, as a misplaced fragment from another work and decided off his own bat, with no manuscript authority whatever, to move the ninth book into the position of the seventh. Such was Gaza's reputation that the Venetian publisher, printer and humanist, Aldus Manutius, in his edition of Aristotle (1495–8), the first to be printed in Greek, branded the tenth book as spurious and reordered the Greek text in conformity with Gaza's Latin version. Aristotle editors down to the present day, moreover, have followed suit.[6]

Aldus, whose press was an important channel for the diffusion of ancient philosophy in the Renaissance, announced in the preface to his Greek Aristotle that he intended to supplement the philosopher's works by publishing all the ancient commentaries on them – just as the Berlin Academy followed up its 1831 edition by bringing out the *Commentaria in Aristotelem Graeca* (1882–1909). Although it took more than one publishing house to complete this ambitious programme, by the mid sixteenth century the corpus of commentaries was in print, both in the original Greek and in Latin translation. This vastly increased access to the ancient commentaries, only a handful of which were known in the Middle Ages, had repercussions on Renaissance philosophy. The corollaries in Book IV of Philoponus' commentary on the *Physics*, for example, provided sixteenth-century opponents of Aristotle with ammunition to attack the philosopher's account of place and his rejection of the void. And the appearance in 1527 of a Latin translation of Alexander of Aphrodisias' commentary on the *Metaphysics* started a controversy over the authenticity of the book called Little Alpha which is still unresolved.

The biggest waves, however, were caused by the publication in 1495 of a Latin translation of Alexander's *On the Soul (De anima)*. Thomas Aquinas, as part of his Christianization of Peripatetic philosophy, had held that according to Aristotle the individual human soul was a substantial form which continued to exist after the death of the

body. Since the thirteenth century, Thomas' interpretation had been
in competition with the view of Averroes that there was only one
immortal soul for all mankind, a stance which effectively ruled out
individual immortality. Alexander's treatise now gave authoritative
backing to a third possibility: that Aristotle had regarded the soul
as essentially mortal. In an attempt to end this confusion on a matter of such vital concern, in 1513 the Church officially sanctioned
Thomas' position and furthermore insisted that philosophers must
support it not only on theological but also on philosophical grounds.
Just three years later Pietro Pomponazzi, a prominent Aristotelian
philosopher at the University of Bologna, who agreed with Alexander
rather than Thomas, wrote a deliberately provocative treatise in
which he accepted the Church's right to regulate his religious beliefs,
but challenged its attempt to control his philosophical views. After
a hard-fought battle, the Church reluctantly backed down, marking
a momentous stage in the liberation of philosophy from ecclesiastical constraints. Aristotelians were now much freer to endorse the
position of Pomponazzi and Alexander or even of Averroes. It was
generally accepted that the job of a natural philosopher was to interpret what Aristotle had written in the light of reason and experience
but without taking account of religious issues, which were rightly
the province of theologians.

The immortality of the soul was a minefield for Renaissance Aristotelians. For Platonists, by contrast, it was a safe haven. They could
point to Plato's clear endorsement of an afterlife, complete with
apposite rewards and punishments, as proof of the essential concord
between Platonic philosophy and Christianity. It was for this reason that in the early years of the fifteenth century Leonardo Bruni
chose the *Phaedo*, also known as 'On the Immortality of Souls', for
his first attempt at translating Plato, even though it was one of the
very few dialogues already available in Latin. As we have seen, this
was an advantage for a Renaissance translator, who could both rely
and improve on the mediaeval version. Bruni, however, explained in
a dedicatory preface addressed to his employer, Pope Innocent VII,
that he had selected this dialogue because in it Plato presented the
philosophical arguments for immortality. It was therefore a work of
particular interest to the supreme pontiff, who had a heaven-sent
mandate to care for the souls of the faithful. And even though sacred
doctrines did not need the support of philosophy, it was nonetheless

reassuring to know that the wisest of all pagan thinkers had agreed with Christian beliefs about the soul.

Bruni went on to translate more dialogues, including the *Crito* and *Gorgias*. The *Republic*, *Apology* and a few other works also became available in Latin versions by humanists. Calcidius' translation of the *Timaeus*, along with his commentary, remained in circulation. As in the twelfth century, the dialogue's perceived similarities to the biblical narrative of creation provided evidence that Platonism was in agreement with Christianity. Plato's Renaissance supporters seized on this issue as further corroboration of his superiority to Aristotle, whose belief in the eternity of the world placed him in direct conflict with the Bible. To counter such arguments, the Byzantine scholar and fanatical Aristotelian, George of Trebizond, in 1458 wrote *A Comparison of the Philosophers Aristotle and Plato* (*Comparatio philosophorum Aristotelis et Platonis*), in which Plato was judged inferior to Aristotle in every respect. George was well acquainted with Platonism, having translated, on commission, the *Laws*, *Epinomis* and *Parmenides*. Familiarity in this case bred not merely contempt but obsessive hatred and paranoid fear. The rise of Platonism, in George's view, was a greater threat to western civilization than the advance of the Turks, not least because Plato's philosophy, in striking contrast to Aristotle's, was completely incompatible with Christianity. Plato's doctrine of immortality, George contended, was undermined by his belief in the pre-existence and transmigration of souls; and in the *Timaeus* he did not describe a creation 'out of nothing', as in Christian theology, since it is clear that the 'receptacle' was already in being.

The most significant result of George's treatise was that it provoked a reply from Cardinal Bessarion, who threw the full weight of his erudition and, no less important, his ecclesiastical position into a defence of Plato against George's slanderous allegations. Bessarion had no grudge against Aristotle, whose *Metaphysics* he himself had translated. His aim, however, was to show that although both Plato and Aristotle were pagans and held beliefs unacceptable to the Church, Plato was by far the closer of the two to Christianity. Among the most avid readers of this work, published in 1469 (one of the first books by a living author to be printed in Italy), was the Florentine philosopher Marsilio Ficino. He was just finishing the first draft of his Latin translation of all Plato's dialogues, which, when revised and published in 1484, would at last make the entire Platonic corpus accessible to western philosophers. Ficino had embarked on this daunting project because he shared Bessarion's conviction that Platonism, rather than Aristotelianism, offered the best philosophical underpinning for Christianity. He backed up this conviction in 1474, soon after entering the priesthood, with a treatise entitled *The Platonic Theology on the Immortality of Souls*. Here Ficino demonstrated in great detail what Bruni had merely pointed out: that Plato's philosophy supported the Christian belief in an afterlife.

Ficino's lifelong commitment to Christian Platonism was also expressed through his commentaries on the dialogues, most notably the *Symposium*. In his interpretation it was about the soul's spiritual ascent to God, the ultimate source of beauty, by means of a chaste love between men. This commentary, which he wrote in Latin but also translated into Italian to ensure a large readership, inspired the cult of Platonic love in sixteenth-century art and vernacular literature. The orientation, however, moved from homosexual to heterosexual love, and the Christian dimension which was central to Ficino's reading of the dialogue grew ever more faint. Our habit nowadays of describing non-sexual relations as 'platonic' is a distant echo of Ficino's revival and re-invention of Plato.

By making all of Plato's works available in Latin and by presenting his thought in a form which accentuated its compatibility (and played down its incompatibility) with Christianity, Ficino hoped to give Platonism the wherewithal to replace Aristotelianism as the dominant force within western philosophy. He was successful to the limited extent that certain Platonic doctrines were absorbed into the general culture of late Renaissance Europe. Aristotle, however, remained firmly entrenched within the universities. True, Plato was taught, but almost exclusively by humanists who explored the dialogues within a linguistic, grammatical and literary context. As for philosophical faculties, Platonism made very few inroads: a chair of Platonic philosophy was established in the late sixteenth century at the University of Pisa; and Francesco Patrizi, the premier Platonist of his age, occupied a similar chair, first in Ferrara, then in Rome. A century after Ficino, Patrizi was fighting the same losing battle to oust Aristotle from the philosophy curriculum and install Plato in his place. In the preface to his *New Universal Philosophy* (*Nova de universis philosophia*) of 1591, dedicated to Pope Gregory

XIV, Patrizi lamented that it was Aristotle's impious writings, rather than the pious dialogues of Plato, which were lectured on throughout Christendom.

Most Renaissance Platonists, from Bessarion and Ficino to Patrizi, were heavily influenced by Neoplatonic authors, whom they regarded as interpreters of Plato rather than philosophers in their own right. For Ficino, Plotinus was the best guide to understanding Plato's thought; and in 1492 he brought out a complete Latin translation of the *Enneads*, with commentary, dedicated to his former student Lorenzo de' Medici, the unofficial ruler of Florence. Five years later a collection of Ficino's Latin versions of other Neoplatonic texts, including works by Porphyry, Iamblichus, Synesius and Proclus, was published by Aldus Manutius. Proclus' *Elements of Theology*, known since the late thirteenth century in William of Moerbeke's Latin rendering, was retranslated by Patrizi in 1583, together with the *Elements of Physics*. After the 1520s, when Erasmus argued forcefully that Dionysius the Areopagite was not a convert of St Paul but rather a late ancient imposture, Proclus' ideas no longer circulated in this Christian guise – at least among Protestants, that is; Catholics were less inclined to accept Erasmus' judgement.

Protestants were also more inclined than Catholics to reject the Neoplatonic interpretation of Plato. The French Calvinist Jean de Serres, who translated and commented on the dialogues for Henri Estienne's celebrated 1578 edition (whose page numbers we still use to cite the Greek text of Plato) railed against exegetes such as Porphyry, Iamblichus and Proclus who obscured Plato's straightforward meaning with their fanciful allegorical readings. On the other hand, the Counter-Reformation Catholic Giovan Battista Crispo, in a treatise of 1594 entitled *On the Need to Read Pagan Authors with Caution (De ethnicis philosophis caute legendis)*, showed that he was aware of certain philosophical differences which separated Plotinus from Plato but on the whole expressed a preference for the former because his doctrines were closer to Christianity.

As in the Middle Ages, Stoicism during the Renaissance retained its number one position in the league table of Hellenistic philosophical schools. Mediaeval scholars had been well supplied with Latin texts on Stoic philosophy; but in the fifteenth century new Greek sources came to light. In the first place, Diogenes Laertius' *Lives and Opinions of the Eminent Philosophers* was translated into Latin in 1433 by the part-time humanist Ambrogio Traversari (his day job was General of the Camaldulensian Order). This work, first printed around 1472,[7] contained valuable information about the lives and doctrines of Aristotle, Plato and a variety of lesser-known Greek philosophers including the Stoics Zeno, Cleanthes and Chrysippus. Another new Greek source was the *Handbook* (*Enchiridion*) of Epictetus which was translated into Latin twice in the fifteenth century: in 1450 by Niccolò Perotti, the secretary of Cardinal Bessarion; and in 1479 by the most learned of Florentine humanists, Angelo Poliziano, whose version was dedicated to his patron Lorenzo de' Medici. To fill in gaps in his defective Greek manuscripts, Poliziano relied on lemmata from the commentary on the *Handbook* by Simplicius. According to Simplicius, a Neoplatonist (though he wrote commentaries on Aristotle), Epictetus had been inspired by reading Plato's *Alcibiades*. This interpretation enabled Poliziano to give Epictetus' Stoic *Handbook* a Platonic spin, ensuring that it would go down well with Lorenzo, who had studied philosophy with Ficino and to whom Poliziano had dedicated his Latin translation of the *Charmides* a year earlier.

Poliziano's translation, which was frequently reprinted both in his own works (including a 1498 edition by Aldus) and on its own, helped to diffuse Epictetus' form of Stoicism,[8] which had a distinctly devout and religious tone that made it attractive to Christians. Though these qualities could also be found in Seneca, some of his views – his condemnation of pity as a vice, for instance, and his acceptance of suicide – aggravated nagging doubts about the compatibility of Stoicism and Christianity. In his 1529 edition of Seneca, Erasmus, who had already rejected the corpus attributed to Dionysius the Areopagite, now declared the Seneca–St Paul correspondence to be forgery – here, too, Catholics were less inclined than Protestants to accept his judgement. In addition he warned Christians, in the preface, to be wary of Seneca's Stoic wise man, so self-sufficient that he had no need of divine grace. The same note was struck towards the end of the century by Michel de Montaigne in his *Essays*. After quoting Seneca's declaration that man is 'a vile and abject thing if he does not raise himself above humanity', Montaigne wrote: 'he will rise by abandoning and disavowing his own means, letting himself be raised and pulled up by heavenly ones'. It was Christian faith, not

Stoic virtue, which enabled us 'to aspire to that holy and miraculous metamorphosis'.[9]

Such complaints, compounded by the charge that Stoic *apatheia* or impassivity was psychologically unfeasible, seriously damaged the ability of Stoicism to compete in the philosophical marketplace. Its stock began to rise, however, in 1584 when the Flemish humanist Justus Lipsius, in his best-selling treatise *On Constancy in Times of Public Calamity*, repackaged Stoic *apatheia* as an antidote to the political and religious passions then tearing the Low Countries and France apart. By transforming ineluctable Stoic fate into Christian divine providence and effecting similar metamorphoses, Lipsius made sure that there was no need to label this remedy with a spiritual health warning: his brand of Stoicism was as suitable for Christians as the Aristotelianism of Thomas Aquinas and the Platonism of Ficino. On the other hand, by concentrating on the therapeutic powers of Stoic philosophy in adversity, he cut its original remit, which included good times as well as bad, in half. The lasting impact of this reduction can be seen in our use of the term 'stoical' to describe a person who is uncomplaining in the face of misfortune but not one who reacts impassively to good fortune. Lipsius continued to campaign for a revival of Stoicism in his magisterial 1605 edition of Seneca, and in two scholarly treatises published the previous year: a guide to the history and doctrines of the sect; and a comprehensive account of Stoic natural philosophy. What is more, in these treatises Lipsius, three centuries before von Arnim, collected together all the known ancient sources for Stoicism, both Greek and Latin.

Epicureanism, like Stoicism, became better known in the Renaissance through Traversari's Latin translation of Diogenes Laertius, whose sympathetic 'Life of Epicurus' included lengthy extracts from the philosopher's writings. New material, particularly regarding the scientific side of Epicureanism, also became accessible with the recovery in 1417 of the complete text of Lucretius' *On the Nature of Things* (*De rerum natura*). Recognized as a masterpiece of Latin literature, the poem was widely read, first in manuscript, then in print; but reluctance to confront Lucretius' controversial views on religion meant that no commentaries were produced in the fifteenth century and very few in the sixteenth. The glaring conflicts between Epicureanism and Christianity which had placed this sect beyond the pale in the Middle Ages were equally damaging to its respectability in the Renaissance.

The stance modern scholars refer to as 'Christian Epicureanism' in truth amounted to little more than a knowing and ironic misappropriation of Epicurean doctrines for Christian purposes. It was a rhetorical strategy rather than a philosophical programme and therefore needs to be clearly distinguished from the serious and sincere efforts of Renaissance scholars to Christianize Aristotelianism, Platonism and Stoicism. The fifteenth-century Italian humanist Lorenzo Valla, in his dialogue *On the True and False Good* (*De vero falsoque bono*), co-opted the Epicurean principle that virtue was pursued for the sake of pleasure. But this was merely a tactic to refute the Stoic doctrine that virtue was its own reward and to defend the Christian position, as he saw it, that virtue was pursued to attain rewards in an afterlife whose existence, both he and his readers were well aware, Epicurus had denied. Erasmus, following in Valla's footsteps, asserted in one of his colloquies that Christians were the true Epicureans. It was on the grounds, however, that the most pleasurable life was one lived not merely in accordance with virtue, as Epicureanism required, but in pious gratitude for a divine providence whose existence, like that of the afterlife, as both Erasmus and his readers were well aware, Epicurus had denied.

Pyrrhonian scepticism, practically unknown in the Middle Ages, was opened up in 1433 by Traversari's Latin version of Diogenes Laertius' 'Life of Pyrrho'. Although the works of Sextus Empiricus were not translated and printed until the late sixteenth century, some Greek manuscripts circulated and were consulted by Poliziano and a few other Italian humanists. These scholars mined his writings for historical and doxographical material, but ignored their philosophical content. The first thinker to spot and exploit the epistemological potential of Sextus' works was the paradoxical figure of Gianfrancesco Pico della Mirandola: a humanist and philosopher like his more famous uncle Giovanni, but at the same time a follower of the fanatical religious reformer Girolamo Savonarola. In his *Examination of the Futility of Pagan Learning and the Truth of Christian Teaching*, published in 1520, Pico's method of defending the unique authority of the Bible, as interpreted by the Catholic Church and safeguarded by the papacy, was to mount a full-scale offensive against ancient philosophy, brandishing weapons plundered from the enemy's arsenals, to which his expert knowledge of Greek and his profound Classical erudition gave him privileged access. Long before Philoponus' commentary on the *Physics* was printed in either Greek (1535) or Latin (1539), Pico used the corollaries on place and void to attack Aristotle, the principal target of his treatise. His biggest guns, however, were raided from the armoury of Sextus Empiricus. In particular, Pico applied Sextus' account of the first of the Agrippan 'Five Modes' of suspension of judgement (see above p. 181), 'deriving from disagreement', to the dissenting views voiced by pagan philosophers on every conceivable issue. Such Pyrrhonian strategies were extremely useful, he believed, 'in repudiating the arrogance of the philosophers and demonstrating the superiority of the Christian faith', whose principles, since they did not depend on reason, sense perception or human invention but rather on 'divine revelation', were, in contrast to those of pagan thinkers, invulnerable to sceptical arguments.[10]

The revival of ancient scepticism was thus founded on its utility for a type of Christian apologetic known as fideism, which sets out to destroy the philosophical pretensions of human reason. The fideistic slant given to Pyrrhonism in this period is usually referred to as 'Christian scepticism', a stance which, like 'Christian Epicureanism', should not be confused with wholehearted attempts to adapt other ancient philosophical systems to Christianity. Although Pico made use of sceptical arguments, he was not attempting to guide his readers on an unbiased quest for an unattainable truth, which would end in a suspension of judgement. Quite the opposite. His aim was to instil an unquestioning, indeed dogmatic, acceptance of Christian truth. The Calvinist scholar and publisher Henri Estienne had the same objective in mind when in 1562 he printed his own Latin translation of the *Outlines of Pyrrhonism*. In the preface Estienne described scepticism as a cure for the disease not only of dogmatism, as Sextus had claimed, but also of impiety: the two, in fact, shared the same pathology, for it was 'the unbridled presumption of dogmatists in making judgements' which caused them 'to lapse into atheism'. *Against the Professors* was soon translated by Gentian Hervet, a Counter-Reformation theologian, whose motives harked back to the more militant fideism of Pico, though in Hervet's eyes the enemy was as much heresy (i.e. Protestantism) as paganism. Despite their confessional differences, Hervet's translation was published together with Estienne's *Outlines* in 1569, so that the complete works of Sextus were now available in Latin (they were not printed in Greek until 1621). Even though the vernacular had not yet over-taken Latin as the language of philosophical communication, the elegant French of Montaigne's *Essays* was probably the most important conduit for the spread of Pyrrhonian scepticism. For Montaigne, too, Pyrrhonism was primarily a philosophical means to a religious end: it showed man 'stripped of all human learning and so all the more able to lodge the divine within him, annihilating his intellect to make room for faith'.[11]

As in the case of other philosophical traditions, the Renaissance recovery of the Presocratics began with Traversari's translation of Diogenes Laertius. The accounts of the early Greek philosophers found in Burley's mediaeval compilation, though they continued to be read and printed until the early sixteenth century, were gradually replaced by the original versions on which they were only loosely based. This new material generated interest in these philosophers, who began to be discussed as a relatively coherent group. The Florentine humanist Bartolomeo Scala, in a letter of 1458 on the different philosophical sects, referred to 'the crowd of very ancient philosophers who devoted all their energy and spent their entire life illuminating the obscurity of nature'. Scala then provided thumbnail sketches, based on Diogenes Laertius, of the views of Thales, Anaxagoras, Parmenides, Empedocles and many others.[12] In the same year, the Byzantine émigré Johannes Argyropoulos, lecturing on the *Physics* at the University of Florence, explained that the study of nature before Aristotle had been unsystematic: 'there were many philosophers who handed down knowledge obscurely and in verse', though they nevertheless produced much that was 'worthy and outstanding'.[13] It was not until 1573, however, that the surviving fragments of early Greek philosophy were collected together and published. The editor and publisher, Henri Estienne, who was assisted by his learned friend Joseph Scaliger, entitled the volume *Philosophical Poetry, or at any rate, the Remains of Philosophical Poetry* (*Poesis philosophica, vel saltem reliquiae poesis philosophicae*) and emphasized in his preface that these writings were both useful, as natural philosophy, and delightful, as poetry. To locate these fragments, Estienne and Scaliger, the Diels and Kranz of their day, ransacked an impressive range of sources: ancient (Aristotle and his Greek commentators, Diogenes Laertius, Plutarch, Porphyry, Proclus, Sextus Empiricus, Galen, Stobaeus and many more), patristic (Clement of Alexandria, Justin Martyr, Theodoretus) and even Byzantine (Tzetzes).

Some of the Presocratics were, of course, more famous than others, though not necessarily for their philosophy. The contrasting images, well known from Latin literature,[14] of Democritus, who laughed at the human predicament, and Heraclitus, who wept over it, were a popular subject for emblems and paintings – Ficino had one in his study. The *topos* also frequently cropped up in literary contexts: Erasmus praised his witty friend Thomas More as someone who played 'the role of Democritus by making fun of the ordinary lives of mortals';[15] and Montaigne, in a chapter of his *Essays* entitled 'On Democritus and Heraclitus', predictably came out in favour of the former. Empedocles, for his part, was generally regarded as the best poet among the group. In the preface to his 1500 edition of Lucretius, *On the Nature of Things*, Aldus, who believed (wrongly) that Empedocles was 'the first of the Greeks to versify philosophical principles', attempted to boost the reputation of Lucretius – and, not incidentally, increase the sales of the book, which he published as well as edited – by claiming that the Roman poet had modelled his elegant and erudite scientific verse on Empedocles.

The most renowned of the early Greek philosophers, however, was Pythagoras. This was in part because, even though he himself committed nothing to writing, more was allegedly known about him – and falsely attributed to him – than any other Presocratic thinker. In addition to the biography in Diogenes Laertius, there were various works on Pythagoras by Iamblichus, which some humanists certainly read – Ficino even made a Latin translation, though it never got into print. The pithy and enigmatic rules of conduct, or *symbola*, which Pythagoras was supposed to have handed down to his disciples ('Do not pare your nails while sacrificing' and 'Abstain from beans' are typical examples), appealed to the Renaissance taste for erudite riddles. They were famous enough in the early 1490s for Poliziano to make fun of them in an inaugural lecture for his lecture course on the *Prior Analytics* at the Florentine university. The spurious *Golden Verses* of Pythagoras became a popular schoolbook for teaching Greek.[16] And a Neo-Pythagorean treatise ascribed to Timaeus of Locri, the principal speaker in Plato's *Timaeus*, carried sufficient weight to accompany the dialogue in the Greek editions of Plato published by Aldus in 1513 and Estienne in 1578.

It was this close connection between Pythagoreanism and Platonism, underscored in many Neoplatonic works, which gave Pythagoras special significance for Renaissance Platonists from Ficino to Patrizi. Pythagoras, for them, was the philosopher who bequeathed to Plato the doctrine of the immortality of the soul, among the best advertisements for Christian Platonism – though this did not prevent them from using him as a convenient fall guy for Plato's embarrassing belief in the transmigration of souls. Pythagoras and his follower Philolaus were vital links in the chain of 'ancient theologians' (prisci theologi), stretching from Hermes Trismegistus, the legendary Egyptian priest believed to be a contemporary of Moses, down to Plato. Through these thinkers a pagan revelation, regarded either as parallel to or as derivative of the revelation to the Jews, was transmitted to fifth-century Greece. This was why, just as the Old Testament prefigured the New, the works of Plato and his predecessors (the latter consisting of forgeries such as the Hermetic corpus and the Golden Verses) contained many anticipations of Christian beliefs. In 1540 Agostino Steuco, bishop of Gubbio and Vatican librarian, proffered an enlarged version of this tradition in his treatise On Perennial Philosophy (De perenni philosophia), in which he described an eternal wisdom that lay hidden under the diverse manifestations of human thought. Guided by the eye of faith and unhindered by any critical instincts, Steuco detected traces of the most sacred dogmas, including the Trinity, in the writings of a broad church of ancient theologians, which included a large contingent of Presocratics: Thales, Anaxagoras, Parmenides, Empedocles and Melissus, as well as the hardy perennial Pythagoras.

THE EARLY MODERN ERA

The rise of modern philosophy in the seventeenth century was paralleled by the decline of ancient philosophy as a living tradition which informed and structured the practice of the discipline. The new style of philosophy which began to take shape in this period no longer rested on the foundations laid by the philosophical schools of Greek and Roman antiquity. It was grounded instead on logically rigorous deductions from self-evident principles or, in the case of natural philosophy, direct observation of nature. For Descartes, Hobbes, Spinoza and their most zealous supporters, the philosophical legacy of antiquity was outmoded, obsolete, dysfunctional – in a word, antiquated. Yet not all seventeenth-century philosophers took such a hard line on ancient philosophy. Some attempted to straddle the ever-widening gap between ancient and modern, keeping one foot planted in the old world of classical and Hellenistic philosophy, while stepping with the other into the brave new world of mechanism, empiricism and heliocentrism.

Aristotle continued to hold sway over philosophy well into the seventeenth century, at least in the universities, where his works or, more often than not, textbooks based on them remained the staple fare of the curriculum. The modernists, as a rule, were convinced that the Aristotelian philosophy in which they had been educated was long past its sell-by date. Leibniz, who declared Aristotle himself to be 'free and innocent' of the ineptitude which 'polluted' his scholastic interpreters,[17] is a well-known exception to this rule. But there were others as well. William Harvey, one of the pioneers of modern anatomy, thought that Aristotle had laid down sound principles of scientific investigation, which had been particularly fruitful in the field of biology. Therefore, in the preface to his 1651 commentary on *Generation of Animals*, he was proud to call the ancient philosopher his 'leader' (*dux*) and 'commander' (*dictator*), though he was prepared to be insubordinate whenever observational evidence, the cornerstone of his own work in the life sciences, proved Aristotle to be in the wrong. Another hero (and very nearly martyr) of the Scientific Revolution, Galileo, also professed admiration for Aristotle's methodological principles, especially the guidelines he had established for avoiding error. In a letter of 1640 to Fortunio Liceti, one of the most eminent Aristotelian philosophers of his day, he claimed that one of the most important of these precepts was that we should not accept the authority of others when it is contradicted by our own sense experience. Galileo therefore considered himself to be a more faithful follower of Aristotle than contemporary Aristotelians, who in adhering to the letter of his philosophy had betrayed its spirit.

It was easy for Galileo and Harvey to make Aristotle relevant to contemporary science by laying stress on his empiricism. Making Aristotle relevant to contemporary philosophy was an altogether more difficult assignment. Nevertheless, Sir Kenelm Digby, who counted Descartes and Hobbes among his correspondents and whose tract on plants was published by the Royal Society, willingly took it on. His version of the fashionable new mechanical philosophy, which explained all natural operations solely in terms of matter in motion, was based, he insisted, on old-fashioned Aristotelianism. So, although Digby's philosophy was atomist, this was compatible, according to him, with the theory of *minima naturalia* (the smallest possible particles of a given substance, but ones which unlike atoms have their own qualitative properties) developed and elaborated by Arabic and scholastic commentators on Aristotle from scattered remarks in his writings. Moreover, there is no void in Digby's system, in accordance with the 'repugnance of vacuities', a principle which was 'exactly and rigorously Aristotle's'.[18] Another seventeenth-century hybrid of ancient and modern philosophy is found in the philosophical textbooks written for French Jesuit schools by Honoré Fabri. Descartes, Hobbes and Spinoza appealed to the axiomatic method of Euclidean geometry as a means of providing their new systems with a certitude that would enable them to supersede the long-standing but gradually diminishing authority of ancient philosophy, above all Aristotelianism. Fabri also adopted this method but as a means of demonstrating the certitude of Aristotelianism, the official philosophy of the Jesuit Order, and thus stanching the slow ebbing away of its authority.

The declining fortunes of Aristotelianism in the seventeenth century did not provide Platonism with an opportunity to step out from the wings on to centre stage. With all the starring roles in the new philosophical drama taken by contemporary thinkers, ancient ones like Plato were left to play only supporting parts. So, for instance, just as Galileo claimed that his empirical scientific method was essentially Aristotelian, he also maintained that his theory of the origin of the cosmos was inspired by Plato's *Timaeus*. In Galileo's account, all he had done, with some (unacknowledged) help from Ficino and other Renaissance Platonists, was to remove the dialogue's 'poetical mask' in order to reveal the 'true story' hidden beneath.[19]

Similarly, just as Digby managed to combine mechanism with Aristotelianism, strange bedfellows on the face of it, so the Cambridge Platonists found a way to unite mechanism with Platonism, an equally odd couple. What attracted the Cambridge group, composed of learned Anglican clergymen, to Plato's doctrines was their usefulness in neutralizing the atheistic tendencies of contemporary philosophy and science, in which they took a keen interest. Ralph Cudworth, for instance, gave his massive, though unfinished, *True Intellectual System of the Universe*, published in 1678, the subtitle: 'Wherein All the Reason and Philosophy of Atheism is confuted: and Its Impossibility Demonstrated'. For him, Platonic ideas, as immaterial substances, were a corrective to atomistic materialism, whether the ancient Epicurean variety or the modern Hobbesian one. They also served to guarantee the existence of an 'eternal and immutable morality' against the ethical relativism of Protagoras and his seventeenth-century acolyte – Hobbes once again.[20] His fellow Platonist and scientific enthusiast, Henry More, attempted to counteract mechanistic determinism with the 'Spirit of Nature', a descendant of Plato's world soul, which pervaded 'the whole matter of the universe' carrying out the orders of divine providence.[21]

The Cambridge Platonists were so steeped in Neoplatonism that, according to Coleridge, they should really be called 'Plotinists'. Nor did the group make any attempt to disentangle Plato's views from those of the Neoplatonists, treating the latter essentially as ancient commentators on the former. Neoplatonism would not be recognized as a distinct philosophical movement until the nineteenth century. Nevertheless, as in the sixteenth century, a few early modern thinkers showed some awareness that Plato's philosophy differed considerably from that of his later interpreters. The most distinguished of these was Leibniz. Not only did he want to scrape away the scholastic accretions from Aristotle's philosophy, he was also convinced that it was necessary to get to know Plato 'from his own writings, not from Plotinus or Ficino, who by striving always to say astounding and mystical things have corrupted the teaching of such a great man'.[22]

The Neo-Stoic movement, which grew out of Lipsius' revival of Stoic philosophy, had an impact on many aspects of seventeenth-century culture, including literature, art and politics. Although Lipsius did not succeed in completely silencing religious objections to Stoicism, his presentation of it as largely in accord with Christianity was widely accepted. This view was reinforced when the *Meditations* of Marcus Aurelius were incorporated into the canon of ancient Stoicism. First published in a Greek–Latin edition of 1559, the work was not regarded as a Stoic masterpiece until the 1634

English translation of Meric Casaubon, who first gave it the title *Meditations*, and Thomas Gataker's Greek edition, Latin translation and commentary, which came out in 1652. Casaubon and Gataker, both Church of England ministers, pointed out innumerable parallels between the *Meditations* and the Gospels, whose force was undiminished by the pagan emperor's regrettable failure to halt the persecution of Christians. Gataker, arguably the best Greek scholar of his day, confidently asserted in the preface to his edition that 'of the surviving works of the ancient pagans, none comes closer to Christian doctrine than the writings and exhortations of Epictetus and Marcus Aurelius'.

The influence of Stoicism on seventeenth-century philosophy, though by no means negligible, is difficult to pin down. Some of the ethical rules in Descartes' 'provisional moral code' have a definite Stoic ring to them: the maxim 'to try always to master myself rather than fortune' can be traced back to Epictetus' injunction, in the first chapter of the *Handbook*, to concentrate on matters within our power, such as the internal state of our souls, while resigning ourselves to those external circumstances which it is not in our power to change.[23] Since, however, Descartes was trying to build an entirely new philosophy, whose authority derived solely from the irrefutable logic with which it was constructed, he had no interest in drawing attention to items he had borrowed from those ancient philosophical systems he was attempting to replace. Such comments as he troubled to make about Stoicism were dismissive.[24] Spinoza, too, had little to say, and none of it good, about the Stoics, even though his complete subordination of the passions to reason and his pantheistic cosmology bear a clear Stoic imprint.

Recent attempts to identify a Stoic contribution to the Scientific Revolution have run into a similar conspiracy of silence on the part of seventeenth-century scientists. The integrated physics of the Stoics, with their fiery and airy *pneuma* pervading both the heavens and the earth, may well have played a part in the downfall of the Aristotelian cosmos, with its strict separation between the sublunary region, made up of the four elements, and the supralunary realm, composed of the fifth element or aether. But given the absence of first-hand testimony and the circumstantial nature of the evidence, the jury is still out in this case.

It was only in the seventeenth century that Epicureanism entered the philosophical mainstream. The suitability of Epicurean atomism to the new mechanical philosophy finally made it imperative to remove the powerful theological objections which had dogged its reputation since the patristic era and which Renaissance humanists like Valla and Erasmus had done little to defuse. In the 1640s and 1650s the French scholar and priest, Pierre Gassendi, almost single-handedly transformed Epicureanism into a viable philosophical option. Using his philological skills, Gassendi drew on Diogenes Laertius' 'Life of Epicurus' and Lucretius, together with a multitude of ancient sources, to produce a detailed reconstruction of Epicurean philosophy – not surpassed until Hermann Usener published his *Epicurea* in 1887. More importantly, using his philosophical and theological expertise, Gassendi made modifications to Epicureanism which brought its false doctrines into line with the truths of Christianity. In natural philosophy, he replaced the infinite, eternal and self-moving atoms of Epicurus and Lucretius with a finite number of atoms, created and set in motion by God. In ethics, he interpreted the Epicurean pleasure principle as part of a divine providential plan for the survival of mankind. The enormous difference which this made to the reception of Epicureanism can be judged by the fact that in 1652 the highly respected physician Walter Charleton could publish to considerable acclaim a treatise entitled *The Darkness of Atheism dispelled by the Light of Nature*, in which he presented Gassendi's version of Epicurean atomism as a bulwark against the irreligious tendencies of modern science, in much the same way that the Cambridge Platonists portrayed the philosophy of Plato.

Gassendi initially became interested in Epicurus because, like other philosophers of the modernist persuasion, he was seeking a replacement for Aristotle. In his earliest work, published in 1624, he attempted to demolish scholastic Aristotelianism with arguments taken from the repertoire of ancient scepticism. Unlike Pico and other sixteenth-century thinkers who had deployed sceptical strategies, Gassendi's aims were epistemological, not fideistic. He and his seventeenth-century colleagues took up Pyrrhonian scepticism for philosophical and scientific, not religious, purposes. In 1625 Gassendi's friend and fellow priest Marin Mersenne brought out a huge tome, *The Truth of the Sciences against the Sceptics* or *Pyrrhonians* (*La Vérité des sciences contre les sceptiques ou Pyrrhoniens*), in which he rehearsed the arguments set out by Sextus Empiricus and accepted their validity. It was indeed impossible, Mersenne admitted, to get beyond appearances and penetrate to the essence of things. Yet this limited knowledge of appearances was sufficient not just for the needs of daily life, as the ancient sceptics would have conceded, but also for the purposes of science and philosophy. Thus, Gassendi, who shared Mersenne's view, declared that the Epicurean philosophy which he had carefully reconstructed was no more than an hypothesis about the nature of reality. Nevertheless, it was enough to be getting on with. This pragmatic approach to scepticism, ideally suited to empirical and experimental science, was the philosophical position endorsed by the Royal Society. The other seventeenth-century response to what came to be known as the Pyrrhonian crisis was to devise sceptic-proof methods of attaining certainty. In pursuit of this goal, Descartes, Spinoza, Leibniz, Locke and others put epistemology at the top of the philosophical agenda, where, at least in the Anglo-American world, it has remained ever since.

The Presocratics, like other ancient philosophers, were at times invoked by early modern thinkers as the distant forebears of their own theories, particularly scientific ones, since they were known as specialists in natural philosophy. Pythagorean cosmology, with its notion of a central fire, was seen to be an antecedent of heliocentrism. This explains why Johannes Kepler stated in the preface to his *Secret of the Universe* (*Mysterium cosmographicum*), first published in 1596 and then revised in 1621, that the subject of his treatise had been dealt with 'two thousand years ago by Pythagoras'. Furthermore, in a poem addressed to the reader, Kepler playfully alluded to the transmigration of souls by describing Copernicus as a reincarnation of Pythagoras. A hundred years later, another great scientist, Sir Isaac Newton, in the so-called 'classical scholia' to his *Principia mathematica*, stated that both Pythagoras and Thales had had some inkling of gravitational attraction. The revival of atomism in the seventeenth century brought Democritus and Leucippus, the predecessors of Epicurus, to prominence. Since, however, these Presocratic atomists were, like Epicurus himself, tarred with the brush of atheism, the Cambridge Platonists preferred to believe that the doctrine predated them and could be traced back to a Phoenician thinker by the name of Mochus, who was mentioned in Iamblichus' *Life of Pythagoras* and, in a 1598 Latin translation of the work, identified with Moses. Such arguments enabled Cudworth to maintain that the 'atomical philosophy' was neither 'Epicurean nor Democritical' but rather 'Mosaical'.[25] He and his Cambridge Platonists were enthusiastic advocates of the new philosophy and science of the seventeenth century; but they were still concerned to establish both the ancient heritage of atomism and its compatibility with the Bible. As the next century progressed, both concerns would become increasingly irrelevant to the practice of philosophy.

EPILOGUE

That great monument of the French Enlightenment, the *Encyclopédie*, printed between 1751 and 1780, contains a number of articles on ancient philosophy, most of them written by the work's energetic editor, Denis Diderot. Relying to a large extent on another landmark of eighteenth-century erudition, Jacob Brucker's *Historia critica philosophiae* (*Critical History of Philosophy*), whose six weighty volumes were published at Leipzig from 1742 to 1767, Diderot relegated ancient thought and its later revivals to the history of philosophy rather than treating it as a part of the philosophical currents of his own day. His lengthy article on Greek philosophy – the Romans are given short shrift – is organized around the different sects, each of which also has an individual entry. Unlike their mediaeval and Renaissance predecessors, recent philosophers such as Descartes, Locke and Spinoza could in no way be considered as belonging to any of these sects and therefore merited articles of their own. Although ancient philosophers continued to be read and studied, even by self-consciously modern ones, their influence was increasingly diffuse and often unacknowledged. The Stoic philosophy of Marcus Aurelius was among the many sources from which Francis Hutcheson, a leading light of the Scottish Enlightenment, drew inspiration for his moral sense theory, yet the annotated English translation of the *Meditations* which he brought out in 1742 did not bear his name.

Even a philosopher such as Hegel, who attached considerable importance to the history of philosophy, above all in antiquity, saw it primarily as a means to corroborate his own account of the logical development of thought. The 'Young Hegelian' Karl Marx was a student of classical philology, a discipline which reached new heights of scholarly professionalism in nineteenth-century Germany. After producing a doctoral dissertation in 1840–1 on 'The Difference between the Democritean and Epicurean Philosophy of Nature', he intended to write a larger work on Epicureanism, Stoicism and scepticism in relation to the whole of Greek speculation. As we know, however, Marx soon decided that the point was not to interpret the world – or still worse, to interpret its interpreters – but rather to change it. This was probably no great loss to the study of ancient philosophy. The field did arguably suffer from its abandonment by a far more talented classical philologist, Friedrich Nietzsche. His promising career began with a doctoral dissertation in 1868 on the sources of Diogenes Laertius' *Lives and Opinions of the Eminent Philosophers*. But the publication of *The Birth of Tragedy*, four years later, signalled that he, like Marx, had chosen to carve an entirely new path for himself, though ancient philosophy was to remain a *leitmotif* in his later writings.

Few philosophers in the twentieth or twenty-first centuries would admit – let alone boast, as Wittgenstein did – that they had never read a word of Aristotle. Although contemporary philosophers, particularly in the Anglo-American analytical tradition, engage relatively infrequently with Greek and Roman thought, the techniques of analytic philosophy had a considerable impact on the study of Plato and Aristotle in the second half of the twentieth century. There have been periodic proposals to bring ancient philosophy to life once again: Alasdair MacIntyre's *After Virtue*, of 1981, made the case for a revival of Aristotelian moral theory, as presented by Thomas Aquinas; while 1998 witnessed Lawrence Becker's updating of Stoic ethics in *A New Stoicism*, not to mention Tom Wolfe's best-selling novel *A Man in Full*, in which the writings of Epictetus play a pivotal role. In the continental European tradition, such major twentieth-century philosophers as Martin Heidegger, Karl Popper and Hans-Georg Gadamer attached unique importance to the classical roots of their own ideas. Ancient thought has not been at the forefront of the philosophical tradition since the seventeenth century. In the background, nevertheless, it remains a powerful presence.

NOTES

1   B. Williams, 'Philosophy', in M. I. Finley, *The Legacy of Greece: A New Appraisal* (Oxford 1981), pp. 202–55, at 202.

2   E.g. the prose writings of the Epicurean Philodemus, found in charred papyrus rolls during the eighteenth-century excavations of Herculaneum; Cicero's *De republica*, published in 1822 from a palimpsest manuscript in the Vatican Library; a collection of *Sayings of Epicurus*, found in 1888 in a fourteenth-century manuscript in the Vatican Library; Aristotle's *Constitution of Athens*, published in 1891 by F. G. Kenyon from a papyrus in the British Museum; and the 74-line fragment of Empedocles discussed above, pp. 69–71.

3   William also translated Simplicius on the *Categories*, Ammonius on *De interpretatione*, Alexander of Aphrodisias on the *Meteorology* and *On Sensation*, Themistius on *On the Soul* and Philoponus on Book III of *On the Soul*.

4   John of Salisbury, *Policraticus*, ed. C. C. I. Webb, 2 vols. (Oxford 1909), II, p. 320.

5   Ibid., II, pp. 412–25.

6   A notable exception is D. M. Balme's Loeb edition of *History of Animals Books 7–10* (Cambridge, Mass./London 1991).

7   There were ten more fifteenth-century editions, together with a further ten in Italian translation. The Greek text was not printed until 1533.

8   The *Discourses* of Epictetus reported by Arrian were first published in Greek in 1535 and in Latin translation in 1595.

9   Michel de Montaigne, *The Complete Essays*, trans. M. A. Screech (London 1993), p. 683 (II.12); see Seneca, *Natural Questions* I, 'Praefatio'.

10 Gianfrancesco Pico della Mirandola, *Examen vanitatis doctrinae gentium et veritatis Christianae disciplinae*, in his *Opera omnia* (Basle 1573), pp. 719–1264, at 852–3.

11 Montaigne, *Essays*, p. 564 (II.12).

12 See 'Epistola de sectis philosophorum', in *Bartolomeo Scala: Humanistic and Political Writings*, ed. Alison Brown (Tempe, Ariz. 1997), pp. 251–61, at 254–5.

13 Quoted in C. S. Celenza, 'Pythagoras in the Renaissance: The Case of Marsilio Ficino', *Renaissance Quarterly* 52 (1999): 667–711, at 678.

14 See, e.g., Juvenal, *Satires* X 28–30 and Seneca, *On Anger* II 10.5.

15 Erasmus, *Praise of Folly*, trans. C. H. Miller (New Haven/London 1979), p. 2.

16 They were first published in Greek in 1495 and in Ficino's Latin version, together with the *symbola*, in 1497; both were Aldine editions.

17 G. W. Leibniz, *Philosophical Papers and Letters*, trans. L. E. Loemker (Dordrecht 1969), p. 127.
18 Kenelm Digby, *Two Treatises* (Paris 1644), p. 343.
19 Galileo Galilei, *Two New Sciences* (English trans., Madison, Wisc. 1974), p. 233.
20 See Ralph Cudworth, *A Treatise concerning Eternal and Immutable Morality*, ed. S. Hutton (Cambridge 1996), in which a connection is made between Hobbes and Protagoras, as portrayed in Plato's *Theaetetus*.
21 Henry More, *The Immortality of the Soul*, ed. A. Jacob (The Hague 1980), Book III, chap. 12.
22 G. W. Leibniz, *Die philosophischen Schriften*, ed. C. J. Gerhardt, 7 vols. (Berlin 1875–90), VII, pp. 147–8.
23 René Descartes, *Selected Philosophical Writings*, trans. J. Cottingham et al. (Cambridge 1988), p. 32.
24 See his comments on Seneca's *On the Happy Life* in his letter of 4 August 1645 to Princess Elizabeth of Bohemia, in René Descartes, *Selected Letters*, trans. A. Kenny (Oxford 1970), pp. 164–7.
25 Cudworth, *A Treatise*, p. 39.

BIBLIOGRAPHY

I GREEK AND ROMAN PHILOSOPHICAL WRITERS IN
ENGLISH TRANSLATION

Ancient philosophy readers (in English translation)

[1] Annas, J., *Voices of Ancient Philosophy: an Introductory Reader* (Oxford 2001)
[2] Cohen, S. M., P. Curd, C. D. C. Reeve, *Readings in Ancient Greek Philosophy* (ed. 2, Indianapolis 2000)
[3] Irwin, T., *Classical Philosophy* (Oxford 1999)

Translation series

[4] The Loeb Classical Library (Cambridge Mass. and London) prints texts of Greek and Latin authors with English translations on facing pages. The great majority of the authors relevant to this volume are included, in whole or in part.

Historical and doxographical authors

[5] Diogenes Laertius, *The Lives and Opinions of the Eminent Philosophers*: see [4]

Presocratics and sophists

Collections

[6] Barnes, J., *Early Greek Philosophy* (Harmondsworth 1987, ed. 2, 2002)
[7] Burnet, J., *Early Greek Philosophy* (ed. 4, London 1930)
[8] Curd, P., R. McKirahan, *A Presocratics Reader* (Indianapolis 1996)
[9] Gagarin, M., P. Woodruff, *Early Greek Political Thought from Homer to the Sophists* (Cambridge 1995)

353

[10] Kirk, G. S., J. E. Raven, M. Schofield, *The Presocratic Philosophers* (ed. 2, Cambridge 1987)

[11] McKirahan, R., *Philosophy Before Socrates* (Indianapolis 1994)

[12] Sprague, R. K., *The Older Sophists* (Columbia, South Carolina 1972)

[13] Waterfield, R., *The First Philosophers* (Oxford 2000)

Individual writers

[14] Anon., *Dissoi logoi*: T. M. Robinson, *Contrasting Arguments: an Edition of the Dissoi Logoi* (New York 1979)

[15] Atomists: C. C. W. Taylor, *The Atomists* (Toronto 1999)

[16] Empedocles: B. Inwood, *The Poem of Empedocles* (ed. 2, Toronto 2000)

[17] Heraclitus: C. H. Kahn, *The Art and Thought of Heraclitus* (Cambridge 1979)

[18] Parmenides: D. Gallop, *Parmenides of Elea* (Toronto 1984)

[19] Xenophanes: J. H. Lesher, *Xenophanes of Colophon* (Toronto 1992)

Socrates

Aristophanes *Clouds*: included in [20] C. D. C. Reeve (ed.), *Plato, Aristophanes, Xenophon. The Trials of Socrates: Six Classic Texts* (Indianapolis 2002)

[21] Brickhouse, T. C., N. D. Smith, *The Trial and Execution of Socrates: Sources and Controversies* (Oxford 2002)

Plato: see below under 'Plato'

Xenophon: [22] H. Tredennick, R. Waterfield, *Xenophon, Conversations of Socrates* (Harmondsworth 1990); see also [4]

Plato

For the citation system in Plato, see above, p. 99.

Complete works

[23] Cooper, J. M. (ed.), *Plato, Complete Works* (Indianapolis 1997)

Reading selections

[24] Chappell, T., *The Plato Reader* (Edinburgh 1996)

Individual works

(see also [4])

Apology: [25] G. M. A. Grube, *Plato, Five Dialogues: Euthyphro, Apology, Crito, Meno, Phaedo* (Indianapolis 1981; rev. ed. J. Cooper, 2002); [26] J. Cooper (ed.), *Trial and Death of Socrates* (ed. 3, Indianapolis 2000); [27] M. C. Stokes, *Plato, Apology* (Warminster 1997)

Charmides: [28] T. G. West, G. S. West, *Plato, Charmides* (Indianapolis 1986); see also [37]

Cratylus: [29] C. D. C. Reeve, *Plato, Cratylus* (Indianapolis 1998)

Crito: see [25], [26]

Euthydemus: [30] R. K. Sprague, *Plato, Euthydemus* (Indianapolis 1993)

Euthyphro: [31] R. E. Allen, *Plato's Euthyphro and the Earlier Theory of Forms* (includes a translation; London 1970); see also [25]

Gorgias: [32] T. Irwin, *Plato, Gorgias* (Oxford 1979); [33] R. Waterfield, *Plato, Gorgias* (Oxford 1994); [34] D. Zeyl, *Plato, Gorgias* (Indianapolis 1987)

Greater Hippias: [35] P. Woodruff, *Plato, Hippias Major* (Oxford 1982); see also [36]

Ion: [36] P. Woodruff, *Plato, Two Comic Dialogues: Ion and Hippias Major* (Indianapolis 1983)

Laches: [37] R. K. Sprague, *Plato, Laches and Charmides* (Indianapolis 1992)

Laws: [38] T. J. Saunders, *Plato, The Laws* (Harmondsworth 1970)

Lesser Hippias: see [39]

Lysis: [39] T. J. Saunders (ed.), *Plato, Early Socratic Dialogues* (Harmondsworth 1987)

Meno: [40] J. M. Day (ed.), *Plato's Meno in Focus* (includes a translation; London 1994); [41] G. M. A. Grube, *Plato, Meno* (ed. 2, Indianapolis 1980); [42] R. W. Sharples, *Plato: Meno* (Warminster 1985)

Parmenides: [43] M. L. Gill, P. Ryan, *Plato, Parmenides* (Indianapolis 1996)

Phaedo: [44] G. M. A. Grube, *Plato, Phaedo* (Indianapolis 1980); [45] D. Gallop, *Plato, Phaedo* (Oxford 1975)

Phaedrus: [46] A. Nehamas, P. Woodruff, *Plato, Phaedrus* (Indianapolis 1995); [47] C. J. Rowe, *Plato: Phaedrus* (ed. 2, Warminster 2000)

Philebus: [48] D. Frede, *Plato, Philebus* (Indianapolis 1993)

Protagoras: [49] S. Lombardo, K. Bell, with introduction by M. Frede, *Plato, Protagoras* (Indianapolis 1992); [50] B. A. F. Hubbard, E. S. Karnofsky, *Plato's Protagoras* (London 1982); [51] M. Ostwald, revision of B. Jowett's trans. with introduction by G. Vlastos, *Plato, Protagoras* (Indianapolis 1956); [52] C. C. W. Taylor, *Plato, Protagoras* (ed. 2, Oxford 1991)

Republic: [53] G. R. F. Ferrari, T. Griffith, *Plato, The Republic* (Cambridge 2000); [54] G. M. A. Grube, *Plato: The Republic* (Indianapolis 1974); [55] the same, rev. C. D. C. Reeve (Indianapolis 1992); [56] P. Shorey's 1930 translation in the Loeb series (see [4]) remains in many ways the most accurate

Sophist: [57] F. M. Cornford, *Plato's Theory of Knowledge* (London 1935); [58] N. P. White, *Plato, Sophist* (Indianapolis 1993)

Statesman: **[59]** J. Annas, R. Waterfield, *Plato, Statesman* (Cambridge 1995);
[60] C. J. Rowe, *Plato Statesman* (Indianapolis 1999)
Symposium: **[61]** C. Gill, *Plato: Symposium* (Harmondsworth 1999);
[62] A. Nehamas, P. Woodruff, *Plato, Symposium* (Indianapolis 1989);
[63] C. J. Rowe, *Plato, Symposium* (Warminster 1998); **[64]** R. Waterfield
Plato, Symposium (Oxford 1994)
Theaetetus: **[65]** M. J. Levett, with introduction by M. Burnyeat, *The
Theaetetus of Plato* (Indianapolis 1990); **[66]** the same, with introduction
by B. Williams (Indianapolis 1992); **[67]** J. McDowell, *Plato, Theaetetus*
(Oxford 1973)
Timaeus: **[68]** F. M. Cornford, *Plato's Cosmology* (London 1937; repr.
Indianapolis 1997); **[69]** D. J. Zeyl, *Plato, Timaeus* (Indianapolis 2000)

Aristotle

For the citation system, see above, p. 129.

Complete works

[70] Barnes, J. (ed.), *The Revised Oxford Translation of Aristotle*, 2 vols.
(Princeton 1984)

Reading selections

[71] Ackrill, J. L., *A New Aristotle Reader* (Oxford 1987)
[72] Irwin, T., G. Fine, *Aristotle: Selections* (Indianapolis 1995)

Individual works

(See also **[4]**)
Categories: **[73]** J. L. Ackrill, *Aristotle's Categories and De Interpretatione*
(Oxford 1963)
Constitution of the Athenians: **[74]** P. J. Rhodes, *Aristotle. The Athenian
Constitution* (Harmondsworth 1984)
De interpretatione: see **[73]**
Eudemian Ethics: **[75]** M. Woods, *Aristotle's Eudemian Ethics Books I, II
and VIII* (Oxford 1982)
Metaphysics: **[76]** A. Madigan, *Aristotle, Metaphysics Books B and K
1–2* (Oxford 1999); **[77]** C. Kirwan, *Aristotle's Metaphysics Books Γ,
Δ, E* (Oxford 1971); **[78]** D. Bostock, *Aristotle, Metaphysics Books Z
and H* (Oxford 1994); **[79]** M. Furth, *Aristotle Metaphysics Books Zeta,
Eta, Theta, Iota (VII–X)* (Indianapolis 1985); **[80]** J. Annas, *Aristotle's
Metaphysics M and N* (Oxford 1976)

Nicomachean Ethics: **[81]** S. Broadie, C. Rowe, *Aristotle Nicomachean Ethics: Translation, Introduction, and Commentary* (Oxford 2002); **[82]** R. Crisp, *Aristotle Nicomachean Ethics* (Cambridge 2000); **[83]** T. Irwin, *Aristotle Nicomachean Ethics* (Indianapolis 1985; ed. 2, 2000); **[84]** M. Pakaluk, *Aristotle Nicomachean Ethics Books VIII and IX* (Oxford 1998)

On Coming-to-be and Passing Away: **[85]** C. J. F. Williams, *Aristotle's De Generatione et Corruptione* (Oxford 1982)

On Dreams: **[86]** D. Gallop, *Aristotle, On Sleep and Dreams* (Warminster 1996)

On Memory: **[87]** R. Sorabji, *Aristotle On Memory* (London 1972)

On the Heavens: **[88]** S. Leggatt, *Aristotle, On the Heavens I and II, with an Introduction, Translation and Commentary* (Warminster 1995)

On the Movement of Animals: **[89]** M. C. Nussbaum, *Aristotle's De motu animalium* (Princeton 1978)

On the Soul: **[90]** H. Lawson-Tancred, *Aristotle: De anima* (Harmondsworth 1986)

Parts of Animals: **[91]** J. G. Lennox, *Aristotle On the Parts of Animals* (Oxford 2002)

Physics: **[92]** W. Charlton, *Aristotle's Physics I, II* (Oxford 1970); **[93]** E. Hussey, *Aristotle's Physics Books III and IV* (Oxford 1983); **[94]** D. Graham, *Aristotle Physics Book VIII* (Oxford 1999)

Poetics: **[95]** S. Halliwell, *The Poetics of Aristotle* (London 1987); **[96]** R. Janko, *Aristotle – Poetics* (Indianapolis 1987)

Politics: **[97]** E. Barker, *Aristotle, The Politics*, revised with an introduction by R. F. Stalley (Oxford 1995); **[98]** S. Everson, *Aristotle, Politics* (Cambridge 1996); **[99]** C. D. C. Reeve, *Aristotle, Politics* (Indianapolis 1998); **[100]** T. J. Saunders, *Aristotle Politics Books I and II* (Oxford 1995); **[101]** R. Robinson, *Aristotle's Politics III and IV* (Oxford 1962); **[102]** D. Keyt, *Aristotle Politics Books V and VI* (Oxford 1999); **[103]** R. Kraut, *Aristotle, Politics Books VII and VIII* (Oxford 1997)

Posterior Analytics: **[104]** J. Barnes, *Aristotle's Posterior Analytics* (Oxford 1975, ed. 2 1994)

Prior Analytics: **[105]** R. Smith, *Aristotle, Prior Analytics* (Indianapolis 1989)

Rhetoric: **[106]** H. Lawson-Tancred, *Aristotle, The Art of Rhetoric* (Harmondsworth 1991)

Topics: **[107]** R. Smith, *Aristotle Topics Books I and VIII* (Oxford 1997)

Theophrastus

Fragments and testimonia: **[108]** W. W. Fortenbaugh, P. M. Huby, R. W. Sharples, D. Gutas, *Theophrastus of Eresos: Sources for his Life, Writings, Thought and Influence*, 2 vols. (Leiden 1992)

Characters: see **[141]**
Metaphysics: **[109]** W. D. Ross, F. H. Fobes, *Theophrastus: Metaphysics, with Translation, Commentary and Introduction* (Oxford 1929); **[110]** M. van Raalte, *Metaphysics: Theophrastus* (Leiden 1993)
See also **[4]**

Hellenistic

Collections

[111] Annas, J., J. Barnes, *The Modes of Scepticism: Ancient Texts and Modern Interpretations* (Cambridge 1985)
[112] Inwood, B., L. P. Gerson, *Hellenistic Philosophy: Introductory Readings* (ed. 2, Indianapolis 1998)
[113] Long, A. A., D. N. Sedley, *The Hellenistic Philosophers*, 2 vols. (Cambridge 1987)

Single authors

Epicurus: **[114]** Inwood, B., L. P. Gerson, with introduction by D. S. Hutchinson, *The Epicurus Reader* (Indianapolis 1994)
Philodemus: **[115]** R. Janko, *Philodemus, On Poems, Book I* (Oxford 2000); **[116]** D. Konstan et al., *Philodemus, On Frank Criticism* (Atlanta 1998); **[117]** D. Obbink, *Philodemus, On Piety, Part I* (Oxford 1996; *Part II* forthcoming)
Sextus Empiricus: **[118]** P. P. Hallie (ed.), *Sextus Empiricus. Selections from the Major Writings on Scepticism, Man and God* (Indianapolis 1985); **[119]** J. Annas, J. Barnes, *Sextus Empiricus, Outlines of Scepticism* (= *Outlines of Pyrrhonism*; Cambridge 1994); **[120]** B. Mates, *The Skeptic Way: Sextus Empiricus' Outlines of Pyrrhonism* (Oxford 1996); **[121]** D. Blank, *Sextus Empiricus, Against the Grammarians* (Oxford 1998); **[122]** R. Bett, *Sextus Empiricus, Against the Ethicists* (Oxford 1997); see also **[4]**
See also below, 'Roman philosophy'

Roman philosophy

For Augustine, Boethius, Cicero, Epictetus, Lucretius, Marcus Aurelius, Seneca, Varro, see **[4]**
Augustine: **[123]** H. Chadwick, *Saint Augustine, The Confessions* (Oxford 1991); **[124]** R. W. Dyson, *Augustine, The City of God against the Pagans* (Cambridge 1998)

Boethius: [125] J. C. Relihan, *Boethius, Consolation of Philosophy* (Indianapolis 2001)

Cicero: [126] P. G. Walsh, *Cicero, The Nature of the Gods* (Oxford 1997); [127] M. Graver, *Cicero's Tusculan Disputations 3 and 4: the Books on Emotion* (Chicago/London 2002); [128] J. Annas, R. Woolf, *Cicero on Moral Ends* (Cambridge 2001); [129] J. Zetzel, *Cicero, On the Commonwealth and On the Law* (Cambridge 1999)

Epictetus: [130] R. Dobbin, *Epictetus, Discourses Book I* (Oxford 1998); [131] N. P. White, *The Handbook of Epictetus* (Indianapolis 1983)

Lactantius: [132] A. Bowen, P. Garnsey, *Lactantius, Divine Institutes* (Liverpool, forthcoming)

Lucretius: [133] M. F. Smith, *Lucretius, On the Nature of Things* (ed. 2, Indianapolis 2001)

Marcus Aurelius: [134] R. Hard, C. Gill, *Marcus Aurelius, Meditations* (Ware 1997)

Seneca: [135] R. Campbell, *Seneca: Letters from a Stoic* (Harmondsworth 1969); [136] J. M. Cooper, J. F. Procopé, *Seneca. Moral and Political Essays* (Cambridge 1995)

Philosophy and literature

Aristophanes: see [4]

Aristotle: see [95]–[96], [106]

Cicero, letters: see [4]

Greek tragedy: [137] D. Grene, R. Lattimore (ed.), *The Complete Greek Tragedies*, 3 vols. (ed. 2, Chicago 1991)

Lucretius: see [133]

Plato: see [23]–[69]

Seneca, tragedies: [138] E. F. Watling, *Seneca, Four Tragedies and Octavia* (Harmondsworth 1966), [139] F. Ahl, *Seneca. Three Tragedies: Trojan Women, Medea, Phaedra* (Ithaca/London 1986); philosophical writings: see [135]–[136] and [4]; *Pumpkinification*: [140] P. T. Eden, *Seneca, Apocolocyntosis* (Cambridge 1984)

Theophrastus, *Characters*: [141] P. Vellacott, *Theophrastus, The Characters; Menander, Plays and Fragments* (Harmondsworth 1967)

Late ancient philosophy

Selected readings

[142] Gregory, J., *The Neoplatonists: a Reader* (London 1991; ed. 2 1999)

[143] Sorabji, R. R. K., *The Philosophy of the Commentators (200–600 A.D.)*, 3 vols. (London/Ithaca, N.Y. forthcoming)

Translation series

A huge range of commentaries by Alexander of Aphrodisias (including his physical and ethical *Quaestiones*), Themistius, Dexippus, Ammonius, (Pseudo-)Philoponus (including *On the Eternity of the World against Aristotle* and *On the Eternity of the World against Proclus*), Boethius, (Pseudo-)Simplicius and Stephanus are available in English translations by various hands, in the ongoing series

[144] Sorabji, R. (general editor), *Ancient Commentators on Aristotle* (London 1989–) Progress of this series can be tracked on *http://www.kcl.ac.uk/kis/schools/hums/philosophy/frames/Research/*

Further individual authors and works

Alcinous: **[145]** J. M. Dillon, *Alcinous. The Handbook of Platonism* (Oxford 1993)

Alexander: **[146]** R. W. Sharples, *Alexander of Aphrodisias, On Fate* (London 1983)

Iamblichus: **[147]** J. M. Dillon, J. P. Hershbell, *Iamblichus: On the Pythagorean Way of Life. Text, Translation and Notes* (Atlanta 1991)

Olympiodorus: **[148]** R. Jackson, K. Lycos, H. Tarrant, *Olympiodorus, Commentary on Plato's Gorgias* (Leiden 1998)

Plotinus: **[149]** A. H. Armstrong, *Plotinus: a Volume of Selections* (London 1953); for full translation, see **[4]**

Plutarch, collected philosophical writings in **[4]**; see also the selection in **[150]** R. Waterfield, I. G. Kidd, *Plutarch: Essays* (Harmondsworth 1992)

Porphyry, *Isagoge*: **[151]** P. V. Spade, *Five Texts on the Mediaeval Problem of Universals: Porphyry, Boethius, Abelard, Duns Scotus, Ockham* (Indianapolis/Cambridge 1994; contains the *Isagoge*); **[152]** J. Barnes, *Porphyry, Introduction* (Oxford, forthcoming)

On Abstinence: **[153]** G. Clarke, *Porphyry, On Abstinence from Killing Animals* (in the **[144]** series; London 2000)

Proclus: **[154]** W. O'Neill, *Proclus. Alcibiades I* (The Hague 1965, repr. 1971); **[155]** G. R. Morrow, *Proclus. A Commentary on the First Book of Euclid's Elements* (Princeton 1970); **[156]** T. Taylor, *Proclus' Commentary on the Timaeus of Plato* (London 1820, repr. 1988, 1998); **[157]** G. R. Morrow, J. M. Dillon, *Proclus' Commentary on Plato's Parmenides* (Princeton 1987)

Philosophy and Science

Selections

[158] Barker, A., *Greek Musical Writings*, 2 vols. (Cambridge 1984, 1989)
[159] Bulmer-Thomas, I., *Greek Mathematical Works*, 2 vols., in **[4]**

[160] Cohen, M. R., I. E. Drabkin, *A Sourcebook in Greek Science* (Cambridge, Mass. 1948)

Individual authors and works

Aristarchus: [161] T. L. Heath, *Aristarchus of Samos* (Oxford 1913)
Euclid: [162] T. L. Heath, *The Thirteen Books of Euclid's Elements*, 3 vols. (ed. 2, New York 1956)
Galen (for the method of citation see above p. 299 n. 3): [163] M. Frede, *Galen: Three Treatises on the Nature of Science* (Indianapolis 1985); [164] P. N. Singer, *Galen: Selected Works* (Oxford 1997); [165] D. J. Furley, J. S. Wilkie (1984) *Galen on Respiration and the Arteries* (Cambridge 1984); [166] R. J. Hankinson, *Galen: On the Therapeutic Method, Books I and II* (Oxford 1991); [167] R. J. Hankinson, *Galen, On Antecedent Causes* (Cambridge 1998)
Hippocrates: [168] G. E. R. Lloyd (ed.), *Hippocratic Writings* (Harmondsworth 1978); see also [4]
Ptolemy: [169] G. J. Toomer, *Ptolemy's Almagest* (London/Ithaca 1984)

Philosophy and Religion

Reading selections

[170] Beard, M., J. North, S. Price, *Religions of Rome: vol. II, a Sourcebook* (Cambridge 1998)
[171] Ferguson, J., *Greek and Roman Religion: A Source Book* (Park Ridge, N.J. 1980)
[172] Rice, D. G., J. E. Stambaugh, *Sources for the Study of Greek Religion* (Missoula, M.N. 1979)

Individual works

Hesiod, *Theogony*: [173] D. Wender, *Hesiod, Works and Days, Theogony; Theognis, Elegies* (Harmondsworth 1973)
Philo of Alexandria: see [4]
See also, among other relevant texts [68], [69], [122], [157]

The legacy of ancient philosophy

Reading selections

[174] Cassirer, E. et al. (eds.), *The Renaissance Philosophy of Man* (Chicago 1948)

[175] Kraye, J. (ed.), *Cambridge Translations of Renaissance Philosophical Texts*, 2 vols. (Cambridge 1997), I: *Moral Philosophy*; II: *Political Philosophy*

[176] Kretzmann, N., E. Stump (ed.), *Cambridge Translations of Medieval Philosophical Texts* (Cambridge 1988), I: *Logic and the Philosophy of Language*

[177] McGrade, A. S. et al., *Cambridge Translations of Medieval Philosophical Texts* (Cambridge 2000), II: *Ethics and Political Philosophy*

Individual works

Aquinas, Thomas, [178] *Selected Writings*, trans. R. McInerny (London 1998)

Bruni, Leonardo: [179] G. Griffiths et al., *The Humanism of Leonardo Bruni: Selected Texts* (Binghamton 1987), chs. 4 and 7

Dionysius, Pseudo-, [180] *The Complete Works*, trans. C. Luibheid (London 1987)

Erasmus, 'The Epicurean': [181] C. R. Thompson, *The Colloquies of Erasmus* (Chicago 1965)

Ficino, Marsilio: [182] *Commentary on Plato's Symposium on Love*, trans. S. Jayne (Dallas 1985); [183] *The Philebus Commentary*, ed. and trans. M. J. B. Allen (Berkeley/L.A./London 1975); [184] *Platonic Theology*, trans. M. J. B. Allen, ed. J. Hankins (Cambridge, Mass./London 2001–)

Kepler, Johannes, [185] *Mysterium cosmographicum. The Secret of the Universe*, trans. A. M. Duncan (New York 1981)

Lipsius, Justus, [186] *Two Bookes of Constancie*, trans. J. Stradling (Brunswick, N.J. 1939)

More, Henry, [187] *A Platonick Song of the Soul*, ed. A. Jacob (Lewisberg 1998)

Valla, Lorenzo, [188] *On Pleasure. De voluptate*, trans. A. Kent Hieatt, M. Lorch (New York 1977)

2 FURTHER READING

The selection that follows is limited to books in English, judged suitable either as relatively introductory reading or as being especially important. So far as possible, books requiring knowledge of Greek and Latin have been avoided. Many of the books listed above in Section 1 contain, in addition to ancient philosophical writings in translation, a great deal of helpful commentary.

Fuller bibliographies will be found in the Cambridge Companions to: Early Greek Philosophy [239], Plato [267], Aristotle [280], the Stoics [301] and Plotinus [337].

*Histories and encyclopaedias including substantial coverage
of ancient philosophy*

[189] Craig, E. J. (ed.), *The Routledge Encyclopedia of Philosophy* (London 1998; online version, *http://www.rep.routledge.com/index.html*)
[190] Edwards, P. (ed.), *The Encyclopedia of Philosophy* (New York/London 1967)
[191] Kenny, A. J. P., *A Brief History of Western Philosophy* (Oxford 1998)
[192] Kneale W. and M., *The Development of Logic* (Oxford 1962)
[193] Zalta, E. N. (ed.), *The Stanford Encyclopedia of Philosophy* (online only: *http://plato.stanford.edu/*)

*Journals and other serials (entirely or mainly in English)
specialising in ancient philosophy*

[194] *Ancient Philosophy* (Pittsburgh)
[195] *Apeiron* (Kelowna, British Columbia)
[196] *Oxford Studies in Ancient Philosophy* (Oxford)
[197] *Phronesis* (Leiden)
[198] *Proceedings of the Boston Area Colloquium in Ancient Philosophy* (Leiden/Boston/Köln)

Histories and encyclopaedias of ancient philosophy

[199] Annas, J., *Ancient Philosopy: A Very Short Introduction* (Oxford 2000)
[200] Brunschwig, J., G. E. R. Lloyd (ed.), *Greek Thought: a Guide to Classical Knowledge* (Cambridge Mass./London 2000)
[201] Friis Johansen, K., *A History of Ancient Philosophy: from the Beginnings to Augustine* (English trans., London 1998)
[202] Gill, C., *Greek Thought*, Greece and Rome New Surveys in the Classics, 25 (Oxford 1995)
[203] Gottlieb, A., *The Dream of Reason: a History of Western Philosophy from the Greeks to the Renaissance* (London 2000)
[204] Guthrie, W. K. C., *A History of Greek Philosophy*, 6 vols. (Cambridge 1962–81; ends with Aristotle)
[205] Irwin, T., *Classical Thought* (Oxford 1989)
[206] Taylor, C. C. W. (ed.), *The Routledge History of Philosophy, vol. I: From the beginning to Plato* (London 1997); D. J. Furley (ed.), vol. II: *From Aristotle to Augustine* (London 1999)
[207] Zeyl, D. J. (ed.), *Encyclopedia of Classical Philosophy* (Westport, Ct. 1997)

*Books covering more than one period or aspect of
ancient philosophy*

[208] Annas, J., *The Morality of Happiness* (Oxford 1993)

[209] Cooper, J. M., *Reason and Emotion: Essays in Ancient Moral Psychology and Ethical Theory* (Princeton 1999)

[210] Denyer, N., *Language, Thought and Falsehood in Ancient Greek Philosophy* (London/New York 1991)

[211] Dover, K. J., *Greek Popular Morality in the Time of Plato and Aristotle* (Oxford 1974)

[212] Everson, S. (ed.), 'Companions to Ancient Thought' (series, Cambridge): [212] *Epistemology* (1990), [213] *Psychology* (1991), [214] *Language* (1994), [215] *Ethics* (1998)

[216] Frede, M., *Essays in Ancient Philosophy* (Oxford 1987)

[217] Furley, D., *Cosmic Problems* (Cambridge 1989)

[218] Hadot, P., *What is Ancient Philosophy?* (English trans., Cambridge Mass. 2002)

[219] Lloyd, G. E. R., *The Revolutions of Wisdom* (Berkeley/L.A. 1987)

[220] Makin, S., *Indifference Arguments* (Oxford 1993)

[221] Nehamas, A., *Virtues of Authenticity* (Princeton 1999)

[222] Owen, G. E. L., *Logic, Science and Dialectic: Collected Papers in Greek Philosophy* (London 1986)

[223] Rowe, C., *An Introduction to Greek Ethics* (London 1976)

[224] Rowe, C., M. Schofield (ed.), *The Cambridge History of Greek and Roman Political Thought* (Cambridge 2000)

[225] Sorabji, R., *Time, Creation and the Continuum* (London 1983)

[226] Sorabji, R., *Matter, Space and Motion* (London 1988)

[227] Sorabji, R., *Animal Minds and Human Morals* (London/Ithaca, N.Y. 1993)

[228] Sorabji, R., *Emotion and Peace of Mind: From Stoic Agitation to Christian Temptation* (Oxford 2000)

[229] Vlastos, G., *Studies in Greek Philosophy*, 2 vols. (Princeton 1993, 1995)

Presocratics and sophists

[230] Barnes, J., *The Presocratic Philosophers*, 2 vols. (London 1979; single-vol. ed. 1982)

[231] Furley, D. J., *The Greek Cosmologists*, vol. 1 (Cambridge 1987)

[232] Furley, D. J., R. E. Allen (ed.), *Studies in Presocratic Philosophy*, 2 vols. (London 1970, 1975)

[233] Hussey, E. L., *The Presocratics* (London 1972)

[234] Kahn, C. H., *Anaximander and the Origins of Greek Cosmology* (New York 1960; repr. Indianapolis 1995)

[235] Kahn, C. H., *The Art and Thought of Heraclitus* (Cambridge 1979)
[236] Kahn, C. H., *Pythagoras and the Pythagoreans* (Indianapolis 2001)
[237] Kerferd, G. B., *The Sophistic Movement* (Cambridge 1981)
[238] Kerferd, G. B. (ed.), *The Sophists and their Legacy* (Wiesbaden 1981)
[239] Long, A. A. (ed.), *The Cambridge Companion to Early Greek Philosophy* (Cambridge 1999)
[240] Mourelatos, A. P. D. (ed.), *The Pre-Socratics: a Collection of Critical Essays* (New York 1974; repr. with addenda, Princeton 1993)
[241] Ring, M., *Beginning with the Pre-Socratics* (Palo Alto 1987)
[242] Romilly, J. de, *The Great Sophists in Periclean Athens* (Oxford 1992)
[243] Salmon, W. C. (ed.), *Zeno's Paradoxes*, (Indianapolis/New York 1970)
[244] West, M. L., *Early Greek Philosophy and the Orient* (Oxford 1971)

See also [10]

Socrates

[245] Benson, H. (ed.), *Essays on the Philosophy of Socrates* (Oxford 1992)
[246] Brickhouse, T. C., N. D. Smith, *Socrates on Trial* (Oxford 1989)
[247] Brickhouse, T. C., N. D. Smith, *The Philosophy of Socrates* (Boulder/ Oxford 2000)
[248] Nehamas, A., *The Art of Living: Socratic Reflections from Plato to Foucault* (Berkeley/L.A./London 1998)
[249] Santas, G. X., *Socrates* (London 1979)
[250] Stone, I. F., *The Trial of Socrates* (Boston 1988)
[251] Taylor, C. C. W., *Socrates: A Very Short Introduction* (Oxford 1998)
[252] Vander Waerdt, P. (ed.), *The Socratic Movement* (Ithaca, N.Y./London 1994)
[253] Vlastos, G. (ed.), *The Philosophy of Socrates: A Collection of Critical Essays* (Garden City, N.Y. 1971; repr. Notre Dame 1980)
[254] Vlastos, G., *Socrates, Ironist and Moral Philosopher* (Cambridge 1991)
[255] Vlastos, G., *Socratic Studies* (Cambridge 1994)

Plato

[256] Allen, R. E. (ed.), *Studies in Plato's Metaphysics* (London 1965)
[257] Annas J., C. J. Rowe (ed.), *New Perspectives on Plato, Modern and Ancient* (Cambridge, Mass. 2002)
[258] Annas, J., *An Introduction to Plato's Republic* (Oxford 1981)
[259] Bambrough, R. (ed.), *Plato, Popper and Politics* (Cambridge 1967)
[260] Crombie, I. M., *An Examination of Plato's Doctrines*, 2 vols. (London 1962–3; repr. Bristol 2002)

[261] Ferrari, G. R. F., *Listening to the Cicadas: a Study of Plato's Phaedrus* (Cambridge 1987)

[262] Fine, G. (ed.), *Oxford Readings in Philosophy: Plato* 2 vols. (Oxford 1999)

[263] Friedlander, H, *Plato*, 3 vols. (Engl. trans. New York 1958–69)

[264] Gill, C., M. M. McCabe (ed.), *Form and Argument in Late Plato* (Oxford 1996)

[265] Irwin, T., *Plato's Ethics* (Oxford 1995)

[266] Kahn, C. H., *Plato and the Socratic Dialogue* (Cambridge 1996)

[267] Kraut, R. (ed.), *The Cambridge Companion to Plato* (Cambridge 1992)

[268] Murdoch, Iris, *The Fire and the Sun: Why Plato Banished the Artists* (Oxford 1977)

[269] Nightingale, A., *Genres in Dialogue* (Cambridge 1995)

[270] Popper, K., *The Open Society and its Enemies: I, The Spell of Plato* (classic critique; London 1945)

[271] Rutherford, R., *The Art of Plato* (London 1995)

[272] Szlezák, T., *Reading Plato* (represents the 'esoteric' interpretation; Engl. trans. London 1993)

[273] Vlastos, G. (ed.), *Plato*, 2 vols. (Garden City 1971)

[274] Vlastos, G., *Plato's Universe* (Seattle 1975)

[275] White, N. P., *Plato on Knowledge and Reality* (Indianapolis 1976)

[276] Williams, Bernard, *Plato: the Invention of Philosophy* (London 1998)

Although only a few books on individual dialogues have been listed above, further seminal studies of individual dialogues were included in [25]–[69].

Aristotle

[277] Ackrill, J. L., *Aristotle the Philosopher* (London 1981)

[278] Allan, D. J., *The Philosophy of Aristotle* (Oxford 1952)

[279] Barnes, J., M. Schofield, R. Sorabji (ed.), *Articles on Aristotle* (4 vols., London 1975–9)

[280] Barnes, J. (ed.), *The Cambridge Companion to Aristotle* (Cambridge 1995)

[281] Barnes, J., *Aristotle* (London 1982)

[282] Gotthelf, A. (ed.), *Aristotle on Nature and Living Things* (Bristol/ Pittsburgh 1985)

[283] Gotthelf, A., J. G. Lennox (ed.), *Philosophical Issues in Aristotle's Biology* (Cambridge 1987)

[284] Grene, M., *A Portrait of Aristotle* (Chicago/London 1963)

[285] Judson, L. (ed.), *Aristotle's Physics: A Collection of Essays* (Oxford 1991)

[286] Kraut, R., *Aristotle: Political Philosophy* (Founders of Modern Political and Social Thought) (Oxford 2002)

[287] Lear, J., *Aristotle, the Desire to Understand* (Cambridge 1988)

[288] Lloyd, G. E. R., *Aristotle, The Growth and Structure of his Thought* (Cambridge 1968)

[289] Nussbaum, M. C., A. Rorty (ed.), *Essays on Aristotle's De Anima* (Oxford 1992)

[290] Reeve, C. D. C., *Substantial Knowledge: Aristotle's Metaphysics* (Indianapolis 2000)

[291] Rorty, A. (ed.), *Essays on Aristotle's Rhetoric* (Berkeley/Los Angeles 1996)

[292] Sherman, N. (ed.), *Aristotle's Ethics: Critical Essays* (Lanham, Md. 1999)

Although only a few books on individual works have been listed above, further seminal studies of individual works were included in [73]–[107].

Hellenistic philosophy

[293] Algra, K., J. Barnes, J. Mansfeld, M. Schofield (ed.), *The Cambridge History of Hellenistic Philosophy* (Cambridge 1999)

[294] Annas, J., *Hellenistic Philosophy of Mind* (Berkeley/L.A./London 1992)

[295] Bett, R., *Pyrrho. His Antecedents and his Legacy* (Oxford 2000)

[296] Branham, R. B., M. O. Goulet-Cazé (ed.), *The Cynics* (Berkeley/L.A./London 1996)

[297] Brunschwig, J., *Papers in Hellenistic Philosophy* (Cambridge 1994)

[298] Burnyeat, M., M. Frede (ed.), *The Original Sceptics: a Controversy* (Indianapolis 1997)

[299] Dudley, D. R., *A History of Cynicism* (London 1937)

[300] Hankinson, R. J., *The Sceptics* (London 1995)

[301] Inwood, B., *The Cambridge Companion to the Stoics* (Cambridge 2003)

[302] Long, A. A., *Hellenistic Philosophy* (London 1974; repr. Berkeley/L.A. 1999)

[303] Mates, B., *Stoic Logic* (Berkeley 1953)

[304] Nussbaum, M., *The Therapy of Desire: Theory and Practice in Hellenistic Ethics* (Princeton 1994)

[305] Sandbach, F. H., *The Stoics* (London 1975)

[306] Sharples, R. W., *Stoics, Epicureans and Sceptics* (London 1996)

[307] Striker, G., *Essays on Hellenistic Epistemology and Ethics* (Cambridge 1996)

[308] Tsouna, V., *The Epistemology of the Cyrenaic School* (Cambridge 1998)

See also [113], [309], [310], [313], [325], [388]

Roman philosophy

[309] Algra, K. A., M. H. Koenen, P. H. Schrijvers (ed.), *Lucretius and his Intellectual Background* (Amsterdam/Oxford/New York/Tokyo 1997)
[310] Brittain, C., *Philo of Larissa: the Last of the Academic Sceptics* (Oxford 2001)
[311] Brown, P., *Augustine of Hippo: a Biography* (London 1967)
[312] Chadwick, H., *Augustine* (Oxford 1986)
[313] Clay, D., *Lucretius and Epicurus* (Ithaca, N.Y./London 1983)
[314] Gersh, S., *Middle Platonism and Neoplatonism: the Latin Tradition*, 2 vols. (Notre Dame 1986)
[315] Griffin, M., *Seneca: A Philosopher in Politics* (Oxford 1976)
[316] Griffin, M., J. Barnes (ed.), *Philosophia Togata I. Essays on Philosophy and Roman Society* (Oxford 1989)
[317] Griffin, M., J. Barnes (ed.), *Philosophia Togata II. Plato and Aristotle at Rome* (Oxford 1997)
[318] Hadot, P., *The Inner Citadel: the Meditations of Marcus Aurelius* (English trans., Cambridge Mass./London 1998)
[319] Long, A. A., *Epictetus: a Stoic and Socratic Guide to Life* (Oxford 2002)
[320] MacKendrick, P., *The Philosophical Books of Cicero* (London 1989)
[321] Osborn, E., *Tertullian: First Theologian of the West* (Cambridge 1997)
[322] Powell, J. G. F. (ed.), *Cicero the Philosopher* (Oxford 1995)
[323] Rist, J. M., *Augustine* (Cambridge 1994)
[324] Rutherford, R. B., *The Meditations of Marcus Aurelius: A Study* (Oxford 1989)
[325] Sedley, D., *Lucretius and the Transformation of Greek Wisdom* (Cambridge 1998)

See also [333]

Philosophy and literature

[326] Halliwell, S., *Aristotle's Poetics* (London 1987)
[327] Halliwell, S., *The Aesthetics of Mimesis* (Princeton 2002)
[328] Lamberton, R., J. Keaney (ed.), *Homer's Ancient Readers: the Hermeneutics of Greek Epic's Earliest Exegetes* (Princeton 1992)
[329] Louden, R. B., P. Schollmeier (ed.), *The Greeks and Us* (Chicago 1996); esp. the chapter by Bernard Williams, '*The Women of Trachis*: fictions, pessimism, ethics'
[330] Nussbaum, M., *The Fragility of Goodness: Luck and Ethics in Greek Tragedy and Philosophy* (Cambridge 1986; ed. 2, 2001)
[331] Williams, Bernard, *Shame and Necessity* (Berkeley 1993)

See also [269], [271], [304], [318], [324]

Late ancient philosophy

[332] Annas, J., *Platonic Ethics, Old and New* (Ithaca, N.Y. 1999)
[333] Armstrong, A. H. (ed.), *The Cambridge History of Later Greek and Early Medieval Philosophy* (Cambridge 1970)
[334] De Haas, F. A. J., *John Philoponus' New Definition of Prime Matter. Aspects of its Background in Neoplatonism and the Ancient Commentary Tradition* (Leiden 1997)
[335] Dillon, John M., *The Middle Platonists. A Study of Platonism 80 B.C. to A.D. 220* (London 1977; rev. ed. Ithaca, N.Y. 1996)
[336] Dillon, J., Long, A. A. (ed.) *The Question of Eclecticism. Studies in Later Greek Philosophy* (Berkeley/L.A./London 1988; repr. 1996)
[337] Gerson, L. P. (ed.), *The Cambridge Companion to Plotinus* (Cambridge 1996)
[338] Haase, W. (ed.), *Aufstieg und Niedergang der römischen Welt* II 36, 7 volumes (Berlin/New York 1972–; devoted entirely to philosophy in the Roman Empire, largely in English)
[339] Lloyd, A. C., *The Anatomy of Neoplatonism* (Oxford 1990)
[340] Merlan, P., *From Platonism to Neoplatonism* (The Hague 1968)
[341] O'Meara, D. J., *Plotinus: an Introduction to the Enneads* (Oxford 1993)
[342] O'Meara, D. J., *Pythagoras revived. Mathematics and Philosophy in Late Antiquity* (Oxford 1989)
[343] Rist, J. M., *Plotinus: the Road to Reality* (Cambridge 1967)
[344] Siorvanes, L., *Proclus. Neoplatonic Philosophy and Science* (Edinburgh 1996)
[345] Sorabji, R. (ed.), *Aristotle Transformed: The Ancient Commentators and Their Influence* (London/Ithaca 1990)
[346] Sorabji, R. (ed.), *Philoponus and the Rejection of Aristotelian Science* (London/Ithaca 1987)
[347] Steel, C. G., *The Changing Self: a Study on the Soul in Later Neoplatonism: Iamblichus, Damascius and Priscianus* (Brussels 1978)
[348] Van Riel, G., *Pleasure and the Good Life. Plato, Aristotle, and the Neoplatonists* (Leiden 2000)
[349] Wildberg, C., *John Philoponus' Criticism of Aristotle's Theory of Aether* (Berlin 1988)

Philosophy and science

[350] Allen, J., *Inference from Signs: Ancient Debates about the Nature of Evidence* (Oxford 2001)

[351] Barnes, J., J. Brunschwig, M. Burnyeat, M. Schofield (ed.), *Science and Speculation: Studies in Hellenistic Theory and Practice* (Cambridge 1982)

[352] Dicks, D. R., *Early Greek Astronomy to Aristotle* (Ithaca, N.Y. 1970)

[353] Hankinson, R. J., *Cause and Explanation in Ancient Greek Thought* (Oxford 1998)

[354] Hankinson, R. J. (ed.), *Method, Medicine, and Metaphysics* (Edmonton 1988)

[355] Heath, T. L., *A History of Greek Mathematics*, 2 vols. (Oxford 1921)

[356] Jouanna, J., *Hippocrates* (English trans. Baltimore 1999)

[357] Lloyd, G. E. R., *Early Greek Science: Thales to Aristotle* (London 1973)

[358] Lloyd, G. E. R., *Greek Science after Aristotle* (London 1973)

[359] Lloyd, G. E. R., *Magic, Reason and Experience* (Cambridge 1979)

[360] Lloyd, G. E. R., *Methods and Problems in Greek Science* (Cambridge 1991)

[361] Pellegrin, P., *Aristotle's Classification of Animals* (English trans. Berkeley 1986)

[362] Sambursky, S., *The Physical World of the Greeks* (London 1956)

[363] Sambursky, S., *Physics of the Stoics* (London 1959)

[364] Sambursky, S., *The Physical World of Late Antiquity* (London 1962)

[365] Staden, H. von, *Herophilus: the Art of Medicine in Early Alexandria* (Cambridge 1989)

[366] Taub, L., *Ptolemy's Universe* (Chicago 1993)

See also [282], [283], [225], [226], [219]

Philosophy and religion

[367] Bruit Zaidman, L., P. Schmitt Pantel, *Religion in the Ancient Greek City* (Cambridge 1992)

[368] Burkert, W., *Ancient Mystery Cults* (Cambridge, Mass. 1987)

[369] Burkert, W., *Greek Religion. Archaic and Classical* (Oxford 1985)

[370] Burkert, W., *Homo Necans. The Anthropology of Ancient Greek Sacrificial Ritual and Myth* (Berkeley 1983)

[371] Buxton, R. (ed.), *Oxford Readings in Greek Religion* (Oxford 2000)

[372] Caird, E., *The Evolution of Theology in the Greek Philosophers* (Glasgow 1903)

[373] Dodds, E. R., *The Greeks and the Irrational* (Berkeley 1951)

[374] Dodds, E. R., *Pagan and Christian in an Age of Anxiety* (Cambridge 1968)

[375] Drachmann, A. B., *Atheism in Pagan Antiquity* (London 1922)

[376] Easterling, P. E., J. V. Muir (ed.), *Greek Religion and Society* (Cambridge 1985)

[377] Gerson, L. P., *God and Greek Philosophy* (London/New York 1990)

[378] Gordon, R. L., *Myth, Religion and Society* (Cambridge 1981)

[379] Jaeger, W., *The Theology of the Early Greek Philosophers* (Oxford 1947)

[380] Nock, A. D., *Conversion* (Oxford 1933)

[381] Nock, A. D., *Essays on Religion and the Ancient World*, 2 vols. (Oxford 1972)

[382] Parker, R., *Miasma: Pollution and Purification in Early Greek Religion* (Oxford 1983)

[383] Parker, R., *Athenian Religion: A History* (Oxford 1996)

[384] Seltzer, R. M. (ed.), *Religions of Antiquity. Religion, History, and Culture: Selections from 'The Encyclopedia of Religion'* (New York 1987)

[385] Versnel, H. S., *Faith, Hope, and Worship. Aspects of Religious Mentality in the Ancient World* (Leiden 1981)

[386] Versnel, H. S., *Inconsistencies in Greek and Roman Religion*, 2 vols. (Leiden 1990–3)

The legacy of ancient philosophy

[387] Baldwin, A., S. Hutton (ed.), *Platonism and the English Imagination* (Cambridge 1994)

[388] Burnyeat, M. (ed.), *The Skeptical Tradition* (Berkeley/L.A./London 1983)

[389] Colish, M. L., *The Stoic Tradition from Antiquity to the Early Middle Ages*, 2 vols. (Leiden 1985)

[390] Floridi, L., *Sextus Empiricus: The Transmission and Recovery of Pyrrhonism* (Oxford 2002)

[391] Grafton, A., *Commerce with the Classics: Ancient Books and Renaissance Readers* (Ann Arbor 1997)

[392] Hankins, J., *Plato in the Italian Renaissance*, 2 vols. (Leiden 1990)

[393] Heninger, S. K., *Touches of Sweet Harmony: Pythagorean Cosmology and Renaissance Poetics* (San Marino, Calif. 1974)

[394] Inwood, B., J. Miller, (ed.) *Hellenistic and Early Modern Philosophy* (Cambridge, forthcoming)

[395] Jones, H., *The Epicurean Tradition* (London/New York 1989)

[396] Kraye, J., M. W. F. Stone (ed.), *Humanism and Early Modern Philosophy* (London/New York 2000)

[397] Lane, M., *Plato's Progeny: How Plato and Socrates Still Captivate the Modern Mind* (London 2001)

[398] Morford, M., *Stoics and Neostoics: Rubens and the Circle of Lipsius* (Princeton 1991)

[399] Oestreich, G., *Neostoicism and the Early Modern State*, ed. and trans. B. Oestreich and H. G. Koenigsberger (Cambridge 1982)

[400] Osler, M. J. (ed.), *Atoms, Pneuma, and Tranquillity: Epicurean and Stoic Themes in European Thought* (Cambridge 1991)

[401] Popkin, R., *The History of Scepticism from Erasmus to Spinoza* (ed. 2, Berkeley/L.A./London 1979)

[402] Popkin, R. H., C. B. Schmitt (ed.), *Scepticism from the Renaissance to the Enlightenment* (Wolfenbüttel 1987)

[403] Pyle, A., *Atomism and its Critics from Democritus to Newton* (Bristol 1997)

[404] Schmitt, C. B., *Aristotle and the Renaissance* (Cambridge, Mass./London 1983)

[405] Sorell, T. (ed.), *The Rise of Modern Philosophy: The Tension between the New and Traditional Philosophies from Machiavelli to Leibniz* (Oxford 1995)

[406] Verbeke, G., *The Presence of Stoicism in Medieval Thought* (Washington, D. C. 1983)

[407] Walker, D. P., *The Ancient Theology* (London 1972)

GLOSSARY

(The italicized terms are Greek except where Latin is indicated)

Academic: a member of the Academy, the school founded by Plato; 'New Academy' and 'New Academic' designate the school's sceptical phase in the Hellenistic period, and the simple 'Academic' was sometimes used in this latter sense

accident, accidental property: see *symbebēkos*

account: see *logos*

activity: see *energeia*

actuality: see *energeia, entelecheia*

aether: *aithēr* (sometimes also 'ether'): the stuff of the heavens; distinguished by Aristotle as a fifth element

affinity: see *oikeiōsis*

ahoristos dyas: see 'Indefinite Dyad'

aisthēsis: 'perception', 'sensation'

aisthētos: 'sensible' (i.e. perceptible), used by Plato in contrast with 'intelligible' (*noētos*)

aitia, aition: literally 'responsibility' and 'thing responsible', respectively, but the standard terms for 'cause' (to which some interpreters prefer the translation 'reason' or 'explanation')

alētheia: 'truth', sometimes 'reality'; in the fifth century BC often used as a philosophical book title

alloiōsis: 'alteration' (specifically, change of quality)

anamnēsis: 'recollection', in the sense of recovery of prenatally acquired knowledge (Plato)

anankē: 'necessity', 'compulsion'

andreia: 'courage' (lit. 'manliness'), one of the 'cardinal virtues'

apatheia: absence of the passions (a Stoic ideal)

apeiron: see '*peras* and *apeiron*'

apodeixis: 'proof', 'demonstration'

appropriate action: see *kathēkon*

appropriation: see *oikeiōsis*

archē: 'principle' (plural *archai*), 'beginning'; used of a primeval originative stuff, an explanatory or causal starting point, and much else

aretē: 'excellence', 'virtue', 'goodness'; frequently spanning functional as well as narrowly moral goodness; cf. 'cardinal virtues'

assent: see *synkatathesis*

ataraxia: 'freedom from disturbance', 'tranquillity' (a Pyrrhonist and Epicurean goal)

atom: *atomos, atomon*; lit. 'uncuttable'

atomism: a modern term for the tradition of atomic physics represented by Leucippus, Democritus and the Epicureans

attunement: see *harmonia*

becoming like god: see *homoiōsis theōi*

being: see *ousia*

belief: see *doxa*

breath: see *pneuma*

canonic: the Epicurean term for epistemology; see *kanōn*

cardinal virtues: now a collective designation for wisdom, courage, justice and temperance (plus sometimes holiness/ piety); not a term used in antiquity

categories: (*katēgoriai*), a set of ten 'kinds of predication' – substance, quantity, quality, relation etc. – classified by Aristotle

catharsis: see *katharsis*

cause: see *aitia, aition*

choice: see *prohaeresis*

change: see *kinēsis, metabolē, alloiōsis*

city, city-state: see *polis*

clearing up: see *katharsis*

clinamen: preferred Latin name for Greek *parenklisis*; the random 'swerve' of atoms postulated in Epicureanism to avoid determinism

coincidence: see *symbebēkos*

collection and division: *synagōgē* and *diairesis*; a Platonic method of analysis, bringing a dispersed plurality under a single genus, then dividing it 'at the natural joints'

compulsion: see *anankē*

conflagration: see *ekpyrōsis*

constitution: see *politeia*

contemplation: see *theōria*

convention: see *nomos*

cosmogony: a (mainly) modern term for any theory about the origin of the *kosmos* (world)

cosmology: a modern term for the study of the *kosmos* (world)

cosmos: see *kosmos*

courage: see *andreia*

criterion: see *kritērion*

daimōn: a semi-divine being intermediary between gods and humans; in Empedocles functioning like a transmigratory soul; plural *daimones*; also written as 'demon'

decision: see *prohaeresis*

demiurge: *dēmiourgos*, lit. 'craftsman'; the world's creator according to Plato's *Timaeus*

demon: see *daimōn*

demonology: a modern term for the ancient discipline of theorizing about *daimones* (see *daimōn*)

demonstration: see *apodeixis*

diairesis: see 'collection and division'

dialectic: *dialektikē* (sc. *technē*), lit. 'conversational expertise'; the question-and-answer method of investigation first developed by Socrates

dikaiosynē: 'justice' (from *dikaios*, 'just'), one of the 'cardinal virtues'; sometimes treated as embracing all virtue, and closer to biblical 'righteousness'

division: see 'collection and division'

dogma: 'doctrine', 'dogma', 'theory'; professed by most philosophers, eschewed by Pyrrhonist sceptics

doxa: 'opinion', 'belief', 'judgement'; typically contrasted, as fallible, with 'knowledge' (*epistēmē*)

doxography: a modern term for the ancient literary genre of cataloguing philosophical doctrines

duty: see *kathēkon*

dynamis: 'potentiality' (in Aristotle, opp. *energeia*), 'power'

ecstasy: see *ekstasis*

efficient cause: a primarily modern designation of what Aristotle usually calls 'the source of change' in his classification of four causes

eidos: see 'Forms', 'matter and form'

ekpyrōsis: 'conflagration'; at the end of a Stoic world cycle

ekstasis: 'ecstasy'; state of contact with the One which transcends human rationality (Neoplatonism, esp. Plotinus)

Eleatic: a follower of Parmenides of Elea (not to be confused with 'Elean', a citizen of Elea)

element: see *stoicheion*

elenchos: a method of 'cross-examination', typical of Socrates; the word also incorporates the notions of 'testing' and 'refutation'

emanation: see *prohodos*

emotion: see *pathos*

enactment: see *mimēsis*

end: see 'final cause', *telos*

endoxa: 'standard views', 'received views', 'reputable views' (Aristotle)

energeia: 'activity', 'actuality' (Aristotle); contrast *dynamis*

entelecheia: (Aristotle) actuality (whether a mere variant for *energeia* is uncertain)

eph' hēmin: 'in our power'; to designate actions for which we are (morally) responsible

epistēmē: 'knowledge', 'science', 'understanding'

epistrophē: 'return' (Neoplatonism); the process by which lower realms turn towards their higher causes; for humans, it constitutes the domain of ethics which aims at becoming godlike

epochē: suspension of judgement, claimed by both Pyrrhonist and Academic sceptics

equivocation: see 'homonymy'

eristic: the technique of verbal dispute and other such confrontational argument; contrasted with 'dialectic'

erōs: love (passionate and/or sexual); cf. *philia*

error: see *hamartia*

essence: see *ousia*; also, in Aristotle, *to ti ēn einai*, lit. 'what was it to be (something)?'

ethics: *to ēthikon* or *ta ēthika*: a recognized sub-division of philosophy at least from the time of Aristotle; literally 'the study of character (*ēthos*)'

eudaimonia: approximately 'happiness' (some interpreters prefer the translation 'flourishing'), typically viewed as lifelong well-being

eudaimonism: a modern term for any ethical approach that views something like *eudaimonia* as the goal

excellence: see *aretē*

familiarization: see *oikeiōsis*

feeling: see *pathos*

final cause: what Aristotle usually calls the 'goal' or 'end' (*telos*) or 'that for the sake of which' in his theory of four causes

flourishing: see *eudaimonia*

form: see 'matter and form'

Forms: *eidē* (singular *eidos*) or *ideai* (singular *idea*); paradigmatic and independently existing universals, the proper objects of knowledge (Plato)

freedom from disturbance: see *ataraxia*

friendship: see *philia*

goal: see 'final cause', *telos*

gnōsis: 'knowledge'; sometimes used interchangeably with *epistēmē*, sometimes implying a religious or mystical knowledge thought able to provide salvation for the soul

god: *theos*; not a proper name in pagan usage (so an initial capital is misleading); varying between singular and plural often without apparent change in meaning

godly man: see *theios anēr*

hamartia: 'mistake', 'error', usually in action; 'wrongdoing'

happiness: see *eudaimonia*

harmonia: 'attunement', 'harmony'; lit. 'fixing'

heaven(s): see *ouranos*

homoiōsis theōi: 'becoming like god' (a Platonic ideal)

homonymy: *homōnymia*, equivocation (Aristotle)

hylē: see 'matter and form'

hylomorphism: a modern term for Aristotelian analysis into form and matter

hypodochē: see 'receptacle'

hypokeimenon: lit. 'what underlies'; either 'substrate' (underlying qualities), or 'subject' (underlying predicates)

hypostasis: level of existence (Neoplatonists)

Ideas: see 'Forms'

imagination: see *phantasia*

imitation: see *mimēsis*

impression: see *phantasia*

Indefinite Dyad: *ahoristos dyas*; a matter-like ultimate principle invoked, alongside the One, by Plato (not in the dialogues, however) and his successors

intellect: see *nous*

intelligence: see *nous*, 'wisdom'

intelligible: see *noētos*

judgement: see *doxa*

justice: see *dikaiosynē*

kalon: the 'beautiful', the 'fine', spanning both the aesthetic and the moral

kanōn: lit. a builder's stick against which straightness is checked; hence an epistemological yardstick or 'criterion' (see *kritērion*); esp. in Epicureanism (see 'canonic') *katalēpsis*: 'cognition' (Stoic)

kataleptikē (*phantasia*): 'cognitive' (Stoicism)

katharsis: 'purgation', 'purification'; a perhaps medical or religious metaphor applied by philosophers to the soul in intellectual and moral contexts; Aristotle, *Poetics* 6, speaks of tragedy's *katharsis* (here possibly 'clearing up') of emotions through pity and fear

kathēkon: (plural *kathēkonta*; Latin *officium*), 'appropriate action', 'duty', 'proper function' (Stoics)

kenon: see 'void'

kinēsis: 'motion', 'locomotion' (more accurately called *kinēsis kata topon*), 'change'

kinship: see *oikeiōsis*

knowledge: see *epistēmē, gnōsis*

kosmos: 'world', 'world-order' (literally 'arrangement', 'ordering'); whether there is more than one *kosmos* was a running debate (contrast 'universe', of which there can be only one)

kritērion: 'criterion', most frequently 'of truth'; the focal concept of epistemology in Hellenistic philosophy

law: see *nomos*

lekton: 'sayable', 'thing said'; Stoic term for the incorporeal significate of a linguistic utterance

limit: see '*peras* and *apeiron*'

locomotion: see *kinēsis*

logic: *logikon, logikē* (derived from *logos*); came to be one of the main branches of philosophy; usually wider in scope than the modern term, embracing epistemology and linguistic theory

logos (plural *logoi*): 'discourse', 'speech', 'language', 'sentence', 'statement', 'account' (sometimes bordering on 'definition'); 'argument', 'reason'; 'ratio'

love: see *erōs, philia*

matter and form: in Aristotle's terminology, respectively *hylē*, and *eidos* (or *morphē*), viz. a constituent stuff plus the structuring principles which make it something definite; see also 'prime matter' mean: *mesotēs*; the middle condition, of emotions and other factors of action, in which Aristotle locates virtue

metabolē: 'change'

metaphysics: by origin the subject that properly comes (lit.) 'after physics' in the Aristotelian curriculum, Aristotle's own name for it being 'first philosophy'

methexis: see 'participation'

metriopatheia: 'moderation of the emotions', recommended by Aristotelians (on the basis of Aristotle's doctrine that virtue lies in a 'mean'), Pyrrhonists, Neoplatonists

mimēsis: 'imitation', 'representation', 'enactment'; a term from aesthetics, especially poetics, first in Plato (*Republic*)

mind: see *nous*, *psychē*

mistake: see *hamartia*

moderation of the emotions: see *metriopatheia*

monism: a modern term for the reduction of any explanandum to a single entity; in ancient philosophy, used variously for element theory (e.g. Anaximenes), ontology (e.g. Parmenides), and psychology (e.g. Socrates)

motion: see *kinēsis*

nature: see *physis*

necessity: see *anankē*

noētos: 'intelligible', i.e. accessible to the intellect (*nous*); used by Plato to contrast with *aisthētos*, 'sensible'

nomos: 'convention', 'custom' (to indicate what is culturally determined, by contrast with *physis*, 'nature'); also 'law'

nous: 'intellect', 'intelligence', 'mind'; used for both divine and human varieties (insofar as these are distinguished)

officium (Latin): see *kathēkon*

oikeiōsis: 'affinity', 'kinship', 'appropriation', 'familiarization' (Stoic ethical term)

One, the: a supreme principle, either incorporating (Parmenides) or standing above the whole of being (Platonists; cf. 'Indefinite Dyad')

opinion: see *doxa*

Organon: 'instrument', became the collective title for Aristotle's logical works *ouranos*: 'heaven(s)'; sometimes used to designate the entire world

ousia: lit. 'being', used especially for (1) 'essence', and (2) 'substance', of which the latter is, in Aristotle, a self-subsistent being or entity, but in Stoicism equivalent to matter

parenklisis: see *clinamen*

participation: *methexis*, *metalēpsis*: the relation in which particulars stand to Platonic Forms

passion: see *pathos*

pathos: 'feeling', 'emotion', 'passion'; also 'property'

peras and *apeiron*: 'limit' and 'unlimited', treated as explanatory principles in a Pythagorean tradition which includes Plato's *Philebus* and Proclus, for whom they rank immediately after the One; elsewhere *apeiron* ranges in use from 'indefinite' or 'indeterminate', via 'boundless', to the mathematically precise 'infinite'

perception: *aisthēsis*

Peripatetic: a follower of Aristotle

peripeteia: 'reversal' of fortune, in tragedy

phantasia: lit. an 'appearing' or 'appearance'; more frequently translated 'imagination' (Aristotle), 'impression' or 'presentation' (Stoics), cf. *kataleptikē* (*phantasia*)

philia: friendship, (friendly) love (cf. *erōs*)

philosophy: *philosophia*, lit. 'love of wisdom'; the term's invention was credited to Pythagoras

phronēsis: see 'wisdom'

physics: the study of nature, constituting one main part of the philosophical curriculum; the Presocratics were sometimes known collectively as the *physikoi* or *physiologoi* ('physicists', 'natural philosophers', 'nature explainers')

physikoi, *physiologoi*: see 'physics'

physis: 'nature', sometimes contrasted with *nomos* ('convention')

pneuma: 'breath', 'wind'; an animating causal principle in Stoicism, Aristotle and some medical writers

poiotēs: 'quality'

polis: often rendered 'city' or simply transliterated; a politically autonomous Greek 'city-state' (as it is better translated)

politeia: 'constitution'; misleadingly (through its Latinization as *respublica*) translated 'republic' in the title of Plato's so-named dialogue

potentiality: see *dynamis*

power: see *dynamis*; cf. also *eph' hēmin*

practical wisdom, practical intelligence: see 'wisdom'

preconception: see *prolēpsis*

prenotion: see *prolēpsis*

prime matter: *prōtē hylē*; irreducibly simple, and therefore quality-free, matter; postulated by Stoics and later Aristotelians and Platonists, but only disputably present in Aristotle

Prime Mover: see 'Unmoved Mover'

principle: see *archē*

procession: see *prohodos*

proēgmenon (plural *proēgmena*): 'preferred' (opp. *apoproēgmenon*, 'dispreferred'); a term for ranking moral indifferents in Stoicism

prohaeresis: 'decision', 'choice' (Aristotle, Epictetus)

prohodos: 'emanation', 'procession'; the coming-to-be of lower realms from, ultimately, the One (Neoplatonism)

prolēpsis: 'preconception', 'prenotion', 'prolepsis'; a generic conception, functioning as a 'criterion of truth' in both Epicurean and Stoic epistemology

proof: see *apodeixis*

proper function: see *kathēkon*

pros ti: 'relative'

prudence: see 'wisdom'

psychē: 'soul', but so used that it is uncontroversial that all animals (and maybe plants too) have one simply in virtue of being alive; sometimes translatable as 'mind' (but cf. *nous*)

purgation: see *katharsis*

purification: see *katharsis*

quality: *poiotēs*

reason: see *logos, aitia/aition*

receptacle: *hypodochē*, the malleable world-stuff in which, according to Plato's *Timaeus*, Forms come to be reflected

recollection: see *anamnēsis*

relative: *pros ti*

representation: see *mimēsis*

return: see *epistrophē*

reversal: see *peripeteia*

sage: see *sophos*

Sceptic: *skeptikos*, 'inquirer'; from approx. first century AD, an alternative title for a Pyrrhonist; not used in antiquity in its modern sense as a common noun

science: see *epistēmē*

sensation: *aisthēsis*

sensible: (in the sense 'perceptible') see *aisthētos*

Skeptic (US spelling): see 'Sceptic'

sophia: see 'wisdom'

sophism: *sophisma*; a fallacious or otherwise deceitful argument; from 'sophist' in its pejorative sense (below)

sophist: a term for (roughly) 'intellectual', applied (often with initial capital) more specifically to the professional teachers of the fifth century BC, but, owing largely to Plato, acquiring early the pejorative sense it carries today; cf. 'eristic'

sophos: 'wise' (cf. 'wisdom'), often used as a noun to designate the paradigmatic 'sage' typically cited as a model by Hellenistic schools

sōphrosynē: 'self-control', 'temperance', 'self-discipline', one of the 'cardinal virtues'; lit. 'soundness of mind'

soul: see *psychē*

stoicheion: a primary element in any system (alphabetic, mathematical etc.); hence, frequently, one of the four primary physical stuffs – earth, water, air and fire

subject: see *hypokeimenon*

sublunary: an adjective designating the region below the moon, governed by the regular laws of physics, distinguished from the heavens, held controversially by Aristotle to consist of aether; the term 'sublunary' (*hyposelēnios*) itself is not found in Aristotle

substance: see *ousia*

substrate: see *hypokeimenon*

suspension of judgement/assent: see *epochē*

swerve: see *clinamen*

syllogismos: a valid deduction of a certain formal kind, as variously specified in Aristotelian and Stoic logic; commonly translated 'syllogism' (see p. 134 for a caution about this)

symbebēkos: (mainly Aristotelian) 'accidental property', 'accident', 'coincidence'

synagōgē: see 'collection and division'

synkatathesis: 'assent', usually to an 'impression', in Stoicism

technē: 'expertise', 'skill', 'craft'; sometimes used for a handbook to an expertise, especially rhetoric

teleology: explanation in terms of the purpose served; not an ancient term, although derived from *telos*

telos: 'goal', 'end'; naming 'the *telos*' became the focal task of ethics, but in Aristotle the term is also one of those used in causal theory

temperance: see *sōphrosynē*

theios anēr: 'godly man'

theōria: 'contemplation'; the highest intellectual activity (Aristotle)

theurgy: lit. 'work of the gods'; a Neoplatonic rite of divinization

tode ti: a 'this something' (Aristotle), implying definiteness and perhaps particularity

tranquillity: see *ataraxia*

truth: see *alētheia*

understanding: see *epistēmē*

universe: properly used to translate *to pan*, lit. 'the all'; it may in principle contain more than one 'world' (*kosmos*) at a time, although for thinkers like Plato and Aristotle who posit just one world 'universe' and 'world' become virtually interchangeable in most contexts

unlimited: see '*peras* and *apeiron*'

Unmoved Mover: the ultimate cause of motion postulated by Aristotle, treated as equivalent to god; also 'Prime Mover'

virtue: see *aretē*

void: *kenon*, lit. the 'empty', often identified with empty space, but sometimes arguably with the emptiness in that space

wisdom: one of the 'cardinal virtues'; *phronēsis, sophia*; usually interchangeable, but in Aristotle respectively practical wisdom (or 'prudence') and theoretical wisdom

wise (man/person): see *sophos*

world: see *kosmos*

wrongdoing: see *hamartia*

INDEX